The *ribbon* places frequently used commands a mouse-click away.

Any Mac can play back Word 5 *voice annotations* recorded on microphone-equipped Macs.

Draw your own illustrations or import clip art and scanned images without leaving Word, thanks to the new *drawing* and *graphics-positioning tools*.

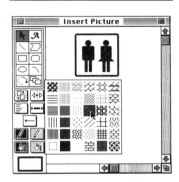

Word 5's improved *find* and *replace* features help you locate and change styles, special characters, formats, and much more.

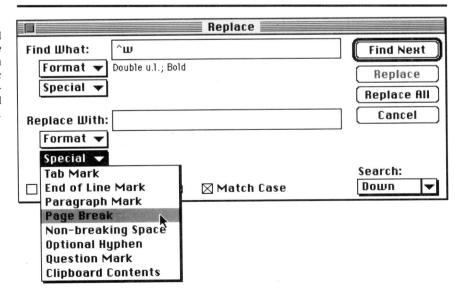

Books that work just like your Mac

As a Macintosh user, you enjoy unique advantages. You enjoy a dynamic user environment. You enjoy the successful integration of graphics, sound, and text. Above all, you enjoy a computer that's fun and easy to use.

When your computer gives you all this, why accept less in your computer books?

At SYBEX, we don't believe you should. That's why we've committed ourselves to publishing the highest quality computer books for Macintosh users. Externally, our books emulate the Mac "look and feel," with powerful, appealing illustrations and easy to read pages. Internally, our books stress "why" over "how," so you'll learn concepts, not sequences of steps. Philosophically, our books are designed to help you get work done, not to teach you about computers.

In short, our books are fun and easy to use—just like the Mac. We hope you find them just as enjoyable.

For a complete catalog of our publications:

SYBEX Inc.
2021 Challenger Drive, Alameda, CA 94501
Tel: (510) 523-8233/(800) 227-2346 Telex: 336311
Fax: (510) 523-2373

SYBEX is committed to using natural resources wisely to preserve and improve our environment. As a leader in the computer book publishing industry, we are aware that over 40% of America's solid waste is paper. This is why we have been printing the text of books like this one on recycled paper since 1982.

This year our use of recycled paper will result in the saving of more than 15,300 trees. We will lower air pollution effluents by 54,000 pounds, save 6,300,000 gallons of water, and reduce landfill by 2,700 cubic yards.

In choosing a SYBEX book you are not only making a choice for the best in skills and information, you are also choosing to enhance the quality of life for all of us.

The Mac Book
of Microsoft Word 5

The Mac® Book of Microsoft® Word 5

RON MANSFIELD

SYBEX®

San Francisco ■ Paris ■ Düsseldorf ■ Soest

Acquisitions Editor: Dianne King
Developmental Editor: Kenyon Brown
Editor: David Krassner
Technical Editor: Celia Stevenson
Word Processors: Ann Dunn and Susan Trybull
Book Designer: Helen Bruno
Chapter Art: Charlotte Carter
Technical Art: Cuong Le
Screen Graphics: Delia Brown and Cuong Le
Typesetter: Elizabeth Newman
Proofreader/Production Assistant: Arno Harris
Indexer: Nancy Guenther
Cover Designer: Ingalls + Associates
Cover Illustrator: Tom McKeith

SYBEX is a registered trademark of SYBEX Inc.

TRADEMARKS: SYBEX has attempted throughout this book to distinguish proprietary trademarks from descriptive terms by following the capitalization style used by the manufacturer.

SYBEX is not affiliated with any manufacturer.

Every effort has been made to supply complete and accurate information. However, SYBEX assumes no responsibility for its use, nor for any infringement of the intellectual property rights of third parties which would result from such use.

Copyright ©1992 SYBEX Inc., 2021 Challenger Drive, Alameda, CA 94501. World rights reserved. No part of this publication may be stored in a retrieval system, transmitted, or reproduced in any way, including but not limited to photocopy, photograph, magnetic or other record, without the prior agreement and written permission of the publisher.

Library of Congress Card Number: 91-68340
ISBN: 0-7821-1056-8
Manufactured in the United States of America
10 9 8 7 6 5 4 3 2 1

To my kind, loving and generous dad who did not take enough time to fish.
We all miss you.

ACKNOWLEDGMENTS

The tough part of writing anything—especially acknowledgments—is deciding when to stop. With apologies to those not mentioned, here goes...

Bill Gates and his growing family have much to be proud of. This book wouldn't exist without the capable assistance of Maria Staaf's good-natured, young Microsoft Word army. Their enthusiasm for Word 5 is well-founded. Microsoft's David (Beta Man) Pearce always cheerfully returned my calls and sent me everything he promised to, despite his hectic "new product launch" schedule.

Alex Maluta, friend, employee, and Macaholic extraordinaire not only contributed portions of this book, he also helped keep our consulting firm's clients happy while I played "author in seclusion." Get some sleep, Alex.

Like Alex, SYBEX never sleeps. Syboids even worked at home through the holidays on this book. Thanks Dianne King for helping me "join the club." Ken Brown's early editorial guidance and attention to detail will make a typesetter out of me yet. Hats off to David Krassner, as likable and capable an editor as I've ever met. Much thanks also to Celia Steveson, technical editor; Ann Dunn and Susan Trybull, word processors; Cuong Le, screen graphics; Elizabeth Newman, typesetter; Charlotte Carter, artist; and Arno Harris, proofreader. Let's do it again soon.

Finally, I want to acknowledge my wonderful family for putting up with an often invisible, but clearly audible husband and dad. It's done! Thanks Nancy and Adam.

Contents at a Glance

		Introduction	xxv
PART	**I**	**THE BASICS**	**1**
	1	Your First Word 5 Document	2
	2	Save Early and Often	14
	3	Printing Basics	20
	4	Copying and Moving	27
	5	Drawing in the Picture Window	34
	6	Quitting and Restarting Word 5	46
	7	How Word 5 Differs from Previous Versions	50
PART	**II**	**PERSONALIZING WORD 5**	**65**
	8	Word 5 Defaults	66
	9	Preferences	72
	10	Adding, Deleting, and Moving Menu Choices	86
	11	Views	102
PART	**III**	**LOOKING GREAT IN PRINT**	**115**
	12	The Chooser, Page Setup, and Print Dialog Boxes	116
	13	Document Margins and Gutters	132
	14	All About Characters and Fonts	142
	15	Paragraphs and Line Spacing	160
	16	All About Tabs	170
	17	All About Styles	178
	18	Headers and Footers	194
	19	Page Numbers and Pagination	200
	20	Annotations	210
	21	Footnotes	216
	22	Hyphenation and Dashes	224
	23	Sections	232

PART IV		**TIME SAVERS**	**239**
	24	Keyboard Features	240
	25	Undo, Redo, and Reverting	248
	26	Finding and Replacing	254
	27	Navigating through a Document	266
	28	Glossaries	274
	29	Stationery and Insert File…	284
	30	Managing Your Files	290
PART V		**WORKING WITH GRAPHICS**	**303**
	31	Positioning Graphics	304
	32	Importing Graphics	312
PART VI		**POWER TOOLS**	**317**
	33	Checking Spelling and Counting Words	318
	34	The Grammar Checker	326
	35	The Thesaurus	334
	36	Multiple Columns	340
	37	Tables	346
	38	Sorting	366
	39	Math and Formula Features	372
	40	Print Merge	386
	41	Creating a Table of Contents and an Index	408
	42	Outlining	418
	43	Working with Large Documents	426
	44	Publish and Subscribe, Link, and Embed	432
	45	E-Mail	448
APPENDICES			
	A	Installing Word 5	451
	B	Word 5 Commands	461
		Index	499

Contents

Introduction xxv

PART I   THE BASICS   1

CHAPTER 1
Your First Word 5 Document — 2
Page and Document Setup   4
Typing Habits to Break   4

CHAPTER 2
Save Early and Often — 14
Summary Information   16
Keyboard Shortcuts   17

CHAPTER 3
Printing Basics — 20
Print Preview   21

CHAPTER 4
Copying and Moving — 27
Cut, Copy and Paste   27

CHAPTER 5
Drawing in the Picture Window — 34
- Opening the Picture Window   35
- A Simple Drawing   36
- Text in Drawings   38
- Drawing Shapes   41
- That's Only the Beginning   44

CHAPTER 6
Quitting and Restarting Word 5 — 46
- Launching Word by Double Clicking on a Document   47

CHAPTER 7
How Word 5 Differs from Previous Versions — 50
- New Features   51
- Enhanced Features   60
- Keyboard Shortcuts Worth Noting   62
- System 7 Support   63

PART II   PERSONALIZING WORD 5   65

CHAPTER 8
Word 5 Defaults — 66
- What Are Defaults?   66
- Designer Defaults   67
- Where Defaults Are Stored   69
- Reverting to Standard Defaults   69

CHAPTER 9
Preferences 72
Reaching Preference Dialog Boxes 72

CHAPTER 10
Adding, Deleting, and Moving Menu Choices 86
A Caution 87
The Commands Dialog Box 87
What's a *Work* Menu? 92
When Are Menu Changes Saved? 97
Command Reference 97
Resetting Word's Standard Menus 97
Adding and Changing Keyboard Shortcuts 98
Using Multiple Command Sets 99

CHAPTER 11
Views 102
Normal View 103
Switching Views 105
Page Layout View 105
Split Screen View 108
Split Screen and Different Views 108
Print Preview 110
Outline View 110
View Defaults 113

PART III LOOKING GREAT IN PRINT 115

CHAPTER 12
The Chooser, Page Setup, and Print Dialog Boxes 116

Printing in Word Is an Interactive Process   117
Choosing a Printer   118
Effect of Page Setup Options on Formatting   119
Print Dialog Box Differences   128

CHAPTER 13
Document Margins and Gutters 132

Document Margins vs. Indents   134
Changing Document Margins   134
Alternate Facing (Mirror) Margins   137
Gutters Facilitate Binding   138
Printer Capabilities Limit Margins   139
Printing in Margins   139
Headers and Footers   139

CHAPTER 14
All About Characters and Fonts 142

Terminology   143
Applying and Removing Character Formats   146
Special Characters   155
More About Fonts   155

CHAPTER 15

Paragraphs and Line Spacing   160

    Paragraphs   160
    Paragraph Formatting with the Ruler   163
    The Paragraph Dialog Box   166

CHAPTER 16

All About Tabs   170

    Five Kinds of Tab Stops   171
    Tables vs. Tabs   172
    Setting Tab Stops   172
    Leading Characters   175
    Default Tab Stop Positions   176
    Clearing Tab Stops   176
    Entering and Editing Tabular Data   176
    Tabs and Data Exchange   177

CHAPTER 17

All About Styles   178

    What Are Styles and Style Sheets?   179
    Style Name Considerations   181
    The Style Dialog Box   181
    When and Where Style Sheets and Styles Are Saved   183
    Basing One Style upon Another   184
    Manual Formatting and Styles   186
    Deleting Styles   189
    Renaming Styles   189
    Finding and Replacing Styles   189
    Using the Same Styles in Different Documents   190
    A Few Style Tips   192

CHAPTER 18
Headers and Footers 194

- Entering Basic Headers in Normal View 195
- Entering Basic Footers in Normal View 195
- Rulers and Ribbons in Headers and Footers 196
- Headers and Footers in Page Layout View 196
- Headers and Footers in Print Preview 196
- Even and Odd Headers and Footers 198
- Different First Page Headers and Footers 199
- PostScript Code in Headers 199

CHAPTER 19
Page Numbers and Pagination 200

- Three Methods for Page Numbering 201
- Page Numbering Formats and Styles 204
- Managing Starting Page Numbers 204
- Removing Page Numbers 206
- Pagination and Page Numbers 207

CHAPTER 20
Annotations 210

- Hidden Text for Annotations 210
- Sound Advice 211

CHAPTER 21
Footnotes 216

- Easy Automatic Footnotes 217
- Viewing Footnotes 218
- Inserting Footnotes ahead of Existing Ones 218
- Copying, Deleting, and Moving Footnotes 218

CHAPTER 22
HYPHENATION AND DASHES 224
- Typing Hyphens 225
- Automatic Optional Hyphenation 226

CHAPTER 23
SECTIONS 232
- Creating Section Breaks 233
- Copying Section Breaks 236
- Deleting Section Breaks 236
- Time-Saving Section Tips 237

PART IV TIME SAVERS 239

CHAPTER 24
KEYBOARD FEATURES 240
- Keyboard Differences 241
- Repeating Keys 243
- Exploring and Modifying Keyboard Shortcuts 244
- Activating Word's Keyboard Menus 246
- Keyboard Tricks in Dialog Boxes 247

CHAPTER 25
UNDO, REDO, AND REVERTING 248
- Undo 249
- Repeat 251
- The Revert to Style Command 251

CHAPTER 26
Finding and Replacing   254
- The Art of Finding   255
- The Art of Replacing   259
- Using the Clipboard with Find and Replace   263
- Replacing Tips   264

CHAPTER 27
Navigating Through a Document   266
- Navigating with Your Mouse   267
- The Go To Feature   267
- Go Back   268
- Using Find to Navigate   268
- Moving Between Document Windows   269
- Keys for Navigation   270

CHAPTER 28
Glossaries   274
- Defining Your Own Glossary Entries   275
- Inserting Glossary Entries in Your Documents   276
- Changing and Deleting Glossary Entries   278
- Word 5's Standard Glossary Entries   278
- How and Where Glossary Entries Are Stored   279
- Special Purpose Glossaries   280
- Merging Glossaries   281
- Glossary Entries and Styles   281
- Printing Glossary Entry Lists   282

CHAPTER 29

Stationery and Insert File...   284

- Why Stationery?   284
- Combining Documents and Boilerplate with Insert File...   288

CHAPTER 30

Managing Your Files   290

- Files, Folders, and Paths   290
- Find File...   293
- Deleting Files from within Word   300

PART V   WORKING WITH GRAPHICS   303

CHAPTER 31

Positioning Graphics   304

- The Easy Way   305
- Frame... on the Insert Menu   306
- The Frame Dialog Box   307
- Frame Positions as Styles   307
- Deleting Frame Objects   308
- Repeating Framed Objects on Multiple Pages   308
- Frame Objects in Views   309

CHAPTER 32

Importing Graphics   312

- Types of Graphics   313
- Importing with Picture...   314

PART VI POWER TOOLS 317

CHAPTER 33
Checking Spelling and Counting Words — 318
Checking Spelling 319
Custom (a/k/a User) Dictionaries 321
The Word Count Command 324

CHAPTER 34
The Grammar Checker — 326
Checking Grammar and Style 327
Changing Preferences 330
Document Statistics 331

CHAPTER 35
The Thesaurus — 334
Looking Up Words and Phrases 334
Replacing Words and Phrases 335
Related Words and Phrases 336
Finding Antonyms 337
Spelling Help from the Thesaurus 338
Exploring the Thesaurus 338

CHAPTER 36
Multiple Columns — 340
Multicolumn Documents from the Ribbon 341
Multicolumn Documents from the Section Dialog Box 342
Column Breaks and Sections 342
Controlling Column Width from the Ruler 344
Controlling Column Breaks 344

CHAPTER 37
Tables 346
- Parts of a Table   347
- Creating a Simple Table   347
- Entering and Editing Text in a Table   348
- Selecting in Tables   349
- Modifying Table Designs   351
- Converting Tables to Text and Vice Versa   361
- Table Tips   363

CHAPTER 38
Sorting 366
- Simple Sorting   367
- Sort Order   368
- Sorts Based on Portions of Lines   368
- Sorting Dates, Names, and Part Numbers   369
- Multilevel Sorts   370

CHAPTER 39
Math and Formula Features 372
- Word's Built-in Math Capability   373
- Formula Typesetting Commands   376
- Introducing the Equation Editor   381

CHAPTER 40
Print Merge 386
- About Data Documents   389
- Overview of a New Print Merge Project   389
- Design Data and Main Documents   390
- Creating a Data Document First   391
- Entering and Editing Data in a Data Document   393

Creating a Main Document 394
Testing and Proofing Before Printing 397
Printing Merged Documents 397
Merge Instructions 398
DATA... 405
If You Don't Use Print Merge Helper 406
Restarting Stopped Merges 406
Word's Predesigned Labels and Envelopes 406

CHAPTER 41
Creating a Table of Contents and an Index — 408
A Quick Table of Contents 409
Index 413

CHAPTER 42
Outlining — 418
Styles and Outlines 419
The Outline View's Tools 419
Creating New Outlines 421
Promoting and Demoting 421
Expanding and Collapsing Outlines 423
Split Views 423
Moving Paragraphs 424
Printing Outlines 425

CHAPTER 43
Working with Large Documents — 426
Planning for Large Documents 427
Connecting Multiple Parts in a Series 427
Printing Multipart Documents 430

CHAPTER 44

PUBLISH AND SUBSCRIBE, LINK, AND EMBED   432

Which, When, and Why? 433
Publish and Subscribe 434
Embedding 439
Link 443

CHAPTER 45

E-MAIL   448

Sending Mail and Word Documents 449

APPENDICES

APPENDIX A

INSTALLING WORD 5   451

What You Need 451
Preparing Your Mac 452
Running the Installer 452
What Gets Installed? 455
Custom Installation 457
Using Old Dictionary and Glossary Files 458

APPENDIX B

WORD 5 COMMANDS   461

Index 499

INTRODUCTION

I've been using Microsoft Word on a Macintosh almost since the two products were first announced. I've looked over the shoulders of a hundred or more people as they learned to use earlier versions of Word. This is the book I've often wished I had in my reference library. It is also one I've wanted to give to Word students. Like the software it describes, *The Mac Book of Microsoft Word 5* is designed for both first time and experienced users.

Word 5.0 is a major upgrade to an already full-featured program. Thanks to Word's new features, you can create documents like Figure I.1 in minutes. Word can integrate information from non-Word programs (spreadsheets, databases, graphics sources, etc.) and assure that Word documents are automatically updated when those outside information sources change.

While writing this book, I imagined some of my favorite Macintosh users. Joanne, for instance, already knows how to make Word 4 sing. She takes "new version" books like this one home and reads them cover-to-cover in a single night. She's heard about the new power offered in Word 5, and hopes to utilize things like the much improved Print Merge, spelling checker, graphics Frames, rulers and ribbons, Word's new drawing features, MathType, voice annotation, etc.

Joanne wants to know more about older Word features too; like page-numbering alternatives, glossaries, the Work menu, print merge tricks, and so on. For instance, she's always wondered why Word's sort feature behaves the way it does when it encounters dates. *The Mac Book of Microsoft Word 5* will help her understand and work around peculiarities like these.

Next, there's Michael, an experienced MS-DOS user who has recently discovered the Macintosh advantage. He understands basic text editing but wants to learn new tricks he can do with Word on a Mac. Michael is a lawyer and a columnist, so he needs to be able to quickly put his finger on instructions for creating footnotes, line-numbered drafts, tables and other advanced page-formatting features. Some of his clients and publishers use MS-DOS and Windows 3.0 products, so he needs to know how to exchange documents with those worlds.

Figure I.1
A typical Word 5 document includes information from many sources.

H&P Au-Pair Finders Interoffice Memo

To: H. Higgins, Col. Pickering
From: E. Doolittle
Subject: Rain in Spain

Gentleman:

As I have been telling you all along, the rain in Spain falls mainly in the mountains, not the plains; and I have created a spreadsheet in *Microsoft Excel 3.0* on my Macintosh to prove it:

Rain in Spain			
	Coast	Mountains	Plains
Summer	0.1	0.2	0.1
Fall	0.1	0.5	0.6
Winter	0.2	0.4	0.5
Spring	0.3	0.9	0.3

I've generated an Excel chart which I am also enclosing here, thanks to *Microsoft Word 5's* recently improved graphics capabilities:

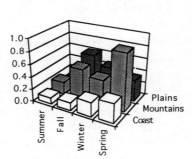

I plan to use System 7's new "publish and subscribe" features to automatically update this memo *over the network*. Just you wait, Henry Higgins!

Moreover, I will no longer need English lessons, since Word 5 has a grammar checker, a spelling checker, and a thesaurus.

Pity, aye?
ED

Then there is Nancy. You could count her Macintosh experience in hours, not weeks or days. She's a busy executive with the occasional need to type professional looking letters and memos. Chances are, she'll read *Part One* and *Part Two* of this book, then bounce around the rest to pick up selected skills like spell-checking and envelope printing. It may be years before she'll use or even wonder about Word's graphics prowess and multi-column features.

Finally, I had Candy in mind when I wrote this book. She's a sophisticated Macintosh user with more projects than time. Among other things, Candy is in charge of her organization's Macintosh network and computer training. She routinely looks for ways to improve office communication and users' skill levels. She makes executive-level presentations, and is always in a hurry, so I expect she'll skim *Part One* and *Part Two,* then dig into *Part Three* and *Part Four.* She'll want to know if Microsoft Word 5's and System 7's Publish and Subscribe features will benefit or confuse her network users. Candy doesn't know it yet, but Word 5's new *Find File...* feature will help her entire company organize its server-resident Word files. Word 5's new drawing tools will catch her eye, as will the new menu layouts and personalization possibilities.

Each of my friends has a delightful sense of humor; something I've tried to keep in mind. That's why the examples and illustrations in this book are intentionally tongue-in-cheek. Learning anything as powerful as Word 5 takes time. I've always felt that if a book weighs more than five pounds and you need to pick it up regularly, it had better be fun to read!

BOOK CONVENTIONS

Most of the examples and exercises in this book are illustrated using Apple's System 7. Except where noted, they'll all work just fine under System 6.

We've tried to adhere to "official" Apple jargon where possible. Apple now calls the ⌘ key the *Apple key,* for instance. Earlier books and Apple manuals called it the *Command key.* We'll use either the words *Apple key* or this symbol: ⌘.

Moreover, Apple would prefer that you and I not use the term *Macintoshes* when referring to a gaggle of Macs. Ooops, *Macs* is also verboten. Henceforth, we'll try to use the term *multiple Macintosh computers,* but may slip in a *Mac* or two just for variety. Please don't tell the authors of the official *Apple Publications Style Guide.*

Finally, when we say "press ⌘-B," we mean hold down the Apple key and press the B key. If we want you to hold down Shift, we'll say "press ⌘-Shift-B."

Where to Go From Here

The book's organization is fairly straightforward; except for a quick detour to *Appendix A* if you need to install Microsoft Word 5. Consider starting with *Part One*. It briefly describes and demonstrates most of Word's features. You'll get your hands on the keyboard almost immediately. Here's an overview of the book and its contents.

Part One: The Basics

Part One dives right into creating and editing your first Word 5 document. Sit at a Mac (sorry)—sit at a *Macintosh* when you read it. You'll soon be creating, saving, and printing some impressive Word examples of your own, beginner or not.

Near the end of *Part One,* you'll find information meant for users of earlier Word versions. Here you'll learn what's different and the same. You'll also see how Word 5 treats non-Word documents and files created under earlier versions of Word and visa versa.

Part Two: Personalizing Word 5

Part Two shows you how to personalize Word 5. Few other programs offer as much opportunity for customization. Word lets you rearrange menus, change default settings, modify dictionaries and grammar rules, and much, much more.

Experienced Word 4.0 users will notice that the designers of Word 5 have made a number of major "interface" changes. Menu locations and contents have changed. Keyboard shortcuts are different. Many of these changes are reversible if you prefer the old interface.

You'll find yourself revisiting *Part Two* of this book from time to time. New Word users will want to just skim it initially so that you'll know what's possible down the road. Experienced Word 4 users may want to start changing things immediately in order to get back the exact look and feel you prefer. That's why this information is near the front of the book.

Part Three: Looking Great in Print

Part Three shows you how to look great in print. It is organized to help you quickly find illustrated answers to specific questions. You'll see how to create outstanding looking documents by supplementing Word's default settings. You'll learn important preliminary document-setup steps that will make it easy to start new projects. You'll read about character, line, paragraph, and section formatting tips.

Tabs, styles, style sheets, headers, footers, hyphenation, and page numbers are covered here. Those of you who need help with footnotes will find it in this part.

Part Four: Time Savers

Part Four is titled *Time Savers*. As you might expect, it is filled with tips and techniques. Here you will learn good habits, explore keyboard-shortcut options, see Word's *Undo* feature in action, and learn to find and replace text or styles. We'll also attempt to unravel the mysteries of Word's new Glossary features, see how to create stationary pads for repetitive tasks, and learn how to manage that exploding collection of Word files on your hard disk.

Part Five: Working with Graphics

Part Five covers Word 5's graphics features—both new and old. You'll learn to create, import, position, and size graphic elements. The process of flowing text around graphics is illustrated. We'll also try to make some sense out of the growing collection of graphics standards (TIFF, PICT, etc.) and show how they relate to Microsoft Word 5.

Part Six: Power Tools

Part Six contains thirteen chapters describing word's "power tools" for authors, including the thesaurus, outliner, and spelling and grammar checkers. You'll learn about multiple columns; when and how to use tables instead of tabs; how to sort, and more.

There are examples of print-merge projects for personalized mailings and similar documents. Word's table-of-contents and indexing features are explored here as well.

Appendices

Appendix A covers the installation of Word 5. Visit this appendix first if you are unsure of how to install the software. *Appendix B* is a list of all word commands, complete with shortcuts and cross-references.

What You Need to Get Started

If you haven't already installed Word 5 on your Macintosh, either follow Microsoft's instructions or read *Appendix A* of this book. If this is your first Macintosh adventure, you might want to prevail upon your Apple dealer or a friend to help with the installation.

This book assumes that you have used your Mac at least briefly and that you know how to click, drag, select text, and make menu choices. The first part of the book reviews these concepts, but you might want to keep your Apple manuals within reach if you are just getting started.

Your Macintosh can run Word 5 in as little as 1 Mb of RAM under System 6, if you don't use MultiFinder, or a minimum of 2 Mb under System 7 (which always runs MultiFinder). Microsoft *recommends* 2 Mb of RAM under System 6 and 4 Mb of RAM under System 7.

While you can run a stripped-down version of Word 5 from a high-density (1.4 Mb) floppy, you cannot run Word 5 from floppies on a machine with only 800K disk drives. The uncompressed program is too big to fit on an 800K diskette.

For all practical purposes, you'll want to run Word 5 from a hard disk. Plan to have at least 6.5 Mb of hard-disk space available before installing Word. You'll need at least one properly installed printer. If you want to practice saving work to floppies, find a spare before you settle down to work. I promised we'd get right to it—so here goes!

PART 1

THE BASICS

Although Microsoft Word 5 has hundreds of features and options, you only need to understand a handful of them to create professional-looking documents. In fact, you can do quite a lot using Word's factory or *default* settings. This part of the book will give you a chance to try Word's major features as you create your first Word 5 document. You'll also learn how to open previously saved Word 5, Word 4, and non-Word documents.

CHAPTER 1

Your First Word 5 Document

FEATURING

- Starting Word 5
- Typing a document
- Inserting and deleting text
- The new ribbon and ruler

In this chapter we'll explore Word's basic text-editing and drawing features using Word's default settings and a Mark Twain quote. You'll type, edit, save, recall, stylize, and print it.

To get started, turn on your Macintosh and locate the Word 5 icon, as shown in Figure 1.1. (Look in the Word folder on the hard disk if you have used Word's installer.) If you can't find the icon, use the *Find File* feature under your *Apple* menu, or get assistance. Once you've located the icon, point to it using your mouse (or trackball), then click on it twice quickly (*double-click*) to launch the program.

Your First Word 5 Document

Figure 1.1
To start Word 5, double-click the Word 5 icon.

You will see a new document window similar to the one in Figure 1.2. The exact size and shape of your window may be different, depending on your monitor and system configuration. If you are a System 6 user or have a black-and-white display, you will not see the shades of gray depicted in many of the illustrations in this book.

Figure 1.2
A new document window appears each time you start Word.

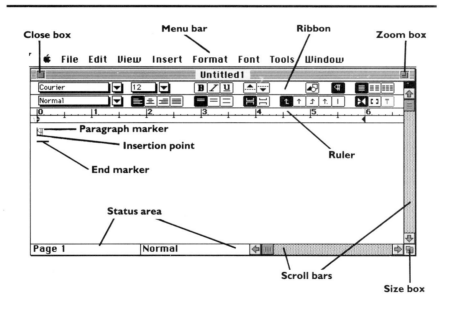

If you are using MultiFinder or System 7 with a large screen, you may see part of your Macintosh desktop in addition to the Word window. This is normal.

An active Word 5 window has standard Macintosh scroll bars, a title bar, zoom boxes, a menu bar, and so on. (If you are unfamiliar with these terms and concepts, take a moment to review your Apple Macintosh manuals.) In addition to the usual Macintosh tools, you should see a Word 5 *ruler, ribbon,* and a flashing *insertion point.* (The insertion point or *cursor* denotes where text will go when you type.) Your mouse pointer should look like an I-beam and move freely about the screen. As you'll soon see, the lower-left corner of your Word window gives additional information about your work.

Page and Document Setup

Word gives you on-screen clues about how your document will look on paper. It shows you line endings, page endings the relative size and placement of text, graphics, margins, and so on. In order to do this, Word needs to know a few things from you. For instance, it needs to know what size paper you plan to print on, as well as the kind of printer you will be using. You may have strong feelings about how much white space you want around the edges of your pages, for example. Once you tell Word these things, it changes the on-screen margins, ruler, and other settings to accommodate and reflect your design. Thus, it is always a good idea to input (at least preliminary) printer, paper, margin, and other document-design decisions before you start typing. In *Part Three,* you will learn how to do this by using Page Setup, the Chooser, the Document menu, and other tools.

If you are lucky enough to have a simple life with only one printer, one paper size, and similar projects, you may be able to make your setup decisions once and forget about them or even use Microsoft's default factory settings for every project. If you do complex tasks or are a perfectionist, you'll frequently change specialized printer and document settings.

That said, let's use Word's default settings for this first example in order to simplify things and get you rolling.

Typing Habits to Break

If you learned to type on a typewriter or even an old word processor, chances are you have established habits that will be counterproductive in your use of

Word 5. Here are a few habits you should try to break:

- Do not use the Tab key or the Spacebar to indent paragraphs. Instead, use the indent control in Word's ruler (the top half of the split triangle at the left side of the ruler). You'll learn more about this in *Chapter 15*.
- Don't use the Spacebar to center text. Use the center-alignment button on the ruler instead.
- Don't use the Spacebar to make columns. Instead use tabs or make a table. See *Chapters 16* and *37*.
- Do not manually space paragraphs. Use Word's paragraph spacing features rather than extra carriage returns, as explained in *Chapter 15*.
- Do not hit the Return key repeatedly to start a new page. Instead, use Word's *Insert Page Break* feature.

Typing Text

Type the following quotation (intentionally type **The the** rather than simply *The* at the beginning). Don't worry if you also make unintentional typing mistakes, you'll learn how to fix them in a moment. Watch the screen as you type. Notice that Word 5 automatically moves text down to the next line when it runs out of room near the right edge of the screen. This is called *automatic word wrap,* a common and useful word processing feature. For this exercise, do not press the Return key until you've typed the period after the word *bug*:

The the difference between the right word and the almost right word is the difference between lightning and the lightning bug.

Finish by typing Mark Twain's name then press the Return key again. When you are done, your screen should look something like Figure 1.3

Selecting Text

Word lets you do a lot with text after you've typed it. You can change its appearance, move it around, delete it, and copy it. The first step is to tell Word which text you want to work with. This is done by selecting it. Word has many, many ways to select text. For instance, you can drag your mouse pointer over the text while holding down the mouse button. There are shortcuts for selecting individual words, lines, sentences, and paragraphs. There is even a *Select All* choice in the *Edit* menu.

Figure 1.3
Type in Mark Twain's unembellished quote.

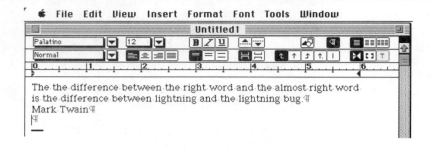

One handy text-editing trick is to simply double-click on a word. Try double-clicking on the second occurrence of *the* in the practice sentence. The word *the* should highlight, along with the space following it. Depending on your system configuration, the selected text will either change color, or be surrounded by a gray or black background. That's how you know what you have selected, as you can see in Figure 1.4.

Figure 1.4
Double-click on a word to highlight it.

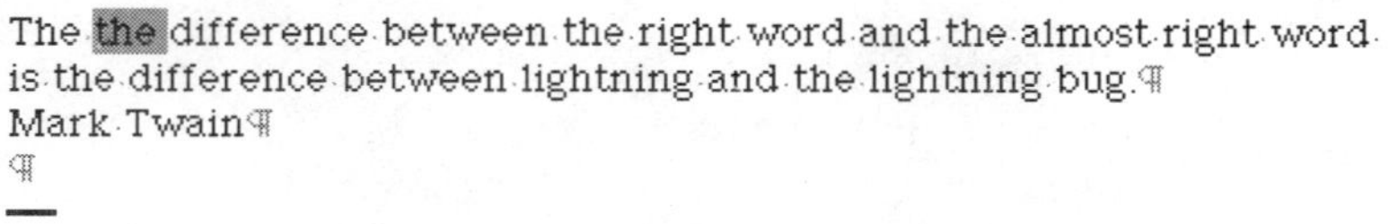

If you are new to the Mac, practice selecting other words, sentences, and single characters with the mouse. It might be frustrating at first, but you'll soon find yourself reaching for the mouse even when using a computer that doesn't have one!

Deleting Text

There are several ways to delete unwanted text like that extra *the* you have typed. If you had spotted your mistake right after typing it, pressing the Delete key (yours may read *backspace*) four times would have removed the unwanted characters and space.

Your First Word 5 Document

Even though you did not make the correction earlier, it is easy to go back now, select the undesired text and remove it.

Once the text is selected, simply press the Delete key once to eliminate the unwanted word and unnecessary space. Try it.

Later, you will learn other ways to delete text, and numerous strategies to reuse deleted text (move it) elsewhere. In this chapter, you are seeing a very simple example of Word's deletion capabilities.

Undoing Actions

Word keeps tracks of the things that you do, and can often undo your most recent change or changes. This is particularly useful when you've made a major mistake and spot it immediately. If you are following along with the example, point to the *Edit* menu with your mouse, then, while holding down the mouse button, slide the mouse down to highlight the *Undo Typing* command as shown in Figure 1.5

In this case, the *Undo* choice will be *Undo Typing*. It will replace the word and space you just deleted. If you haven't already done so, try it. (The keyboard shortcut is ⌘-Z.)

Now, visit the *Edit* menu again and notice that the *Undo Typing* command has been replaced with a new *Redo Typing* command which would, in effect, undo the undo.

Word modifies *Undo* and some of its other menu names and functions based on what you've last done. (You'll learn more about *Undo* in *Chapter 25.*)

Inserting Text

Word offers several ways to insert new text into an existing document. The most straightforward approach is to move the insertion point to the desired location, then start typing. Word accommodates the new text by pushing the existing text to the right and down as necessary.

Figure 1.5
Choose the *Undo Typing* command to undo your most recent edit.

Suppose you wanted to add the word *obviously* between *the* and *right* in the first line of Mark Twain's quote. You would start by placing the mouse pointer (the I-beam) where you want to begin inserting text—between the space and the *r* in *right* for this example. Next, press and release the mouse button to move the insertion point to the desired position.

Beginners sometimes forget to press the mouse button after pointing with the I-beam. Don't confuse the I-beam with the insertion point. First you use the I-beam to point to where you want the insertion point placed. Then you must press and release the mouse button to actually move the insertion point.

Place the insertion point properly and type the word **obviously,** including the space that follows it. Your screen should look something like Figure 1.6.

Figure 1.6
You must position the insertion point and then insert the text.

> The real difference between the obviously right word and the almost right word is the difference between lightning and the lightning bug.¶
> Mark Twain¶
> ¶

Replacing Text

Word also makes it easy to *replace* text. It combines the steps of deleting unwanted text, positioning the insertion point and inserting replacement text. Simply highlight the unwanted text and start typing. The old text disappears and the new text snakes across the screen as you type it.

For example, watch the screen while you highlight the word *almost* (double-click on it) and type **nearly.** See how easily you can turn great prose into drivel? Since we'll be using this text for some future exercises, take a moment now to restore Mark Twain's actual words using the text editing tricks you've learned so far.

Style Changes

Let's take a quick look at a few of Word's most often used style options. Word 4 users are accustomed to going to the menu bar to make style changes. You'll still need to do that occasionally, but Word 5 contains something new called the *ribbon,* shown in Figure 1.7

The Ribbon

Among other things, the ribbon lets you make style changes by clicking buttons or pulling down single level menus, rather than going to the more crowded menu bar. *Chapter 15* describes the ribbon's features in detail. But don't wait that long to try using it.

As always you must select text before working with it. For this exercise, select all the text either by dragging, choosing *Select All* from the *Edit* menu, or by

Figure 1.7
The ribbon makes changing styles easy.

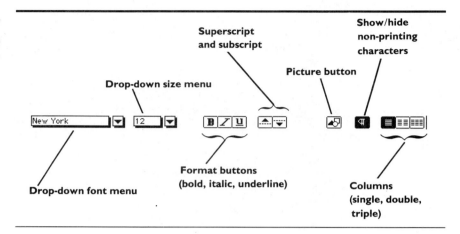

using the keyboard shortcut ⌘-A. Let's start by increasing all of the type from 12 to 24 points. The second triangle in the upper left corner of the ribbon reveals a list of type sizes, shown in Figure 1.8.

To reveal them, point at the triangle and press and hold the mouse button. Slide the pointer down to highlight *24* and release the mouse button. Your screen should look something like Figure 1.9.

You can change as much or as little text as you like this way. Highlight just the first letter *T* in the quote and make it 48 point type. Your text will look like Figure 1.10.

Figure 1.8
You can quickly change the type size with the ribbon.

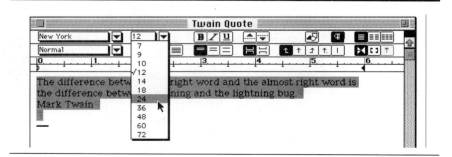

Figure 1.9
The type size has been enlarged to 24 points.

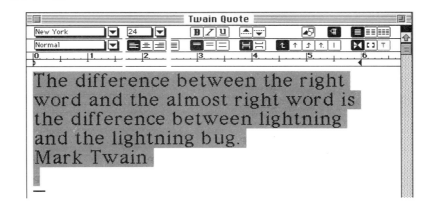

Figure 1.10
Single characters can be changed for emphasis or decoration.

Notice the wider space between the first and second lines now. The space between the *T* and the *he* look unnatural too. That's because different type sizes and fonts have different inter-character (kerning) and inter-line (leading) space specifications. These can be overridden. You will learn how in *Part Three*.

Let's make Mark Twain's name appear in boldface. Start by selecting his first and last names by double-clicking or dragging. Then press the bold button on the ribbon (the uppercase *B*).

The button to the right of the bold button italicizes text. The underscore button is next to the italic button and the next two buttons are for super- and sub-scripting text.

The remaining buttons on the top row access the drawing tools, toggle the display of symbols, and create multi-column layouts.

The Ruler

The ruler is used to control margin settings, line spacing, tab settings, and more. Word 4 users will spot some changes here too. Let's use one of the ruler buttons now and postpone a complete ruler tour until later.

Notice the group of four buttons on the left of the ruler containing horizontal lines (see Figure 1.2). These let you select left-justified, centered, right-justified, or fully-justified text alignment.

With *Mark Twain* highlighted, press the right justification button and watch what happens. Your screen should look like Figure 1.11.

Figure 1.11
Clicking here right-justifies Mark Twain's name.

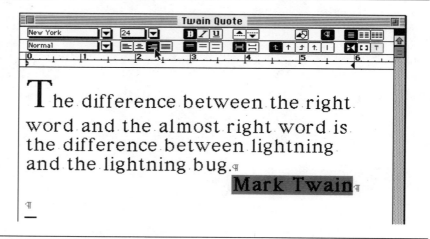

There's much more to learn about the ribbon and the ruler, as you'll see in *Part Three*. You are probably itching to print by now, and you will in a moment, but it would be a good idea to save your work first. That way if you have a printer or system problem, you won't need to re-do the entire exercise.

CHAPTER 2

Save Early and Often

FEATURING

- Saving your work
- Summary information box

The words that you have typed and stylized so far exist only on your screen and in your computer's volatile RAM (random-access memory). That is to say, if you were to switch off the computer, or experience a power failure or other malfunction, your work would be forever lost. By saving your work to disk as you go, you can pick up where you have left off.

Many experienced computer users save every fifteen minutes or whenever they are interrupted by phone calls or visitors. That's a good habit to establish.

Once you are happy with the appearance of the Mark Twain quote, select *Save* from the *File* menu (or press ⌘-S). You will see the Save dialog box, illustrated in Figure 2.1.

This box tells you where Word plans to store your work and requests a name for the file. It also gives you several other save options, which are discussed in *Chapter 30*.

Figure 2.1
You see the Save dialog box the first time you save a file.

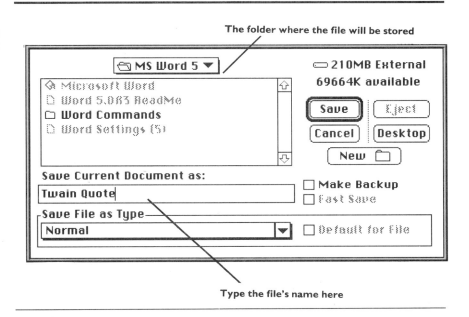

Let's keep things simple for now and use Word's default save options. Start by noticing where Word is proposing to put your document. This is a very important habit to establish. If you do not think about *where* you and Word save documents, you will misplace them. When saving to a floppy disk or your own small, uncluttered hard disk, this can be a minor annoyance. If you work on a far-flung network with multiple servers and gigabits of storage space, it can take hours or days to locate lost files.

In Figure 2.1, Word is proposing to store our new document in a folder called MS Word 5. You can tell this from the picture of a folder next to its name (MS Word 5) near the top of the dialog box.

Look at your screen. Take a moment to see where Word plans to save your work. Chances are you will see something slightly different from the folder location shown in Figure 2.1. If you think you might forget the location, write down the folder name or other location information.

Like any good Macintosh program, Word lets you specify save locations. If you don't know how to change the save location (the path), you will learn in *Chapter 30*. For now, let's use Word's default path.

Type a name for your document in the Save Current Document as: box, then simply click the Save button.

Here's a handy shortcut: Instead of clicking on the Save button, tap the Return key. This will have the same effect as clicking Save. With Microsoft Word 5, like most Macintosh programs, pressing the Return or Enter key will execute the button with the bold border in the active dialog box.

One way or the other, Word will save your document and, assuming you are using Word's default settings, you will see a Summary Info dialog box similar to the one shown in Figure 2.2.

Figure 2.2
The Summary Info dialog box helps categorize documents.

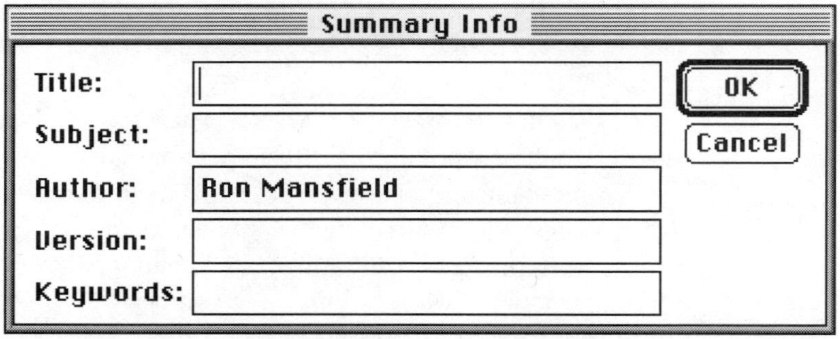

SUMMARY INFORMATION

You needn't type anything in this dialog box, and you can prevent it from even appearing. But if you plan to keep many documents on your hard disk, and particularly if you will be storing things on a crowded network server, it is a good idea to use this new Word 5 feature. It will help you quickly locate typing projects when you want to round them up for later use.

Save Early and Often

Start by typing **Twain Quote** as the document title. Do *not* press Return yet. Instead, tab or point with the I-beam to move the insertion point to the next blank and type **Writing** as the subject. Tab or point again and enter your name if it does not already appear in the author box. Tab again and enter **Draft**. Tab once more and enter some keywords (such as **Twain** or **lightning**) from the document. Your finished summary information should look something like Figure 2.3.

Figure 2.3
The specific summary information will be saved with your document.

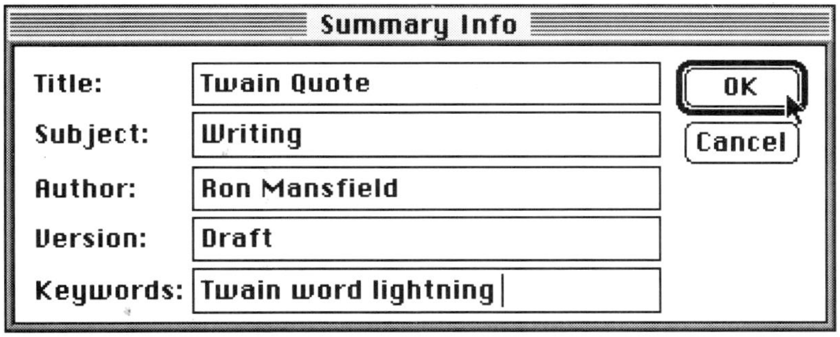

```
┌─────────────── Summary Info ───────────────┐
  Title:     [Twain Quote         ]   [ OK ]
  Subject:   [Writing             ]   [Cancel]
  Author:    [Ron Mansfield       ]
  Version:   [Draft               ]
  Keywords:  [Twain word lightning|]
```

Click the OK button or quicker still, press the Return or Enter key. You will learn more about the Summary Info feature in *Chapter 31*.

Once you have saved a document's summary information, you will not be asked for it again when you save your work. Summary information can be viewed and modified by picking the *Summary Info...* choice from the *File* menu.

KEYBOARD SHORTCUTS

Some Word menu choices are used frequently; Word has built-in keyboard shortcuts for these. Notice the ⌘ symbol and the letter S to the right of the *Save* command in the *File* menu. Word is telling you that there is a keyboard shortcut for this menu choice. You can save without visiting the menu by holding down ⌘ and pressing the S key. Word has many keyboard shortcuts like this one, and you can design your own as you will see in *Part Two* of this book.

Try the Save keyboard shortcut, ⌘-S, and get into the habit of using it early, whenever you make major changes, and often. You'll be glad you did.

So, Ron... when are we gonna print?

CHAPTER 3

Printing Basics

FEATURING

- Printing your document
- Using Print Preview

Finally, it is time to print. Be certain that your printer is turned on and ready to go. Most laserprinters need to warm up, so if you are using one and have just turned it on, wait for the ready light before attempting to print.

If you have more than one printer, use the *Chooser* item under the *Apple* menu to select the desired printer, as shown in Figure 3.1.

Your *Apple* menu will look somewhat different from the one in Figure 3.1. It will show different choices and won't contain icons if you are running under System 6. There will be a *Chooser* somewhere on your *Apple* menu, though. Pick it. Soon, your screen will look something like Figure 3.2.

Here too, your display might look quite different from the illustration. You might have different printer icons, may or may not have Mail or AppleShare icons, and so on. Click on the desired printer. Then, close the Chooser by clicking in the close box in the upper-left corner of the window.

Printing Basics

Figure 3.1
Pull down the *Apple* menu to reach the *Chooser.*

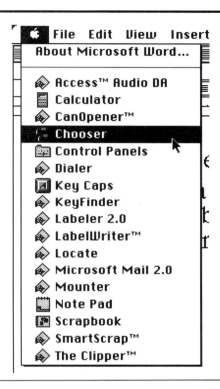

Remember that you normally make your printer choice right when you start designing and creating a document.

RINT PREVIEW

Let's take a look at the Print Preview feature before you actually print your first Word 5 document. You *can* bypass the Print Preview and print immediately to hardcopy, but previewing is advised. It lets you see a screen representation of one or more entire pages before you print them, often saving paper and time. (As you'll see in a moment, Print Preview has other uses as well.) Pull down the *File* menu and choose *Print Preview* (or key ⌘-Option-I). Your screen will look like Figure 3.3

22 The Mac Book of Microsoft Word

CHAPTER 3

Figure 3.2
You use the Chooser to select a printer.

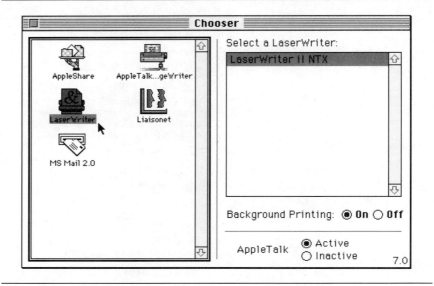

Figure 3.3
Print Preview shows a lot of detail on a big screen.

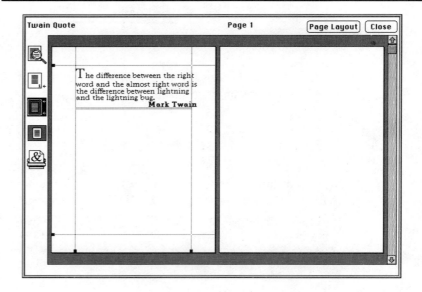

Printing Basics

This will give you an excellent idea of *where* the text will print on the paper. You will be able to see margins as well. If your document contains headers, footers, line numbers, and other embellishments you will see them represented here.

Notice the icons along the left of your screen. They are actually buttons, as explained in Table 3.1.

TABLE 3.1
Print Preview Action Icons

Icon	Function
	Magnifies part of a page
	Adds page numbers
	Displays or hides margins
	Displays one or two pages
	Prints the document

The top button lets you zoom in and out to better read a portion of a page. The second button is used for simple page numbering. The third button turns margin lines on and off. The fourth button switches between a one- or two-page view. The final button is an icon for your chosen printer. Pressing it will print the document.

If you spot a problem in your work, click on either the Page Layout or Close buttons near the top right of the screen to quit previewing. Then you can fix the errors and preview again.

Moving Margins in Print Preview

While a complete explanation of margins will have to wait until *Part Three*, here is a quick trick you can try in Print Preview. Notice the margin lines in Figure 3.4.

Figure 3.4
Drag the margin lines to adjust the margins.

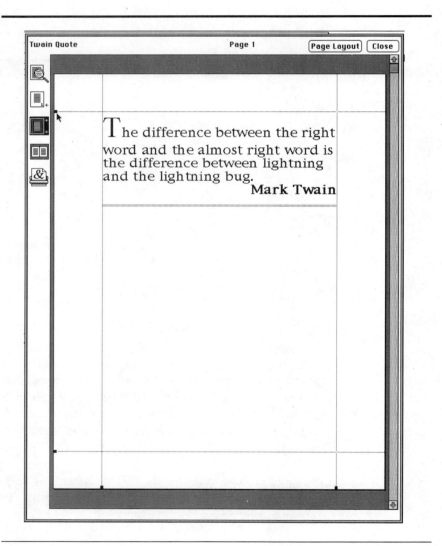

There are small blocks called handles at their left and bottom ends. You can move the margins by dragging them with your mouse. Try centering the text by pulling the top margin down. If you like, switch to one-page view first by pressing the fourth button. After you've moved the margin, turn off the margin lines and see what the printed page should look like.

Print Dialog Boxes

Before printing begins, you will see a Print dialog box similar to those depicted in Figure 3.5.

Figure 3.5
Print dialog boxes differ from printer to printer.

```
LaserWriter  "LaserWriter II NTX"                    7.0    [ Print ]
Copies: [1]         Pages: ◉ All  ○ From:      To:          [ Cancel ]
Cover Page:    ◉ No ○ First Page ○ Last Page
Paper Source: ◉ Paper Cassette   ○ Manual Feed
Print:              ◉ Black & White   ○ Color/Grayscale
Destination:   ◉ Printer           ○ PostScript® File
Section Range: From: 1      To: 1      ☐ Print Selection Only
☐ Print Hidden Text   ☐ Print Next File   ☐ Print Back To Front
```

Your dialog box may look different, depending upon the printers you own and the system version you are using. All Macintosh Print dialog boxes have a few things in common, though. They all give you the opportunity to print one or multiple copies; they let also you print the entire document or just a selected range of pages.

If you are sharp, you may have noticed that Word has added one or more choices to Apple's standard dialog boxes. Can you spot any? They are explained in *Part Three*.

It is finally time to print. Click the Print button (or press Return or Enter) and prepare to admire your work.

CHAPTER 4

Copying and Moving

FEATURING

- Cut, copy, and paste
- The new Move Text command
- Drag-and-Drop

Word 5 supports all of the usual Macintosh techniques for copying and relocating things. It also provides two unique move commands that leave your Macintosh Clipboard undisturbed. One is called *Move Text*. The newest addition, not available in versions before Word 5, is called *Drag-and-Drop*. It's a handy one-step, mouse-assisted mover. This chapter will review conventional moving and copying both within Word and between Word and other programs. You will also learn about Word 5's new Move Text and Drag-and-Drop commands.

CUT, COPY, AND PASTE

The traditional way to move or duplicate things on a Macintosh is to select the items of interest, cut or copy them to the Clipboard, move the insertion point to the new position, and paste them in. For example, suppose you wanted to move the second paragraph in Figure 4.1 in front of the preceding paragraph. You would start by selecting the entire paragraph.

Copying and Moving

Figure 4.1
First, select the items you wish to to move.

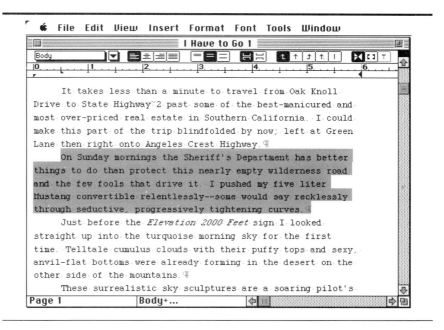

Next, use the *Cut* command found under the *Edit* menu or the ⌘-X shortcut. (If you have an extended keyboard, F2 will work, too.)

The selected text will disappear from the screen and be placed on the Clipboard. Text on your screen below the cut paragraph will move up.

Once the item to be moved is on the Clipboard, place the insertion point at the desired location, as illustrated in Figure 4.2.

Figure 4.2
You must position the insertion point *before* pasting.

Next, paste the paragraph, using either the *Paste* command on the *Edit* menu, the ⌘-V shortcut, or the paste key (F4) on your extended keyboard. Text will flow to the right and down as the Clipboard's contents move into place. In our example, the resulting move would look like Figure 4.3.

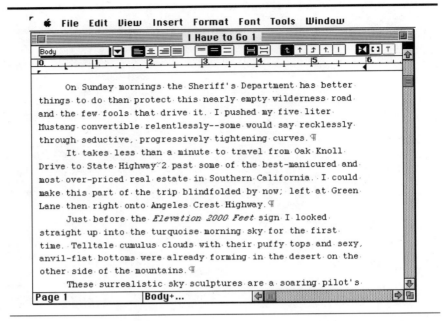

Figure 4.3
The pasted material forces the other material down.

Copying from One Word Document to Another

Since you can open and work on multiple Word documents at the same time, it is easy to move things from one document to another. For example there are two contracts open in Figure 4.4.

With a large screen, it is easy to size and position multiple windows in plain sight and quickly move back and forth, simply by clicking in the window of interest. You can arrange your desktop by clicking and dragging the size boxes in the lower-right corners of windows to adjust their size and shape. You can move windows around as usual, by pointing to their title bars and dragging them.

Remember, while it is possible to have many windows in view at the same time, you can have only one *active* window. You can tell the active window by the lines in its title bar. In Figure 4.4, the bottom window is the active one.

Copying and Moving

Figure 4.4
You can open several documents simultaneously.

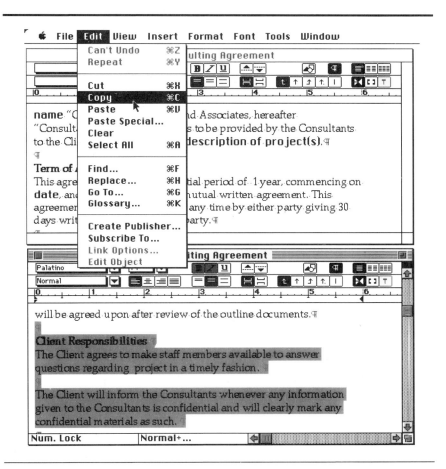

Word's Window Menu

Sometimes your screen may not be big enough to display multiple Word documents in useful sizes. Word provides the *Window* menu for these instances. As you can see in Figure 4.5, the *Window* menu lists the open documents and lets you switch between them. A checkmark denotes the active window. Using this menu, you can activate one window to copy information, go back to the *Window* menu to activate and display another window, and then paste.

Figure 4.5
The *Window* menu allows you to switch between documents.

Activating Windows by Pointing

Even if only a small portion of an inactive window is showing, clicking on it will activate it and bring it forward.

Some Reminders about the Clipboard

It is important to remember that when you cut or copy to the Clipboard, you replace whatever is stored there. If you do this by accident and spot your error immediately, the *Edit* menu's *Undo* command will restore the Clipboard's contents.

The Clipboard can store text, graphics, even sound and animation. While you normally don't need to see the Clipboard to use it, you can view the Clipboard by choosing *Show Clipboard* from the *Window* menu.

Remember also that the contents of the Clipboard disappear when you turn off your Macintosh. If you want to save something permanently, consider pasting it to the Scrapbook, which saves items to disk.

The contents of your Clipboard usually stay the same when you switch from program to program, as long you do not turn off or restart your computer. Thus, you can copy items from a spreadsheet, quit the spreadsheet program, launch Word, and paste the spreadsheet information into your Word document.

MultiFinder users and System 7 users with enough RAM to run more than one program at once often use the Clipboard to pass information back and forth without quitting any of the programs. Here's an example.

Copying and Moving

Suppose that you have created invoices using a spreadsheet, and you want to copy a customer's mailing information from the spreadsheet to a letter you are writing. Assuming you have enough RAM to run both programs, you might open the customer's invoice spreadsheet and a new Word document, as shown in Figure 4.6.

Figure 4.6
The spreadsheet program and Word are running together.

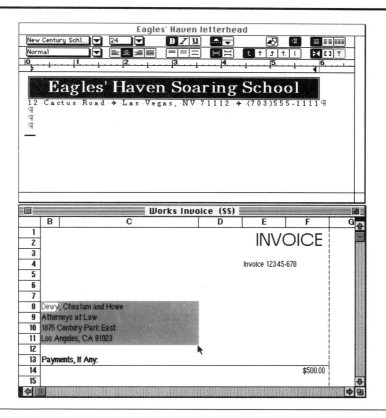

You could copy the customer's address from the spreadsheet onto the Clipboard, then paste it into the Word document. The results might look something like Figure 4.7. Notice that Word has changed the typeface in the process. You will learn more about this in *Part Three*.

Figure 4.7
It's easy to paste information from a spreadsheet into a Word document.

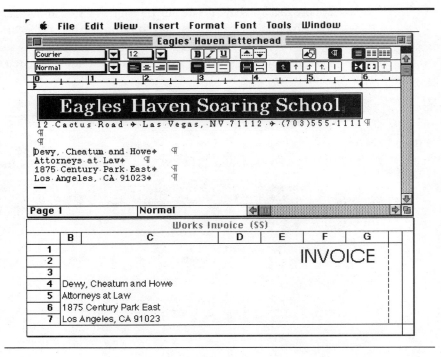

The Move Text Command

While cutting and pasting is the traditional Macintosh way to move items, Word has an additional tool which does not affect the Clipboard's contents. It's called the *Move Text* command. Although you'd never guess from its name, Move Text will also move graphics and sounds. Unfortunately, Move Text is not one of the default choices on the *Edit* menu. However, you can access it by using a keyboard shortcut. If, after you've tried the command, you like it, you can use Word's *Commands...* command to add Move Text to the *Edit* or other menu. Adding commands to menus is described in *Chapter 10*.

To use the Move Text feature via the keyboard shortcut, highlight some text or a graphic to be moved. Then hold down three keys at once—the ⌘, Option, and X keys. The lower-left corner of the active window will display the message *Move to*. Place the insertion point at the desired location and press the Return or Enter key. The text or graphic will move without affecting the Clipboard's contents. *Undo* works here if you need it.

Copying and Moving

The process can work in reverse, if you like. Start by moving the insertion point to the desired location then press ⌘-Option-X and select the item to be moved. Pressing Enter or Return will move the selection to the insertion point.

You can use Move Text to move things from one Word window to another, but it cannot exchange information with other programs.

Drag-and-Drop

Word 5's new *Drag-and-Drop* move feature lets you highlight text or other movable objects and drag them to a new location. For instance, in Figure 4.8 the word *almost* has been highlighted with Drag-and-Drop enabled. With the mouse button depressed, the mouse pointer changes appearance slightly. Notice the small rectangle near the arrow. Notice also the long pointer. The arrow, box, and pointer move as one when you move the mouse with the button held down. Once you release the mouse button, the selected items will be moved to the Drag-and-Drop insertion point. In Figure 4.8, the word *almost* would be inserted between *the* and *right*. If you Drag-and-Drop while holding ⌘, you will move a *copy* of the highlighted text.

Figure 4.8
The pointer and insertion point change when Drag-and-Drop is enabled.

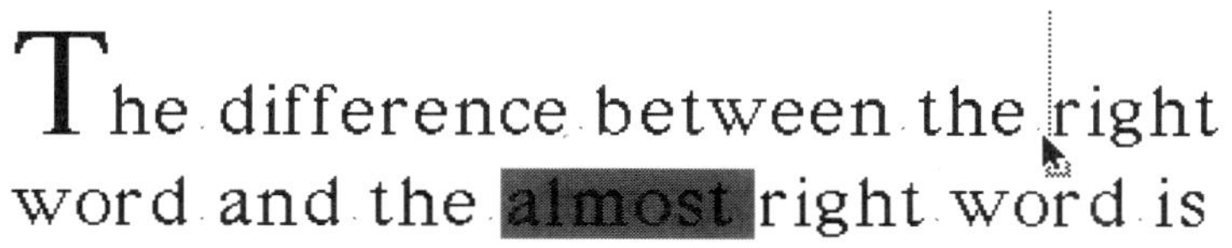

The difference between the right word and the almost right word is

Now let's take a look at Word 5's new Picture window. It's a built-in drawing and painting program.

CHAPTER 5

Drawing in the Picture Window

FEATURING

- Drawing shapes
- The tool palette
- Rotating and flipping objects

Version 5 of Word lets you do more with graphics than any preceding version. The *picture window* is one example of that added power. You can use it to draw diagrams, create forms, design logos, and more. For example, Figure 5.1 shows an organizational chart created entirely in the Word 5 picture window.

This chapter shows you how to use the picture window's drawing tools. *Part Five* will go into more detail about Word's graphic features.

In general, the process works like this. With a Word document window open and active, you open the picture window and draw. Drawings made in the picture window are automatically pasted into a frame (you'll learn more about frames in *Part Five*). The graphic will appear at the insertion point in your Word document when you close the picture window. In order to save a picture thus drawn, you must save the Word document itself.

Drawing in the Picture Window

Figure 5.1
This hierarchy chart is a typical picture window creation.

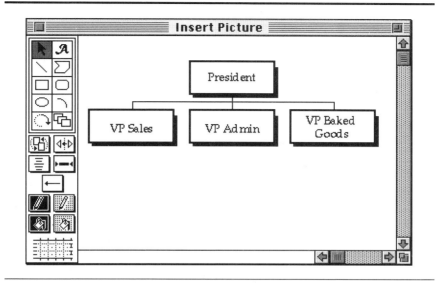

OPENING THE PICTURE WINDOW

Open the window either by clicking on the picture icon in the ribbon or choose *Picture...* from the *Insert* menu. If you use the *Picture...* command, you will also need to click the New Picture button in the resulting dialog box, as shown in Figure 5.2.

Figure 5.2
Click the picture icon or choose *Picture...* from the *Insert* menu to get the New Picture dialog box.

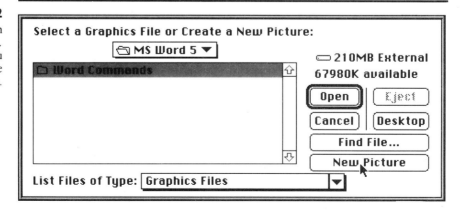

The Tool Palette

Figure 5.3 shows the picture-window tool palette. These tools let you draw objects, add text to drawings, and restyle drawn elements.

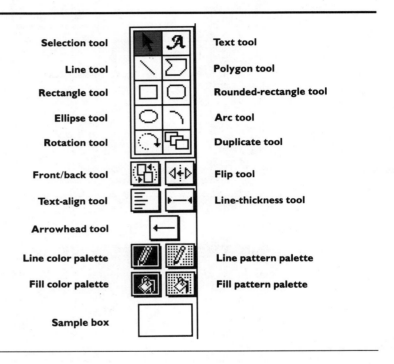

Figure 5.3
The picture-window tool palette may look familiar to those who have used drawing programs.

A SIMPLE DRAWING

The easiest way to learn any drawing program is to use it. To recreate the organization chart shown in Figure 5.1, you might start by drawing a rectangle. Then you could duplicate the rectangle several times, connect the boxes with lines, and add text and shading effects. Here are the steps in more detail with added information about the tools.

The Rectangle Tool

Click on the *rectangle* tool button. It will darken. This is how you know which tool you are using. Next, click and drag with your mouse to form a box of the desired size and shape, as shown in Figure 5.4. To draw a square, hold down the Shift key while you drag. Notice the status area in the lower portion of the window. It displays the height and width of the box as you drag. (When you let go of the mouse button the box will be selected, with *handles* in the corners and in the center of all four sides. These can be used to resize the rectangle.)

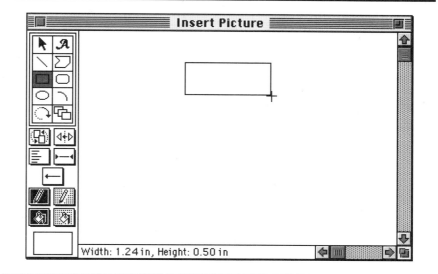

Figure 5.4
Draw a rectangle about the same size as the one in the figure.

Selecting Objects

The upperleft-most tool in the palette (the arrow) is the *selection* tool. Click on it to darken it, then click on the object you want to select. With objects like the rectangle, you may need to click on or near a line. Holding down the Shift key lets you select multiple objects.

To deselect an object, click outside of it or select something else without holding down the Shift key.

Duplicating Objects

To create the organizational chart, you could attempt to draw three more boxes exactly the same size and shape as the first. But there's an easier way.

If the object you wish to duplicate (the rectangle in this example) is not already selected, select it. Then click on the *duplicate* tool, which looks like three staggered rectangles. Each time you click on the duplicate tool, it creates a copy of the selected objects. Click this button three times. Notice how the tool staggers or *cascades* the copies.

Moving Objects

To move an object, first select it, then drag it with your mouse. Do not point to the selection handles when you are attempting to move an object (see Figure 5.5). This will resize it. *Undo* can restore an object's original size and shape if you act immediately. Once selected, objects can be "nudged" a pixel at a time by using the four arrow keys on your keyboard.

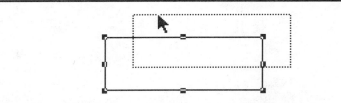

Figure 5.5
Don't point to the resizing handles when moving an object.

Drawing and Sizing Straight Lines

Use the *line* tool to draw straight lines. It is located under the selection tool in the palette. You can draw horizontal, vertical, or angled lines. If you hold down the Shift key while dragging, Word will help you draw straight horizontal or vertical lines, as illustrated in Figure 5.6.

As you drag a line, the status box shows its length. Once you have drawn a line, you can make it longer. First select the line. Handles will appear at each end. Use them to drag the line to the desired length.

EXT IN DRAWINGS

Word permits text in the picture window with a few style and formatting restrictions. By the same token, it is possible to do things with text in the picture window that you can't do in a document window. For instance, you can

Drawing in the Picture Window

Figure 5.6
To draw straight horizontal or vertical lines, hold down the Shift key while dragging.

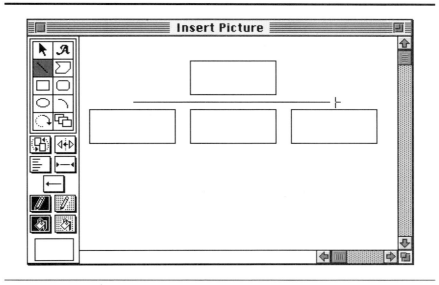

rotate text in the picture window, then insert it into a Word document. When working in the picture window, you create text in text *blocks* or boxes. These are rectangles with invisible sides and exaggerated handles. The word *President* in Figure 5.7 is an example.

Figure 5.7
Text is typed in blocks.

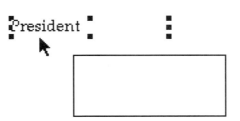

Click on the *text* tool (the letter *A* in the palette) and click in the picture window. Word automatically creates a text block as you start typing. You can resize text blocks by dragging their handles, and the text will wrap to fit in different block sizes. You can change the shape and size of text blocks by dragging the handles; text reflows to fit new text-block sizes and shapes.

Text blocks can be moved like any other picture element. In Figure 5.8, the *President* block has been dragged on top of a chart box, then resized to the length of the box. Dragging the text block to the length of the organizational box will make it easier to center the text, as you will see in a moment.

Figure 5.8
This text block has been moved and resized.

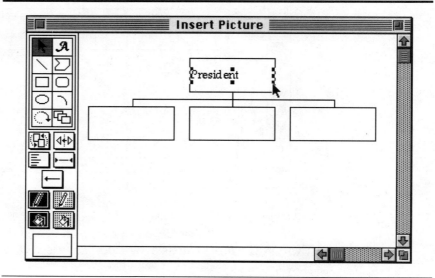

Editing Text

You edit text in text blocks as you might expect. Highlight the text of interest and cut, paste, apply formatting, and so on.

Text Style and Size When Drawing

Many of the format choices on Word's menu bar function with picture text. Plain, Bold, Italic, and Underline each work. All of your Mac's fonts and font sizes are available. *Undo* is often available. You can tell which menu items are available by pulling down the menus. Dimmed choices won't work.

None of the ruler or ribbon features is available, for instance, so you can choose a font from the *Font* menu but not from the Font list on the ribbon. The same is true for point-size selections.

Aligning Text in the Picture Window

While you cannot use any of the ruler's text-alignment buttons, there is a drawing tool that will let you center, left-, or right-align text. The titles in the sample organizational chart were centered by dragging the text blocks to make them the length of the boxes, then selecting the text blocks and picking Align Center from the drop-down *text alignment* button menu.

Groups of Objects

While there is no "group objects" feature, it is possible to act upon multiple picture elements if you select them simultaneously. For instance, if you wanted to move the entire organizational chart you could do that by choosing *Select All* (⌘-A) from the *Edit* menu, then drag all the elements at once.

Line and Fill Colors and Patterns

The picture window offers a variety of fill patterns and colors if your Mac is equipped to support them. Simply select the desired object, then use the appropriate color or pattern tool to apply your choice.

DRAWING SHAPES

Figure 5.9 shows examples of most of the picture window's shape drawing tools at work. The head was drawn using the *polygon* tool. The eyeglasses were drawn with the *rounded rectangle* and *line* tools. The eye was drawn with the *ellipse* tool; the smile with the *curve* tool. Our friend's hair was created with the *arc* tool, then filled.

Line Thickness and Arrowheads

Word 5 offers a choice of nine line thicknesses and three types of arrowheads. They are specified by choosing from pop-up menus, which are reached from the *arrowhead* and *line-thickness* buttons on the palette.

In Figure 5.10 we've drawn a horizontal line with a right arrowhead and are about to make it thicker. Arrowheads and line thickness can be specified before you start to draw a line or added later by selecting an existing line and specifying the arrowhead or new thickness

Figure 5.9
You can create a variety of shapes with the drawing buttons and tools.

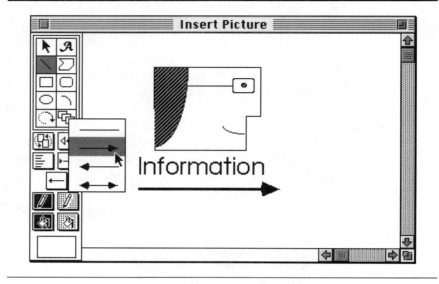

Figure 5.10
Specify line thickness with the line thickness pop-up menu.

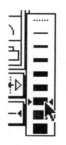

Bring to Front, Send to Back

You've already seen items stacked on top of each other. The text blocks were placed on top of the organizational chart boxes, for instance. Generally, the last thing you draw ends up on top. Sometimes this is not what you want. Suppose, for example, that after creating the information sign, you decided to draw a box to enclose it like the one in Figure 5.11

Drawing in the Picture Window

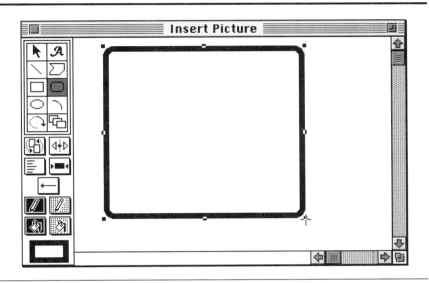

Figure 5.11
An opaque box covers the information drawing

After drawing the box over the sign you could use the Send to Back choice on the *front/back* tool to place the box behind the sign. The finished picture would look like Figure 5.12.

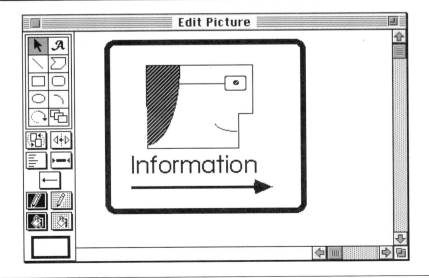

Figure 5.12
The opaque box has been moved to the back.

Rotating and Flipping

The picture window lets you rotate and flip objects as you can see in Figure 5.13. Here we've typed the words *You will flip over Word 5.0*, duplicated them once, flipped them vertically, and changed the flipped words to a lighter color to create a reflection effect. We've also pasted a fly from a Scrapbook collection, duplicated it twice, flipped the right copy vertically and have rotated the center one.

Figure 5.13
Both text and graphics can be rotated and flipped.

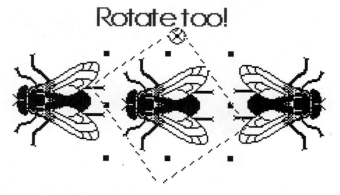

And that's only the beginning!

This chapter has given you only a hint of Word 5's graphic prowess. In *Part Five, Working with Graphics*, you will learn much more about positioning, importing, and manipulating graphics from the picture window and other sources.

CHAPTER 6

Quitting and Restarting Word 5

FEATURING

- Quitting Word
- Launching from a document
- Making aliases

There are several ways to completely quit Word. You can choose *Quit* from the *File* menu or simply use the ⌘-Q keyboard shortcut, as shown in Figure 6.1. Try one or the other method now.

If you have made any changes since the last time you saved, Word will ask if you want them saved. Select Yes to save changes, No to ignore the most recent changes, or Cancel to abort your quit request and return to word processing.

After you have satisfied Word that you have saved everything of value, Word will quit and you'll be returned to your Macintosh desktop.

Figure 6.1
Quit by visiting the *File* menu or using the ⌘-Q shortcut.

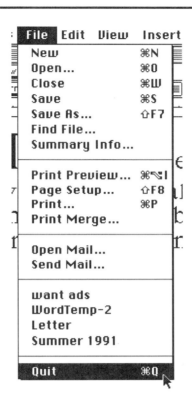

LAUNCHING WORD BY DOUBLE-CLICKING ON A DOCUMENT

Now that you've quit Word, you will need to restart the program before you can use it again. You could double-click on the Word 5 program icon as you did before, then tell Word to load the document that you want to revise. But there is a shortcut. It is possible to load Word by double-clicking on a Word document icon. Try this by double-clicking on your Twain Quote document icon. It will look like Figure 6.2 if you are viewing *by Icon*.

Find your Twain document (hopefully in your Word 5 folder) and double-click on it. After a moment, Word 5 should be on your screen, along with the Twain document, ready for you to edit.

Figure 6.2
You can double-click a Word 5 document icon to start Word.

It is even possible to launch Word 5 by double clicking on documents created with Word 4 and earlier versions. It's a good idea to make sure certain that Word 5 is the only Word version on your hard disk.

Using System 7's Alias Feature

One of the most useful new features of System 7 are its *aliases,* which you can use to launch Word 5. For example, you might keep the actual Word 5 icon tucked away in the Word folder and make an alias of the Word icon for your desktop. System 7 will remember where you've stored Word and will find and launch it when you double-click on the alias icon. Here's how to make an alias for Word.

Start by locating and highlighting the Word 5 icon. Choose *Make Alias* from the *File* menu, as shown in Figure 6.3.

A new icon will appear in the folder along with the Word icon. This is the alias icon. Notice that the file name is italicized and contains the word *alias,* as shown in Figure 6.4.

Drag the icon to a convenient location. Many people place them out on their Macintosh desktop. Close the Word folder and double-click on the alias. It will launch Word without your needing to open up any folders. It is also possible to make alias icons for Word documents. Using this approach, you could have an alias for your letterhead, another for proposals, etc. Also, you can open any document by dragging its icon on top of the Word 5 icon or its alias.

Quick Access to Your Last Four Projects

Once you have saved some Word 5 documents, Word facilitates quick access to the last four of them. Word "remembers" the names and locations of the last

Quitting and Restarting Word 5

Figure 6.3
Making an alias in System 7 can make it easier to launch programs.

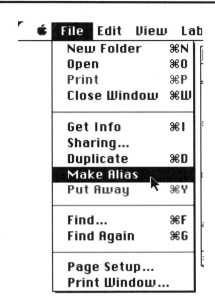

Figure 6.4
You can place an alias anywhere for easy access.

four documents you have worked with and lists them at the bottom of your *File* menu. It even remembers them after you quit Word.

Choose the file of interest and Word will attempt to locate and load it. If you have changed the document's name or moved it since your last Word session, Word may ask for help locating it.

CHAPTER 7

How Word 5 Differs from Previous Versions

FEATURING

- New features
- New commands

In the past, Microsoft has been criticized for adding and changing features without much regard for input from users. Recently they have taken steps to remedy this. For instance, Microsoft's researchers have set up high-tech "useability labs" where they unobtrusively record and analyze peoples' reactions to existing products and to proposed new features. Microsoft also visits users in their offices and tracks calls to the Microsoft help lines. Moreover, as any Microsoft programmer or product manager will tell you, a single letter written by a user carries plenty of weight in "features" meetings.

The results of this renewed attention to user needs can be seen in Word 5. The product "feels" right. At a recent Word Users Conference in Seattle, experienced Word 4 users "oooed and ahhhed" aloud when they saw Word 5's improvements demonstrated for the first time. You might have the same reaction. This chapter assumes you've had experience with Word 4, and explores Word's major modifications. They've been grouped into five categories:

- New features
- Enhanced features
- Menu changes
- Keyboard shortcut changes
- System 7 support

You may find a few of the changes annoying at first. If you are like most people, however, after a week or less of using Word 5, you'll never want to go back to an earlier version.

EW FEATURES

It's hard to know which new feature to explore first. One of the most intriguing—*Drag-and-Drop*—was a last minute addition to Word 5. Let's start with it.

Drag-and-Drop

Drag-and-Drop lets you highlight text, pictures, or other Word elements and drag them, simply by holding down the mouse button. As you do this, the insertion pointer gets very large and moves with the mouse. When you release the mouse button your highlighted material will be moved (copied, cut, and pasted) to the right of the insertion pointer. This action will not affect the contents of your clipboard. Alternately, you can drag a copy of the text by holding down the ⌘ key while dragging, again without affecting the contents of your clipboard.

When you unintentionally Drag-and-Drop something (and you will...), the *Undo* command can restore things if you catch your mistake in time. Drag-and-Drop is enabled when you first install Word 5. You can turn it off permanently from the General category of the Preferences dialog box; or you can use Word's *Commands...* feature to add Drag-and-Drop to the *Tools* or other menu.

Thereafter, you can turn the feature on and off from the menu bar. Drag-and-Drop is demonstrated in *Chapter 4*.

The Ribbon

As you learned in *Chapter 1,* the ribbon puts frequently used style features like bold, underscore, and font choices a mere mouse-click away. Excel 3 users will find that it looks vaguely familiar.

Triple-Click Paragraph Selection

Here's a feature guaranteed to start a fight at a users' meeting. Clicking three times quickly in succession will highlight any paragraph you click in. Most people love it. Others don't, at least not at first. There is no way to disable triple-click selection.

Insert Symbols

Are you tired of trying to remember the key combination required to type the trademark symbol (TM) or have you forgotten how to make an umlauted *u* (ü)? Word 5's *Symbol...* feature (found on the *Insert* menu) displays all special symbols available for the current font. As shown in Figure 7.1, clicking on the symbol of interest places it in your document at the insertion point.

In the lower-left corner of the Symbol window, you will see the ASCII decimal code for the symbol you've entered. (Thanks to another new Word feature, this is only of passing interest now, unless you are a programmer or trained troubleshooter.) See *Chapter 14* for more information about inserting symbols.

Special Character Replacement

In the past, if you wanted to replace tabs, paragraph markers, or other special characters in a Word document, you needed either to know the ASCII code for the special character or to copy the sample character to the Clipboard and paste it into the Replace dialog box.

As you can see in Figure 7.2, Word 5's new Replace dialog box contains dropdown lists of special characters that make them much easier to change.

How Word 5 Differs from Previous Versions

Figure 7.1
Clicking on a symbol places it in your document.

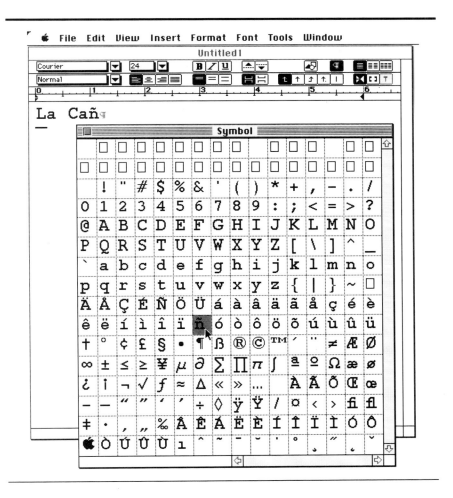

See *Chapter 26* for more information about this feature.

Style Replacement

How often have you wished you could easily change all the underlined text in a document to italic, or change one heading level to another, or modify certain indents throughout a document? Word 5's improved *Replace...* feature simplifies that too. See *Chapter 26* for more information about style replacement.

Figure 7.2
Replacing special characters is much easier now.

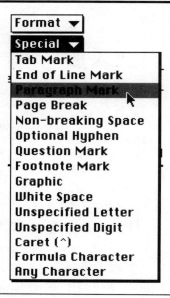

Summary Info

This one will grow on you after you use it for a while. It works in conjunction with Word 5's new *Find File...* feature, (described next). If enabled, the *Summary Info...* feature presents a dialog box like the one shown in Figure 7.3 when you first save a document.

Figure 7.3
Word's Summary Info dialog box helps you locate and organize documents.

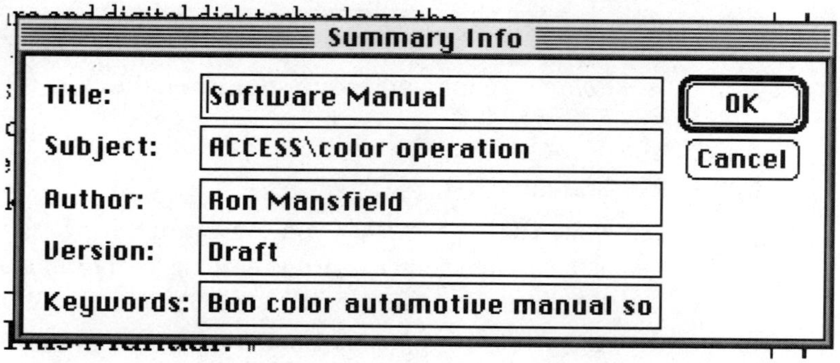

How Word 5 Differs from Previous Versions

Word 5 asks you for information about the document (author's name, subject matter, key words, etc.) If you enter summary information for all of your Word 5 documents, it will be easy to use the new *Find File...* feature to round up all of the invoices you've typed or to find proposals written by your boss.

If you want to include old Word 4 or other non-Word 5 documents in summary searches, you will need to open them under Word 5, save them as Word 5 files, and add summary information when prompted to do so. See *Chapter 30* for more details.

Find File...

"I lost my file!"

How many times have you said or heard that? Today's big hard disks and widespread networks, and the ease with which things can be accidentally dragged into folders has made file hunting a popular pastime. *Find File...* can help. Don't confuse this new Word feature with the *Find...* command located on the *Edit* menu. And, don't confuse it with the *Apple* menu item called *Find File* either. Figure 7.4 gives you a glimpse of this powerful new Word feature.

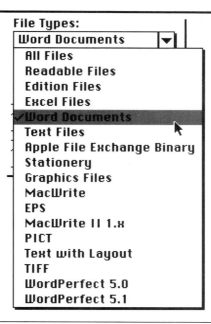

Figure 7.4
Don't confuse Word's *Find File...* command with the *Find...* menu choice or Apple's *Find File* desk accessory.

Word 5's *Find File...* command lets you search your disks and other disks on your network using a wide variety of criteria. *Find File...* lets you list, browse, open, and even copy the contents of files once you have located them. There are some limitations, however. This is one feature you will want to understand fully. See *Chapter 30* for details.

Quick Access to Last-Used Files

This'll be an instant hit once you remember it is available. Word adds the names of the last four documents you've worked on to the bottom of the *File* menu, as shown in Figure 7.5.

Figure 7.5
Your last four projects appear at the bottom of the *File* menu.

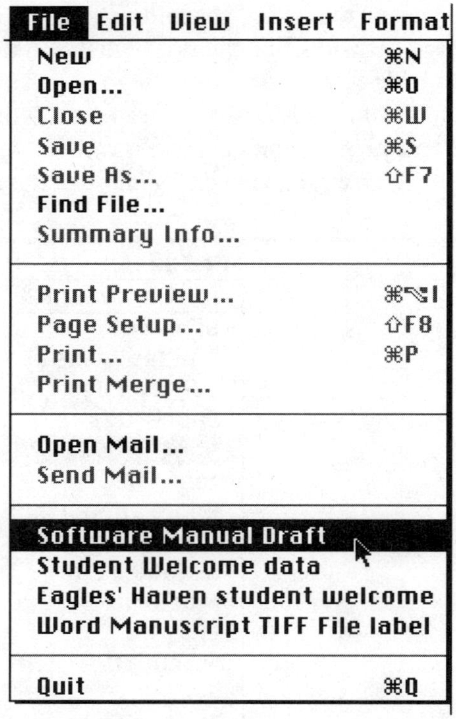
File Edit View Insert Format
New ⌘N
Open... ⌘O
Close ⌘W
Save ⌘S
Save As... ⇧F7
Find File...
Summary Info...
Print Preview... ⌘⌥I
Page Setup... ⇧F8
Print... ⌘P
Print Merge...
Open Mail...
Send Mail...
Software Manual Draft
Student Welcome data
Eagles' Haven student welcome
Word Manuscript TIFF File label
Quit ⌘Q

To resume working on a recent project, just pick its name from the Word 5 *File* menu. Word remembers where the file is stored, retrieves it, and puts it on your screen faster than you can say "Now which folder was that in?" This even works if the file is on a server or on someone else's System 7-shared disk. Naturally, if you have changed the name of a file since using it, or if you move a file, or if you have not mounted the drive containing the requested file, Word cannot automatically find the document for you. You will be asked to participate in the search, which you can cancel if you so desire. Learn more about this feature in *Chapter 30*.

Don't Embarrass Yourself

While the last-used-file feature is a real timesaver, it *can* be a source of embarrassment and security leaks as well. Realize that if the last documents you worked on were titled *Resume, 10 Things I hate about my boss, Confidential salary memo,* and such, anyone viewing your Word *File* menu would learn a lot.

You can remove items from the list by either opening non-controversial documents (which will replace the earlier ones) or by using the Remove Menu Items techniques described in *Chapter 10*. You can disable the last-used-file feature from the View Category in the Preferences dialog box. See *Chapter 9* for details.

The Insert Menu's File... Command

Here's a quick new way to assemble new documents from old ones. Place the insertion point at the appropriate place in your new document, then use the *Insert* menu's *File...* command to automatically copy-in one or more other files. You can even import certain non-Word files this way. See *Chapter 30* for details.

Drawing Features

In the past, if you wanted to place drawings in your Word documents you needed to use other Macintosh programs to create them. As you know from *Chapter 5,* Word 5 offers a very functional built-in drawing package that lets you create logos, forms, and much more. If you have ever used another Macintosh drawing program, Word 5's features will seem familiar. If this is your first drawing program, it may be all you'll ever need.

Paragraph and Cell Shading

Users asked for paragraph shading. Word 5 has it. When used in combination with Word's Border features, shaded paragraphs can create impressive, easy-to-use forms like the one in Figure 7.6.

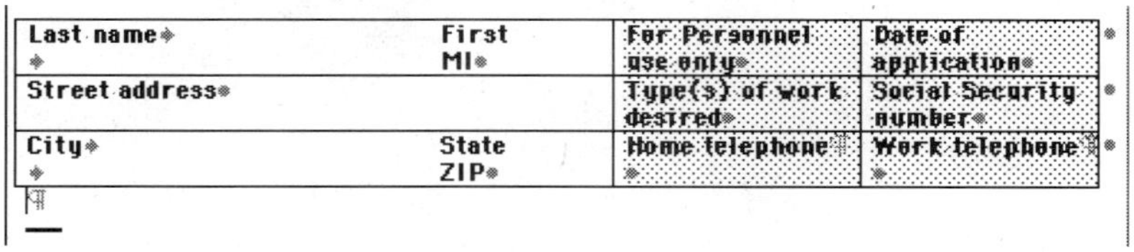

Figure 7.6
Paragraph shading is a new way to highlight important information. Use it with paragraph borders to create forms.

Last name	First MI	For Personnel use only	Date of application
Street address		Type(s) of work desired	Social Security number
City	State ZIP	Home telephone	Work telephone

Thesaurus

Do you wish you could find a new way to say *however*? Word 5 can suggest *nevertheless, yet,* and *moreover* thanks to its new built-in thesaurus from Houghton. Highlight the word you want to replace, choose *Thesaurus...* from the *Tools* menu and click on the replacement word of your choice, as shown in Figure 7.7.

Word 5 will even insert the new word for you. If you ask about an ambiguous word like *duck,* Word's thesaurus feature will let you tell it whether you mean the noun *water fowl* or the verbs for *crouch to avoid* or *plunge into water.* Read all about it in *Chapter 35*.

Grammar Checker

While professional editors won't be summarily unemployed by this feature, Word 5's built-in Grammar Checker can help improve your prose. It will analyze your document for redundant expressions, cliches, over-used phrases, long sentences, the ever-dreaded passive voice, and more. You get to turn rules off if they don't fit your style.

Beware: The Grammar Checker needs a lot of RAM. With the Grammar Checker installed, Word 5 may not run properly with less than 2 Mb of RAM under System 6. It won't always run with 4 Mb under System 7! Fortunately, memory is inexpensive these days.

How Word 5 Differs from Previous Versions

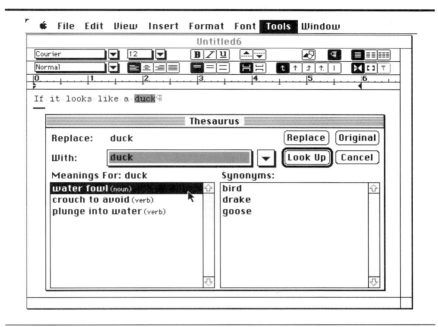

Figure 7.7
The Word Thesaurus helps find the "just right" word.

Print Merge Helper

Better than an industrial-size bottle of aspirin, Word 5's Print Merge Helper and related Print Merge improvements will relieve mass-mailing headaches. Print Merge has other interesting applications even if you don't create junk—er, sorry—"targeted direct mail." Read about these improvements in *Chapter 40*.

Annotations

The electronic equivalent of Post-it™ notes, Word's two annotation features let you add non-printing notes to yourself or others in the document-production loop. You can type the notes or, if you have a microphone-equipped Macintosh, leave spoken notes for your colleagues. See *Chapter 20* for examples of these features at work.

Equation Editor

Rocket scientists rejoice! Microsoft heard you grumbling about the difficulties of equation typing. If you create tests, class notes, journal articles, or dissertations, you will probably enjoy the new Equation Editor described in *Chapter 39*.

Non-Word 5 File Converters

Word is now better able to share files with other word processors, including earlier versions of Word, WordPerfect, and MacWrite, to name a few. *Chapter 45* gives you the inside scoop.

Enhanced Features

For every new Word feature, ten existing features have been enhanced. Here are some examples.

Ruler Improvements

The ruler is slimmer now and it takes up less screen space. The ruler numbers are closer to your text. Tab buttons are grouped to the right for easy access.

Better Spelling Checker

Now you can stop cursing Word's spelling checker. The new one is quick, and it usually guesses exactly what you meant to type. It even knows how to spell *Microsoft!*

More Standard Glossary Entries

All of your old favorite glossary entries remain, and dozens have been added. It is even possible to print dates without days in the usual American format (*November 7, 1947,* for instance). You can choose standard or user entries. Items from the Summary Info dialog box are also glossary entries (*author,* for instance). Read more about the glossary in *Chapter 28*.

Larger Fonts

Word no longer has a ceiling on font sizes of 127 points. If you want, you can recreate a billboard sign at full scale!

Easier Default Changes

Default settings are more logically grouped and are easier to see and change. Word even asks you to pick a default font for Normal when you install the program. Defaults are discussed throughout this book, but primarily in *Part Two*.

Improved Graphics Positioning

The Position feature has been replaced by the much more intuitive *Frame* technology. See *Chapters 31* and *32*.

Improved Tables

There have been many subtle improvements to Word's various table features. Together they make tables much more powerful and easier to use. Frequent table makers will particularly enjoy Word's ability to automatically match column widths when you type **Auto** in the Column Width space of the Table Cell dialog box. See *Chapter 37* for examples of this and other table improvements at work.

Better Small Screen Support

Owners of Macintosh computers with traditional (9-inch diagonal) screens will be happy to know that there are abbreviated menu names available. This makes it possible for you to see Word's menus and have a clock and other icons on your menu bar.

The magnifying glass is back in Word's Print Preview mode. Now small screen users will be able to zoom in and actually read text in Print Preview mode.

A Kinder, Gentler Print Preview

Speaking of Print Preview, there have been other improvements here, too. Icons are bigger and more meaningful. Double clicking on a Print Preview page returns you to the Page Layout view (formerly called *Page View*).

Enhanced Dialog Boxes

Many of Word's dialog boxes have been improved. Labels and buttons and messages are often more meaningful. Features are more logically grouped. Some boxes, like Find, have added features resulting in new buttons and menus. And, you will now be able to tab from place to place within more dialog boxes.

Rearranged and Renamed Menus

Word's menus have been revised and in some cases combined or renamed. Figure 7.8 compares Word 4's and Word 5's menus. With a few exceptions, you will find most of the changes logical.

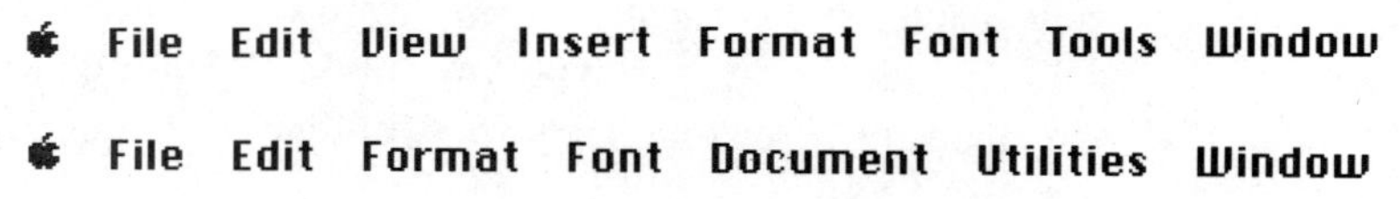

Figure 7.8
Word's menus have changed from Word 4 (bottom) to Word 5 (top).

🍎 File   Edit   View   Insert   Format   Font   Tools   Window

🍎 File   Edit   Format   Font   Document   Utilities   Window

Keyboard Shortcuts Worth Noting

A number of keyboard shortcuts have changed. The good news is that shortcuts are now more "Mac-like". The bad news is, users of earlier Word versions have developed some bad habits through no fault of their own.

For instance, ⌘-B is now the shortcut for bold text. In Word 4, that key combination put you into Page View mode. The Word 5 key combination for Page Layout view (formerly called *Page View*) is ⌘-Option-P.

The ⌘-I combination now creates italic text and ⌘-U creates underlined text. Previously ⌘-U took you to Outline View and ⌘-I placed you in Print Preview. The new key combinations for those are ⌘-Option-O and ⌘-Option-I respectively.

You can change these shortcuts, but you might want to try changing your habits first. The new combinations are better to know in the long run. Table 7.1 lists the most commonly confused ones in Word 5:

TABLE 7.1

Word 5's Most Commonly Confused Keyboard Shortcuts

Normal	⌘-Option-N
Page Layout	⌘-Option-P
Outline	⌘-Option-O
Print Preview	⌘-Option-I
Bold	⌘-B
Italic	⌘-I
Underline	⌘-U
Select All	⌘-A
Repeat Formatting	⌘-Y
Show Paragraph	⌘-J

System 7 Support

While you don't need System 7 to use Word 5, they work well together. If different people in your organization contribute portions of whole documents, you may benefit from the fact that Word 5 takes advantage of System 7's Publish and Subscribe features. They are described in *Chapter 44*. Word also has its own Balloon help.

PART II

PERSONALIZING WORD 5

Word has hundreds of features. Usually, there are several different ways to do the same thing. Realizing that people will have strong and differing preferences, Word's designers have given you the ability to turn features on and off. You can also rearrange menus. It's possible to add keyboard shortcuts for Word's commands and change the ones Microsoft has assigned. You can determine which view Word starts in and pick your favorite font. The chapters in this part show you how to customize Word to make it the product *you* would have designed had they put you in charge.

Word 5 Defaults

FEATURING

- Choices Word's designers have made for you
- Where default are stored
- How to change and restore standard settings

WHAT ARE DEFAULTS?

The computer industry has been misusing the term "default" for several decades; but even the publishers of Webster's weighty New Lexicon edition of the English dictionary haven't noticed.

For our purposes, *defaults* are choices that Word's designers made in your absence regarding key features. These decisions affect the look and feel of Word when you first install it. For instance, by default, Word 5 opens with the ruler and ribbon displayed. If you are using a small Macintosh display, Word's installation program notices that fact and *defaults* to short menu names.

You can overrule many of Word's defaults. Ironically, once you override default settings and save new ones, we usually still refer to the new collection of settings as "defaults", rather than "user preferences" or "start-up settings" or something more precise.

Designer Defaults

Word's original (factory) settings are referred to as "Microsoft Standard Settings". The designers of Word 5 have chosen settings that they feel will work for the majority of people doing general typing and correspondence. For instance, they assume you will use standard letter size (8½ × 11") paper. They have specified generous right, left, top and bottom margins that should accommodate most binding, header and footer needs. They have turned on popular Word features and turned off more esoteric ones that annoy some people. They have organized the menus for you and held back many potential menu choices.

But even the research-laden folks in the Microsoft Useability labs couldn't come to a consensus on the "best" font default, so Word lets you pick your favorite at installation. Table 8.1 lists some (but not all) of Microsoft Word 5's standard settings for the American version. Most can be found in various categories of the Preferences dialog box.

As you can see from the table, some defaults, like Fractional Widths and Most Recently Used List (MRU List), change based on your machine's configuration. Things like the dictionaries and thesaurus change in international versions.

TABLE 8.1 Word 5's Factory Defaults (American Version)

Feature	Default Settings
Allow Fast Saves	On
Always interpret RTF files	On
Always Make Backups	Off
Always suggest spellings	On
Background Repagination	On
Custom dictionary	Selected
Default font	New York (user prompt at installation)
Drag-and-Drop	On
Fractional Widths	On (if LaserWriter is chosen)
Grammar rules (all)	On

TABLE 8.1

Word 5's Factory Defaults (American Version) (continued)

Feature	Default Settings
Hyphenation Dictionary	English (US)
Ignore Uppercase (spell checking)	Off
Ignore Numbers (spell checking)	Off
Include formatted text in Clipboard	On
Main dictionary	English (US)
Most Recently Used Files list	On (off for small-screen Macs)
Open in Page Layout view	Off
Page margins in Print Preview	On
Picture placeholders	Off
Prompt for Summary Information	On
Ribbon	On
Ruler	On
Save Option	Normal Word file format
Save reminder	Off
Section Start	No Break
Short menu names	Off
Show Document Statistics (grammar)	On
Show function keys on menus	Off
Show Hidden Text	On
Show paragraph markers	Off
Show table gridlines	On
Smart Quotes	Off
Text boundaries in Page Layout view	Off
Thesaurus	English (US)
View	Normal view

Where Defaults Are Stored

Defaults are stored in the *Word Settings* (5) file in your System Folder. If you are using System 7, the file is stored in the Preferences folder *within* the System Folder. The Word Settings (5) icon is shown in Figure 8.1. You will learn how to change these settings and work with more than one collection of settings in *Chapter 9* and *Chapter 10*.

Figure 8.1
Word's defaults are stored in the Word Settings (5) file.

Reverting to Standard Defaults

Be aware that reverting will change other things besides the Microsoft standard settings you hope to regain. For instance, if you have a list of most recently used files, they will not be on the file menu after you revert to Microsoft's standard settings. If you have reassigned some keyboard shortcuts, those changes will also be lost. Your default-font choice will need to be made again as well.

That said, there are several ways to revert to Microsoft's standard defaults. The brute force method is to reinstall Word, but you needn't go to that extreme.

Whenever Word starts, it looks in your System Folder for a Word Settings (5) file. If it can't find one, it makes a new one. Thus, dragging the Word Settings (5) file from the System folder into the trash (or renaming the settings file) *before* you start Word will cause Word to create a new "standard" Word Settings (5) file. There is one potential gotcha, however. You *must* do this when Word is *not* running.

If you do trash the undesirable settings file while Word is running and then quit Word, it will save the undesirable settings in a new settings file.

Finally, Word has a built-in feature for resetting. Open the Commands dialog box with the *Commands...* choice on the *Tools* menu (or the ⌘-Shift-Option-C shortcut), and click the Reset... button. You will see a dialog box like the one in Figure 8.2. Choose Revert to Microsoft Standard Settings and things should be back to Microsoft's suggested defaults!

Figure 8.2
Choose the standard-settings option to revert to the "factory" configuration.

CHAPTER 9

Preferences

FEATURING

- Changing the default settings
- Customizing Word's appearance and functionality

Word 5 gives you considerable control over its various features. For example, you can dictate default view settings, menu appearance, default font settings, and much more. Many of these choices are made using Preference dialog boxes. This chapter will introduce you to Word's Preference dialog boxes. Preferences are saved in Word Settings files, so it is possible to have more than one set of preferences.

REACHING PREFERENCE DIALOG BOXES

There are eight Preferences dialog boxes. Unless you have moved the *Preference...* choice somewhere else on your menu bar, begin by selecting *Preferences...* from the *Tools* menu. This brings up a dialog box like the one shown in Figure 9.1. Notice the icons and scroll bar on the left side of this dialog box.

By clicking on these icons you move from one Preferences category to another. Microsoft calls these *preferences categories.* You'll always see the General category first. To quit, click in the close box. Let's look at all eight categories (General, View, Open and Save, Default Font, Spelling, Grammar, Thesaurus, and Hyphenation).

Preferences

Figure 9.1
The Preferences dialog box allows you to customize settings.

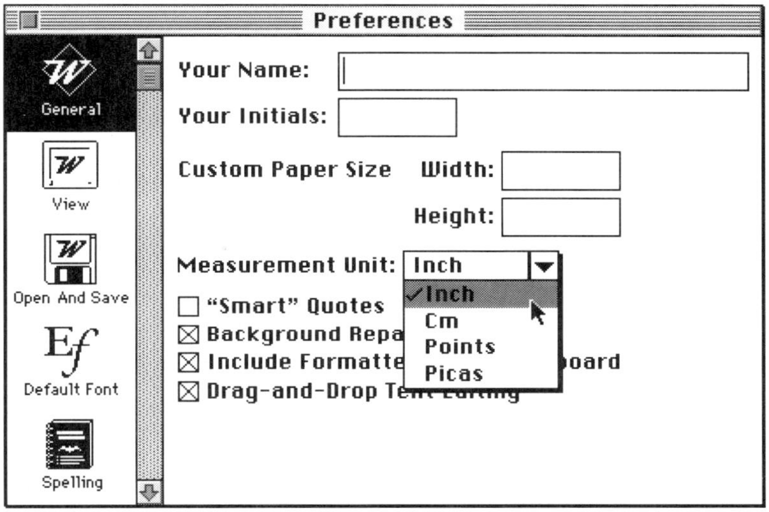

The General Category

The General Preferences category lets you enter or edit your name and initials, define custom paper sizes, toggle "smart" quotes, control automatic repagination, and control clipboard formatting.

Name   The name is used by the Summary Information dialog box and the Glossary for the author glossary item. If you get your name right here, you will not need to retype it each time you create Summary Information or use the author glossary item. If necessary, edit your name using normal Macintosh editing and navigation techniques.

Initials   The initials you type here will be displayed when you record a voice annotation. See *Chapter 20* for more information about voice annotation.

Custom Paper Size   Notice the custom paper-size boxes below the name and initial boxes. They will be dimmed unless your chosen printer supports custom paper sizes. Most laserprinters do not, ImageWriters and the ImageWriter LQ do.

If your printer supports custom sizes and you wish to define them, but the choices are dim, close the Preferences dialog box and visit the Chooser to select the appropriate printer icon. Then return to the General Preferences category to continue.

Measurement Unit Beneath the custom paper size boxes you'll find a drop-down menu used to define the units of measure used by the ruler, text boxes, and for margins and tab settings, as shown in Figure 9.1. Spacing measurements such as super- and subscripts, line spacing and inter-character spacing are not controlled here.

"Smart" Quotes An *X* in this box tells Word to replace simple quotes with curly "typsetter's" quotes as you type. This option does not affect previously typed quote marks. To turn off "smart" quotes, remove the *X* from the checkbox by clicking on it.

Background Repagination With this option checked, Word will automatically repaginate your document (compute new line and page endings) whenever you are not typing. On some slower Macs you may find that automatic repagination slows certain operations. If this is an annoyance, remove the check mark and Word will only repaginate when you tell it to or before you print or do other tasks requiring repagination.

Include Formatted Text in Clipboard Normally you will want this box checked. It carries text attributes (bold, italic, etc.) with the text on the Clipboard. Paragraph formatting carries over as well if you copy the appropriate paragraph markers to the Clipboard. Removing the checkmark from this box copies plain text to the Clipboard.

Drag-and-Drop Text Editing This box determines whether the Drag-and-Drop feature defaults to off or on when you start Word. No matter which preference you choose here, you can always turn Drag-and-Drop off and on from the menu bar if you have installed it there. (See *Chapter 10* to learn how.)

The View Category

Figure 9.2 illustrates the View category. It determines how hidden text, grid lines, text boundaries, and picture placeholders appear. It gives you control

Figure 9.2
The View Preference choices range from non-printing character display to menu appearance.

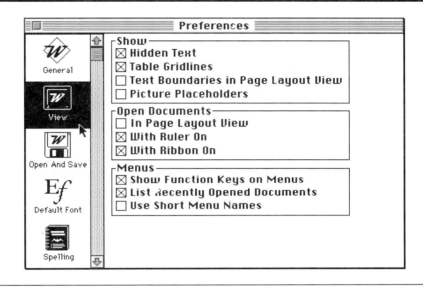

over the appearance or absence of the ruler and ribbon in new documents. This category also controls several items relating to menu appearance. With most choices in this category, regardless of what you set here, you can control the option from the menu bar.

Show Hidden Text This choice determines whether hidden text will be displayed by default. It does not affect the default printing of hidden text.

Show Table Gridlines An *X* here means that you will see dotted lines between rows and columns in tables. These lines will not print.

Show Text Boundaries in Page Layout View An *X* here means that when you are in the Page Layout view, you will see dotted lines around document elements like text areas, headers, footers, and framed objects. These lines will not print. Note that even though the choice contains the word *text,* it affects non-text elements as well (like graphics).

Show Picture Placeholders On slower Macs, Word can slow to a crawl if your document contains large graphics. It is possible to speed up work in drafts by displaying gray rectangles instead of the graphics themselves while editing. *Chapter 31* has more information on this topic. The picture placeholders choice determines whether or not these placeholders are used by default.

Open Documents in Page Layout View   With this box checked, Word 5 will always open your documents in Page Layout view (called *Page View* in Word 4). In Page Layout view, you will see headers, footers, page numbers, and so on. There is a performance penalty. Scrolling and other tasks can be noticeably slower in this view. That's why you have a choice of default views.

Open Documents with Ruler On   With this box checked, Word 5 will always open your documents with the ruler in view. The ruler shows tabs, indent styles, etc., but takes up room, particularly on small screens.

Open Documents with Ribbon On   With this box checked, Word 5 will always open your documents with the ribbon in view. The ribbon shows font choices, lets you show paragraph markers, lets you quickly apply bold, underscore, and other embellishments. Like the ruler, the ribbon takes up room, particularly on small screens.

Show Function Keys on Menus   Notice the difference between the left and right menus in Figure 9.3. The *Save As...* choice on the left lists Shift-F7 as a keyboard shortcut.

The other menu does not. This choice toggles the display of function key shortcuts. If your keyboard does not have function keys, or if you have redefined the use of your function keys, you may want to remove the *X* in the *Show Function Keys in Menus* box to make your menus consistent with your keyboard.

List Recently Opened Documents   This box controls the feature that appends the names of the last four Word documents you've used to the *File* menu. An *X* in the box assures that the file names will appear. See *Chapter 6* for more about this feature.

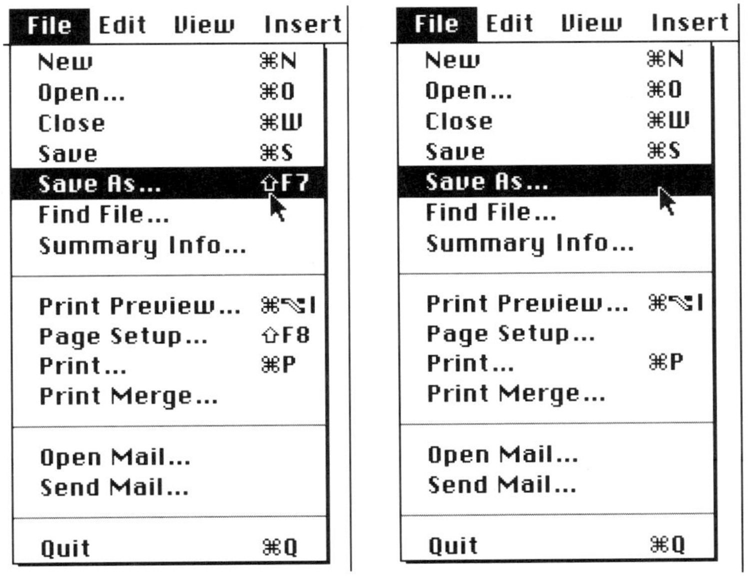

Preferences

Figure 9.3
The *Save As...* choice shown with the function keys option on (left) and off (right)

File	Edit	View	Insert
New			⌘N
Open...			⌘O
Close			⌘W
Save			⌘S
Save As...			⇧F7
Find File...			
Summary Info...			
Print Preview...			⌘⌥I
Page Setup...			⇧F8
Print...			⌘P
Print Merge...			
Open Mail...			
Send Mail...			
Quit			⌘Q

File	Edit	View	Insert
New			⌘N
Open...			⌘O
Close			⌘W
Save			⌘S
Save As...			
Find File...			
Summary Info...			
Print Preview...			⌘⌥I
Page Setup...			
Print...			⌘P
Print Merge...			
Open Mail...			
Send Mail...			
Quit			⌘Q

Use Short Menu Names   Notice the difference in the length of the menu names, shown in Figure 9.4. With the short menu box checked, menu names are reduced in length to facilitate small screens and non-Word menu additions (clocks, for instance.)

The Open and Save Category

This category deals with the way Word reads and writes disk files. The dialog box in Figure 9.5 gives you control over automatic prompts for Summary Information and lets you enable or disable reminders to save your work.

Always Interpret RTF   Word will automatically open documents saved in the Rich Text Format (RTF) if this box is checked. If you remove the checkmark from this box, Word will ask if you want RTF files converted each time you attempt to open one. RTF files are created by many different word-processing, spreadsheet, and other programs. RTF is an industry standard for certain formatting features (bold, italic, etc.)

Figure 9.4
You can choose short (top) or long (bottom) menu names, depending on your preferences.

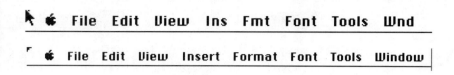

Figure 9.5
In the Open and Save category, you can set an option that reminds you to save your work.

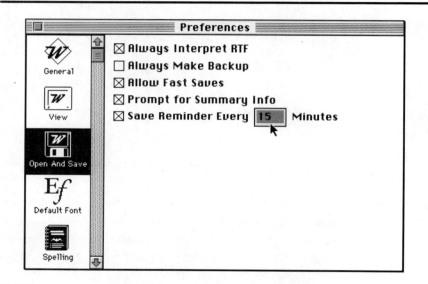

Always Make a Backup   With this box checked, Word 5 will always make a backup copy of the previous version of your document whenever you save your current work. It does not make a backup when you first save a document. That is to say, it only makes backups on second and subsequent saves.

The backup file created by Word is a copy of your document before your last save, and does not contain your most recent changes. In other words, the backup feature lets you "go back in time" one generation.

Preferences

For instance, suppose you created a new document containing only the word *Test,* and saved it as a file called *Example 1.* There would be no backup created at this point. Suppose that you then modify the text to read *Test two.* Now when you save, Word creates two files in your folder—one called *Example 1* and another called *Backup of Example 1.* If you were to open Backup of Example 1, you would find that it contained only the word *Test.* Example 1 would contain the words *Test two* and would be the most recent version of your work.

Keep file names short if you plan to use this feature, and note that automatic backup disables Fast Saves (see the next topic).

Allow Fast Saves   This feature speeds the saving process. Rather than writing the entire document to the disk each time you save, Word writes and keeps track of just the changes. Eventually, Word performs a slower, full save to clean up the document file and reclaim some memory. Quick saves are particularly useful if you work with floppies, save over a network, and so on. The always backup feature disables fast saves.

Prompt for Summary Information   This box turns on and off Word 5's new Summary Information feature. See *Chapter 30.*

Save Reminder Every *n* Minutes   With this box checked, Word asks you how often you wish to be reminded to save your work. Enter the number of minutes between saves. Whenever the specified number of minutes passes without your saving your work, you'll see a dialog box like the one in Figure 9.6.

Figure 9.6
The save reminder box pops up if you neglect to save your work.

The Save reminder dialog box lets you save by simply clicking OK (or by pressing Return). If you want to postpone the save and be reminded again, you can specify a length of time to be left alone. The cancel box postpones the reminder for the default period. That is to say, if you have entered *15* minutes in the save reminder box, then you would be interrupted again in 15 minutes. To stop the interruptions entirely, go back to the Open and Save Preferences category and remove the *X* from the save reminder box.

Default Font Category

The Default Font category lets you pick a font and size for new documents. It defines the font and size used by the Normal style. Press on the appropriate triangle to reveal the font or size menu. Slide the mouse pointer down the menu and release the mouse button on the desired item. Your choice will be highlighted and a checkmark will appear next to it, as shown in Figure 9.7. See *Part Three* for more information about styles.

The Spelling Category

This category lets you pick dictionaries and instruct Word's spell checker to ignore certain words or combinations of words and numbers, as shown in Figure 9.8.

Main Dictionary   A drop-down list shows all main dictionaries in your Word Commands folder. The one you check will be used when you run the spelling checker. Contact Microsoft for information about additional dictionaries.

Custom Dictionaries   This is where you specify which custom dictionaries Word's spelling checker will automatically use. Custom dictionaries might include technical phrases, client names, etc. It is best to keep custom dictionaries in the Word Commands folder, since Word looks for them there first. See *Chapter 33* for more information about dictionaries and spelling checks.

Always Suggest   An *X* in this box causes Word's spelling checker to always suggest replacement words when it detects a possible misspelling. If you

Figure 9.7
The default font and size are shown with checkmarks.

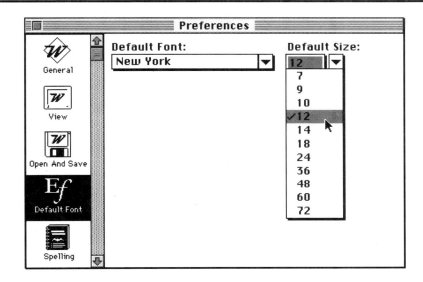

Figure 9.8
The Spelling category lets you choose your dictionary.

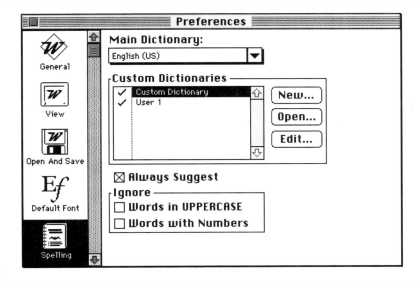

turn off this option, you can still ask Word to suggest when the spelling checker is running. Start with this feature turned on, even if you were disappointed with earlier Word versions. Word 5's suggestions are much better and appear more quickly than prior versions'.

Ignore   A checkmark in the *Words in UPPERCASE* box will cause word to ignore acronyms like *ASAP, RAM,* etc. Word will still check text that has been given the *appearance* of being captialized by the All Caps and Small Caps style features.

Words with Numbers tells the spelling checker to skip techno-babble like *800K* and words containing numbers, such as *10cm.*

The Grammar Category

You will probably need to scroll down using the scroll bar to bring the Grammar and remaining category icons into view. The Grammar category lets you specify which writing style and grammar rules will be used by the Grammar checker. An Explain... button offers brief explanations of each option.

Rule Groups: Style   Clicking on the Style button reveals a scrollable list of style tests that can be turned on or off. Click to the left of choices you wish to toggle. A checkmark indicates that the grammar checker will watch for the indicated problem.

Rule Groups: Grammar   Clicking on the Grammar button replaces the list of style issues with a scrollable list of grammar rules. Those with checkmarks are enabled. See *Chapter 34* for more information about grammar checking.

Catch   The Grammar Preferences dialog box provides a way to fine-tune the flagging of split infinitives, consecutive nouns, and prepositional phrases, as shown in Figure 9.9. Choose the appropriate menu and scroll down the list of choices. Release the mouse button to highlight your choice. See *Chapter 34* for more information about flagging these items.

Figure 9.9
You can turn off unwanted grammar and style rules.

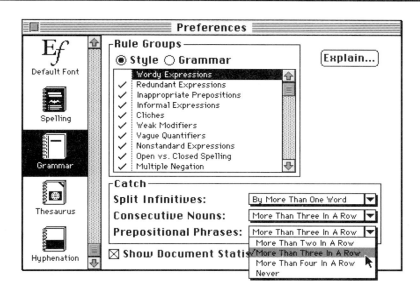

Thesaurus Category

You will probably need to scroll down using the scroll bar to bring the Thesaurus and remaining category icons into view, as illustrated in Figure 9.10.

The Thesaurus category lets you pick a default thesaurus language. Press on the appropriate triangle to reveal the language choices, if any. Slide the mouse pointer down the menu and release the mouse button on the desired item. Your choice will be highlighted and a checkmark will appear next to it. Thesaurus files should be located in the Word Commands folder, since that is where Word looks for them. See *Chapter 35* for more information about the thesaurus.

Hyphenation Category

This dialog box lets you pick a default hyphenation language and is almost identical to the Thesaurus category. Press on the appropriate triangle to reveal the language choices, if any.

Figure 9.10
The Thesaurus category

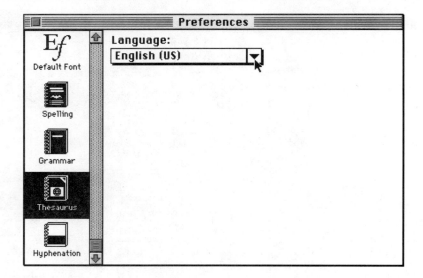

Slide the mouse pointer down the menu and release the mouse button on the desired item. Your choice will be highlighted and a checkmark will appear next to it. Hyphenation files should be located in the Word Commands folder, since that is where Word looks for them. See *Chapter 23* for more information about hyphenation.

CHAPTER 10

Adding, Deleting, and Moving Menu Choices

FEATURING

- Customizing Word 5's menus
- Saving your settings
- Creating a *Work* menu

Word lets you control the appearance and arrangement of its menus. You can add, delete, and reposition menu items. It is possible to change the keyboard-shortcut assignments for most menu items. Your revised configurations can be stored in one or more *Settings files* for quick access. This gives your one copy of Word 5 the potential to have "multiple personalities."

In this chapter you will learn about Word 5's standard menu settings and how to change them. You will learn about an optional *Work* menu, and about predefined menu-settings files provided by Microsoft that make users of other word processors feel at home with Word 5. In *Appendix B* you'll find a complete list of each Word command, a description of its function, some tips on use, and information about where in this book to go for more help.

Adding, Deleting, and Moving Menu Choices

▲ CAUTION

Imagine living in a community where everyone made their own laws. One driver could decide that red traffic lights mean go and yellow lights mean stop. Your neighbor could declare his or her backyard a toxic-waste dump site. Similarly, changing Word's menus is not without risk.

Adding an extra command like *Screen Test* to Word's standard menus normally does not cause problems. Word's standard optional features like these are well documented in this and other books.

Deleting menu items will normally not create big problems either. However, you can cause frustration and inconvenience by deleting certain items.

Moving items from menu to menu may make things easier and more logical for you; but it will make life difficult for others that need to use your machine. Imagine being a temporary worker trying to figure out a completely reorganized set of Word menus... The training of new-hires can be slowed by undocumented, department-wide changes to menus as well.

And, if you are using third-party macro programs like QuicKeys or Apple's now discontinued MacroMaker, changes in menus can sometimes cause your old macros to malfunction.

If you work in a large organization, your systems manager may have strong feelings about changing Word's menus and shortcuts. Check first.

With that out of the way, let's look at menus and how to change them. There are two ways to modify menus. You can use the Commands dialog box or some menu changing keyboard shortcuts. Let's look at the dialog box method first.

Reach the Commands dialog box by choosing *Commands...* from the *Tools* menu or using the ⌘-Shift-Option-C keyboard shortcut.

THE COMMANDS DIALOG BOX

Take a moment to study your screen's Commands dialog box, shown in Figure 10.1. It is one of the most crowded you will find in Word. There is a scrollable

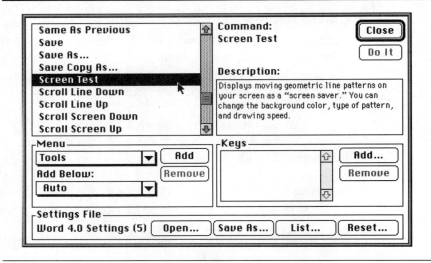

Figure 10.1
You use the Commands dialog box to customize menus.

list of commands in the upper-left corner. You select commands by scrolling them into view and clicking on them once or by typing the first few unique characters in their names. You will see a description box to the right of the command list that tells about each command as you select it. Beneath the list and the description box you will find two more boxes; one titled *Menu,* the other *Keys.* The Menu box lets you tell Word where you want to place or remove items. The Keys box is used to assign keyboard shortcuts.

At the bottom of the Commands dialog box you will see the Settings File section. It contains four buttons. These are used to manage multiple settings files and to restore Word's default settings.

The upper-right corner of the Commands dialog box contains two buttons and an information area. We'll learn about the tools here by using them to add the *Screen Test* menu item.

The Scrollable Command List

Take a moment to scroll through the Commands list. Select a command or two and read the corresponding descriptions. When you are ready to try adding a command to your menus, select the Screen Test command either by scrolling

Adding, Deleting, and Moving Menu Choices

and clicking or by typing **sc**, the first two letters in *Screen,* as shown back in Figure 10.1.

Specifying Menu Positions

With Screen Test selected, look in the Menu section of the Commands dialog box. Word is telling you that it plans to *automatically* position the Screen Test item in the *Tools* menu at a menu position that Word's designers suggest. You can overrule these defaults by picking a different menu or menu position. For this exercise, let's let Word position *Screen Test* in the *Tools* menu, but let's force the choice to appear just beneath the *Word Count...* choice instead of the automatic, default position, as shown in Figure 10.2.

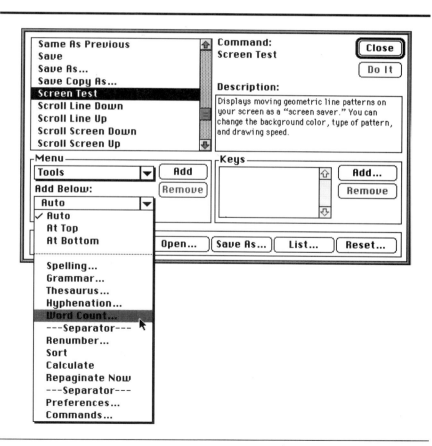

Figure 10.2
Force the *Screen Test* choice to appear beneath the *Word Count...* choice on the *Tools* Menu.

Do this by pointing to the *Add Below:* menu triangle, then sliding the mouse pointer down to highlight *Word Count*.... Finish-up by clicking the Add button in the Menu area and click the close button at the top of the Command dialog box. *Screen Test* should appear in your *Tools* menu, as shown in Figure 10.3.

Try using your new menu item. As soon as you select the *Screen Test* menu choice, your screen will go black and geometric patterns will swirl around. To see the available Screen Test options, press the Esc key or your mouse button to view and use the Screen Test dialog box. To cancel the screen test, bring up its dialog box and click on the cancel button, as shown in Figure 10.4.

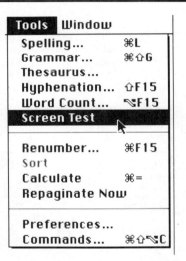

Figure 10.3
Here's the *Screen Test* item in place on the *Tools* menu.

Removing Menu Items

To remove menu items, bring up the Commands dialog box. Scroll the command list if necessary and select the menu item you want to remove. Click the Remove button and close the dialog box.

Some menu choices like "About Microsoft Word" cannot be removed. The Remove button will remain dim in these instances. Obviously, if a command has not been added to a menu it cannot be removed; therefore, the Remove

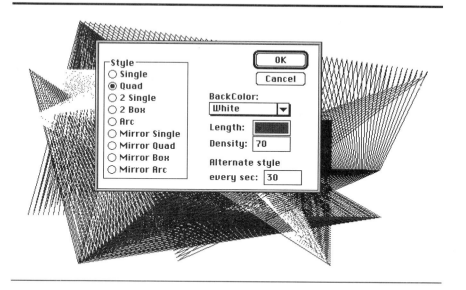

Figure 10.4
To cancel the Screen Test, just click Cancel.

button will be dim in these cases as well. Removing commands from menus does not remove them from Word. You can still use their keyboard shortcuts or open the Commands dialog box and use them from there. That is the purpose of the Do It button in the Commands dialog box.

A Shortcut for Adding or Removing Menu Items

If you wish to add or remove menu items from the keyboard, there is a handy shortcut. To add an item, locate the command you wish to add in its dialog box; then press ⌘-Shift-+ and click on the command once with the mouse. The item will be added to a default menu. To remove an item, press ⌘-Shift-–; then choose the doomed menu item. It will flash and disappear.

What if I Remove the *Commands...* Menu Choice?

At first you might think that removing the *Commands...* menu choice would prevent you and others from reaching the Commands dialog box and modifying Word's menus. In fact, some system managers use this trick to "secure" the menu layout.

If someone has accidentally or intentionally removed your *Commands...* menu choice, you can get it back by using the keyboard shortcut (⌘-Shift-Option-C) to bring up the Commands dialog box. Then, if you so desire, you can re-add *Commands...* to the *Tools* menu.

Moving Menu Items

To move a menu item, first remove it, then reinstall it at the desired new location using the Menu and Add Below features discussed above.

Adding and Removing Separator Lines

Most menus contain separator lines that help you spot groups of related choices. For instance, there are three separator lines on the standard Word *File* menu. You have some (but not total) control over their quantity and location.

You add, remove, and position separator lines just like any other menu item. Suppose, for instance, you wanted to add a separator below the *Open...* command in the *File* menu.

Bring up the Commands dialog box as before. Then scroll down and select the ---*Separator*--- choice in the commands list. Specify the desired menu (*File* for example) in the Menu box. Then pull down the *Add Below:* menu to specify the position of the new separator, as shown in Figure 10.5.

When you click on Add and close the Commands dialog box, the new separator will be placed in the appropriate position, under the *Open...* command in the *File* menu.

It is not possible to remove Word's default separator lines. Custom lines can be removed, though. To do so, press ⌘-Shift- – , click the menu, and drag down to the separator you want to delete. The separator will flash and disappear.

HAT'S A *WORK* MENU?

The *Work* menu is a powerful but sometimes overused and often misused tool. The addition of Word 5's new ribbon and ruler features further reduces the need for *Work* menus, but they are still worth understanding. The *Work* menu is a place

Adding, Deleting, and Moving Menu Choices

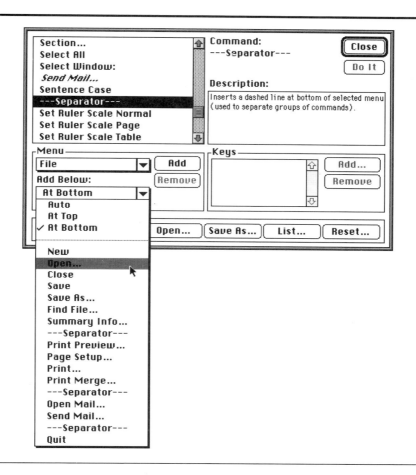

Figure 10.5
Specifying the location of a new separator line is easy.

for you to display the names of frequently used documents, glossary entries and styles. (You'll learn more about glossaries and styles later). A typical *Work* menu is shown in Figure 10.6.

This sample *Work* menu lists two documents (*Agreement Cover Letter* and *M&A Letterhead*); three glossary entries (*Biz address, Biz Phone,* and *Logo*); and a style (*Invoice tabs*). Notice how Word segregates listings into similar groups. All of the documents are together, the glossary entries are kept together, and so on.

Figure 10.6
A typical *Work* menu contains documents, glossary entries, and styles that you use often.

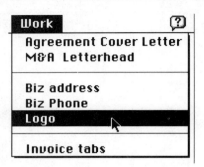

Once you've created a *Work* menu, you can open documents, paste glossary entries, or apply styles by visiting the *Work* menu. Sometimes, this technique is quicker than using other methods of doing the same thing. For instance, suppose that you have been working on a new agreement and want to write an accompanying cover letter. If you did not have a *Work* menu, you would have to go to Word's *File* menu and use the *Open...* command to sift through the various folders on your disk until you found the appropriate boilerplate cover letter. But if you've set up a *Work* menu containing the name of the boilerplate document, you can simply pick *Agreement Cover Letter* from the *Work* menu. Based on things you tell it when you set up the *Work* menu, Word will remember, quickly locate, and open the document. This may be the best way to use the *Work* menu—as a shortcut for loading frequently used documents.

Remember, however, if you rename files or move them to different folders, Word will not be able to find them. If you select such a file from the *Work* menu, you will see a dialog box asking you to help find the files.

The *Work* menu can do other things. Suppose you are designing a new brochure using Word and you want to paste in a copy of your logo. If you have stored a copy of the logo in your glossary and if you have added the *Logo* glossary item to your *Work* menu, you could go to the *Work* menu rather than the glossary to paste the logo. Similarly, you could list glossary items like address lines, signature lines, and so on in your *Work* menu. As you will see when you work with glossaries later, you may prefer to add keyboard shortcuts for your favorite glossary entries instead. See *Chapter 28* for more about glossaries.

Finally, suppose you've created a very involved paragraph style for invoicing or some other purpose. You might be able to place its name on the *Work* menu, then visit the *Work* menu rather than the ruler's *Style* menu when you want to apply the style. However, this technique works only if the document you are editing contains the style listed on the *Work* menu. See *Chapter 17* for more about Styles.

Creating a *Work* Menu

With that background, let's see what is involved in creating a *Work* menu. In most cases, you start by opening a dialog box. For instance, to add a file name to the *Work* menu, start by opening the Open dialog box (from Word's *File* menu, ⌘-O), as shown in Figure 10.7. Locate the file you wish to add to the *Work* menu using the usual Macintosh navigation tricks; then highlight the file name by clicking on it.

Figure 10.7
Highlight the name of the file you want to add to the *Work* menu.

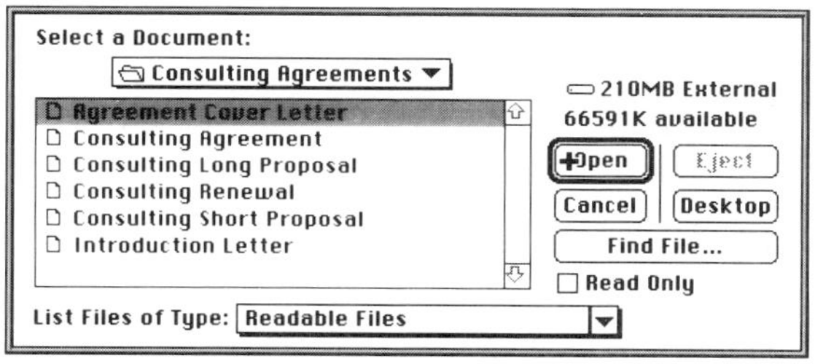

Next, while holding down the Option and ⌘ keys, press the plus (+) key on the top row of your keyboard (not on the 10-key pad). Your mouse pointer will turn into a large, bold "plus" sign, as shown in Figure 10.7 next to the file name. Click on the Open button in the dialog box. Your menu bar will flash. A *Work* menu will appear on the menu bar, if there wasn't one there already, with the file name you selected added to the menu.

Use the same technique with glossary entries. Open the Glossary dialog box (on the Edit menu, ⌘-K), select an entry of interest, press Option-⌘-+, and proceed as above. Styles are added the same way. Before getting carried away with adding glossary and style entries to your *Work* menu, though, consider creating keyboard shortcuts for these items instead. If you have multiple glossaries, you can list them in the *Work* menu and flip between them quickly. See *Chapter 28* for more information about multiple glossaries.

Removing *Work* Menu Items

To remove a *Work* menu item, hold down the Option and ⌘ keys and press the "minus" key on the upper row of your keyboard (not on the key pad). The mouse pointer becomes a bold, black minus sign. Go to the *Work* menu and pick the doomed item. Your display will flash and the item will disappear. *Undo* will not make it reappear.

Listing Commands

As you can imagine, it is important to document the commands you are using with Word, particularly if you have made changes to the standard setup. Word 5 has a feature that lets you do this quickly. It is the List... button located near the bottom of the Commands dialog box.

Clicking it will create a new Word document containing a table listing either just the commands on your menus or all possible Word commands. You decide by clicking the appropriate button, as shown in Figure 10.8.

Figure 10.8
Choose what kind of command list you want Word to generate.

The resulting list will look something like Figure 10.9. It can be saved, printed, and edited like any other Word document. Notice that the table in Figure 10.9 even contains the names of choices in the *Work* and *Font* menus. The table also lists menu locations and keyboard shortcuts when appropriate. In cases where a command has more than one keyboard shortcut, all possibilities are listed.

Adding, Deleting, and Moving Menu Choices

Figure 10.9
A typical command list shows commands with their keyboard shortcuts.

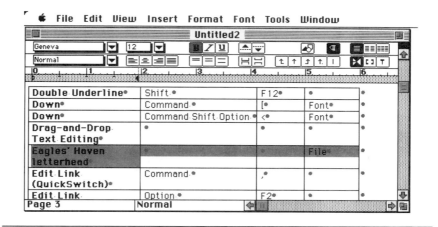

WHEN ARE MENU CHANGES SAVED?

Menu and other settings changes are saved when you quit Word. You can force Word to save sooner by clicking on the Save As... button in the Commands dialog box. This will preserve your changes in case of a computer malfunction prior to your quitting Word normally.

COMMAND REFERENCE

Now that you know how to add, move, and delete commands, take a few moments to browse Table B.1 in *Appendix B*. It lists *all* available Word 5 commands and offers some tips on their use. The table also shows you where to go in this book for more detailed information. If you find some commands that interest you, add them to your menus and experiment.

RESETTING WORD'S STANDARD MENUS

There are several ways to restore Word's standard menus. The brute force method is to use the Reset function found in the Commands dialog box. After clicking on the Reset... button you will be given three choices, as shown in Figure 10.10.

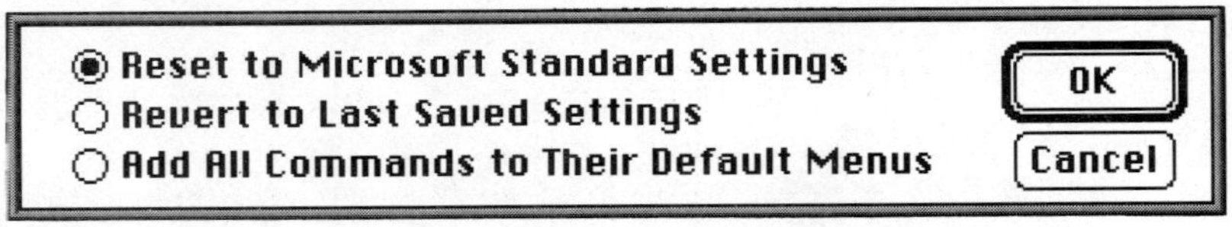

Figure 10.10
There are three Reset choices. Use them prudently!

```
● Reset to Microsoft Standard Settings        [ OK ]
○ Revert to Last Saved Settings
○ Add All Commands to Their Default Menus    [ Cancel ]
```

Besides restoring the "factory" menus, Reset can restore other things, such as default preferences. This may or may not be desirable. If you've just spent the afternoon getting margins, typestyles, grammar rules, and other preferences the way you like them, avoid the temptation to use the *Reset to Microsoft Standard Settings* choice. There are better ways to restore menus, as you will see in a moment.

The top choice restores all of Words standard settings, not just menus. The second choice returns you to your last group of saved settings. The third choice leaves your non-menu preferences as is, and adds *all* of Word's commands (one hundred plus) to their default menus.

Because of Word's limitations in restoring settings files, it is a *very* good idea to make a copy of your favorite settings file and store it in a safe place on your hard disk. You may even want to store it on another computer or on a backup floppy disk. This way, even if your settings file gets messed up, you'll have a backup copy.

Adding and Changing Keyboard Shortcuts

The Commands dialog box lets you assign or change standard Word 5 keyboard shortcuts. Do this in the area of the Commands dialog box shown in Figure 10.11. Start by selecting the command of interest from the scrolling list. If one or more keyboard shortcuts already exist for a selected command (like ⌘-P and F8 for Print...), they will be displayed in the Keys list as illustrated in Figure 10.11.

To add a new shortcut, click the Add... button. You will be asked to demonstrate the desired new shortcut. Press the new key combination. If the combination you press has not been assigned to another command, Word will assign it to the selected command and add it to the Keys list.

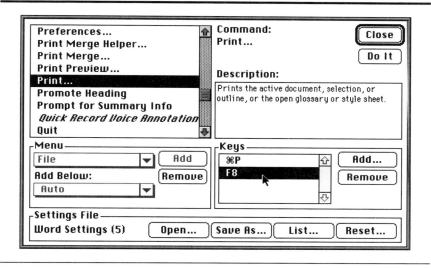

Figure 10.11
You can assign and change keyboard shortcuts to make your work easier.

Since the designers of Word have already assigned most of the easy keyboard combinations, you may need to be creative. Word will warn you if you attempt to use an already assigned combination. You will be given a chance to pick a different combination or re-assign an existing shortcut to a new command. Consider using the Control key if you have one. The program will not let you assign the same key combination to two different commands.

To remove existing shortcuts, choose the command of interest from the scrolling list, then highlight the combination you wish to remove (like F8 in Figure 10.11). Click the Remove button. Undo does not work here.

Word will automatically update the current settings file to reflect your changes. You may want to print out a new command list to use as a reference.

USING MULTIPLE COMMAND SETS

As you know, menu configurations (and much more) are stored in Word Settings files. Normally, Word 5 uses the settings file called *Word Settings (5)*, located in your System Folder. But suppose you want to have different Word 5 configurations for specific tasks like script writing? Or suppose you share your computer with someone who wants to have more or different menu choices? It is possible to create multiple settings files, then switch to the one that best suits your needs. Microsoft has even provided some alternative settings files you may find useful.

The bottom of the Commands dialog box contains controls that let you save and load different settings files. Clicking on the Open... button in the Settings File area of the Commands dialog box brings up an Open dialog box, as shown in Figure 10.12.

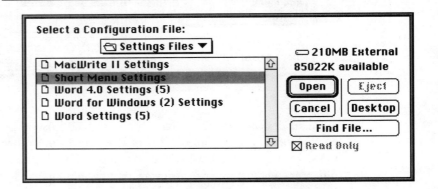

Figure 10.12
You can use different settings files for different applications or user skill levels.

Use the dialog box to locate and load alternate Word Settings files of interest. (The alternate files provided by Microsoft are normally in a folder called *Settings Files,* which will probably be in your Word 5 folder.) Once you locate the settings file you desire, either double-click on its name or select the name and click on the Open button in the dialog box.

For instance, Word 5 comes with a settings file that provides abbreviated menus, much like the old *Short Menus* feature in Word 4. Some casual users may find these simplified menus less confusing. Another settings choice emulates MacWrite II settings. Notice that the list in Figure 10.12 includes a settings file called *Word Settings (5)*. This is *not* the one Word normally uses. This is normally an unmodified version of the standard factory settings. Your settings file is in your System Folder.

CHAPTER 11

Views

FEATURING

- Changing views
- Previewing documents before printing
- Keyboard shortcuts for views

Word now provides five different ways to display documents on your screen:

- Normal view
- Page Layout view
- Outline view
- Print Preview
- Split screen

When drafting or making major revisions to documents, you will probably use *Normal* view. But when you polish your work it will usually be more efficient to use *Page Layout* view (formerly called *Page View*) and the *Print Preview* feature.

In addition, you will want to learn about *Outline* view even if you do not use formal outlines when your write. Outline view can help you quickly rearrange your document. This chapter will explore all of these options.

Regardless of which view you use, you will want to take advantage of Word's split-screen feature. As you will see, it's the next best thing to being in two places at once.

Normal View

Unless you are very patient, or have a fast Macintosh with a large screen, use Normal view for most of your heavy-duty text entry and editing. Word's other views respond noticeably slower to typing, editing, and scrolling. That's because, in order to display documents as they will print, Word must "paginate" them, using complex computations that take into consideration page size, font specifications, line-spacing, and many other design elements. This process can consume most of your Mac's resources.

As illustrated in Figure 11.1, Normal view keeps repagination and screen redraw delays to a minimum. It shows your text as you have typed it, and displays graphics at the points in the text where you've inserted them (which is not necessarily where they will print).

In earlier versions of Word, Normal view was called *Galley* view, a sometimes inaccurate homage to the phototypesetting profession. It was the default view. Normal view depicts things like type sizes, line spacing, indents and so on with reasonable accuracy. It does not show side-by-side column positioning, footers,

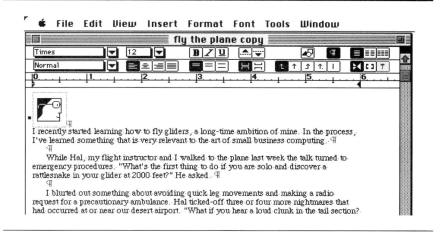

Figure 11.1
Normal view is the best for ordinary editing and text entry.

headers, nor the printing position of framed items. Columns are shown at their actual width, but not side-by-side. Automatic page breaks are shown as dotted lines. Manual page breaks, if you've defined any, are shown as darker lines.

Editing in Normal View

You can create and edit text, columns, and graphics as usual in Normal view. To work on headers or footers, though, you must open Header or Footer windows from the *View* menu. To add date, time, and page numbering to headers and footers, use glossary entries or the icons provided in the Header and Footer windows. (See *Chapter 28* for information about glossary entries.)

Line Numbers Do Not Show in Normal View

If you have instructed Word to number lines, the numbers will *not* appear in this view. Use Print Preview to see line numbers.

Multi-column Text in Normal View

It is possible to prepare multiple-column text for printing while in Normal view, as shown in Figure 11.2.

Here the previously rough text has been justified, hyphenated, and so on, all in Normal view. Even the column margins and indents have been defined. To get a

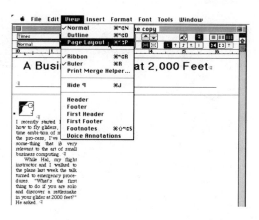

Figure 11.2
In Normal view, multi-column text is shown at the correct width, but not side-by-side. To view the columns side-by-side, you must switch to Page Layout view, as discussed next.

true sense of how this document will look without printing it, though, you must switch to Page Layout view or use Print Preview.

Switching Views

Word 5 has a *View* menu (shown in Figure 11.2) that you can use to select Normal, Outline, or Page Layout views. The keyboard shortcut for Normal view is ⌘-Option-N (for normal). The shortcut for Page Layout view is ⌘-Option-P (for Page). You can probably guess the keyboard shortcut for Outline—⌘-Option-O.

Switching to Print Preview either requires a trip to the *File* menu or use of a not-so-intuitive keyboard shortcut. Press ⌘-Option-I to enter Print Preview mode from the keyboard.

Page Layout View

Figure 11.3 shows what happens to the text from Figure 11.2 when it is displayed in Page Layout view. The ruler and ribbon have been hidden for this example. You can make this the default view in the Preferences dialog box.

In Page Layout view, the screen resembles a white sheet of paper, or at least a portion of a sheet. Look closely at the top, bottom, left, and right edges of the screen in Figure 11.3. You will see a dark background that Word places behind the "paper". On a large enough screen, you will see the whole page. On smaller screens or when using a large paper setting in Page Setup, you may need to scroll to see these representations of the paper's edges.

Editing in Page Layout View

Generally, you edit as usual in Page Layout view. Text and graphics are positioned where they will print. Headers and footers can be both seen and edited. Click in a header, footer, or body text to position the insertion point. Page breaks, be they automatic or forced, are represented by new pages on the screen rather than by dashed lines in the text.

You can scroll only one page at a time. That is to say, you cannot see the bottom of one page and the top of the next at the same time in this view. Two small arrows at the bottom of the window—called the Page Forward and Page

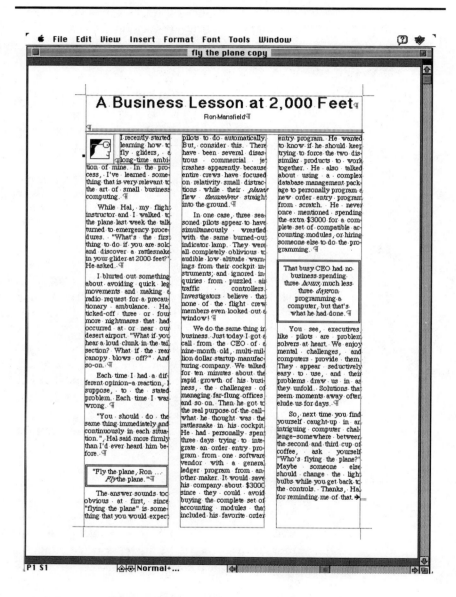

Figure 11.3
In Page Layout view, you can see text as it will print.

Backward arrows—let you scroll up or down one page at a time. When you move to a new page you must click somewhere in the new page to move the insertion point before typing. If you *have* been typing, the insertion point will move automatically.

Showing and Hiding ¶ in Page Layout View

If you have selected the Show ¶ (*show non-printing characters*) feature (located on the *View* menu) you will see shaded lines around text areas, headers, footers, and graphics as illustrated in Figure 11.3.

You can toggle these things on and off either with *Hide* ¶ on the *View* menu or with the keyboard shortcut ⌘-J. The ribbon button that resembles a paragraph mark will also toggle hidden text and lines.

Hidden Text in Page Layout View

If you have hidden text in your document and you reveal it, Page Layout view will display line and page endings adjusted to include the hidden text. This may not correspond to pages that you print if the Print dialog box's *Print Hidden Text* box is unchecked. In order to see what your pages will look like without the hidden text, you must hide the text by unchecking the *Show Hidden Text* box in the Preferences dialog box.

Headers and Footers in Page Layout View

You can see and edit headers and footers in Page Layout view. To add date, time, and page numbering to headers and footers, use glossary entries. (See *Chapter 28* for information about glossary entries.)

Line Numbers Do Not Show in Page Layout View

If you have instructed Word to number lines, the numbers will *not* appear in this view. Use Print Preview to see line numbers.

Repagination in Page Layout View

It is wise to enable automatic background repagination when working in Page Layout view. (This is the default condition.) Otherwise, Word will not always display correct page and line endings. If you have turned background repagination off, you can use the General category of the Preferences dialog box to re-enable it. You can use *Repaginate Now* on the *Tools* menu to update line and page endings whenever you want, even if you have turned off background repagination.

Split Screen View

Regardless of which view you prefer, you can profit from using Word's split-screen feature. With it, you can keep two widely separated portions of a document in view at the same time. To split the screen, simply point to the small black rectangle in the upper-right corner of your Word document window. The pointer will change to the Split-bar pointer shape as shown in Figure 11.4. Drag the Split-bar pointer down to divide the screen.

Figure 11.4
Splitting the screen can be handy when you want to see different portions of the same document.

When you release the mouse button, your screen will split into two independent windows, each with its own scroll bar. To return to a single screen, double-click the Split-bar or drag it to just below the title bar.

Why Split Screens?

With the screen split you can see two parts of your document at once. Use this feature to refer to different portions of a document as you write or to speed copying, cutting, and pasting. But here's another powerful use of split screens.

Split Screen and Different Views

You can use a different view in each portion of the split screen. For instance, you might want to speed scrolling and editing by working in a window pane set to Normal view while watching the effects of your changes in a Page Layout view pane, as shown in Figure 11.5.

Views

Figure 11.5
You can arrange the document with Normal view in the top pane and Page Layout view in the bottom.

Print Preview

As you learned in *Chapter 3,* Print Preview is more than just another way to view documents. Choose *Print Preview* from the *File* menu or with the ⌘-Option-I keyboard shortcut.

Depending on your screen size and settings, you will see either an unreadable birds-eye view of a page or two (with *greeked* text) like Figure 11.6, or you will see a full, readable page like the one in Figure 11.7. The buttons along the left of the Print Preview screen are explained in *Chapter 3*.

In either case, you will be able to reposition margins in Print Preview. It is also possible to force page numbering in this view. Notice that line numbers are displayed in Print Preview but not in any other view type. You cannot edit text or headers or footers in Print Preview. You will not be able to see certain Page Setup printer tricks like image flips in Print Preview.

Outline View

A complete description of Word's Outline feature can be found in *Chapter 42*. For now it is enough to know that if your document is properly formatted,

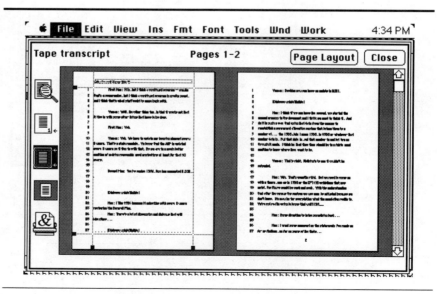

Figure 11.6
With Print Preview on a small screen, the text is often too small to read.

Figure 11.7
With Print Preview on a larger screen, the text and other elements are readily visible.

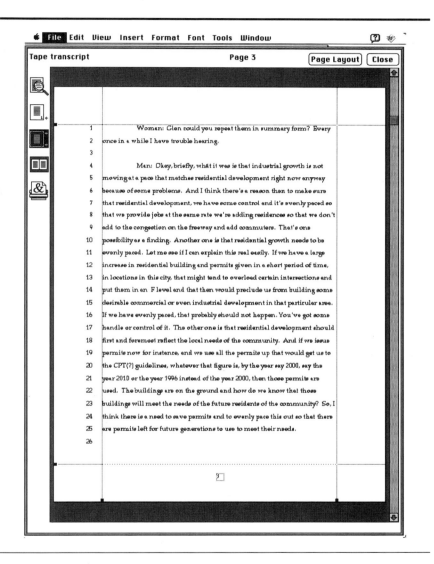

switching to Outline view lets you quickly navigate and reorganize even large, complex documents. Outline view allows you to see the entire contents of the document, just chapter headings, or just section headings, and so on. For instance, Figure 11.8 shows a book outline down to paragraph headings, but does not include the text of the book itself.

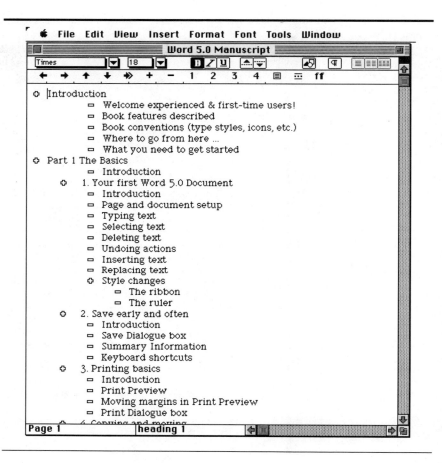

Figure 11.8
A book outline viewed at paragraph heading level

If you wanted to move all of *Part 4* so that it came before *Part 3,* you might ordinarily use Normal or Page Layout view to scroll through and select the complete text of all chapters contained in *Part 4;* then you would cut and paste it ahead of *Part 3*. But by using Outline view, you could simply "collapse" the view, as shown in Figure 11.9.

With the document thus collapsed, you could use Word's Outline tools to move the entire contents of *Part 4* by simply dragging the line *+ Part 4 Time Savers* above *Part 3*.

Views

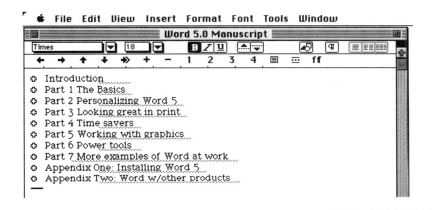

Figure 11.9
A collapsed Outline view allows you to move large sections of a document

You need not begin projects by creating an in-depth outline, as you will see later when you read about styles and outlines. By creating and applying appropriate styles for various heading levels, you can quickly create a document that can be expanded or compressed for viewing and editing with Outline tools.

VIEW DEFAULTS

Normal view is the default for new documents unless you change the default to Page View by using the View category of the Preferences dialog box (see *Chapter 9*). In Word 5, unlike earlier versions, Word remembers the view you were using when you last saved a document and opens the document in that view. If you have opened a new document in Normal view, done some work, switched to Page Layout view, saved, and quit, the next time you open the document it will appear in Page Layout view.

PART III

LOOKING GREAT IN PRINT

Word was designed with the understanding that, frequently, Macintosh computers would be attached to world-class, precision printers. It is obvious when you look at Word's features that its creators want to help you look great in print. In the right hands, Word can rival many desktop-publishing programs. The chapters in this section show you how Word interacts with your printers. You'll gain a better understanding of fonts. You'll explore powerful paragraph features and learn how to create headers and footers. Page numbering is discussed, and you will learn how to unlock the power of Word's style sheets.

CHAPTER 12

The Chooser, Page Setup, and Print Dialog Boxes

FEATURING

- Using the Chooser
- Choosing different paper sizes
- Using special effects
- Printing ranges of pages

Word creates screen representations of each printed page to help you visualize documents before you print them. To do this, it takes into consideration choices you make in the

- Chooser
- Page Setup box and
- Print dialog box

The number of new Macintosh-compatible printer models and options is staggering and grows almost daily. This chapter will discuss typical printers along with their Page Setup and Print dialog-box options. It is beyond the scope of this book to cover all possible features of every printer on the market. You may want to experiment with the choices provided by your printers.

The terms and concepts in this chapter can be confusing. For instance, it is easy to confuse the *Print* dialog box with the *Page Setup* dialog box or printer *effects* with printer *options*. Even experienced users visit the wrong box now and then.

Document appearance both on screen and in printouts is sometimes affected by the font sizes you have installed in your system folder; particularly when using non-laserprinters. You can learn more about this in *Chapter 14*.

PRINTING IN WORD IS AN INTERACTIVE PROCESS

It is a good idea to get into the habit of visiting the Chooser, Page Setup dialog box, and possibly the Print dialog box whenever you *begin* to create a new document, particularly if you work with a variety of printers or paper sizes. If you wait until you have finished working on your document to choose a printer, your page and line endings may change considerably from those you initially saw on your screen. This can mean a minor annoyance or a major disaster.

As an example, if you write a long document, create a table of contents, then change printer models or choose different printing features, you will find that line and page endings may change. This will require you to redo the table of contents. Otherwise it will not agree with the printed document. The following printer-related items affect pagination and should be selected or determined when you begin a project:

- Printer model
- Paper size
- Reduction/enlargement
- Page orientation
- Fractional widths
- PostScript over text
- No gaps between pages

- Larger print area
- Printing/not printing hidden text

Other changes affect the appearance of printed pages, but have little impact on pagination.

If you have only one printer and it works properly, you can skip ahead to *Effect of Page Setup Options on Formatting*.

Choosing a Printer

As you may already know, the *Chooser* is located in your *Apple* menu. It will look something like the one in Figure 12.1. Your Chooser may have different icons than the ones illustrated here. Since the Chooser is used to select things in addition to printers, you might see non-printer choices here. For instance, in Figure 12.1 the AppleShare and Liaisonet icons are not printers. The *printer drivers* shown in Figure 12.1 include an AppleTalk-connected ImageWriter and an Apple LaserWriter.

Sometimes you will see printer driver icons for printers that are not connected to your computer. The Chooser icons represent printer-driver software that is installed in your computer's system folder, not the actual hardware. (You can remove unwanted icons from the Chooser by dragging the unnecessary drivers out of your System Folder.)

You choose an available printer driver by clicking on the desired icon, and possibly on the name of the specific printer in the box to the right of the icons.

Choosing Printers on a Network

If you have a complex network, your Chooser dialog box may ask you for additional choices like zones. You may need to scroll to see the desired printer icon. See Figure 12.1.

In Figure 12.1 there are seven LaserWriters available in the LocalTalk zone. The Mobile LaserWriter has been selected. If you have questions about using printers on your network, contact your Systems Manager.

The Chooser, Page Setup, and Print Dialog Boxes

Figure 12.1
Click on a printer's icon to select it.

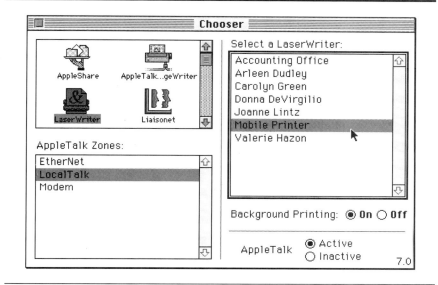

Printer Port Selection

Some printers, like the Personal LaserWriter LS, require serial connections rather than LocalTalk connections. Usually, these printers are dedicated to one computer, and not easily shared. In these cases, when you choose a serial printer, you are given a choice of serial connections or "ports" to use.

EFFECT OF PAGE SETUP OPTIONS ON FORMATTING

Different printer types offer different capabilities. Some let you print at a range of reduction and enlargement percentages, for instance, while others do not Programs like Word take this into consideration when they represent documents on screen. For this reason your Macintosh will remind you to open the Page Setup dialog box whenever you choose a different printer type. *It is important that you do that, even if you do not make any changes in the new Page Setup box.*

The Page Setup Dialog Box

Figure 12.2 shows a typical laserprinter Page Setup dialog box. Let's examine its options in detail.

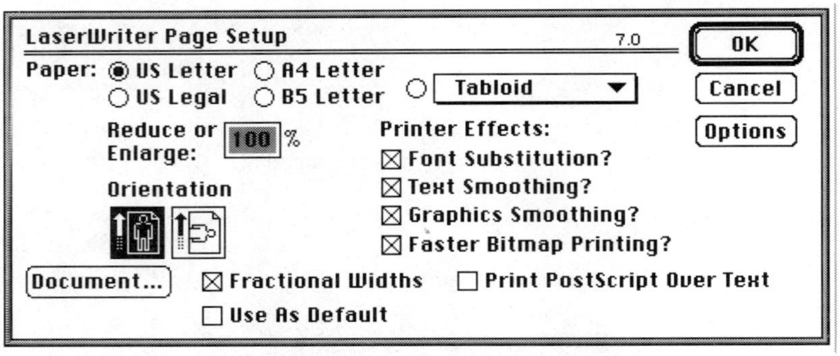

Figure 12.2
The Page Setup dialog box gives you many subtle ways of controlling your printed output.

Many companies besides Apple make laserprinters. They have a variety of features. Most are quite compatible with Word, but your dialog box may look different. If so, check your manual.

The Use As Default Check Box

Normally, changes you make in a Page Setup dialog box are saved only with the document you are working on. New documents are usually opened using Word's standard, default settings.

It is possible, however to define a non-standard collection of Page Setup choices as the default for all new projects. Clicking to place an *X* in the *Use As Default* box will use the current Page Setup information for *all* subsequent new Word projects. This will not affect documents created earlier with different settings, nor will it affect printer settings used by other programs like Excel or Quicken, even if you are running them along with Word 5 under MultiFinder or System 7.

Page Orientation

Most printers offer a choice of portrait or landscape printing. Clicking on one or the other of the pictures beneath the word *Orientation* in most Page Setup dialog boxes tells Word whether you want to use the tall narrow (*portrait*) or wide, short (*landscape*) paper setting. Portrait is the default. For everyday correspondence like letters and memos, you'll want to use portrait orientation.

Landscape orientation is handy for wide tables, spreadsheets, and envelope printing, among other things.

The only way to place an occasional landscape page in a portrait-style document is to create a separate document in landscape mode and link it using Word's File Series features, which can be cumbersome. See *Chapter 43* for more information.

Reduce or Enlarge %

The Page Setup boxes for most printer types offer at least some way to reduce the size of the printed image. Other printers let you both enlarge and reduce.

Be aware that changes you make to the reduction/enlargement controls in your Page Setup box affect the available work area on the document screen. For instance, if you plan to reduce a document 50% when you print it, it stands to reason that if the image on your screen is eight inches long, it will print four inches long. This has some practical application, so you may find it worth taking the time to overcome what might be some initial confusion.

Suppose, for instance that you wanted to print inserts for audio cassette boxes. The inserts can be no wider than four inches, the inside dimension of a cassette box. You could set up a document with a four-inch text area and type tiny characters into the four-inch screen representation of the cassette insert. But it would be better to set the Print dialog box to a 50% reduction, then type in eight inches of space on the screen. This way you can work with large, easy-to-read characters onscreen, and the text will print out at four inches. Figure 12.3 shows just such a printout at actual size.

Obviously enlargements, when available, work the opposite way. Small items on the screen print bigger.

If you do a lot of this work, purchase a reduction/enlargement calculation wheel from a graphic arts store to help you choose the correct ratios. There are also some public domain programs that will help you compute reduction and enlargement settings.

Ruler margin markers and page-ending markers do respond to changes in the reduce/enlarge box. Page Layout view and Print Preview features reflect size

Figure 12.3
You can reduce the size of your printed output.

Crusin • Smokey Robinson	Rocket 88 • Jimmy Cotton Blues Quartet
Concrete & Steel • ZZ Top	Runaway • Bonnie Raitt
I Need You Tonight • ZZ Top	I Love L. A. • Randy Newman
Expressway to Your Heart • Soul Survivors	Road Runner • Bo Diddley
Little Honda • Beach Boys	Master Mechanic • Johnny Winter
Too Many Drivers • Rob Rio	Taxi • J. Blackfoot
Drive • The Cars	Bring it on Home • Led Zeppelin
Thunderbird • Hans Zimmer	Tobacco Road • Junior Wells
Mustang Sally • Wilson Pickett	Baby You Can Drive My Car • Beatles
Fun, Fun, Fun • Beach Boys	One More Mile • Muddy Waters
Life in the Fast Lane • Eagles	409 • Beach Boys
Radar Love • White Lion	Run Me Down • Notting Hillbies
Ride Accross the River • Dire Straits	

changes, but do not display images in their exact dimensions. You need to actually print and measure to determine the results of your changes.

Paper Sizes

Many of Apple's LaserWriter's offer nine or more paper-size and positioning options, as shown in Table 12.1 and in Figure 12.4. In this example, a drop-down menu reveals five of the nine choices.

TABLE 12.1 Common Paper Sizes

Choice	Size in Inches	Size—Metric (mm)
US Letter	11 × 8½	216 × 279
US Legal	14 × 8½	216 × 356
A4 Letter	8¼ × 11⅔	210 × 297
B5 Letter	6.9 × 10.8	176 × 250
Tabloid	11 × 17	279 × 432

Printer Effects

Most laserprinter dialog boxes also have choices called Printer Effects. Here are examples of common Apple LaserWriter Effects.

Figure 12.4
You have a wide selection of sizes to choose from.

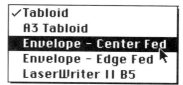

Font Substitution   Laserprinters have built-in fonts. Different printers have different built-in font collections. If your document calls for only the fonts built-in to your printer, font substitution will have no effect.

However, when you ask Word to print using a font that is not in your printer's collection, the font substitution effect will choose a similar laser font. For instance, if your printer does not have New York (most don't), the printer will use Times instead. The lack of printer-resident Geneva will result in Helvetica printing, and so on. Word and your Mac do a pretty good job of maintaining line and page endings in these instances, but you may cringe at the resulting appearance of things like character spacing. Figure 12.5 shows what happens when New York is specified and Times prints due to font substitution.

Figure 12.5
When Times (bottom) is substituted for New York (top), the spacing can be off.

Font Substitution

Font   Substitution

If you turn off font substitution, bitmap characters will print instead. Printing can be considerably slower, and you may not like the final appearance of the characters. If you are planning to use a laserprinter, it is best to stick with printer-resident or downloadable laser fonts, thereby avoiding font substitution. You will learn more about fonts in *Chapter 14*.

Text Smoothing   Text smoothing removes the "jaggies" from bitmapped fonts. As you can see in Figure 12.6 there are times when this improves the appearance of non-laser (bitmapped) fonts.

Figure 12.6
Text smoothing (bottom) removes "jaggies" from bit-mapped fonts (top).

You may want to disable this effect if you use only laser fonts, since text smoothing can sometimes blur them.

Graphics Smoothing   Graphics smoothing removes the sharp edges from bitmapped graphics, as you can see in Figure 12.7.

Figure 12.7
Graphics smoothing (right) makes bit-mapped graphics (left) look nicer.

There may be times when you will want to turn off this effect. It sometimes distorts or degrades graphics—experiment.

Faster Bitmap Printing   This effect assigns more built-in printer memory for bitmap-graphic printing, thereby speeding up the printing of pictures. Memory is taken from other printing tasks. Sometimes this causes the printer to malfunction. If pages fail to print, disable this effect and try again.

Apple LaserWriter Options

In addition to printer *effects* many printers have printing *options*. (If there is a reason to call some printing features *effects* and others *options*, it is not obvious.) Like effects, options change the way your printer prints.

The Chooser, Page Setup, and Print Dialog Boxes

In the case of most Apple laserprinters, the options are contained in a dialog box reached by pressing the Options button in the Page Setup box. Figure 12.8 shows the Options dialog box for an Apple LaserWriter NTX.

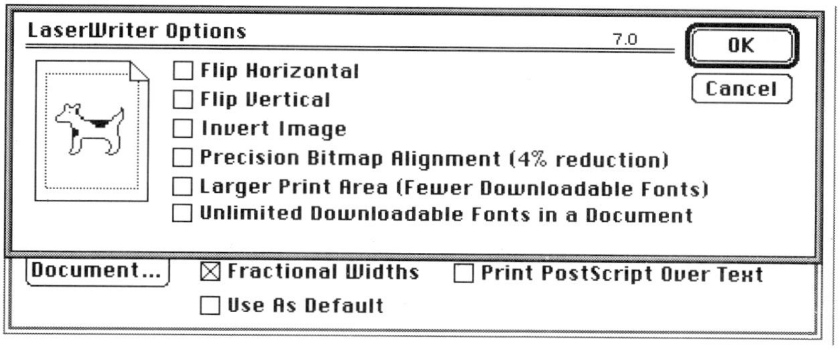

Figure 12.8
A typical Options dialog box—for more fine-tuning!

```
LaserWriter Options                          7.0     [ OK ]
                                                     [Cancel]
   [ ] Flip Horizontal
   [ ] Flip Vertical
   [ ] Invert Image
   [ ] Precision Bitmap Alignment (4% reduction)
   [ ] Larger Print Area (Fewer Downloadable Fonts)
   [ ] Unlimited Downloadable Fonts in a Document

[Document...]  [X] Fractional Widths    [ ] Print PostScript Over Text
               [ ] Use As Default
```

Flips The first two options on the LaserWriter list are *Flip Horizontal* and *Flip Vertical*. They can be used alone or in combination, as shown in Figure 12.9. Except for making signs for the front of ambulances in Australia, it is difficult to imagine a use for these features.

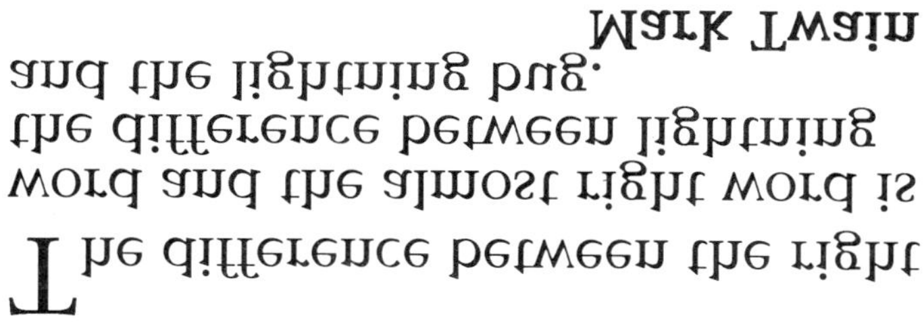

Figure 12.9
Horizontal and vertical flips are useful in making signs for Australian ambulances.

T̲he difference between the light show
is brow thgil tsomla eht dna worg
the difference between lighturing
and the lighturing bug.
Mark Twain

Invert Image The *Invert Image* feature makes black areas (including text) print white and white areas print black. Gray shades are reversed, as well. That is to say, the lighter a shade is the darker it prints.

Precision Bitmap Alignment   Your screen displays 72 dots-per-inch. Most laserprinters print 300 dots-per-inch. This disparity can distort the printed appearance of bitmap graphics that have been created on-screen. Use of the Precision Bitmap Alignment feature reduces the printed size of bitmap images by 4%, making them less distorted. Neither Page Layout view nor Print Preview accurately displays this size reduction.

Larger Print Area   Many laserprinters require a ½" area of white space around the edges of an 8½ × 11" printed page. This is partly because the printers do not have enough memory to image the entire sheet. The *Larger Print Area...* option frees up internal printer memory that is normally reserved for downloaded fonts, making it possible to print to within approximately ¼" of the edge of the sheet. It is very helpful when you want to place page numbers and other header or footer information near the edge of the paper.

Turning this option on and off *does* affect screen representations and pagination of your document: The changes in available printable space are reflected in screen views of document margins, headers, footers, line endings, and so on. So toggle this option when you *begin* your project.

You will be able to use few, if any downloadable fonts with this feature enabled.

Unlimited Downloadable Fonts   This option makes available as much memory as necessary for downloadable fonts. The printer will purge and reload fonts as necessary at the expense of printing speed. Consider adding printer memory or an external disk drive for your printer if you use this feature regularly. It has no effect on how documents are displayed.

Fractional Widths

During printing, this feature improves the appearance of proportionally spaced fonts. It also provides better inter-character spacing. (See *Chapter 14* for more on this topic). Because of display limitations, the Fractional Widths feature sometimes adversely affects the on-screen appearance of fonts. It also affects line endings, and thus pagination. For these reasons, many experienced users turn Fractional Widths off while drafting, then turn it back on while performing hyphenation, or creating the table of contents, index, and final drafts.

The Chooser, Page Setup, and Print Dialog Boxes

Print PostScript Over Text

This choice determines whether embedded PostScript (EPS) images will print on top of or beneath text and other graphics. Figure 12.10 shows a file with EPS information.

Figure 12.10
Embedded PostScript printed over and under other items can have a startling effect.

Mansfield and Associates Clients & Publishers

AMERICAN BROADCASTING CORPORATION (ABC)
AMERICAN INDUSTRIAL REAL ESTATE ASSOCIATION
ASK MR. FOSTER,/FIRSTOURS (CARLSON CORP.)
BEAR STERNS
BERGER & NORTON
CABLE NEWS NETWORK (CNN)
CHILDRENS HOSPITAL OF LOS ANGELES
COLDWELL BANKER
CONSUMER GUIDE COMPUTER BUYING GUIDES
EPSON AMERICA
FADEM & DOUGLAS
FOX TELEVISION
GILLETTE/PAPERMATE
GRUBB & ELLIS
HORVITZ & LEVY
INDUSTRIAL ELECTRONIC ENGINEERS
LASER MEDIA
LOS ANGELES COUNTY COURTS
LOS ANGELES DODGERS
LOS ANGELES OLYMPIC ORGANIZING COMMITTEE
LOVE CONNECTION (ERIC LIEBER PRODUCTIONS)
NORTHROP
OCCIDENTAL PETROLEUM CORPORATION
PARTY PLANNERS WEST
PETER NORTON COMPUTING
PRUDENTIAL STEVENSON
QUE PUBLISHING
QUICK TALLY
ROGERS & COWAN PUBLIC RELATIONS
SCIENCE RESEARCH ASSOCIATES (SRA)
SYBEX PUBLISHING, INC.
WARNER COMMUNICATIONS
XEROX

The Word 5 Document Button

Clicking on this button brings up Word's Document dialog box, which lets you modify margins, hidden-text printing, and more. See *Chapter 13* for details.

PRINT DIALOG BOX DIFFERENCES

The Print dialog box is the one you see whenever you choose *Print* from the *File* menu or click on the printer icon in Print Preview. Don't confuse it with the Page Setup dialog box. Here too, dialog-box appearance changes with printer model. Word 5 adds some of its own features to Print Dialog boxes. Sometimes non-Apple printer manufacturers make their own modifications.

The Print Dialog Box

A typical Print Dialog box is shown in Figure 12.11. We'll examine some of its more popular features in detail.

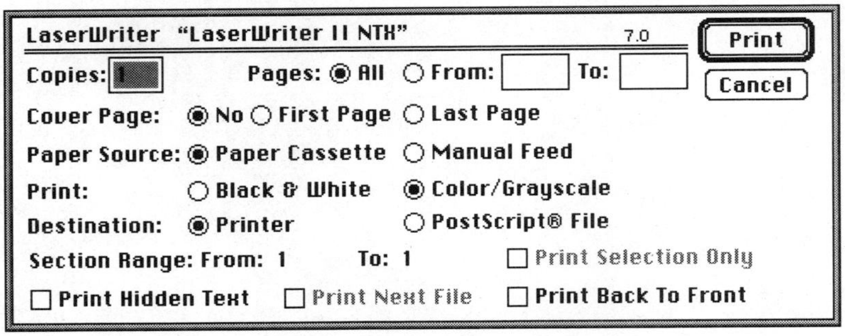

Figure 12.11
A Typical Print dialog box—note the additional instructions provided by Word.

Copies

This area is where you type in the number of copies you want to print. The default is one copy while the maximum is 999 copies.

Pages: All or a Range

You can specify that all pages in a multiple-page document print (the default), or you can ask for selected pages. If you decide to print only selected pages, it is a good idea to repaginate the document before specifying a desired page range.

If your document has sections, you can print the whole document, one or more sections, or *page ranges* within *section* ranges. (You will learn more about sections in *Chapter 23*) Use the Pages: From:/To: boxes and the Section Range: choices in combination to specify the desired page range.

Specifying printing ranges, while normally quite easy, can be confusing at times. For example, to print the entire document, simply check the All button. This is the default condition.

To print only section three in a four-section document, leave the Pages: choice set to All, then place a *3* in the From: section range and a *3* in the To: section range.

To print the entire contents of sections three and four, leave the Pages: choice set to All, then place a *3* in the From: section range and a *4* in the To: section range.

To print only pages 6 through 10 in section three, place a *6* in the Pages: From box and a *10* in the Pages To: box. You must also place a *3* in the section Range From: and another *3* in the To: sections range boxes.

Cover Pages

Laserprinter dialog boxes often offer you the choice of printing a cover page. Cover pages help separate jobs as they pile up in the printer's output tray. You can choose to have cover pages print at the beginning or end of jobs. This makes it easy to spot the beginnings and ends of jobs when they are piled together. It also helps people know where to deliver finished jobs in work groups with shared printers. If you don't need help like this, save a tree: turn off the cover-page feature.

Paper Source

Most Print dialog boxes let you select a method of feeding paper. The default is usually cassette or "tray" feeding for laserprinters and automatic or continuous feeding for dot-matrix printers. Some non-Apple printer makers and sheet-feeder manufacturers modify this area of Print Dialog boxes. Check your manuals for explanations.

Black and White vs. Color/Grayscale Printing

Many, but by no means all Macintosh computers and printers can represent color and shades of gray. If your system is color or grayscale capable, you may want to use these features to improve the appearance of your documents. An in-depth look at color and grayscale issues is beyond the scope of this book. But the information presented here should be enough to help you understand Word 5's color and grayscale capabilities.

Even if your computer cannot *display* color or grays, your printer may be able to print them. Thus, Word 5 lets you define text colors even on black-and-white–only computers. See *Chapter 14* for more information about this feature. Moreover, you can *paste* color and gray graphics into your Word documents. (Word supports up to eight colors or shades of gray in graphics.)

Printing colors and shades of gray is usually slower, and some would say less reliable than printing black and white only. Thus you will have the option in most printer dialog boxes to turn color printing on or off.

Printing Selected Items

If you have selected text or graphics in a document the *Print Selection Only* choice will be available in the Print dialog box. An *X* in this checkbox instructs Word to print only the selected text.

PostScript File Printing

The LaserWriter Print dialog box has a Destination: button that lets you send your document to a disk file, which can be used by phototypesetting machines and other PostScript-compatible devices. Normally, you should leave the default Printer button activated.

Print Hidden Text

This checkbox toggles the printing of hidden index-entry codes, PostScript instructions, notes to yourself, and so on. With this box *X*'ed the hidden text will be printed along with visible text and graphics. Pagination is affected.

Print Next File

This choice is used when you have created a series of "connected" documents and want to print them all. For instance, some authors create separate document files for each chapter of a book, then use this feature to print the entire manuscript. See *Chapter 43* for details.

CHAPTER 13

Document Margins and Gutters

FEATURING

- Ways to adjust the white space around pages
- Tips for documents that will be bound
- Tips for two-sided printing
- How headers and footers affect margins

The white spaces around the four edges of a Word 5 page are determined primarily by *margin* and optional *gutter* settings. (Gutters add extra white space for bound documents) One set of margin and gutter settings is used for an entire document. Your choice of paper size, paper orientation (portrait vs. landscape), and margin and gutter settings work together to determine the size and shape of the text area of the pages in your document.

Larger margins and gutter settings decrease the available *text area* while increasing the surrounding *white space* on each page. Figure 13.1 shows the

Document Margins and Gutters

Word 5 default margin and text-area dimensions for both portrait and landscape orientations when creating U. S. letter-size documents without gutters.

Since margin settings affect pagination, it is a good idea to define them right when you begin a new project. This will give you a better grasp of the page count and overall "look" of the document as you work. You can always fine-tune margin settings just before final printing.

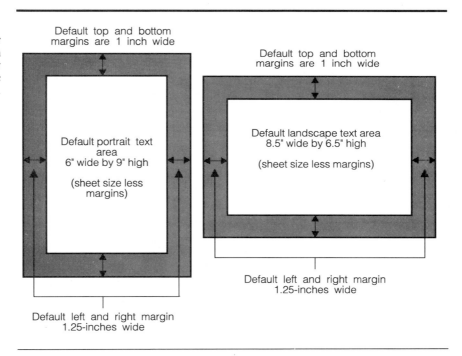

Figure 13.1
Margin settings, paper size, and orientation are three of the many factors that affect the available text area.

Margins need not all be the same dimensions. It is possible, for instance, to have a 1½" left margin and a 1.0" right margin, a ½" bottom margin and a ¾" top margin, or just about any combination you desire.

When printing two-sided documents, you may want to use Word's Mirror Even/Odd margin feature and possibly add gutters to place extra white space near the center of your book. (Note that it is convention to have odd-numbered pages on the right and even on the left—just look at any book!) If you plan to have different left and right margins in a two-sided document (a wide left and narrow right, for instance), it is useful to think of these as *inside* and *outside* margins rather than left and right margins, since the wide margin will be on the left side of odd-numbered pages and on the right side of even-numbered pages. You'll learn how in this chapter.

If you use headers and footers, you will want to know how they interact with margin settings. Word makes this all fairly painless.

Some printers cannot print at the extreme edges of a page. This can be a consideration when setting margins.

DOCUMENT MARGINS VS. INDENTS

Don't confuse Word's margin settings with its paragraph indentation feature. A Word document can have only *one* user-specified left margin setting and only *one* user-specified right margin setting, but each *paragraph* can have a different left and right *indentation* setting.

Indents are added to margin settings. That is to say, if you specify a 1.0" left margin and a ½" left indent, your text will print 1½" from the left edge of the paper. If you set a 1.0" right margin and indent the right edge of a paragraph 1.0", the text will stop 2.0" from the right edge of the paper. See *Chapter 15* to learn more about indenting.

CHANGING DOCUMENT MARGINS

There are three ways to set margins. The most straightforward method is to use the Document dialog box reached from the *Format* menu. (If you have an Extended keyboard you can use the ⌘-F14 keyboard shortcut to bring up the box.)

It is also possible to drag margins using the margin handles in Print Preview. This lets you see the results of margin changes after a slight repagination delay.

Finally, you can drag *margin brackets* in Normal and Page Layout views. The margin brackets are located on Word 5's ruler. Let's look at all three techniques, starting with the dialog box.

The Document Dialog Box Margin Settings

Figure 13.2 shows the Document dialog box. You are invited to enter new Left, Right, Top, Bottom, and Gutter margins. After you type in each new setting, press Tab to move to the next box. As with other Word dialog boxes, enter fractions as decimals (¼" would be *0.25*, and so on).

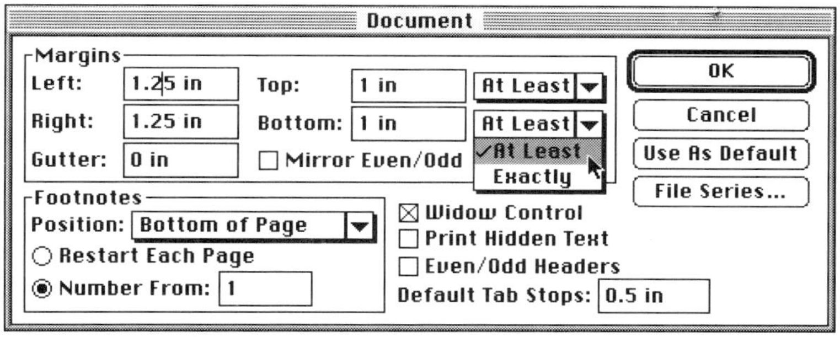

Figure 13.2
You have complete control over margins in the Document dialog box, found under the *Format* menu.

Dragging Margins in Print Preview

If you did the practice exercises in the first few chapters of this book, you've already changed margins while in Print Preview mode. Drag any of the margin handles, as shown in Figure 13.3, then wait a moment for your Mac to redisplay pages with your new margin settings.

If you don't see the margin handles in Print Preview, click the third icon from the top of the Print Preview icon stack as shown in Figure 13.4. This will display the margin guidelines and handles. When displaying two side-by-side pages in Print Preview, you will need to click in one page or the other before adjusting margins. The handles and guidelines will move to the page where you click.

Figure 13.3
Drag margin handles in Print Preview to change your margins.

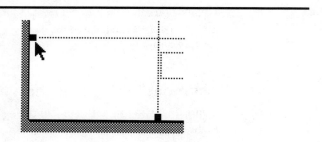

Figure 13.4
Click here if necessary to reveal margin guidelines and handles.

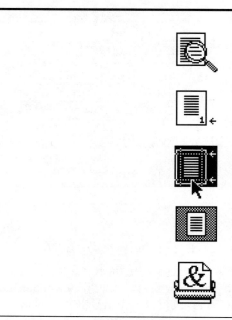

Dragging Margin Brackets on the Ruler

The bottom edge of the Word 5 ruler normally displays left and right paragraph-indent markers. You can display document-margin markers instead, then move them. Start by clicking on the margin-marker button (the middle one), highlighting it as shown in Figure 13.5. With the margin markers (the square brackets) displayed on the ruler, simply drag them to the desired position with your mouse.

Document Margins and Gutters

Figure 13.5
Click on the middle ruler marker button to reveal margin markers, then drag margin markers to change document margins.

Alternate Facing (Mirror) Margins

Select the Mirror Even/Odd feature in the Document dialog box when you have different left and right margin widths and your final output will be two-sided. Word makes inside margins of odd- and even-numbered pages the same size and does the same with the outside margins of odd and even pages, as illustrated in Figure 13.6. This is how you get white space on the appropriate side of even and odd, two-sided pages.

Figure 13.6
Mirror Even/Odd margins compensates for two-sided documents with dissimilar left and right margins.

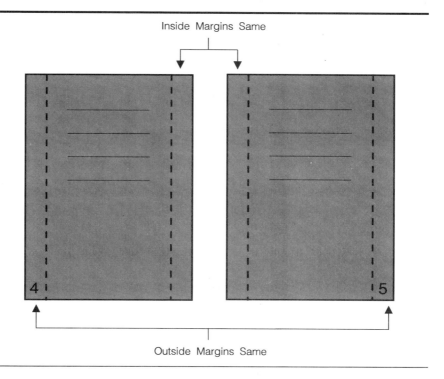

When you choose Mirror Even/Odd, the Document dialog box refers to margins as *Inside* and *Outside* rather than *Right* and *Left*. Word takes care of all the margin details for you, even if you tell it to start new sections on odd pages.

When adjusting margins in Print Preview, if you've chosen the Mirror Odd/Even feature, be sure you display two pages in Print Preview. This will let you see how facing pages look.

Gutters Facilitate Binding

Here's one of those features that apparently exists simply because other products have it. Gutter margins compensate for the paper tucked away in the binding of a two-sided book that would be unreadable. Gutters are additional white space in the inside margins. The gutter width, which you specify in the Document dialog box, reduces the text area, as shown in Figure 13.7.

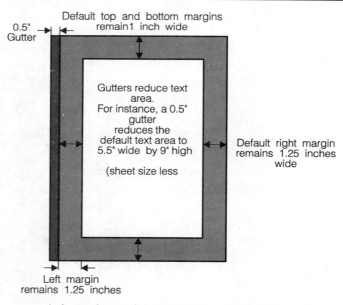

Figure 13.7
Gutter space compensates for paper used in the binding process by adding space to inside margins in two-sided documents.

In Print Preview, you can see the effect of gutter margins, but you cannot adjust them. To adjust the gutter, leave Print Preview and visit the Document dialog box. Instead of using gutters, consider simply increasing the size of the inside margins to accommodate binding.

PRINTER CAPABILITIES LIMIT MARGINS

Many printers, including Apple's LaserWriters, are incapable of printing all the way to the edge of the paper. Keep this in mind when setting margins. If, for instance, your printer cannot print past the last half-inch of a page, any margin of less than 1/2" will result in *cropped* (chopped-off) text.

Some printers offer ways to increase printing area. For instance, many laserprinters let you trade font memory for larger printing areas. See *Chapter 12* or your printer manual for details.

PRINTING IN MARGINS

As you can see from Figure 13.8, it is possible to place text, graphics, and page numbers in margins. You can drag indent markers into margins as described in *Chapter 15*, and text or graphics will follow. You can also use Word's *Frame* command to place things in margins, as described in *Chapter 31*. Page numbers can also be positioned in margins, as you will learn in *Chapter 19*.

HEADERS AND FOOTERS

Headers and footers print in the top and bottom margins. The inclusion of headers and footers causes Word to automatically adjust top and bottom margins when necessary. For instance, if you use the Document dialog box to specify a *minimum* top margin of 1/2", then create a header that is 1.0" high, word will increase the top margin size to make room for the big header. You can override this feature by specifying *exact* top or bottom margins in the Document dialog box. This will force Word to limit top and bottom margins, headers and footers be damned! This can create some interesting effects, desired and otherwise. Read about headers and footers in *Chapter 18*.

Figure 13.8
It's easy to print in the margins.

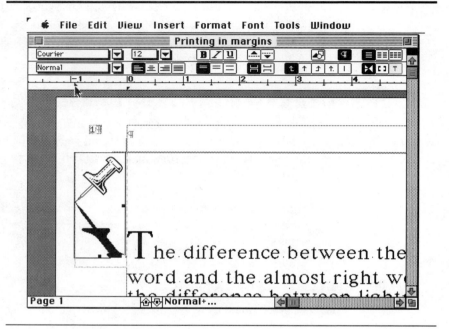

CHAPTER 14

All About Characters and Fonts

FEATURING

- Point sizes
- Serif vs. sans serif
- Character formats

Specialists called "typographers" spend their whole lives studying and improving the appearance of printed words. It is a complex profession steeped in tradition and romance. Computers have added to the trivia and mystique surrounding typography. Word 5 provides considerable typographic prowess. For instance, you can

- Specify fonts (type designs)
- Specify character size (points)
- Apply formats like bold, italic, and underline
- Adjust inter-character spacing (kerning)

- Specify colors for characters
- Change the case of text (e.g., lowercase to uppercase)
- Super- or subscript characters
- Copy and repeat character formatting
- Insert international accent marks and special symbols
- Hide and reveal text selectively (annotations)

For you, it may be enough to know how to print desired characters in appropriate sizes and styles. Other readers will want to know how to get just the right look. Some will need to know about TrueType and kerning. You may need to be aware of compatibility issues when moving documents from one computer or printer to another.

This chapter progresses from simple, non-technical techniques to fairly complex issues. Feel free to jump from topic to topic as need arises. There are very few hard-and-fast rules where the art of typography is concerned. The best way to learn is to experiment.

TERMINOLOGY

We often use the terms *font* and *typeface* and *typeface families* and *typestyles* interchangeably. They are not really synonymous. Word's own, unique, nomenclature and its ability to simulate things like bold and italic characters from plain fonts add to the confusion. With apologies to professional typographers, let's start with some slightly over-simplified definitions.

Fonts and Character Formatting

Characters are the letters, numbers, punctuation marks and special symbols (@, #, etc.) that you type from the keyboard. For our purposes, we'll define a *font* as a collection of character and symbol designs in one size. 18-point Courier is an example. In Word 5, effects like bold, italic, small caps, and shadow can usually be thought of as *styles* or *character formatting*. Figure 14.1 shows many of the character variations possible when using Word 5's character format tricks on the 18-point Courier font.

Figure 14.1
With Word 5's formatting capabilities, you can enhance a font in many ways.

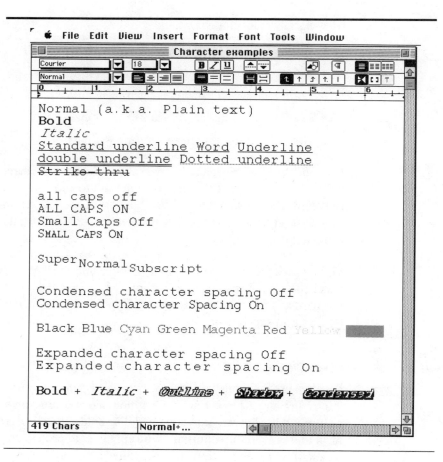

Don't confuse the character formatting tricks shown in Figure 14.1 with true bold, italic, and compressed *fonts*. If you don't know already, you will soon learn that there is more than one way to create a bold character on your Macintosh.

Monospaced vs. Proportionally Spaced

Some fonts are said to be *monospaced* or *fixed-pitch*; others *proportionally spaced* or *variable-pitch*. Monospaced fonts like Courier use the same amount of horizontal space on a line for each character, regardless of the width of a character. With a monospaced font like Courier a letter *i* takes the same amount of horizontal space as the letter *W*. Thus, if, you can fit seventy *W*s on a line in Courier, you can only fit seventy *i*s in the same space. Obviously this is an inefficient use of space and sometimes causes "sloppy" looking words. Since people like lawyers, art directors, and publishers usually want to fit as many words as possible on a page, they turn to proportionally spaced fonts that "tuck" narrow letters in closer to their neighbors.

In Figure 14.2 the same word is printed first in 72-point Courier, a monospaced font and then in 72-point Times and Helvetica, both proportionally spaced fonts. Notice the ocean of white space on either side of the letter *i* in the Courier example. A long base has been added to the bottom of the *i* in an attempt to distract you from this untidiness. Compare the white space on either side of three *i*s in Figure 14.2.

Figure 14.2
Notice that Courier (top) is much less elegant than Times (middle) or Helvetica (bottom).

Wimp

Wimp

Wimp

Incidentally, not all printers have identical looking fonts, even when the font names are the same. The Courier installed in Apple's LaserWriters looks quite different from the Courier in Pacific Data's PostScript products, for instance. Occasionally (but rarely) this can cause differences in line endings.

Point Sizes

The various sizes of type (9-point, 10-point, 12-point, etc.) are referred to as *point sizes*. You should know that 9-point type is smaller than 10-point type, and that there are 72 points to an inch. Thus, 72-point type will print 1-inch high, 36-point type will print ½" high, and so on.

Point size is measured from the top of the tallest *ascending* character (the *W* in Figure 14.2) to the bottom of the longest *descending* character (the *p* in Figure 14.2). Sometimes different fonts appear to be taller or shorter than they really are, due to the amount of space the designer has allowed for ascenders and descenders, and the visual "weight" of the characters. Notice how the 72-point Courier *looks* shorter than the 72-point Helvetica in Figure 14.2.

Ironically, the monospaced Courier font uses less *horizontal* space on the line than either of the proportionally spaced fonts, due mainly to the much wider *W*s and *m*s in the proportional faces. This is not usually the case.

Your choice of point size affects the amount of space between lines (called *leading*), as well as the height of the characters. You can have more than one point size on a line, but Word will adjust the line spacing to accommodate the largest character on the line. You can override this feature as you will see in the next chapter.

Serif vs. Sans Serif

The horizontal cross lines on the *W, i,* and *p* in Figure 14.2's Courier and Times examples are called *serifs*. (The fonts themselves are called *serif fonts*.) Popular Macintosh fonts with serifs include Courier, New York, Palatino, and Times. Fonts without these embellishments are said to be *sans serifs*. Avant Garde, Chicago, Geneva, and Helvetica are examples.

APPLYING AND REMOVING CHARACTER FORMATS

Word offers many ways to choose character formats. These include the ribbon, menu choices, dialog boxes, and keyboard shortcuts. You can change the formatting of single characters, entire words, or whole documents.

Character Changes from the Ribbon

The most immediately visible way to modify character appearance is to use the buttons and font menu on the ribbon as illustrated in Figure 14.3.

All About Characters and Fonts

Figure 14.3
You can format characters right from the ribbon.

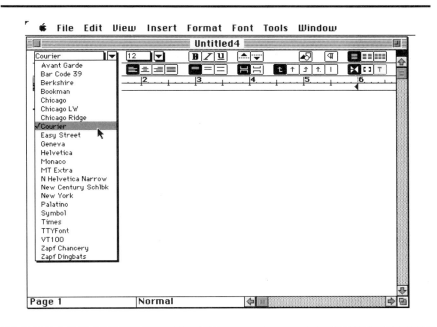

From the ribbon you can pick a font, change to a different point size, toggle bold, italic, and underline. You can also superscript or subscript characters. Simply click on the appropriate ribbon button or pick the desired menu item. It is possible to modify existing text or specify the way you want subsequently typed text to appear.

The Font Menu

Word 5's *Font* menu (located between the *Format* and *Tools* menus) lists all of the fonts installed on your Macintosh, as illustrated in Figure 14.4. (Yours may have fewer fonts.) Don't confuse this with the smaller font menu on the ribbon.

Changing Character (Point) Size

When you pick a font, the *Font* menu also displays the available point sizes. There will be a check mark next to the selected size for standard-size fonts. Non-standard sizes are shown in the Font menu on the ruler. You can change the point size from this menu by clicking on the desired new size.

Figure 14.4
The *Font* menu lists all fonts installed on your Mac.

All About Characters and Fonts

The Word 5 *Font* menu also displays the choices *Up, Down, Other...,* and *Default Font....* The *Up* and *Down* choices (⌘-] and ⌘-[) change the point size. As you would expect, if the current type size is 12-point (indicated by the checkmark in Figure 14.4), choosing *Up* would change to 13-point while choosing *Down* would switch to 11-point type.

Default Font... brings up the Default Font Category of the Preferences dialog box. Closing the box switches to the default font and size you've specified.

The *Other...* choice brings up the Character dialog box.

Character Options in the Format Menu

The *Format* menu (shown in Figure 14.5) contains several character-related choices including *Plain Text,* which removes things like bold, italic, and underlining. Notice the keyboard shortcuts for *Plain Text, Bold, Italic,* and *Underline* in Figure 14.5. The *Format* menu also has the choice *Character...* which will bring up the Character dialog box. Finally, notice *Change Case...*

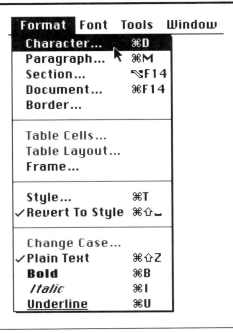

Figure 14.5
The *Format* menu contains character choices, too.

Changing Case from the Format Menu

The *Change Case...* choice is available on the *Format* menu only when you have selected (highlighted) text. Figure 14.6, shows the resulting dialog box which offers five choices.

Figure 14.6
The *Change Case...* dialog box gives you five choices.

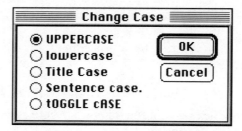

Look closely at the dialog box. It demonstrates the results of the five choices in use. For instance, UPPERCASE changes all selected characters to uppercase letters, and the choice *UPPERCASE* itself appears all uppercase in the dialog box. Title Case changes the first letter of each selected word to uppercase, as illustrated in the dialog box.

Alas, the Title Case feature is not context-sensitive, so it capitalizes prepositions and articles, including *of, the,* and so on.

When you change case by using this dialog box, the characters themselves change to the specified case. It is just as if you had retyped the characters yourself using the new capitalization scheme. As you will see in a moment, there is a different case-changing feature (found in the Character dialog box) that changes only the *appearance* of letters without actually changing the letters themselves.

The Character Dialog Box

The Character dialog box can be reached from the *Format* menu, as shown in Figure 14.5, or with the ⌘-D keyboard shortcut. It can also be reached by using the *Other...* choice on the *Font* menu. This dialog box lets you specify and combine a potentially gaudy array of character effects. It also presents yet another way to pick fonts; and it lets you fiddle with inter-character spacing. Drop-down menus provide you with underline and color choices. You can even enter non-standard font sizes from here. This is one busy box! Take a good look at Figure 14.7.

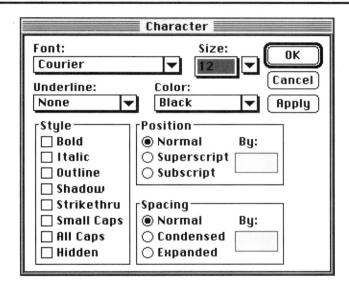

Figure 14.7
The Character dialog box has something for everyone.

Choosing Fonts

While there are many easy ways to specify fonts without visiting the Character dialog box, notice that you can specify fonts here by using a drop-down menu. Click on the *Font:* triangle to reveal the menu.

Custom Point Size

Just as there are many easy ways to specify fonts, there are quicker ways to specify point sizes than from the Character dialog box. But it offers an important additional point-size option: you can type *any* point size from 4 through 16,383 in the Size: box. This corresponds to character heights ranging from approximately $1/18$th of an inch to about 19 feet!

Underline Options

There are five underline choices on the drop-down menu illustrated in Figure 14.8. They include Single, Word, Double, Dotted, and None. The effect of these choices is illustrated back in Figure 14.1. Unfortunately, underline choices cannot be combined; it is not possible to choose double word underline, for instance.

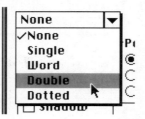

Figure 14.8
There are five underline options.

Character Styles

Notice the Style section of the Character dialog box. It contains eight choices, from Bold to Hidden. You can apply one or more of these choices to selected characters and to subsequently typed text. Simply click to place Xs in the boxes next to the desired effects. You can remove effects by clicking on an X to clear the box.

Effects can often be combined; it is usually possible to have text that is bold *and* italicized *and* underscored. Not all fonts accept all formatting options though, and occasionally you will see combinations on screen that will not print.

If you open the Character dialog box and see gray boxes next to the formatting options, it simply means that you have selected text with different formatting combinations. For instance, some of your selected text may be bold, other parts plain, part underlined, and so on.

Character Color Choices

Even if you cannot display or print color, Word 5 lets you specify six character colors plus black or white. You can then take copies of your disk files to color-capable hardware for display and printing.

All About Characters and Fonts

To specify a color, start by selecting text. Then choose the desired color from the drop-down *Color:* menu in the Character dialog box. If your display supports color, you will see color characters on screen. If your display or printer supports shades of gray, colors will be converted to grays.

You may need to visit the Monitor portion of your Mac's control panel to enable shades of gray. Some people turn off gray-display features to save memory and speed-up video performance. See your Macintosh manuals for details. The actual appearance of your Monitor control panel dialog box may differ from the example in Figure 14.9—a portrait monitor on a Macintosh IIcx.

Figure 14.9
You must visit your Monitor control panel to show grayscales.

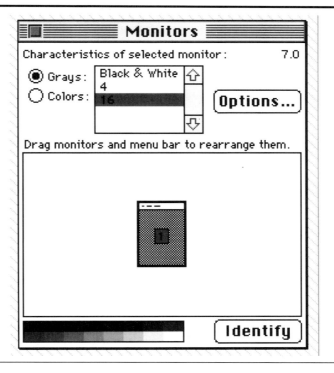

If you have a color printer (or even an Apple ImageWriter with a multicolor ribbon), characters will print in their specified colors. Gray-capable printers, including most LaserWriters, convert colors to shades of gray. You can see an example of this in figure 14.1 near the beginning of this chapter.

Remember, not all Macintosh computers can display gray or colors, but you need not display color to print it.

Position (Superscript and Subscript)

Normally, any characters that you type are placed on an invisible line called the *baseline*. Superscripted characters are usually moved 3 points above the baseline; subscripted characters are generally placed 2 points below the baseline.

There are several ways to super- and subscript characters. You can use the new Super- and Subscript ribbon buttons, or you can use the corresponding buttons in the Character dialog box. Both of these techniques *retain* the current *font size*, but *reposition* the characters above or below the baseline. The Character dialog box lets you type in changes to the defaults of 3 points above and 2 points below in the By: box.

There is a better way to make supers and subs, though, which uses keyboard shortcuts. ⌘-Shift- + is the superscript shortcut (you cannot use the plus on the keypad). ⌘-Shift- – is the subscript shortcut. Rather than just repositioning text in relation to the baseline, both shortcuts decrease the selected type to the next smaller font size. This is very handy for exponents and molecular notation.

Inter-character Spacing

Word lets you override the standard spacing between characters (the *kerning*) defined by their designers. You can either move characters closer together (condensed) or move characters farther apart (expanded). The default for Expand is 3 points. The Condense default is 1.5 points.

Removing Character Formats with the Plain Text Feature

You can remove formats like bold and italic either by choosing *Plain Text* from the *Format* menu or by using the keyboard shortcut: ⌘-Shift-Z.

Copying and Repeating Character Formats

To copy character formatting, select only the characters of interest (but *not* the paragraph marker at the end of the paragraph), then press ⌘-Option-V. The words *Format To* appear in the lower-left corner of the screen. Position the insertion point to begin typing or highlight the text you want to format. Then press Enter (not Return).

Special Characters

Special characters, like the copyright symbol (©), ligatures, and foreign accents have always been fairly easy to type and print on a Macintosh. Word 5 makes it even easier. Let's look at the new *Symbol...* feature and review the old reliable keyboard shortcuts.

The Symbol Command

A new dialog box appears whenever you choose *Symbol...* from the *Insert* menu (see Figure 7.1). ⌘-Option-Q is the keyboard shortcut. It shows you all available characters in the current font. Clicking on a symbol does two things. First, it inserts the character at the insertion point in your document. Then it shows you the ASCII decimal code and, if there is one, a keyboard shortcut

To see which symbols are available in different fonts, simply choose a font from the *Font* menu and use the *Symbol...* command to view the choices.

Typing Symbols from the Keyboard

If you know the key combinations you can enter them directly from the keyboard without using the *Symbol...* feature. For instance to type the bullet character (•), hold down the Option key and press the *8* key (not the one on your numeric keypad). Different fonts sometimes have different key combinations, so you will need to consult the documentation that comes with your fonts or use Word's *Symbol...* command, the *Key Caps* desk accessory, or more powerful third-party accessories like KeyFinder, to show you the combinations.

More About Fonts

Fonts used on the Macintosh fall into two general categories: bit mapped (sometimes called screen fonts) and outline fonts.

Bitmapped Fonts

Bitmapped fonts were the first to be used on Macintosh computers. They are still very popular. When your Macintosh System was installed, a number of standard bitmapped fonts were automatically included. You or someone else may have added others.

Bitmapped fonts create a character by turning on and off the appropriate pixels on your screen and dots on your printer. There is a limitation, though: bitmapped fonts can represent one size and style only. A separate bitmap is required to display a font in a each specific point size or style (bold, italic, etc.). Furthermore, if you plan to use bitmapped fonts to print directly to printers, additional font sizes and styles often need to be installed to support the higher resolution of these devices.

When you install bitmapped fonts on your Macintosh, their names will be added to the *Font* menu, which will also list the available point sizes for any given font.

If you ask Word to use a font in a point size for which a bitmap has not been installed (by typing a non-standard size in the Character Dialog box), Word will attempt to scale an available point size to approximate your request. This often results in jagged, nasty-looking characters.

Since obtaining the best quality from bitmapped fonts requires installing many different versions of the same font, and since bitmapped fonts must record every single dot that makes up a character, a font collection can quickly use up a lot of disk space. That's why outline fonts were invented.

Outline Fonts

Outline fonts can reproduce *any* point size from a single font description. Instead of storing the font as a series of dots, the font is represented by mathematical formulas describing the lines and curves which make up the characters. This enables outline fonts to be displayed at any point size by scaling the outlines. The pixels that fall within the resulting outline are then turned "on" and become part of the character.

The Macintosh currently supports two types of outline font formats: TrueType and PostScript Type 1. TrueType is a font format developed by Apple, while Type 1 was developed by Adobe.

Special Bold Condensed and Italic Fonts

There are two ways to create font variations like bold and italic. You've just seen how Word and your Mac can create these effects from normal fonts by using various mathematical transformations which are applied to either bitmap or outline fonts. That's what happens when you click the bold or italic buttons on the ribbon. That's also what happens when you choose bold or italic from Word's *Format* menu. However, these transformations are generic and do not always provide the best looking results. Some font designers intentionally disable the Mac's ability to create bold and italic type this way, either to protect the "integrity" of their designs, or to get you to purchase additional fonts.

If you are a purist, or if you need an effect not possible with the Mac's standard font and format tricks, you can install specialized bold, italic, condensed, and other fonts. For instance, you may prefer the appearance of B Helvetica Bold (the bold variation of Helvetica); I Times Italic (the italic version of Times), and so on.

The results can be quite impressive. For instance, the top line in Figure 14.10, shows the letter *a* as displayed in the plain, bold, and italic styles in the normal Times font at 72 points. The bottom line shows the same three letters when separate Times Bold and Times Italic fonts were also installed.

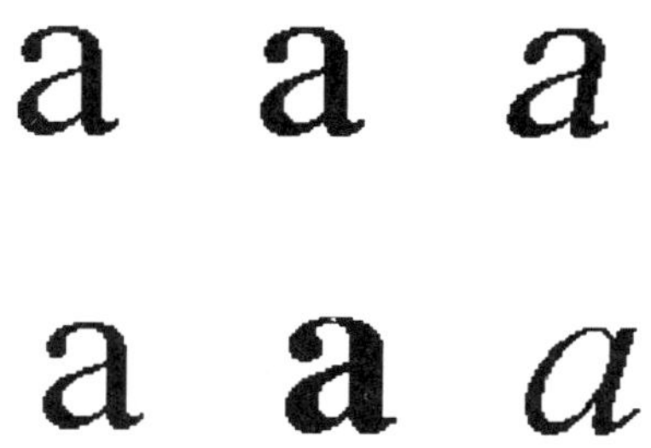

Figure 14.10
Font effects vs. the "real thing".

a a *a*

a **a** *a*

Note that the "bold" version in the first example is simply a darkening of the original font and does not contain detail of the "true" bold typeface. Likewise, the "italic" version, in the first example, is simply a slanted version of the original character, while the "true" italic letter takes on a completely distinctive style.

Once you've installed these extra fonts, whenever you specify bold Helvetica; Word will first attempt to find a font called *B Helvetical Bold* in your system. If it can not find that font, it will use the plain Helvetical font and attempt to simulate a bold effect by darkening some strokes of the letter. Likewise, when asked to italicize characters in the Times font, the Mac will look for a font called *I Times Italic.* If it cannot find the font, it will try to approximate an italicized look by slanting the plain Times font. These built-in transformations seldom result in the true appearance of a font as intended by the font designers.

Even if the Mac could not find the correct font to display on-screen, when you *print* your document, it will perform the search again, this time trying to determine the best font located in the printer.

For example, if you are printing to a Postscript printer, *B Helvetica Bold* is included in most PostScript printers, so the font would be used even if Word were unable to display a true B Helvetica Bold on-screen.

This results in the best looking type, but inter-character and inter-line spacing may not be ideal since Word has formatted the document based on the transformed font.

Problems can arise when you move documents from one machine to another unless both machines have the same fonts installed. Word will reformat the page based on the characteristics of the available fonts. This may create different line endings and page breaks.

CHAPTER 15

Paragraphs and Line Spacing

FEATURING

- Word's unique definition of a paragraph
- How to format paragraphs
- Using the ruler for quick formatting

In this chapter we'll explore Word 5's paragraph-formatting tools and adjustable line spacing. You can save collections of formatting decisions as styles, discussed in *Chapter 17*.

PARAGRAPHS

Your English teachers taught you that paragraphs are collections of sentences on a related topic. Word uses a somewhat more liberal definition. A Word paragraph can be a single text character, a graphic, or even a blank line consisting only of the *paragraph mark* (¶) that appears in your document when you press the Return key. Paragraph-formatting features are an important part of Word 5's arsenal. Figure 15.1 contains five Word paragraphs, each ending with a paragraph mark. Can you find them all?

Figure 15.1
Word paragraphs always end with a paragraph mark (¶).

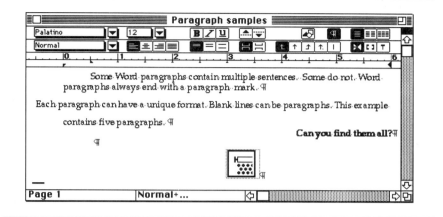

Each Word paragraph in your document can be uniquely formatted, and need not contain text. For instance, the first paragraph in Figure 15.1 is *single* spaced with the first line *indented* about ½". The next paragraph contains a *hanging indent*, and is *double* spaced. The third paragraph is *right justified*. The fourth paragraph is a *blank line* created by pressing just the Return key. The final paragraph is a graphic (without text), followed by a paragraph mark. Notice that this last paragraph has been *centered*.

Other paragraph formatting options include adjustments to *line* and *paragraph spacing*. You can also add *paragraph shading* and *paragraph borders*, and force Word to *keep lines together* when repagination occurs.

Applying Paragraph Formats

When you open a new document, Word applies the default format to all paragraphs until you tell it to do otherwise. You modify paragraphs using Word's ruler button or the Paragraph dialog box. The ruler is easy to use and readily available. When precise formatting is required, consider using the Paragraph dialog box rather than the ruler. Some formatting features have keyboard shortcuts.

If you want to reformat only one paragraph, simply place the insertion point anywhere within the paragraph, then make formatting changes.

To alter multiple paragraphs, select them first. Your changes will affect all selected paragraphs, *including* any partially selected paragraphs.

The Paragraph Mark Knows All

One of the few things that all five paragraphs in Figure 15.1 have in common is a paragraph mark at the end. It is a good idea to display paragraph marks when you work. If you can't see them now, click on the ribbon's paragraph-mark button (the ¶ symbol); or pick the *Show/Hide* ¶ choice in the *View* menu; or use the ⌘-J keyboard shortcut.

While not technically correct, it is useful to think of paragraph marks as "containers" of the paragraph formatting information for the paragraph preceding them. For instance, the first paragraph mark shown in Figure 15.1 "remembers" that the author wants to indent ½″ and single-space the first paragraph. The second paragraph mark "knows" to create a hanging indent and double-space.

If the first mark is deleted, the text from the two adjacent paragraphs combine to form one paragraph. In the process, the text above the deleted paragraph mark takes on the characteristics contained in what *was* the second paragraph mark. Figure 15.2 illustrates the results.

Since the second paragraph has a hanging indent, and since the old first paragraph has taken on the characteristics contained in the remaining paragraph

Figure 15.2
Deleting a paragraph mark causes the paragraph above to take on the characteristics of the next mark below.

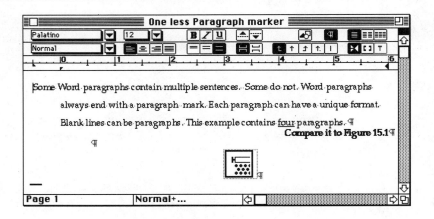

mark, the word *some* is now a hanging indent. The originally single-spaced text is double-spaced now.

The lesson here is simple. When deleting text, if you also delete the associated paragraph mark, things above it will take on the characteristics of the next paragraph mark below. Copying a paragraph marks copies paragraph styles. If you accidentally delete a paragraph mark, use *Undo* to restore formatting.

Paragraph Formatting with the Ruler

The ruler contains a number of handy paragraph-formatting tools. Figure 15.3 shows you their location and function.

When you select a button, it will darken on the ruler. If the ruler is not showing, use the keyboard shortcut ⌘-R or choose *Ruler* from the *View* menu.

Big tip: You must tell Word which paragraph or paragraphs you wish to format before using the ruler's tools.

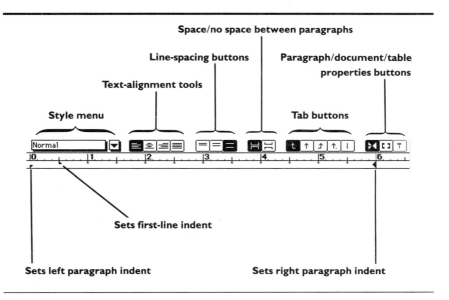

Figure 15.3
The ruler places a number of paragraph-formatting tools at your fingertips.

Indenting Paragraphs with the Ruler

To adjust left and right paragraph indents from the ruler, point to and drag the triangular indent marker to the desired locations. You will see the text move when you release the mouse button.

Notice that the left indent marker is a split triangle. To indent the entire left edge of a paragraph, point to and drag the *bottom* half of the left indent marker. That's the part that adjusts the overall left indentation. The top half of the triangle is used for indenting the first line of each paragraph, as you will see in a moment. When you drag the bottom half of the left indent marker, the two halves stay the same distance apart.

It is possible to drag the right marker past the right margin. This is one way to print text in margins. It is also possible to drag the left marker past the left margin, but expect to scroll very slowly.

As you may recall from *Chapter 13,* indents are added to margin settings. Thus, if you have a 1.0" right margin and drag the right indent marker an additional 1.0" to the left, your text will print 2.0" from the right edge of the paper.

Keyboard Shortcuts Speed Left Indenting

There are keyboard shortcuts for moving the left indent. Use ⌘-Shift-N to move the left indent marker to the right. Pressing ⌘-Shift-M moves the marker to the left. Movements are in the increments used for default tab settings (usually ½"). This is a great way to create nested indents! (Note that ⌘-Shift-M will not go past the left margin.)

Indenting First Lines

To indent the first line of a paragraph, point to and drag the top half of the split, left indent marker to the right. The first line will move when you release the mouse button. The ruler will show the position of the first-line indent, as illustrated in Figure 15.3.

Hanging Indents with the Ruler

Sometimes it is desirable to have the first line in each paragraph "stick out". This is particularly useful for creating bulleted lists, numbered paragraphs, and so forth.

Simply drag the top half of the left indent marker to the left, past the left indent, and release the mouse button when you reach the desired point. The ruler will scroll to show you the hanging indent's position with relation to the rest of the paragraph. The ruler in Figure 15.2 demonstrates this.

Aligning and Justifying Text with the Ruler

The four buttons near the left end of the ruler let you quickly justify, center, right- and left-align text. The lines in the buttons demonstrate the expected results. As always, you must first either select multiple paragraphs or place the insertion point in the paragraph you want to align.

Left Alignment   Left alignment is Word's default. Text sits right up against the paragraph's left indent position. If you have specified a first line indent, the left alignment feature does not override it. Instead, it uses the specified first line setting, then left-aligns the remaining text.

Centering   Don't use spaces to center. Type words at the left margin then click the Center button, which places the text or graphics smack dab between the *indent markers* for the paragraph being centered. If you want to center things between *document margins*, be sure the left and right indent markers are sitting on their respective document margins. Moving the first line indent marker will effect centering.

Right Alignment   Clicking on the Right alignment ruler button places selected items flush against the right *indent position* for the paragraph. Use this feature for correspondence dates, inside addresses, and for added impact.

If you want to right-align things with the *document's* right margin, be sure the paragraph's right indent marker is sitting on the right document margin.

The first-line indent feature works in conjunction with right-aligned text. That is to say, text can be both right-aligned and have the first line indented.

Justification   Clicking on the Justify button causes Word to add space between words in the selected paragraphs. This results in what some people consider to be a "typeset" look.

With the exception of the last line in a paragraph, all of the justified lines will have exactly the same length and will all be flush left and right with the paragraph's left and right indent markers. Justified text can also have the first line indented.

If the uneven spacing and "rivers" of white space caused by justification annoy you, consider inserting hyphens to "tighten up" the text. See *Chapter 22* for details.

Line Spacing with the Ruler Buttons

The ruler provides three buttons for simple but effective control of the space between lines under most circumstances. The buttons contain lines that demonstrate the relative effect of single, one-and-a-half, and double line spacing. Single spacing causes 12-point line spacing, 1½-line spacing is 18 points, and double-spaced lines will be 24 points apart. (There is little or no effect for text larger than 24 points.)

When you use these ruler buttons, Word will compensate for graphics, superscripts, and large or small type sizes. To force exact line spacing, use the line-spacing features found in the Paragraph dialog box (described in a moment). You will find them particularly helpful when working with very large or very small type sizes.

Paragraph Spacing with the Ruler

The ruler's two paragraph spacing buttons add and remove space above selected paragraphs. To change the space at the bottom of paragraphs, visit the Paragraph dialog box.

The Add Space ruler button adds 12 points of white space at the top of each paragraph. The Delete Space button removes any extra space. If you have set the space before to something other than 12 point, neither button will be darkened.

HE PARAGRAPH DIALOG BOX

The Paragraph dialog box shown in Figure 15.4 is reached with the *Paragraph...* choice on the *Format* menu or with the ⌘-M keyboard shortcut.

Figure 15.4
The Paragraph dialog box is where you can fine-tune your paragraph settings.

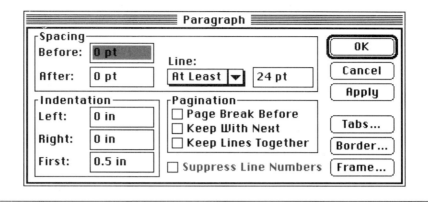

Double-clicking paragraph-related buttons or the ruler's left or right indent markers will also call up the dialog box! Choices, choices...

Besides being the launching pad for several other formatting features (Tabs, Borders, and Frames, all discussed in later chapters), it lets you precisely specify inter-line and inter-paragraph spacing. You can dictate exact indentation measurements here. This is also where you turn off line numbering for specific paragraphs and specify pagination guidelines.

Spacing Before and After Paragraphs

Many people place white space between paragraphs by pressing the Return or Enter key several times—"typewriter style." While this works just fine, there is a preferred method.

The Paragraph dialog box (*Paragraph...* from the *Format* menu) has an area called Spacing. It lets you define the amount of white space Word places before and after paragraphs. You can enter spacing settings in points (*pt*), picas (*pi*), inches (*in*), centimeters (*cm*), or lines (*li*). Thus, 12 points would be entered as *12pt*, 25 centimeters would be entered as *25cm*, and so on.

Each paragraph can have unique *before* and *after* spacing if you wish. One advantage to adding space this way is that the spacing before and after paragraphs does not change when you change the point size of your text. Another advantage is that you can use different spacing combinations for different purposes. Headings often have different spacing requirements from body text, for instance. You may wish to create different before and after spacing designs for figures and figure captions as well.

As you will learn in *Chapter 17*, you can save unique spacing specifications as part of a style, making it easy to keep the look of your documents consistent.

When adding space, remember that if a paragraph has space added after it, and the paragraph beneath it has space added before, the white space between them will be the *combination* of the two settings. For example, if one paragraph has 12 points of spacing after it and its successor has 6 points of spacing before, the white space between will be 18 points.

When you print, Word ignores the before space in paragraphs that automatic pagination starts at the top of a page. If you force a page or section break that starts a new page, however, Word retains the before space. It will also retain before space if you check the *Page Break Before* option in the Pagination section of the Paragraph dialog box.

Paragraph Borders and Shading

Word 5 bristles with paragraph border and shading features. They are covered in detail in *Chapter 37*, but are worth mentioning here since they are paragraph related. As you can see from Figure 15.5, Word lets you apply various border treatments and shading to paragraphs.

Start by selecting the paragraphs you wish to format. Then, either by clicking on the Border... button in the Paragraph dialog box or by choosing *Border...* from the *Format* menu, bring up the dialog box shown in Figure 15.6.

Click on combinations of line types, locations and styles to build a border design of your choosing, or click on one of the preset border icons. To add extra space between the text and borders, specify a point measurement in the From Text box before choosing a border type. To add paragraph shading, pick a shading percentage from the drop-down Shading: menu, or enter a percentage in the entry box.

Paragraphs and Line Spacing

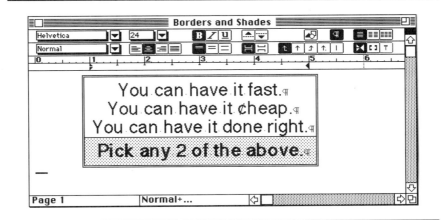

Figure 15.5
Word 5 bristles with paragraph border and shading features. Reach them from the Paragraph dialog box or the *Format* menu.

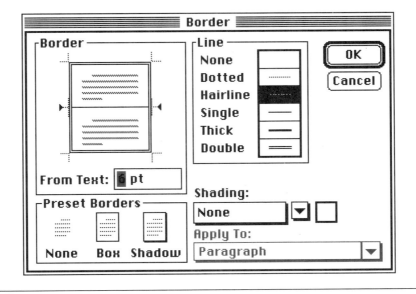

Figure 15.6
You have many shading and border options.

CHAPTER 16

All About Tabs

FEATURING

- Five kinds of tab stops and when to use them
- Tables vs. tabs
- Setting and moving tab stops
- Tab tricks your typewriter can't do
- How tabs facilitate data exchange

Word novices often either under- or overuse *tabs*. Primarily a quick way to position text or graphics, tabs have lots of competition in Word 5. Some people use the *Spacebar* instead of tabs. (Power users cringe when they see this.) Lovers of Word 5's *table* features (discussed in *Chapter 37*) often abandon tabs altogether in favor of tables. This is probably a mistake too. Moreover, your typing teacher may have told you to use tabs to indent the first line of each paragraph. You may prefer Word's split *left indent marker*.

Tabs do some things in Word you can't do on a typewriter. For instance, they can help you exchange Word data with spreadsheets, databases, and other programs. So turn off that MTV and let's explore the wonderful world of tabs and tab stops!

All About Tabs

Five Kinds of Tab Stops

Word offers five specialized tab stop types. They each work with tabs to help align text, and are particularly useful for making simple columnar lists like the one in Figure 16.1.

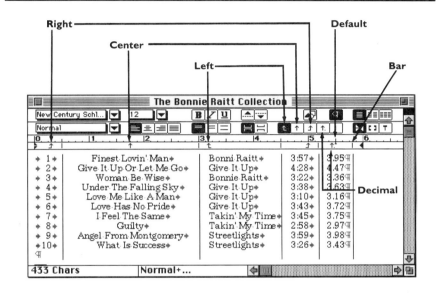

Figure 16.1
Word 5 provides left, center, right, decimal, and bar tabs.

Left Tab Stops

Left tab stops are like the plain vanilla ones you find on your old Smith Corona. Text typed at these tab stops bumps up against the left edge of the stop. A left tab was used to align the album-name list (the third column) in Figure 16.1.

Center Tab Stops

A center tab stop centers your text around the tab stop. In Figure 16.1 the song titles (in column two) are aligned with a center tab stop.

Right Tab Stops

Right tab stops push whatever you type to the left of the tab. As you can see in the first column of Figure 16.1, this is a great way to type long lists of numbers.

Decimal Tab Stops

Don't you wish you had had *these* in college? (On second thought, perhaps you do.) Decimal tab stops behave as you'd expect. They align columns of numbers on the decimal point and are perfect for simple financial reports.

Bar Tabs

The Bar button creates those nice, thin vertical lines you see separating items in Figure 16.1. They aren't actual tab *stops,* (that is, you cannot use them to align text) but they can be placed and moved like stops.

TABLES VS. TABS

Simple tabular columns are great if you have items that *always* fit on one line. But suppose that Bonnie had recorded a song with a very long title—*How Can I Miss You If You Won't Go Away?*, for instance. The title wouldn't automatically wrap to fit the format. You would need to redesign the tab layout, shorten the song title, or cobble things up with a carriage return. Ugh. Long items like these give tab typists fits. As you will see in *Chapter 37,* tables make it easy to deal with this and other problems. Serious typists will probably choose table solutions over tabs most days. The price is speed and complexity. Word's table features can be slow at times; and you may scratch your head in the beginning. Tables require an understanding of tabs too. So, for simple projects like the example here, you might want to stick with tabs alone, at least until you've mastered them.

SETTING TAB STOPS

Tab setting is easiest with the ruler showing. If it's not, use the ⌘-R shortcut to turn on the ruler or choose *Ruler* from the *View* menu.

It is also handy to have the Show ¶ feature on, since that will enable you to see tabs themselves as you type them. Use ⌘-J to display paragraph markers and *tab markers,* which look like bold arrows.

Tab *stops* are stored with the paragraph mark for each paragraph, thus all of the rules about paragraph markers apply. If, for example, you set tab stops once and type returns at the end of each typing line, each new line (actually a paragraph) will use the same tab stops as the preceding one, until you tell Word otherwise. This is discussed in more detail in *Chapter 15*.

Setting Tab Stops with the Ruler

With the ruler in view, click the button with the picture of the desired tab-stop type, which will darken. Hold down the mouse button and drag a new tab stop onto the lower portion of the ruler as shown in Figure 16.1. If you make a mistake, drag the stop off of the ruler and try again.

Moving Tab Stops on the Ruler

Very important point: To move tab stops *before* you've entered text, simply point to the stop of interest and drag away. If you have already entered text that uses the tab stops you want to move, first select *all* of the text before moving the tab stop.

For instance, if you had already typed the ten lines in figure 16.1 and wanted to move the left tab stop, you would need to highlight all ten lines before moving the tab stop. Otherwise, some lines (paragraphs) would have different stops than others. Incidentally, you'd want to also highlight the *paragraph mark* beneath the tenth line too if you plan to enter more items. Otherwise the last paragraph marker won't "know" about the change and subsequent entries would be off.

If you highlight paragraphs with different tab-stop settings, the bottom portion of the ruler will be dimmed. Only the stops for the top paragraph will be displayed.

Setting Tab Stops with the Tabs Dialog Box

While using the ruler is easy, you may want to use the Tabs dialog box for some projects. It provides ways to precisely set tab stops and it offers some additional tab-related options. Figure 16.2 shows the Tabs dialog box at work.

Figure 16.2
The Tabs dialog box gives you precise control and additional tab-related features.

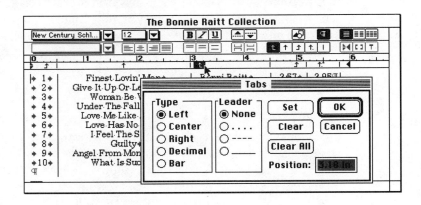

You can reach the Tabs dialog box in several ways. Click the button in the Paragraph dialog box. Or, you could add the *Tabs...* menu item (see *Chapter 10*); but there are easier methods.

Double-clicking in the *tab stop area* of the ruler will place a new left tab stop where you have clicked and bring up the Tabs dialog box. The position of the new tab stop will be shown in the Position: area of the dialog box and will change as you move the tab stop. Note that you can actually manipulate the ruler while the dialog box is open.

Double-clicking any *tab stop button* on the ruler will bring up the Tabs dialog box with the corresponding Tab Type button activated. For instance, if you double-click on the ruler's Center tab stop button, the dialog box will open with the Center choice activated.

If you double-click on an actual *tab stop* on the ruler the Tabs dialog box will open and display the exact position and type of the tab stop, as shown in Figure 16.2.

You can precisely reposition any stop by selecting it this way and typing in the desired new position in the Position: portion of the Tabs dialog box. Click okay, and the stop will move. Remember to select *all* affected text and paragraphs markers before moving tab stops. *Undo* (⌘-Z) will save you when you forget.

All About Tabs

Measurements in the Tabs dialog box are assumed to be in inches unless you type another legal abbreviation (*cm* for centimeter, *pt* for point, or *pi* for pica). As an example, 5 *cm* would position a tab stop five centimeters from the left margin.

Press the Set button in the Tab dialog box when you are happy with your work. The tab changes will be made. You will need to click OK to cast aside the Tabs dialog box and change the text. The advantage of using Set first is that you can then assign more tabs from the dialog box.

Leading Characters

Were not talking Julia Roberts or Robin Williams, here. Word 5's leading characters are dots, dashes, and solid lines. These leaders *precede* tabbed entries, producing the effect demonstrated in Figure 16.3. They make it easy to read wide, sparsely populated lines without losing your place. Select the paragraphs you want to pretty-up. Double click on the tab *to the right* of where you want the leaders. Choose the leader style you desire from the Tabs dialog box. Click OK.

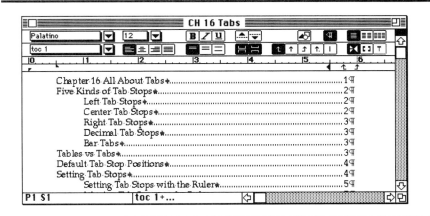

Figure 16.3
Word provides tab leaders that make it easy to read wide, sparsely populated lines without losing your place.

You can apply this effect when defining new tab stops or double-click on existing stops to bring up the Tabs dialog box as an afterthought.

Default Tab Stop Positions

The Microsoft standard settings specify tabs every half-inch (½″). You can change this by setting new stops in the Document dialog box. (Use the *Document...* command on the *Format* menu, or press ⌘-F14 on your extended keyboard. Enter dimensions in inches, centimeters, picas, or points. The example in Figure 16.4 shows default stops set every three-quarters of an inch (¾″).

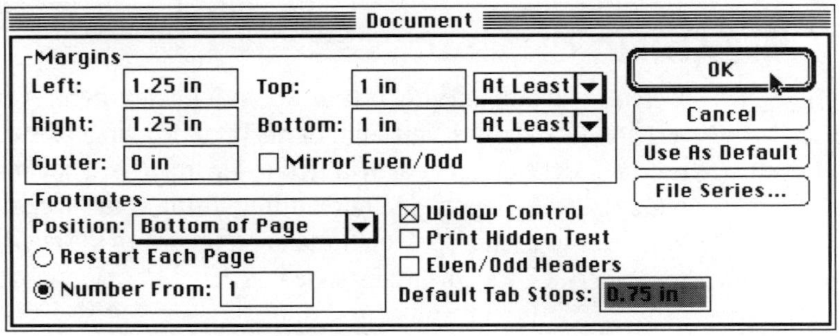

Figure 16.4
Enter new default tab positions and click OK to use them for the current document or click Use as Default to use from now on.

Clearing Tab Stops

You can drag the occasional tab off of the ruler if you don't need it. The Tabs dialog box (see Figure 16.2) provides facilities for clearing multiple tabs at once. If you do choose a specific tab, the Clear button in the Tabs dialog box will still remove it.

Then, there is the Clear All button. It removes all of your custom tabs. Defaults remain. This can make an absolute mess of your pride and joy. *Undo* or Cancel should work if you accidentally clear all custom tabs, but it is always a good idea to save your work before experimenting with major changes like these. Remember, these features only work on paragraphs you have selected.

Entering and Editing Tabular Data

Once you have set up tab stops, simply press the Tab key to reach the stop and begin typing. Word will position the text as you type. If you are typing at a center or right stop, text will flow appropriately as you type. When you type at decimal stops the insertion point sits to the left of the decimal position until you hit the period key; then it hops to the right side.

To leave an entry blank, simply tab past it by pressing the Tab key. To move the insertion point *backwards* one tab at a time, hold down the Shift key and press Tab.

TABS AND DATA EXCHANGE

Tabs and carriage returns are often used by Macintosh databases and spreadsheets. Tabs usually separate fields in records and carriage returns usually separate records. If you use Word 5 to type a list of tab-separated names, addresses, and phone numbers, for instance, you might be able to export the list to your favorite database or time-management program. Check out the "importing" sections of your other Macintosh program manuals.

CHAPTER 17

All About Styles

FEATURING

- Ways to capture and re-use complex formats (styles)
- Word's standard styles explained
- Style-sheet tricks and strategies
- How to base new styles on existing ones

Word 5's style-related features are responsible for much of its power and popularity. They also confuse and initially frustrate most new users. It is possible to plug-along in Word for the rest of your life without knowing a whit about styles. That would be a shame. Learning about *styles* and *style sheets*, Word's *standard styles*, and the concepts of *normal* and *base styles* can save you hundreds or even thousands of hours. When you couple that know-how with Word's glossary and stationery features (covered elsewhere in this book), Word can make you a dramatically more efficient author and typist. If you work with other people on large, complex projects, or if your organization wants a uniform look for all of its printed documents, styles are essential.

Consume this chapter a little at a time. Try a few style experiments when you are not working on a rush project. If your eyes begin to glaze over or you find yourself pounding the desk with your fist, take a break. It will all make sense sooner than you think.

WHAT ARE STYLES AND STYLE SHEETS?

Styles are collections of paragraph and character formatting decisions that you make and save using meaningful names. Styles make it easy for you to reuse complex paragraph formats without laboriously recreating them each time. The sales letter in Figure 17.1 contains five examples of *styles*. Their associated *style names* appear in the drop-down list at the left edge of the ruler.

Each *document* has its own collection of styles. A document's collection of styles is called its *style sheet*.

Figure 17.1

The five styles in this letter (Body, Bullets,b, From Address, Normal, and To Address) are listed in the style menu at the top.

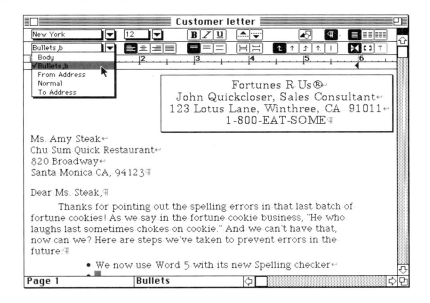

Some styles in this example are very simple. For instance, the style used for *Dear Ms. Steak* is called *Normal*. It uses Word's standard default settings (flush left, single-spaced text in the 12-point New York font). The letter's *Body* style is only slightly more complex. It looks like normal text, except that the first line has been indented ½" and 4 points of space have been added to the *beginning* of the paragraph. (That's why the salutation and the body copy are slightly separated.)

The bulleted paragraphs near the bottom of the window are also normal text, this time indented 1.0″, with extra space preceding them. You may have noticed that the name for this style is *Bullets,b*. The *b* following the comma in the style name is a second name for the same style. (More about this later.)

The most complex collection of formatting tricks in Figure 17.1 was used to create the *From* information. A style named *From Address* includes 14-point New Century Schoolbook rather than 12-point New York. Characters have been expanded. The paragraph is indented 2½″ from the left margin and sticks out ½″ past the document's right margin. The text is centered in a shadowed paragraph border, and extra spacing separates the text from the border.

Creating and naming styles is very easy. Developing clever style strategies takes more forethought. Here's how it all works.

Defining Styles from the Ruler

With the ruler in view (press ⌘-R, or select *Ruler* from the *View* menu if necessary), you can quickly define new styles. Place the insertion point in the formatted paragraph whose style you'd like to capture, then click once on the style box (the name portion of the drop-down style-name list). As shown in Figure 17.2, the style box will turn gray, indicating that you can type a new style name. Type a meaningful style name and press Return twice. Word will save the style information and add the new name to both the style sheet and the drop-down style list for the current document.

Figure 17.2
To define styles from the ruler, click in the style box.

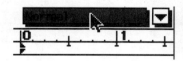

Applying Styles from the Ruler

Once you've defined styles, you can easily apply them to one or more paragraphs. Either place the insertion point in a paragraph or select several paragraphs, then scroll through the drop-down style list to pick the desired style. Your text will be reformatted using the selected style. Note that the style name appears in the status area. That's all there is to it.

Applying Styles from the Keyboard

Instead of scrolling through style names on the drop-down list to apply a style, you can apply a style by typing its name in the status area of the document window. To do this, press the ⌘-Shift-S key combination. The word *Style* will appear in the status area at the lower-left corner of the document window. Type enough of the style's name to uniquely identify it. Press Return. Your paragraphs will be reformatted.

The *Repeat* keyboard shortcut (⌘-Y) works when applying styles. After you apply a style once, you can move the insertion point to other paragraphs and press ⌘-Y to apply the new style where needed.

STYLE NAME CONSIDERATIONS

Style names can be up to 254 characters long, but shorter is often better. Names can contain any legal Macintosh characters including spaces, (although commas and semicolons have special functions in style names).

As you've seen, styles can have more than one name. For instance, you could call the same style *Bullets* and *b*. This is particularly useful if you use the keyboard method of applying styles. You might use a long name to accurately describe the style on the drop-down menu, and a short name for quick keyboard selection. You can assign as many names to a single style as you wish, keeping in mind the 254 character limitation. When you assign multiple style names to the same style, separate them with commas (or semicolons for some non-English Macintosh systems).

Word cares about capitalization in style names: *Figure* and *figure* are two different names. Try to be consistent when naming similar styles in different documents. You'll learn why later in this chapter.

THE STYLE DIALOG BOX

As is often the case with Word, there is a dialog box for styles which contains powerful features not found on the ruler. Reach the Style dialog box by using the ⌘-T keyboard shortcut, or pick *Style...* from the *Format* menu. You will see something like Figure 17.3.

Figure 17.3
Reach the Style dialog box by pressing ⌘-T, or choose *Style*... from the *Format* menu.

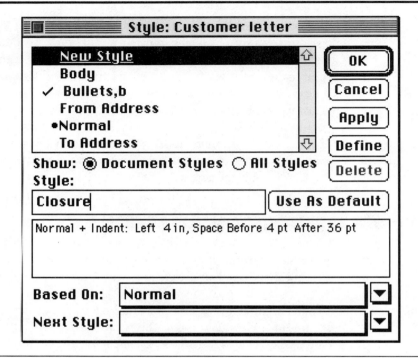

This dialog box lets you define new styles and rename, explore, list, or delete existing ones. It also serves other purposes, as you will soon see.

Defining Styles in the Style Dialog Box

To define a style via the Style dialog box, place the insertion point in or select a paragraph containing the desired format, then open the Style dialog box. Highlight *New Style*, then type a legal style name in the box provided. In Figure 17.3 a new style named *Closure* has been defined. It will be used for the *Sincerely* section of the letter. Text will be positioned 4.0" from the left margin, there will be 4 points of space before the *Sincerely* paragraph and 36 points after, leaving room for a signature. You can tell all of this by looking at the description in the box beneath the new style name. Word's developers call the cryptic formatting shorthand contained here "banter". Finally, click Define to record the style.

Printing Out a Style Sheet

It is often useful to have a printed list of styles and their descriptions. This can help you keep things consistent in a large organization, and it can help you troubleshoot formatting problems in complex documents. To print style information, display the document's Style dialog box, then choose *Print...* from the *File* menu or use the ⌘-P keyboard shortcut. The style list for our sample document is shown in Figure 17.4. Take a moment to compare it to Figure 17.1. Pretty slick, eh?

Figure 17.4
You can print out a list of styles as a handy reference.

Body
    Normal + Indent: First 0.5 in, Space Before 4 pt

Bullets,b
    Normal + Indent: Left 1 in, Space Before 4 pt

Closure
    Normal + Indent: Left 4 in, Space Before 4 pt After 36 pt

From Address
    Normal + Font: New Century Schlbk 14 Point, Expanded 1.5 Points, Indent: Left 2.5 in Right -0.5 in Centered Border: Top Bottom Left Right (Single Shadowed 6 pt Spacing)

Normal
    Font: New York 12 Point, Flush left

To Address
    Normal + Space After 12 pt

WHEN AND WHERE STYLE SHEETS AND STYLES ARE SAVED

Styles are saved with your document and they are saved only when you save the document. This is yet another good reason to get in the habit of saving early and often. If your computer crashes after you've spent several hours setting up a complex style sheet, or if you accidentally click No to the *Save Changes?* prompt when you close a document, you will *not* be happy.

BASING ONE STYLE UPON ANOTHER

This timesaver is often a source of bewilderment for newcomers. It occasionally catches old pros off-guard too. Word lets you build upon styles, or "base" one upon another. You've seen examples of this in the sample customer letter at the beginning of the chapter. The letter's style called *Body* is built by starting with the Normal style and adding instructions to indent the first line of each paragraph. In other words, The style Body is *based* on the style Normal.

If you change the Normal style so that it uses Helvetica instead of New York, any paragraphs formatted with the Body style will change to Helvetica too. That's the good news and the bad news.

Word "watches" you as you develop new styles and bases new styles on the style you modify. For instance, if you type the last paragraph of your customer letter in Body style, and decide when you get the end that you want to create a Closure style, you would probably drag the left indent marker for the paragraph containing the word *Sincerely*. Unless you tell Word otherwise, it will base the Closure style on the Body style, since that's the style you modified to create the Closure.

Since Body contains a ½" first-line indent, your Sincerely will be indented an extra ½". Later, if you change the distance that the Body style indents first lines, the Closure paragraph will move too.

Unless you are careful, you can create quite a chain reaction this way. Experienced users try to create one or two "base styles" and tie most of the rest of their styles to those base styles, rather than basing each new style on the previous style.

The Style dialog box lets you force specific styles to be based upon other styles of your choosing. Pick the appropriate base style from the drop-down *Based On:* menu, found near the bottom of the Style dialog box. Figure 17.5 shows that the From Address style is based on Normal.

What's the appropriate base style? That will vary with your project. At first, you may find it less confusing to base all of your styles upon Normal. Then experiment and observe carefully. You will soon learn from experience which

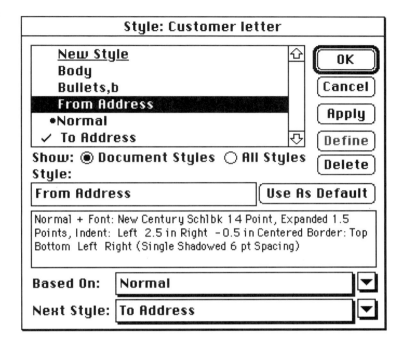

Figure 17.5
Word lets you specify which style each style is based upon.

combinations work best for you. Newcomers, beware. Play with *copies* of important documents, especially if it is ten minutes before the Federal Express person is due to pick up your document.

Next Style:

Frequently, you can predict the order in which styles will be used. When you type letters, for instance, you know that the *To* style will always be used after the *From* style. In reports and manuals, headings are usually followed immediately by body text, and so on.

The Style dialog box let's you specify which style Word will ''flip to'' when you finish typing a paragraph and press Return. Often, you want a paragraph to be in the same style as its predecessor. This is the default condition when creating styles, since paragraphs normally take their style information from the preceeding paragraph mark.

But, as shown in Figure 17.5, it is possible to specify different "next" styles simply by highlighting a style in the style list and picking the desired style from the drop-down *Next Style:* list. In our example, Word will switch to the To Address format when you press the Return key after typing the From Address.

In order for this trick to work, you should hold down the Shift key when you hit Return to terminate all but the last line in your From address. This way, Word treats all of the lines in the From address as one continuous paragraph and places different looking return marks at the end of all but the last lines, as you can see in Figure 17.1.

To override the next style when typing, end your paragraph by pressing ⌘-Return, rather than just return. The next paragraph you type will use the format of its predecessor.

Word's Standard Styles

Word's designers have created 32 special "standard" styles that are used by its footnote, outline, index, table-of-contents, page-numbering, header, and footer features. These standard styles do not automatically appear in your style sheet until you use the associated features in a document. It is possible, though, to force Word to place them in your style sheet by using the All Styles button in the Style dialog box. Try it now.

Note that the standard styles show up in the Style dialog box, but not in the menu on the ruler. The particulars of these standard styles are discussed in their related chapters. For instance, the Outline-related styles (headings 1 through 9) are discussed in *Chapter 42*.

For now, realize that you can modify standard styles, change their base styles and, with few exceptions, otherwise treat them like the custom styles you create. You cannot delete standard styles. Standard styles are all based on Normal, so changes to the Normal style (or your Word default font) will affect all standard styles.

MANUAL FORMATTING AND STYLES

It is possible to override or embellish styles with additional character formatting. But there are some caveats. Consider the From portion of our customer

All About Styles

letter example, for instance. It would be nice to make the company name bigger and bold. The registered symbol (®) could be a little smaller and subscripted. The finished product would look like Figure 17.6.

Figure 17.6
Character formatting can be added to stylized paragraphs, but they may not be permanent.

> **Fortunes R Us**®↵
> John Quickcloser, Sales Consultant↵
> 123 Lotus Lane, Winthree, CA 91011↵
> 1-800-EAT-SOME¶

You already know how to make these character-based changes from the ribbon, and obviously they work in stylized paragraphs. But they may not be permanent. Read on.

Reapply/Redefine Styles

If you ask Word to apply a style to a paragraph that already uses that style (applying Normal to an already Normal paragraph, for instance), you will be visited by a strange and powerful dialog box. It is shown in Figure 17.7.

Figure 17.7
Word wants to know if you want to modify the paragraph or the style itself.

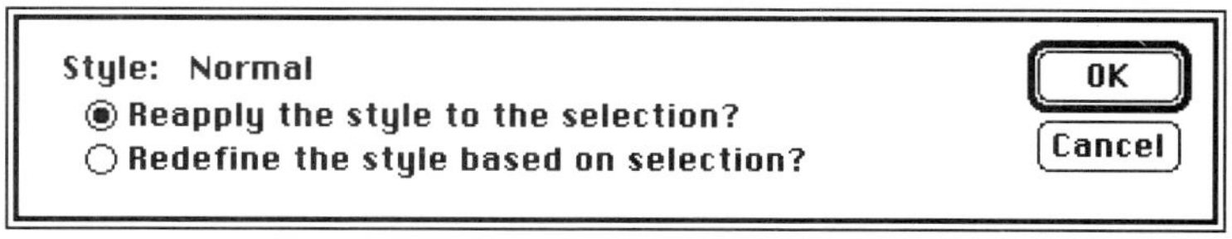

> Style: Normal
> ● Reapply the style to the selection?
> ○ Redefine the style based on selection?
> [OK]
> [Cancel]

This box serves two purposes. First it lets you reapply a style to a paragraph that you have inadvertently messed up. Suppose you accidentally dragged the first line indent marker in a Body paragraph and the paragraph no longer looks like the others. By choosing the Body style again from the ruler you will get a chance to "reapply" your Body style and *repair* the errant paragraph.

The second use of this dialog box is to let you quickly *redefine* a style. Suppose you hate the first line indent you've used for body text. Change the indent in any one Body style paragraph, then pick Body from the Style list. Click on the Redefine button and click OK. Word will redefine the Body style using the new indent from your sample paragraph. All of your Body paragraphs will be changed.

Strange things sometimes happen when you redefine or reapply styles to embellished paragraphs, however. Figure 17.8 shows what happens when the embellished From paragraph has the From style *reapplied*.

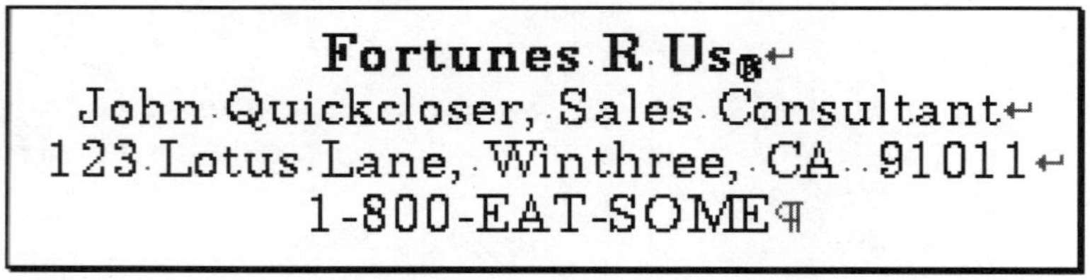

Figure 17.8
Reapplying a style to paragraphs containing additional character embellishments can cause unusual results.

> **Fortunes R Us**®↵
> John Quickcloser, Sales Consultant↵
> 123 Lotus Lane, Winthree, CA 91011↵
> 1-800-EAT-SOME¶

The bold attribute remains. The registered mark is still small and subscripted, but *Fortunes R Us* is now the same type size as the rest of the address.

Figure 17.9 shows the effect of *redefining* the paragraph after making the same text embellishments. This time most of the small text gets bigger.

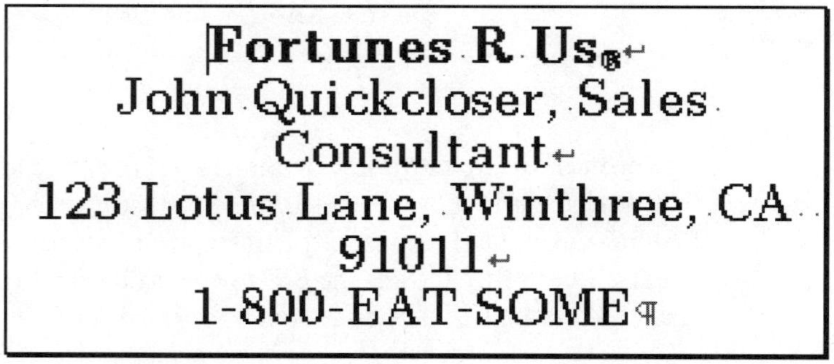

Figure 17.9
Redefining a style in an embellished paragraph can cause problems too.

> **Fortunes R Us**®↵
> John Quickcloser, Sales Consultant↵
> 123 Lotus Lane, Winthree, CA 91011↵
> 1-800-EAT-SOME¶

Deleting Styles

You cannot delete Word's standard styles, but you can remove the custom ones you've created. Unwanted styles can be deleted by selecting them in the Style dialog box and clicking on the Delete button. You will be asked to confirm; press OK. All paragraphs formatted with a deleted style will revert to the document's Normal style.

Undo does *not* work here. Thus, you cannot undo (re-establish) a deleted style, but you can sometimes work around this. Save the document just before you attempt any style deletion. Inspect the document immediately after deleting styles. Do *not* save the document again until you are certain that the deletion of styles hasn't caused problems. If there are problems, close the document without saving by answering No to the *Save Changes?* prompt. Reopen the document and your styles should all be intact. Or, better yet, you can experiment on a *copy* of your document.

Renaming Styles

Styles can be renamed in the Style dialog box. Click on the style name you want to change. Use the Style: name-text box to select and edit or replace the name. Click Define and OK to confirm the change. The style name changes, but the style remains intact, with one possible exception.

If you change a style's name to one that already exists in the document, the style that you have renamed will take on the characteristics of the pre-existing style. For instance if you have a double spaced style called *Draft*, and you change the name of a single spaced style from Body to Draft, all of the paragraphs formatted as Body will be double-spaced and take on any other style characteristics associated with the original Draft style.

Finding and Replacing Styles

Style-change junkies rejoice. Word 5 lets you search for and replace styles. While Word 5's vastly improved replace feature is fully described in *Chapter 26*, here's a quick style replacement how-to.

Open the Replace dialog box from the *Edit* menu or use the ⌘-H keyboard shortcut. It will look like Figure 17.10.

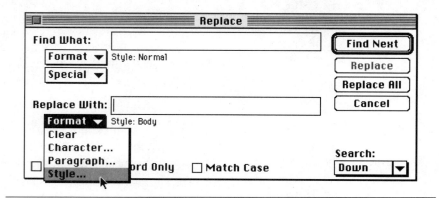

Figure 17.10
The *Replace* feature lets you locate or swap styles.

Visit the two drop-down menus that start with the word *Format*. In both cases, pick *Style...* from those drop down lists. You will be presented with a list of possible styles. In the Find What: portion of the dialog box, you will be shown all styles used in the document. In the Replace With: portion of the dialog box, you will also see Word's standard styles.

Pick the style you want to locate, and, if appropriate, the style you want to replace it with. Use Find Next or Replace All, as appropriate. Consider experimenting on a *copy* of important documents.

Using the same styles in different documents

After you've spent time setting up complex styles, it would be nice to re-use them in new projects. Word provides several ways to do this. For repetitive tasks, consider setting up stationery documents containing styles as described in *Chapter 29*, and glossary entries, described in *Chapter 28*.

If you have just a style or two you want to copy from one document (the source) to another (the destination), select some text from a source paragraph containing the style of interest and paste it into the destination document needing the style. Word will bring over the style with the text. Be aware, however, that if the destination document has a style name identical to the style being copied from the source, the destination document will reformat the incoming text rather than take on the new style. Moreover, if you copy more than fifty styles at once, the source document's entire style sheet will be automatically copied to the destination document.

Other Word commands that exchange style information will bring over styles as necessary. For instance, *Subscribe*, *Link*, *Glossary*, and *Paste Special* all attempt to bring styles with them if you copy paragraph marks.

It is also possible to "merge" different style sheets, which copies unique styles from one document to another and modifies styles with identical names.

Here's how to do it. With styles properly named and saved, work in the destination document. Open the Style dialog box and then choose *Open...* from the Word *File* menu. Select the source document and click Open. Word will update the destination document as described above.

When you are sure that the desired results have been achieved, save the destination document to record the changes to its style sheet. There are a few land mines, though.

First, you must save any changes to the source document before attempting a merge. This "records" the current styles for the source document. Next, inspect the source and destination documents for possible style name problems. Remember that Word styles are case sensitive. "body" and "Body" are *different* style names. As you may have guessed, this can work for or against you. Consider printing out both style sheets and comparing them before you merge.

When you merge, styles on the *destination* style sheet with names identical to those on the source style sheet will take on the characteristics of the *source* style sheet. Styles not found on the destination style sheet will be imported from the source style sheet.

A Few Style Tips

- Establish organization-wide style sheets and style-naming conventions. This will make it easy to work on projects together.

- Use the Space Before and Space After paragraph features along with Shift-Returns rather than creating white space with multiple carriage returns. See *Chapter 15*.

- When experimenting with styles, work on document copies. This is particularly important for new users working on complex documents containing interrelated styles.

- Combine styles with the power of Word's glossary and stationery features. See *Chapter 28* and *29*.

- Establish one or two base styles for complex documents. They need not be based on Word's Normal style, particularly if the look of the document is radically different from your normal work.

- Styles are saved with paragraph marks.

CHAPTER 18

Headers and Footers

FEATURING

- Placing repeating text and graphics in margins
- Adding styles to headers and footers
- Facing page variations
- Steps for spell-checking headers and footers

*H*eaders and *footers* are places to put repetitive information in a document's top and bottom margins. (Don't confuse *footers* with *footnotes*; they are different).

You can use headers and footers to print something simple on each page, like your name, or something complex, like a graphic. Stylized text, dates, and automatic page numbering can all be included in headers or footers.

Headers and footers can be identical on all pages in your document, or you can specify different contents for each section of the document. Odd and even pages can have different designs if you wish. The first page of each document or each section can be unique.

Editing takes place in special Header and Footer windows, opened from the *View* menu. It is possible to apply virtually any paragraph or character style

Headers and Footers

using ribbons and rulers in these windows. Once headers and footers have been added to a document, it is possible to see and edit them in Page Layout view. They are also displayed in Print Preview, but in Normal view, you must open a separate window.

ENTERING BASIC HEADERS IN NORMAL VIEW

To enter a header that repeats on all pages in your document, choose *Header* from the *View* menu. Assuming you're in Normal view, a new *Header window* will open. Create and edit header text as you would any other. You can paste graphics, apply styles and otherwise format your work normally. Figure 18.1 shows an example of centered text, and a small graphic in a header. The bottom of the header contains a line created with Word's paragraph border feature.

ENTERING BASIC FOOTERS IN NORMAL VIEW

Footers are entered the same way as headers, except that you work in a *Footer window*. (Again, we assume you are in Normal view.) Choose *Footer* from the

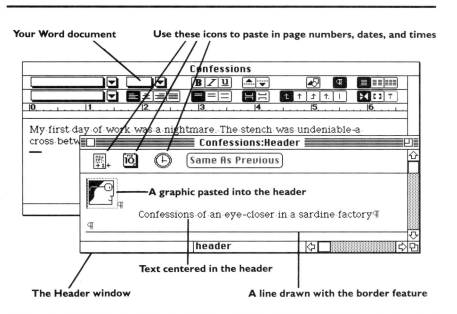

Figure 18.1
A Header window can contain stylized text and graphics.

View menu and use your Word editing and style skills. In Figure 18.2 a page number has been inserted in a footer by clicking on the page numbering icon at the top-left of the footer window. (The date and time can be appended by clicking the appropriate icon.) The page number was then centered by using a *footer ruler* (⌘-R with the Footer window active).

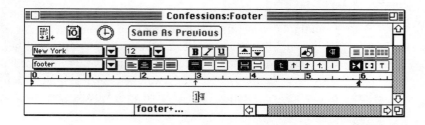

Figure 18.2
A page number has been specified and centered in this Footer window by using the page numbering icon and a special footer ruler and ribbon.

RULERS AND RIBBONS IN HEADERS AND FOOTERS

You don't use your regular document ruler or ribbon when working in header and footer windows. You display special ones by placing the insertion point in your header or footer window and choosing *Ribbon* or *Ruler* from the *View* menu. The keyboard shortcuts (⌘-Option-R and ⌘-R respectively) work here too.

HEADERS AND FOOTERS IN PAGE LAYOUT VIEW

If you are in *Page Layout* view when you choose the *Header* or *Footer* command from the *View* menu, Word will move the insertion point to the header or footer and, if necessary, make room for you to work. (You won't see the page-numbering, date, and time icons in Page Layout view.) This is a good way to visualize the relationships between headers, footers, and the rest of your page.

In Figure 18.3, the header is taller than the specified top margin, so Word has pushed the header down into the text area. You can get an even better view of this in Print Preview, where you can also change the margins to accommodate the tall header.

HEADERS AND FOOTERS IN PRINT PREVIEW

It is a good idea to switch to *Print Preview* when designing headers and footers. As you can see from Figure 18.4, the footer fits properly in the bottom

Headers and Footers

Figure 18.3
When you view documents in Page Layout view, you get a good idea of where headers and footers will print.

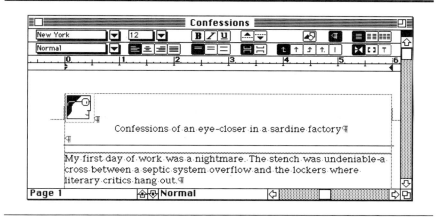

Figure 18.4
Use Print Preview to view and fine-tune header and footer page relationships. Drag margin handles or headers and footers themselves in this view.

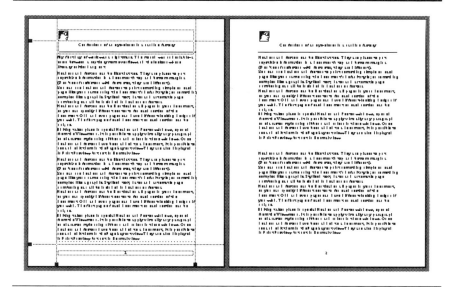

margin, but either the top margin or the header or both need work. You can drag the top margin handle in Print Preview to enlarge the top margin. It is also possible to drag the entire header up and down within the existing margin. To do this, place the pointer in the header. It will change into a "plus" sign (+). Hold down the mouse button and drag the header up or down.

Remember that many printers cannot print at the very edges of the paper; and that it is possible to drag a header or footer into non-printing areas. If you have selected the correct printer (from your Chooser), Word does a pretty good job of showing you when a header or footer will be cut off by your printer.

Seeing those two pages side-by-side in Figure 18.4, it becomes obvious that since this document will be printed two-sided and then bound, it would look better with different odd and even headers.

EVEN AND ODD HEADERS AND FOOTERS

To create different even and odd headers or footers, first place the document in Normal view. Next, check the Even/Odd Headers choice in the Document dialog box, reached from the *Format* menu or with the ⌘-F14 shortcut if you have an extended keyboard. Your *View* menu will change to include additional header and footer choices.

You now have four header and footer windows in which to work. Use them to change text alignment for mirrored pages or even add different graphics for odd and even pages, as illustrated in Figure 18.5.

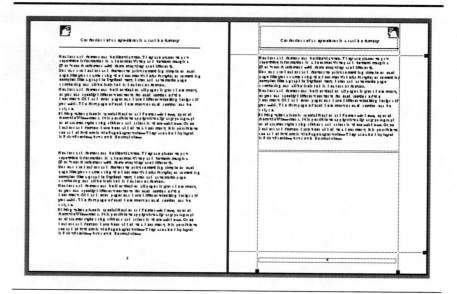

Figure 18.5
Different graphics have been used here for even and odd pages.

So far so good, but now the little face will be looking off the page on the document's first page! Fortunately, Word offers a Different First Page option that can be used to fix this.

DIFFERENT FIRST PAGE HEADERS AND FOOTERS

The Section dialog box contains a choice called *Different First Page*. (*Chapter 23* goes into more detail about sections.)

To create unique headers and footers for the first page of your document, first place the document in Normal view. Reach the Section dialog box from the *Format* menu or use the Option-F14 shortcut on an extended keyboard. Place an *X* in the Different First Page box. Two more choices appear on your *View* menu for this document. They are cleverly titled *First Header* and *First Footer*. It doesn't take a physics degree to know what happens next. Use these choices to create a first page with headers or footers that differ from the rest.

POSTSCRIPT CODE IN HEADERS

If you are using a PostScript printer and want to send PostScript code from Word documents, you can insert the code as hidden text in your headers. Figure 18.6 shows code that will print the word *CONFIDENTIAL* diagonally across an 8½″ sheet of paper over your Word text. Remember to turn off *Print Hidden Text* in the Print dialog box if you try this.

Figure 18.6
PostScript code entered as hidden text in headers can be sent to your printer when you print.

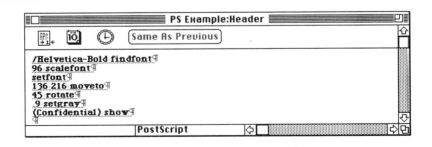

CHAPTER 19

Page Numbers and Pagination

FEATURING

- Three ways to number pages
- Word's many numbering formats
- Controlling pagination

Word offers a variety of tools to help you automatically number pages. You are given many page numbering format and style choices. It's possible to position page numbers nearly anywhere that pleases you. This chapter explores these features and discusses the effects of document sections and pagination on page numbering.

Here's an important timesaving tip. If you plan to break a document into multiple sections, you may want to insert page numbers *before* you split the document into sections. Otherwise, you will have to repeat the page-numbering process for each section of your document (see *Chapter 23*). That said, let's dig right in.

Page Numbers and Pagination

THREE METHODS FOR PAGE NUMBERING

Word provides three page-numbering techniques. Each has advantages and disadvantages. Normally, you will use only one for a particular document. Otherwise, you might end up with two or more sets of page numbers!

The Print Preview Method

The *Print Preview* method of page numbering is *too easy*. To insert simple page numbers in the default location, (1/2″ from the top and right sides of the page), choose *Print Preview* from the *File* menu (⌘-Option-I), then double-click on the page-numbering icon, as shown in Figure 19.1. An automatic page number will appear quicker than a cat's sneeze.

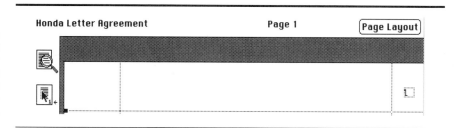

Figure 19.1
Double-click on the page-numbering icon in Print Preview to apply page numbers to the upper-right hand corner of all pages in a single-section document.

Page numbers thus inserted use a Microsoft standard style called *page number*. This style will appear in your document's style list and can be modified like any other style. (See *Chapter 17* for more style information.)

If you know before you insert a page number that you want to position it in other than the default location, *don't double-click the page-numbering icon*. Instead, point to the page-numbering icon and click the mouse button. Your pointer will turn into a bold *-1-* which can be dragged anywhere you wish. When you have it where you want it, click once to anchor the page number.

Once you've created a page number using the Print Preview method, you can move it by pointing to the number. Your pointer will change to a crosshair. Use the pointer to drag your page number to a new position. All of the numbers on all of the pages (in a single-section document) will move to the new position. It will take a moment for the number to reappear after you release the mouse button. Be patient.

The disadvantage of this incredibly simple page numbering method is that you don't have easy control of embellishments. And there is no easy way to include text with page numbers, like *Page 1*. The Header/Footer method offers this flexibility.

The Header/Footer Method

Word makes it easy to place page numbers in headers and footers. (If you are unfamiliar with headers and footers, you might want to read about them in *Chapter 18* before continuing.)

To add page numbers using the *header/footer* method, simply open a Header or Footer window in Normal view and click on the page-numbering button. A number will be inserted for you in your header or footer at the insertion point.

Like anything else placed in headers and footers, page numbers can be stylized, repositioned, surrounded with borders, accompanied by text, and otherwise embellished. Word uses the standard style *header* or *footer* to format page numbers placed therein. You can override this by applying additional character and paragraph formats or by changing the standard *header* or *footer* style.

Headers and footers have tab stops, which you may find useful for page number positioning. Or, you can open rulers and ribbons and use their formatting tools for headers and footers. Figure 19.2 shows an automatic page number centered in a footer, accompanied by the word *Page* and surrounded by a paragraph border. (You need not have other text in a header or footer.)

The Section Method

The Section dialog box provides a third easy way to insert page numbers, which we'll call the *section* method. It uses the Microsoft standard style *page number*. You don't have to use the section method for numbering documents broken into sections, but you might find it convenient to do so.

Page Numbers and Pagination

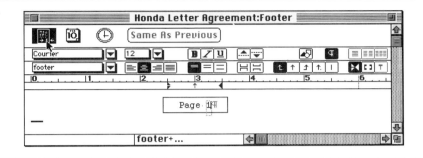

Figure 19.2
Click on the page-numbering button in a header or footer. Numbers placed here are easy to format and embellish.

Start by placing the insertion point in the section you want to number. Next, display the Section dialog box by choosing *Section...* from the *Format* menu or use the Option-F14 shortcut on extended keyboards. The center of the Section dialog box will look something like Figure 19.3.

By default, Word places *section* method page numbers in the upper-right corner of your document (½" from the top and right edges of the paper), but you can specify different positions in the From Top: and From Right: entry boxes. You will probably not want to enter dimensions that will place page numbers within the text area of the document, although this is possible. Moreover, remember that not all printers can print at the extreme outer edges of the paper.

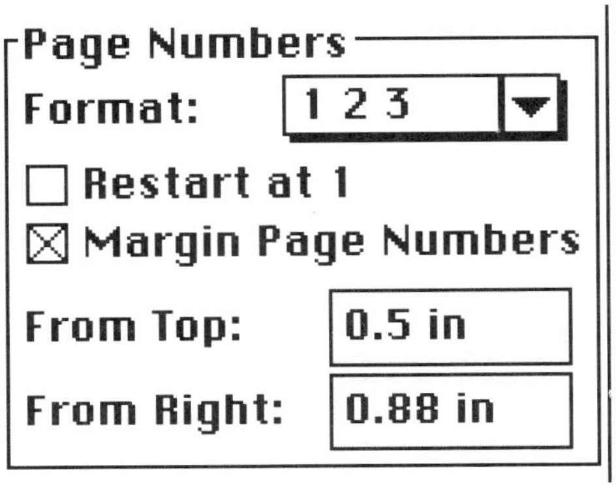

Figure 19.3
The Section dialog box contains several useful page-numbering options.

When the *Restart at 1* box is checked, each new section of your document will start with page *1*.

PAGE NUMBERING FORMATS AND STYLES

Word supports three page-number *formats*. Standard Arabic numbers (*1, 2, 3*...) are the default. It is also possible to number with Roman numerals (*I, II, III*...) or with letters (*A, B, C*...). All of these formats are available, regardless of which page-numbering technique you choose.

You can use Word's many character and paragraph embellishment features to spruce up page numbers. Pick the font of your choice, make numbers bold, align them, put boxes around them. Text can appear next to the numbers (*Pg. 1*, for instance)

Picking a Numbering Format

After inserting page numbers, visit the Section dialog box (*Section...* in the *Format* menu) and use the drop-down Format: menu to choose the one of your choice.

To make the choice your new default page-number format, click on the *Use As Default* button in the Section dialog box. This will record the format, position, and other page choices in a Word Settings (5) file.

Documents containing multiple sections can have different formats in each section. That's both good and bad news. If you want all sections to have the same format, you will want to pick a format *before* you break up the document. Otherwise you must place the insertion point in *each* section and pick the same format for every one. Plan ahead.

MANAGING STARTING PAGE NUMBERS

Usually you will want Word to place the number *1* on your first printed page, but not always. For example, many people prefer their multipage letters to be printed *without* a *1* on the first page. They still want the second page numbered *2*, the third *3*, and so on. Let's call this *first page number suppressed*.

Or, you may wish to start each new section in a multisection document with *1*. Let's call this *restart sections with 1*.

Sometimes you may want your first page to be printed without a number (a cover page, for instance) and then you want the next page to contain the number *1*. Let's call this *begin second page from 1*.

Finally, you might want to use some other number for the first page, like *25* or *100*. This is helpful when you are combining your work with other documents. Let's call that *starting page other than 1*.

Note that in all the following examples, we assume that your document does *not* already have page numbers.

First Page Number Suppressed

This one's easy. Place the insertion point in the desired section. Check *Different First Page* in the Header/Footer portion of the Section dialog box (reached from the *Format* menu). No page number will print on the first page and the second page will be numbered *2*.

Restart Sections with 1

Place the insertion point in any section. Open the Section dialog box and check the *Restart At 1* box.

If you want only certain sections to start this way, repeat the steps as many times as necessary with the insertion point placed in the pertinent sections. To make all sections start with *1*, use the *Select All* (⌘-A) choice from the *Edit* menu. Then check the *Restart at 1* box.

Begin Second Page from 1

This one's tricky and requires an understanding of sections and pagination. You may want to review those topics first. Start by being certain that your first page is perfect and requires no further editing. (You will need to repeat this every time you change the contents of the first page.)

1. From the *Tools* menu choose *Repaginate Now*.
2. Now place a section break between the bottom of the first page and the top of the second.
3. Place an *X* in the *Restart at 1* check box in the Section dialog box. While still in the Section dialog box, pick New Page from the drop-down *Start:* menu.
4. Click OK to close the Section dialog box. Phew!

You may prefer to create a separate document for the first page and number the remaining pages normally. This is an efficient way to create covers.

Starting Page Other Than 1

To start numbering pages with numbers other than *1*, open the Document dialog box from the *Format* menu or press ⌘-F14. Choose File Series. A small dialog box will appear. Type the starting number in the Number From: entry box. Click OK.

Removing Page Numbers

If you've created numbers using the Print Preview method, go back to Print Preview and drag the numbers off of the page.

To remove page numbers inserted using the header/footer method, open the header or footer and delete numbers as you would any other text.

Numbers inserted with the section feature are removed by "unchecking" the *Margin Page Numbers* box in the Section dialog box.

Regardless of which method you've used to insert numbers in documents containing sections, you will need to place the insertion point in each section with page numbers you wish to delete, and repeat the process.

PAGINATION AND PAGE NUMBERS

Word more or less continuously computes things like line endings, page endings, and page numbers as you work. It decides where to split paragraphs when they are too large to fit on a page.

At a minimum, it does these computations whenever you ask it to print a document or compile an index or table-of-contents. Page Layout view and Print Preview need to know correct page endings as well.

This process is called *repagination* or simply *pagination*. Unless you shut off the feature, Word does this automatically whenever there is an opportunity. This is called *background repagination* and it is enabled or disabled from the General category of the Preferences dialog box. Generally you want to leave background repagination on.

Once in a while, as Word repaginates, it will break a table or a paragraph that you want to keep intact. Sometimes you will want certain items to begin at the top of a new page, or on an odd- or an even-numbered page. For this reason, Word lets you specify things that you want to keep together, and it lets you force new pages.

Visualizing Page Breaks

You can see page breaks in all views. They appear as heavy dotted lines in Normal and Outline views. Since both Page Layout view and Print Preview simulate sheets of paper, page breaks are easy to visualize in those views.

Forcing Page Breaks

When you want to force a page break, you can insert *manual page breaks*. In Normal and Outline views they look thicker than Word's automatic page breaks.

To insert a manual page break, move the insertion point to where you want to place the break. Then either select *Page Break* from the *Insert* menu or use the Shift-Enter shortcut. Be sure you hit Shift-*Enter* and not Shift-*Return*. (PowerBook owners will need to hunt for their tiny Enter key.) Text or graphics below the manual page break will appear on the next page of your document.

Generally speaking, forcing a page break is not a great idea. If you must do it, wait until you have done *all* of your formatting.

Moving and Deleting Page Breaks

Manual breaks can be highlighted and deleted like text. Select a break line and press Delete. The *Replace...* command will also let you search for and delete manual breaks; it will even find section breaks if the section break is supposed to begin a new page! (See *Chapter 26* for details.)

Manual breaks can be dragged up or down in Print Preview. They look heavier than Word's margin lines. In other views you will need to cut and re-insert manual breaks.

Annotations

FEATURING

- Using hidden text for annotations
- Recording and playing back voice annotations

Are you one of those people with Post-it™ notes stuck all over your documents? Word 5 offers several alternatives. *Hidden text* was available in earlier Word versions. It has been joined by *voice annotation,* a way to record and play back sounds "attached" to specific locations in Word documents.

Even if you can't record voice notes on your Mac, you will be able to play notes other people include with copies of their document files. Let's look at hidden text first.

HIDDEN TEXT FOR ANNOTATIONS

Hidden text might be better named "hideable" text, since it is not always hidden. In fact, many people leave hidden text in view most of the time. So, with apologies to Microsoft, let's call it "hideable" text here.

Authors often use hideable text to make notes to themselves or to colleagues. They leave the notes in view while working, then hide them when they print their work. Figure 20.1 shows an example of a hideable note.

Annotations

Figure 20.1
Hidden text has dotted lines under it (top). It is only visible when you check the *Show Hidden Text* box in the View category of the Preferences dialog box. Otherwise it is truly hidden (bottom).

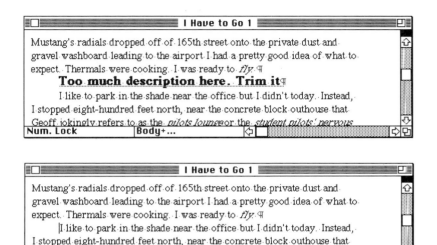

In the example, *Too much description here. Trim it.* is hidden text. As you can see, it is possible to embellish hidden text just as you can embellish regular text.

To define text as hideable, select it, then visit the Character dialog box (choose *Character...* from the *Format* menu) and check Hidden in the Style area. The keyboard shortcut to define text as hideable is ⌘-Shift-X. This command "toggles" hidden text. If you use it with hideable text, the text will revert to non-hideable text.

When printing, check the Print Hidden Text choice in the Print dialog box (*Print...* on the *File* menu) if you want the annotations to print.

SOUND ADVICE

New Macs like the IIsi, LC, and the high-end of the PowerBook portable line come with microphones. They let you *record* sounds to disk, then play them back. Owners of earlier Macs can purchase sound recording accessories like Voice Impact, MacRecorder, or Voice Impact Pro, available from computer dealers and mail order firms. *All* Macs can *play* sounds recorded by any of these new devices.

Word 5 provides a built-in software feature to control the recording of voice annotations. It saves voice annotations with your Word documents. But before you toss out your pocket dictating machine, there are some things you should know. Sound files are pretty big. One second of speech requires nearly 30K of disk space when recorded in the Best Quality mode. That means a minute of sound might require as much as 2 Mb of disk space. There are RAM considerations as well.

If you use a Mac with 8 Mb of RAM and a huge hard disk, you will be able to record reasonably long, wonderful sounding voice annotations. Smaller machines and hard disks will necessitate shorter notes and slightly degraded sound quality.

Once the appropriate sound-recording hardware is installed and configured (check your manuals for these things) Word makes it easy to record.

Recording Voice Annotations

Place the insertion point where you want to attach a voice annotation. From the *Insert* menu, pick *Voice Annotation*. If all goes well, you will see a dialog box like the one in Figure 20.2. It looks like the controls on a cassette recorder. Clicking on record records.

Figure 20.2
If your Mac is sound-savvy, you will see this dialog box when you pick *Voice Annotations* from the *Insert* menu.

Speak so that the Level meter stays in the left three-quarters of its range, as shown in the illustration. This makes sounds easy to hear without distorting them.

Word decides how much time you will be permitted to speak based on available memory and sound-quality decisions you make in the Voice Annotation preference settings. Based on these factors, the circular time meter will show you how much time you have left as you record. It starts out all white and turns progressively blacker as time runs out. In Figure 20.2 about one-quarter of the permitted time has elapsed. Stop slightly before the circle turns completely black, or you risk being cut off abruptly.

To pause while recording, click on either the Record or Pause buttons. A second click resumes recording.

You can play an annotation immediately after you've recorded it by clicking the Play button in the Voice Record dialog box, which will not be dim after you have recorded something. If you are satisfied, click OK to save the annotation in your document at the insertion point. If you want to re-record your note instead, either click Record again or pick *New* from the Voice Record's *File* menu, then click Record again.

Sound Quality

Word provides three sound quality levels—Good, Better, and Best. The better the sound the bigger your files. Experiment, keeping in mind my grandfather's favorite saying: "There's good and there's good enough."

Playing Voice Annotations

First open the Word 5 document containing voice annotations. Each annotation is flagged with a tiny speaker like the two shown in Figure 20.3. The little varmints are only visible if you have the *Show Hidden Text* preference selected in the View category of your Preferences dialog box.

Once you have a voice-annotated document in view, either pick *Voice Annotations* from your *View* menu, or double-click on a voice-annotation marker. A Voice Annotations dialog box like the one in Figure 20.3 will appear.

Figure 20.3
Voice annotations are flagged with little speakers, visible only with Show Hidden Text enabled.

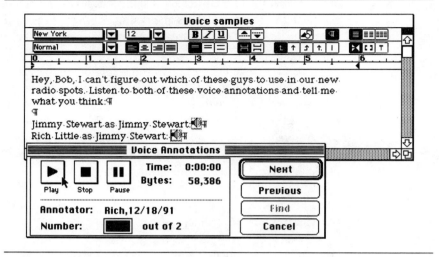

If the person recording the note has entered his or her initials or nickname in the Your Initials section of the General category of the Preferences dialog box, the initials will appear next to *Annotator:*.

You will also see how many annotations the document contains (two in our example) and how much disk space the selected note takes (more than 58K in Figure 20.3).

To hear the note, click Play. To move to the next note click Next. Previous takes you back one note. Cancel closes the dialog box.

To adjust the playback volume, visit the Sound portion of your Mac's control panel. Check your Apple manual if you need help with this.

Keyboard Shortcuts

Shortcut fanatics will be pleased to know that the Voice feature is riddled with key combinations. With the Voice Record dialog box in view, the ⌘-R combination records, Tab pauses, and ⌘-. (period) stops. To play, press ⌘-Y.

Annotations

You can bypass the Voice Record dialog box altogether by holding down the Option key while picking *Voice Annotation* from the *Insert* menu. Start speaking immediately. The status area will give you a running description of what's happening.

CHAPTER 21

Footnotes

FEATURING

- Creating, editing, and moving footnotes
- How Word automatically numbers footnotes
- Personalizing footnote appearance

Word's footnote features make Word popular in the legal, academic, and technical communities. Choosing *Footnote...* from the *Insert* menu or pressing the ⌘-E keyboard shortcut puts Word's standard footnotes to work quick as a wink.

Footnotes consist of in-text *footnote-reference markers* (usually, but not necessary sequential numbers), the *footnotes* themselves, and footnote *separators*, lines that separate footnotes from the document text. When footnotes are long and spill onto other pages, you may want to include Word's footnote *continuation notices*.

Since footnote text can be embellished just like other Word text (italicized, made smaller, etc.), you already know how to modify the appearance of footnotes. Positioning, inserting, editing, and deleting footnotes, separators and markers is equally painless.

Easy Automatic Footnotes

Figure 21.1 shows an automatic (default) Word footnote. It should take you less than ten seconds to add your first footnote to existing text.

Start by placing the insertion point where the footnote marker is needed (after the word *companies* in our example). Next, choose *Footnote...* from the *Insert* menu or press the ⌘-E key combination.

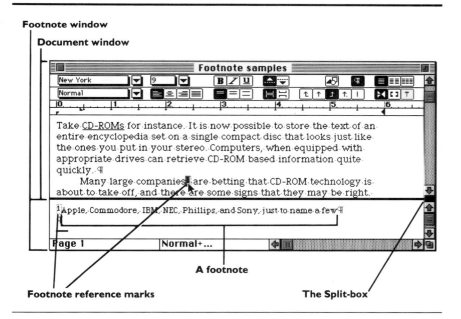

Figure 21.1
Standard footnotes like these require very little effort.

You can dismiss the *Footnote dialog box* by clicking OK, since Word's defaults are fine for this project.

The document window automatically splits into two panes and a footnote reference number (*1* in this case) appears both at the insertion point and in the footnote area of the split document window. The insertion point automatically moves to the footnote window where you can type the footnote.

To return to the main document, move the insertion point with the mouse, or press ⌘-Option-Z. If your keyboard has a numeric keypad *and* if Num Loc is off, pressing zero on the pad will also return you to the main document's insertion point.

Viewing Footnotes

Footnotes are *always* displayed in Page Layout view and Print Preview. If they are not visible in Normal or Outline view, choose *Footnotes* from the *View* menu, (not *Footnote...* from the *Insert* menu) or use the ⌘-Option-Shift-S shortcut.

If you are constantly entering or referring to footnotes, you can leave the footnote window visible while you work. Scrolling in your document will cause corresponding scrolling in the footnote window. Use the footnote scroll bars if necessary to view notes. Feel free to resize the footnote window to suit your taste and screen size. Drag the bar separating the two windows the same way you resize other Word split screens (point to the Split-box and drag).

To hide the footnote window, choose *Footnotes* from the *View* menu or use the four-fingered, ⌘-Option-Shift-S "shortcut".

Double-clicking on a footnote marker in your document will display the footnote and place the insertion point at the end of the footnote. If necessary, Word will open the footnote window and scroll to the appropriate note. There may be a slight delay so be patient.

Inserting Footnotes Ahead of Existing Ones

Whenever you insert footnotes, Word renumbers the existing ones properly, as shown in Figure 21.2.

Copying, Deleting, and Moving Footnotes

You can copy, move, or delete entire footnotes as easily as you would a single character. Select the footnote *marker* of interest in the *document text*. (This might take a steady hand, particularly if you have Drag-and-Drop enabled.) Then cut, copy, paste, or Drag-and-Drop the footnote *mark*.

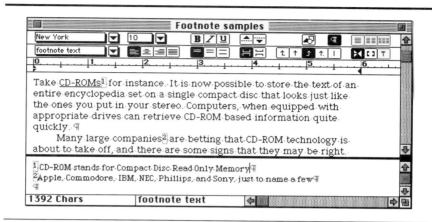

Figure 21.2
Inserting a footnote before the first note automatically renumbers all affected notes.

Word does the rest. If you have Numbering turned on, Word will update the numbers in your text and in the corresponding footnotes. If you copy and paste a mark, a corresponding new footnote will magically appear in the right spot in your footnotes. Deletion works as you would expect.

Editing Footnote Text

Visit the footnote window. Use Page Layout view or open the footnote window itself. Cut, paste, and Drag-and-Drop away to your heart's content. (Note that you cannot cut a footnote's entire text; you must cut the footnote *mark* if you wish to delete or move it.)

Personalizing Footnotes

Word lets you modify many footnote parameters via the Footnote dialog box shown in Figure 21.3. You make other footnote-related decisions in the Footnote section of the Document dialog box (*Document...* on the *Format* menu), also shown in Figure 21.3.

Important tip: This dialog box comes up automatically the first time you insert a note. But there is no *obvious* way to bring it up again without intentionally inserting a footnote marker. Fortunately, there *is* a way. Highlight an existing footnote mark, *then* Choose *Footnote...* from the *Insert* menu or use the ⌘-E shortcut.

Figure 21.3
Personalize footnote appearance using the Footnote dialog box and the Footnote choices in the Document dialog box.

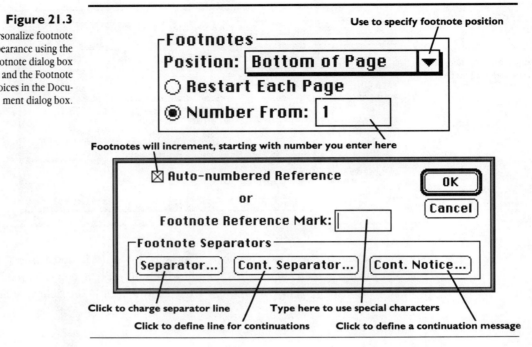

Controlling Footnote Numbering

You can specify the starting number for footnotes in the Footnotes area of the *Format* menu's Document dialog box. Only Arabic numbers are permitted.

Footnote numbering can restart on each page if you check the Restart Each Page button in the Footnotes area of the Document dialog box.

Footnote Text Style

You can embellish *selected* footnote text as you would expect. Highlight the text of interest, then use the ruler, ribbon, or format-related menu choices (bold, italic, and so on).

To change the size or font or other footnote style elements for *all* footnotes, modify the Microsoft standard *footnote text* style. (Footnote text is based on Normal style.) To change the footnote reference marks, modify the *footnote reference* style.

Footnote Position

There are four possible positions for footnotes:

- At the bottom of each page (the default)
- Directly beneath the last text on a page
- At the end of a section in multisection documents
- At the end of your document

Specify footnote position by using the drop-down *Position:* list in the Footnotes section of the Document dialog box on the *Format* menu. Phew! See Figure 21.3.

Incidentally, in multicolumn sections, footnotes print below each *column*.

Footnote Separators

The little black lines that separate document text from the footnotes themselves are cleverly called *footnote separators*. Edit them by clicking the Separator... button in the Footnote dialog box, illustrated in Figure 21.4.

Figure 21.4
Change the separator by opening the separator window.

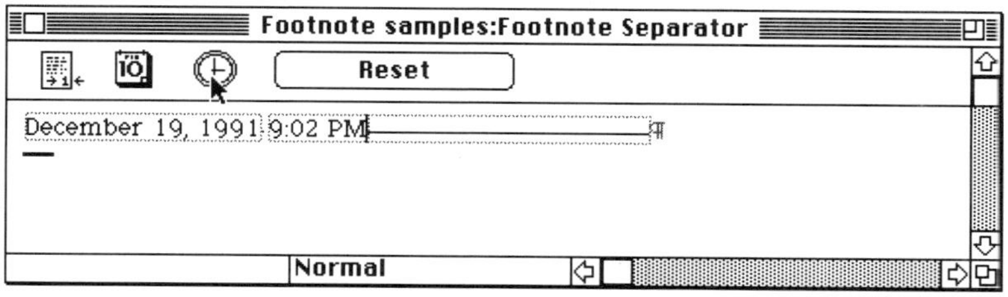

When you click the Separator... button you will see a new window containing a sample of the current separator. The default is a short, thin, black line.

This is just like any other Word window. You can edit the length of the line (it's a paragraph). Insert a graphic, if you like. You can even use Word's drawing tools here. Double lines look nice. Use Word's Paragraph Border feature to create them. It is possible to use a ruler and ribbon in the separator window.

When you are happy with your creation, close the separator window and view the results in Print Preview or Page Layout view.

Footnote Reference Marks

Footnote reference marks appear wherever you place them in your document's text area, and at the beginning of each footnote in the footnote area itself.

By default, Word uses numbers for reference marks. If you turn off the Numbering feature, Word defaults to an asterisk as the footnote reference mark. You can type any character of your choosing in the Footnote Reference Mark: portion of the Footnote dialog box. In fact, it is possible to use as many as ten characters for a footnote reference mark.

Footnote Continuation

Continuation separators appear whenever footnotes carry over onto the next page. These notices can be modified the same way you change regular separators when performing the steps outlined in the section *Footnote Separators*.

Footnote Tips and Cautions

- Word does not automatically spell-check footnotes, but you can select footnotes and run the spellchecker.
- Do not place index or table-of-contents entries in footnotes. They will be ignored.
- Word's new Find and Replace features can help you search for and reformat footnotes. See *Chapter 26*.
- Save frequently used footnote entries in your glossary to eliminate tedious retyping. See *Chapter 28*.

Chapter 22

Hyphenation and Dashes

FEATURING

- Kinds of hyphens and their uses
- Word's automatic hyphenation feature
- What you see vs. what you get
- How to type long (*em*) dashes

Normal hyphens are used to *connect* words like Corky Sherwood-Forest's last name or the three groups of digits in your social security number. You always want these hyphens to print. Sometimes you don't want hyphenated text to word-wrap. For instance, you might want all nine digits of your social security number to appear on the same line. Hyphens that prevent word wrapping are called *nonbreaking* hyphens.

Then there are *optional hyphens*, used to split long words only when they appear at the right edge of a line. Splitting words with these optional hyphens cleans up the right margin of your document. Optional hyphens are also used to "tighten up" justified text. You only want hyphens like these to print if the words are at the *right margin*.

There are rules of grammar and style governing the breakup of words with optional hyphens. For example, typographers cringe when they see hyphens in the right margin of more than two successive lines (called a *ladder*). Editors and English teachers will tell you not to break up proper names with hyphens. Thus, *Mans-field* and *SY-BEX* are verboten.

Word 5 will suggest optional hyphens and even do optional hyphenation automatically. To the best of its ability it will try not to hyphenate proper nouns. Figure 22.1 is an example of a paragraph that could profit from judicious application of optional hyphens.

Figure 22.1
Optional hyphenation could improve the appearance of this text.

> Those priceless few moments before the sun sets always remind him of fine brandy or New England in the fall. Everything and everyone around the two of them was bathed in orange and red and hues without names. Photographers call it *magic light*.

Notice the acres of white space between the words *hues*, *without*, and *names* in Figure 22.1. There are other examples of excess space meandering through the paragraph. Perhaps that's why typographers refer to this phenomenon as a *river*. Notice the *widow* word (*light*) at the end. Even with Word's Widow Control feature enabled (in the Document dialog box) you'll end up with an occasional lonesome word. You can fix these things with Word 5's help.

TYPING HYPHENS

To type hyphens, simply use the minus key (to the right of the zero key at the top of your keyboard). Hyphens typed this way will always print.

Typing Em Dashes (Long Hyphens)

Em dashes are used to indicate an abrupt change of thought—or did you know that already? Hyphens and dashes are often confused. Type the longer *em* dashes by holding down Option, Shift, and the minus key (-). In some fonts *em* dashes are very long and obvious.

Incidentally, *em* dashes get their name from their width. In most fonts an *em* dash is the length of a letter *m*. That's an easy way to remember what it's called.

Typing Nonbreaking Hyphens

Nonbreaking hyphens keep hyphenated text together on the same line. *Never* press the minus key (-) to enter a nonbreaking hyphen! Instead, hold down the ⌘ key and press the tilde key (~).

Since nonbreaking *spaces* are typed by holding down the Option key when you press the Spacebar, you may be tempted to type nonbreaking hyphens by holding down the Option key and pressing the minus key. Big mistake! The Option-minus key combination is used for *en* dashes (a little brother of the *em* dash).

Typing Optional Hyphens

An optional hyphen will always be *displayed* whenever you have the Show Paragraph feature enabled, but it will *print* only if the word it is in sits on the right margin. Most people use Word's *automatic hyphenation* feature to enter optional hyphens, but you can enter them from the keyboard. Hold down the ⌘ key and press the minus key (-). If all this talk of dashes and hyphens is sounding like Morse code, take a moment to peruse Table 22.1.

Automatic Optional Hyphenation

Word 5 has an automatic feature based on certain built-in rules and a hyphenation dictionary that will work with you to place optional hyphens in words. You can supervise the process or let Word take things into its own hands. Word's hyphenation feature is neither the best nor the worst in the industry. If you use it, there are some things you will want to do first.

TABLE 22.1 Word's Hyphens and Dashes	Hyphen	Key Combination	Appearance*
	Normal	- (hyphen)	-
	En dash	Option- – (minus sign)	–
	Em dash	Option-Shift- – (minus sign)	—
	Nonbreaking	⌘-~ (tilde)	≃
	Optional	⌘- – (minus sign)	≃

*With Show ¶ on.

Preparing for Automatic Optional Hyphenation

Optional hyphenation is one of the last things you want to do when preparing a document. Finish everything else that affects line endings first. Otherwise, you may need to rehyphenate one or more times.

For instance, be sure that your document is complete and properly organized. Do the spelling check. Polish the appearance of your text (fonts, sizes, character expansion, etc.). Apply justification, if that's part of your plan. Break the document into sections if you need them. Set up columns. Have someone else proofread your work one last time. You may, however, want to hold off on final page-break decisions until after hyphenation.

Entering Optional Hyphens

Word will hyphenate an entire document or just selected text. When you choose *Hyphenation...* from the *Tools* menu, Word will open a small dialog box like the one in Figure 22.2. Click the Start Hyphenation button.

Working from the insertion point, Word will move through your document (or selected text) looking for a word possible to hyphenate. In Figure 22.2 it has found *remind*.

The dialog box offers several alternatives. The Change button will place an optional hyphen between the *e* and *m*.

The No Change button tells Word not to hyphenate this word and to continue. Cancel quits the hyphenation.

Figure 22.2
Word is suggesting that *remind* be hyphenated between the *e* and the *m*.

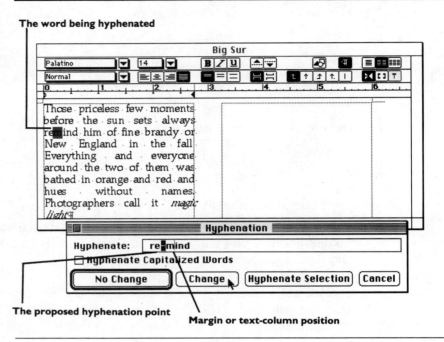

Optionally, you can move the hyphenation point yourself. Use your mouse to point to where you want to place the hyphen. Press the mouse button once. A non-blinking pointer will appear between the characters you've chosen. Click on the Change button to place the optional hyphen and continue the automatic search.

As you can see from Figure 22.3, Word suggested only one hyphenation point in our example. It left the rest of the unsightly white holes (between *Everything and everyone*, *hues without names*, etc.). It didn't solve the widow problem, either. Big help.

Moreover, some editors and style manuals will tell you not to hyphenate words in ways that leave only one syllable on a line, yet Word has done just that. There are few hard-and-fast hyphenation rules.

Hyphenation and Dashes

Manually breaking the one-syllable rule twice more creates a much nicer looking paragraph, as you can see in Figure 22.4. The combination of manual and automatic hyphenation even found a home for the widow. If you like tight copy, you may want to run the auto-hyphenation feature and then fine-tune a bit by hand.

Figure 22.3
Word's automatic hyphenation may not solve all your problems.

> Those priceless few moments before the sun sets always remind him of fine brandy or New England in the fall. Everything and everyone around the two of them was bathed in orange and red and hues without names. Photographers call it *magic light*.

Figure 22.4
Adding two hyphens manually really improves the final appearance of the paragraph.

> Those priceless few moments before the sun sets always remind him of fine brandy or New England in the fall. Everything and everyone around the two of them was bathed in orange and red and hues without names. Photographers call it *magic light*.

Undoing Automatic Hyphenation

The *Undo Hyphenation* command (located on the *Edit* menu) will remove optional hyphens if you use it immediately after you run the auto-hyphenation feature.

You can delete hyphens like any other character. Select them and cut or delete. Word's Find and Replace features will also help you delete hyphens of all sorts. See *Chapter 26* for details.

CHAPTER 23

Sections

FEATURING

- Reasons to break your documents into sections
- How to make section breaks
- Ways to save time when creating sections

When you think of *sections*, you probably imagine traditional book sections—collections of several related chapters, for instance. Word's section features can help you organize large projects this way, of course, but they do much more. Word sections are designed to let you change major formatting features at places you decide in your document.

Sections need not be used only for books or reports. It is a shame sections aren't called "zones" or something less ambiguous.

You can start a new section whenever you want to change the format, position, or progression of page numbers. Sections can be used to turn line numbering on and off. Since footnote positioning can be different in each section, sections are sometimes used for this purpose. Headers and footers can also vary from section to section. Last, but by no means least, sections can be used to change the number of columns in a document. You'll see practical applications of these tricks in a moment.

Sections

There are no firm rules about when to create new sections. Experienced Word users often create multiple sections in a one-page document. Others use a single section for an entire 100-page report.

CREATING SECTION BREAKS

Prepare to create a new section by placing the insertion point where you want the break. Next hold down the ⌘-Enter key combination or pick *Section Break* from the *Insert* menu. This places a double-dotted, *non-printing* line called a *section break* at the insertion point on your screen. Figure 23.1 contains an example.

Figure 23.1
Section marks are double-dotted, non-printing lines like this one. Notice the section number next to the page number in the status area.

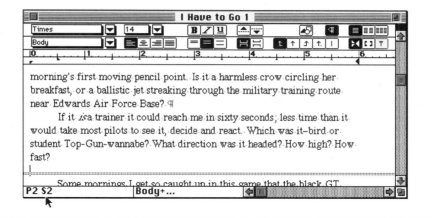

Sections as Chapter Elements

It is very common to create a new section for each chapter in a large publishing project like a manuscript or report. This makes it possible to change header and footer information like chapter names. If you were creating an employee handbook, Chapter One's header might contain the words *Welcome new employees,* while the headers in Chapter Two might say *Your health plan explained,* and so forth.

Sections also make it possible to customize page numbers within chapters. Your document's frontmatter might be numbered in lowercase Roman numerals (*i, ii, iii,* etc.) Page numbers within chapters might contain chapter-related numbers that restart at the beginning of each chapter (1-1, 2-1, and so on). Remember from *Chapter 19* that you can use different page-numbering styles in each section of your document, and that you can restart page numbering at the beginning of any new section.

Sections as Formatting Tools

You probably know that Word can produce multi-column documents, but did you know that you can have different numbers of columns on the same page? The trick is to break a single *page* into multiple sections. Figure 23.2 shows an example of this technique. There's a section break separating the single- and three-column text from one another. See *Chapter 36* for more about columns.

Figure 23.2
You can mix column formats on the same page by inserting section breaks where you want to switch formats.

> I spend lots of time looking over people's shoulders. It's amazing how much computer power goes untapped. Many users learn the basic features of one or two popular programs, then put away their manuals forever. When more advanced projects come along these users (often painfully) apply their basic skills rather than cracking the books to learn about advanced features that could make them much more efficient. This is particularly true of spreadsheet and database users.
>
> Take a "beginner's" program like Microsoft Works for the Macintosh. Works provides over 75 "functions" that simplify and speed development of spreadsheets and databases. Other "more advanced" programs like
>
> It is a much better (and as you'll soon see, safer) way to add-up columns of numbers than specifying each cell that needs to be included in the total. Suppose, for instance that you wanted to add the contents of the ten
>
> Blocks are permissible. You can sometimes list non-contiguous cells to create a range. You can even reference multiple ranges. Here are some range examples using the Works Sum function:

The Section Dialog Box

Reach the Section dialog box by double-clicking on the section break *below* the section you are designing. It is also possible to place the insertion point in the section being designed and choose *Section...* in the *Format* menu. (You owners of big keyboards can press the Option-F14 shortcut, if you prefer.)

Many of the choices in the Section dialog box are covered elsewhere in this book, but the *Start:* drop-down menu of the dialog box contains a number of section-specific items worth exploring. It is shown in Figure 23.3.

This is how you tell Word where you want it to start *printing* the various sections of your document. You can make a different choice for each section. Here are explanations of your options.

Figure 23.3
Choose one of the options from the *Start:* menu to specify how Word should break your section.

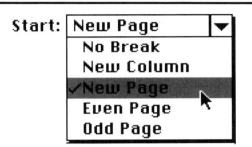

No Break
This is Word's default section-printing strategy. Text from preceding sections occupy the same page as the section being designed, if there is enough room for the text from both sections.

New Column
In multi-column formats, Word breaks a column when it encounters a section mark. It prints the subsequent text at the top, of a new column. (See *Chapter 36* for more about columns.)

New Page
Word will *always* start new sections on a new pages when it encounters this choice.

Even Page
Word starts printing the new section on an even-numbered page, even if it means leaving an odd-numbered page blank.

Odd Page

Word will start the new section on an odd-numbered page. This is a great way to ensure that new sections start on right-hand pages when designing documents for two-sided printing.

COPYING SECTION BREAKS

Section-formatting information is stored with section breaks much the same way paragraph formatting is stored with paragraph marks. And you can copy section information by copying and pasting section breaks. It is even possible to place section breaks as glossary items. See *Chapter 28* for information about glossaries.

Section breaks differ from paragraph marks (¶), in that a section break controls the information *below* it, while a paragraph mark controls the information that precedes it.

It takes some practice to highlight section breaks. You may find it easiest to do this in Normal view. When you move the mouse pointer to the left edge of a section mark it turns into an arrow. Click to highlight the mark as shown in Figure 23.4. You can then copy, cut, etc.

Figure 23.4
Point to a section break from the left margin to select it for copying or deletion.

DELETING SECTION BREAKS

Select a section break as described above. Then press the backspace or Delete key. Text after the removed section break will take on the characteristics of the material following.

TIME-SAVING SECTION TIPS

- Documents start out as one big section and it is often best to wait until you are nearly finished with a document before breaking it into smaller sections. Do, however, *think* about the divisions in your document early on.

- Section formatting done when there is only one section affects the entire document. For instance, header and footer choices will be applied throughout. If you want most of the document to print in multiple columns, make that choice while the document contains only one section. Then break the document into sections and modify things like page numbers within each section.

- Set up stationery and glossary entries for complex section designs. See *Chapter 29* and *Chapter 28*.

PART IV

TIME SAVERS

Do you ever wish you had more hours in the day? Word can't give them to you, but it can do the next best thing. It is packed with time-saving features that can help you get rush documents out the door on time. This section explores Word 5's keyboard shortcuts, Find and Replace features, tricks for navigating documents, ways to minimize repetitive typing, and stationery. Spend an hour or two experimenting with the techniques described in these chapters and save days over the next year.

Keyboard Features

FEATURING

- How Word handles different keyboard designs
- The Keyboard Menu feature
- Exploring and changing keyboard shortcuts
- Tips for the disabled user

The first Macs were like Ford's Model T—simple and utilitarian. You had no choice of keyboards. Today, Apple manufactures two sizes of detached keyboards called *standard* and *extended*, each providing different layouts and features. There are also *international keyboards* labeled with accent marks and configured with special characters for a variety of languages. In addition, Apple's original *portables* and new *PowerBook* notebook computers have unique keyboard layouts and keys. Recently, third-party vendors have started selling keyboards with additional features. Fortunately, Word accommodates most of these differences.

Most newer Macintosh keyboards have *numeric keypads* and *screen editing keys* (Home, Page Up, etc.). Many people prefer Macintosh Extended keyboards containing *special function keys*. Word 5 uses the numeric keypad and fifteen

Keyboard Features

extra special function keys to help you be a more efficient user. Unfortunately, PowerBooks and very early Macs do not have these features, making a few Word functions slightly less convenient.

Touch-typists often dislike taking their hands off of the keyboard for anything, so Word offers a variety of *keyboard shortcuts*, like ⌘-X for *Cut*. These make it unnecessary to reach for the mouse. Shortcuts are mentioned throughout this book, and many are shown on Word's menus. The Commands dialog box (*Commands...* from the *Tools* menu) will help you explore all of Word's keyboard shortcuts. It is possible to change or delete shortcuts or add your own new ones, as you learned in *Chapter 10*. This chapter will give you some additional tips.

Another feature appreciated by some touch-typists and disabled users is called *Keyboard Menus*. It lets you visit and use Word's menus without using a mouse! Speaking of disabled users, Word works well with *Easy Access*, a collection of Apple features that make it easy to press multiple-key combinations with one hand or even one finger. See your Apple manuals for details on Easy Access

KEYBOARD DIFFERENCES

If you work on only one Mac, keyboard differences are probably a trivial matter to you. But if you work in a large office with new and old Macs, there are some things you should be aware of. For instance, in-house computer trainers and system managers need to understand the importance of differences in keyboards when creating user documentation.

And, if you plan to assign new keyboard shortcuts as part of Word Settings files distributed throughout a mixed Mac office, you need to make certain you don't assign combinations that are unavailable to some users. For instance, early keyboards don't have Control or Escape keys. The Delete key was labeled *Backspace* in the good old days. The ⌘ key did not have an Apple logo on it. This sometimes confuses users when they read about the "Apple" key in newer documentation. It is tempting to use these keys when setting up custom keyboard shortcuts. Similarly, if you assign numeric keypad keys to shortcuts, realize that users without numeric pads won't be able to use your new shortcuts. Test new combos and review user documentation on each keyboard type in you organization.

Numeric Keypads and Word

Numeric keypads serve *two* functions in Word. With the Num Loc feature enabled, you can use the pad to enter numbers. With Num Loc *off* (the default) you use the numeric pad to navigate. Pressing *9* on the numeric pad scrolls the screen up, *3* scrolls down, and so on. This is particularly confusing to people in the habit of using the numeric pad with *spreadsheet* and *database* programs. Many of *those* programs default to Num Loc *on*. New Word users often try to enter numbers from the numeric pad and find themselves bouncing around their Word document instead.

The key in the upper-left corner of the numeric keypad toggles Num Lock on and off. Newer keyboards contain *both* the word *clear* and the abbreviation *num lock*. On some keypads it is labeled just *clear* or *Clear*.

Some Mac keyboards have a light that tells you when Num Lock is enabled, others do not. Word's status area at the lower left of a document window will often tell you when Num Lock is enabled.

A few Word keyboard shortcuts are unavailable to users without numeric keypads. For instance, many of the move commands (move down one text area, move to start of line, etc.) are available only from the numeric pad. The Unassign Keystroke command shortcut is also unavailable without a numeric keypad. If you don't have a numeric keypad, and you want to assign your own keyboard shortcuts to replace the ones you are missing, you may. *Appendix B* lists all of Word's standard and numeric-keypad shortcuts.

Extended Keyboards and Word

Extended keyboards cost more and take up extra desk space, but in return you get 105 keys instead of 85 or fewer. Fifteen of the extra keys are special function keys, which are fully exploited by Word 5. You also get a collection of screen-editing keys (Home, End, etc.) and a Help key that Word supports.

Function Keys

The top row of keys on extended keyboards contains fifteen function keys. Word has implemented Apple's standard definitions for the first four keys: F1 is *Undo*, F2 cuts, F3 copies, and F4 pastes. In addition, Word's designers have

Keyboard Features

assigned a number of additional function-key shortcuts. Generally, these are shortcuts that can be accomplished with other key combinations as well. So those of you without function keys have alternatives. For instance, you can apply bold character formatting by pressing the F10 function key. The key combination ⌘-B does the same thing. So does ⌘-Shift-B.

A few commands, like the shortcut for the *Document...* and *Section...* menu choices, are available only if you have an extended keyboard. Obviously, if you don't have function keys and you want to assign your own keyboard shortcuts, that is possible. *Appendix B* shows how Word's designers have utilized function keys.

REPEATING KEYS

Most of the character keys and many of the navigational keys (like arrows) will repeat if you hold them down. This is an easy way to type a series of keystrokes. You can change the speed of this feature from your Keyboard control panel, located under the *Apple* menu, as illustrated in Figure 24.1.

Fig 24.1
Repeating-key rates and delays can be personalized in the Keyboard control panel, found under the *Apple* menu.

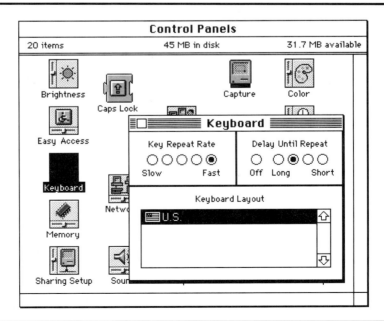

The *speed* with which identical keystrokes are issued is called the *Key Repeat Rate*. There are five choices, ranging from Slow to Fast. The length of time your Mac waits between your first key depression and the rapid-fire insertion of identical keystrokes is called the *Delay Until Repeat* setting. You can specify off or a long to short delay by clicking the appropriate button. You can shut off the delay feature entirely by clicking the Off button in this dialog box. See your Apple manuals for details.

Exploring and Modifying Keyboard Shortcuts

Appendix B lists Word's standard keyboard shortcuts next to the commands they invoke. A shortcut can be a combination of up to four keys.

There are several ways to have Word show you which keyboard shortcuts do what. You can also edit and enter your own shortcuts.

Exploring Keyboard Shortcuts

One way to learn about shortcuts in general is to display or print and study a command list using the List... feature in the Commands dialog box.

There is also a quick way to see what a *specific* key combination does. Start by opening the Commands dialog box, found under the *Tools* menu. With the Commands dialog box in view, type the key combination of interest. The associated command (if there is one) will scroll into view in the commands list. A description of the command will appear in the Description: portion of the dialog box. Since any Word command can have many different keyboard shortcuts, they will all be listed in the Keys area of the dialog box. Scroll if necessary.

Assigning and Changing Keyboard Shortcuts

You can assign a new shortcut from the Commands dialog box. There is also a quicker way. Let's start with the dialog-box technique.

Assigning Shortcuts from the Commands Dialog Box

To assign or change shortcuts from the Commands dialog box, open the dialog box and scroll and select the command you wish to modify. In Figure 24.2 *Screen Test* is selected.

Keyboard Features

Figure 24.2
Select the command you want to assign a keyboard shortcut (*Screen Test* in this case), then click Add... in the Keys area of the Commands dialog box.

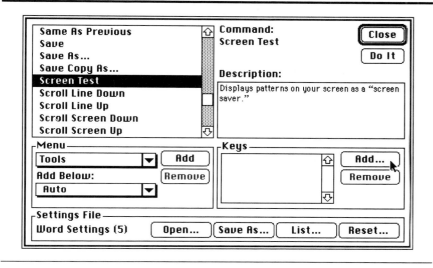

Notice the Keys area of the dialog box. This command does not yet have a shortcut. Click on the Add... button. You will be asked to demonstrate the key combination you want to use for the command. To assign Control-S as the shortcut, press that combination. Word will add it to the Keys area of the dialog box. Henceforth, Control-S will activate the Screen Test.

Suppose, however, that when defining the Screen Test shortcut, you decided to assign ⌘-S, forgetting that ⌘-S is the *Save* command shortcut. When you press ⌘-S, Word will ask you if you want to remove the combination from the *Save* command to use it for Screen Test. Since ⌘-S is an Apple-wide shortcut, you would probably click Cancel to prevent the change.

Shortcuts are stored with your Settings File, which is saved to disk only when you quit Word. If you have spent a long time defining shortcuts, it is good idea to quit Word to save the changes.

Removing Shortcuts in the Commands Dialog Box

To remove shortcuts, highlight them in the Commands dialog box and click the Remove button in the Keys area, as shown in Figure 24.3.

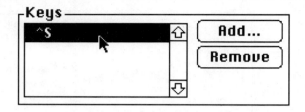

Figure 24.3
You remove shortcuts by highlighting them in the Keys area of the Commands dialog box, and then clicking Remove.

Quickly Changing Shortcuts

You need not visit the Command dialog to add or delete shortcuts if you have a numeric keypad. To *add* a shortcut, hold down ⌘-Option- + (on the numeric pad). Your cursor will change to a large ⌘ symbol. Pick the menu item you want to add a shortcut to. Demonstrate the key combination when Word asks you.

To *remove* shortcuts without visiting the Commands dialog box, hold down ⌘-Option- – (on the numeric pad). Word will ask you to type the key combination you wish to remove. After you demonstrate the shortcut, Word will ask you to confirm the deletion. For instance, if you had pressed ⌘-N, Word would ask *Is it OK to remove* ⌘-N from the "New" command? Click OK to confirm or Cancel to leave the shortcut alone.

Activating Word's Keyboard Menus

If you *really* hate to reach for your mouse when typing, (or have a disability), you can use Word 5's *Keyboard Menus* feature. It lets you use the right- and left-arrow keys to flit from menu to menu and the up- and down-arrow keys to make menu choices.

Activate the feature by pressing the period on your numeric keypad (if you have one) or by holding down ⌘ and pressing the Tab key.

The Word menu bar will turn black for five seconds. At this point, you can press the first letter of the desired menu (*V* for *View*, *W* for *Window*, etc.), or you can use the left- and right-arrow keys to display the desired menu. Menus drop down and stay down as you pick them. Since three of Word's menu choices start with the letter *F* (*File*, *Format*, and *Font*), you will need to hold down the Shift key when you press *F* to move from *File* to *Format* and from *Format* to *Font*. When you get to *Font* the next *F* will take you back to *File*.

With the desired menu displayed, (*Insert*, for example), either use up- and down-arrow keys to highlight an *Insert* menu choice, or type the first letter of a choice (*S* for *Symbol...*, *T* for *Table...*, etc.). Here, you need not hold down the Shift key to move among choices with the same first letters. Pressing *S* the first time in the *Insert* menu gets you to the *Section Break* choice. Pressing *S* a second time takes you to *Symbol....*

Pressing the Return or Enter key is equivalent to releasing the mouse button. Your choice will be carried out. To cancel the Keyboard Menu feature without taking any action, press the Esc (escape) key, or press the ⌘-. (period) shortcut.

KEYBOARD TRICKS IN DIALOG BOXES

- Word supports the usual Apple keyboard tricks in dialog boxes. For instance, in dialog boxes where you are asked to type text or dimensions, you can tab from box to box. Holding down the Shift key will move you backwards when you press Tab.

- Anytime you see a button with a dark border, pressing Return or Enter will work in place of clicking on the button.

- If you are unfamiliar with tricks like these, consult your Macintosh manuals or try the tutorial programs that came with your Mac.

CHAPTER 25

Undo, Redo, and Reverting

- Ways to recover from mistakes
- Ways to repeat operations
- Reverting to styles (removing Character formatting)

Do you know what a *damnosecond* is? It's that fleeting instant when you realize you've done something really stupid on your computer—like accidentally deleting or reformatting twenty pages of text.

Everyone make choices they wish they could undo. Like few other things in life, Word often lets you. Two features—*Undo* and *Revert To Style* are designed specifically for this purpose. You can also form some work habits that will help *you* undo things when Word can't.

And when those tasks are repetitive and complex, it is nice to have your computer take some of the drudgery out of *repeating* tasks. That's where Word's *Repeat* features can help. Since Word gives you so much control over formatting, it is easy to get carried away. When that happens the *Revert To Style* command can make things right. Let's begin by looking at *Undo*.

NDO

Word "watches" as you work. With surprising attention to detail, it "remembers" which steps you last took. When asked, it can frequently undo your errors. You undo things by choosing *Undo* from the *Edit* menu or by using the ⌘-Z keyboard shortcut. The exact name of the *Undo* choice on the *Edit* menu changes as you work. Sometimes it says *Undo Typing*. Other times it says *Undo Formatting* or *Undo Sort*.

Here are some examples of things Word can undo if you ask soon after you discover a problem:

- Editing changes (typing, cutting, pasting, etc.)
- Most formatting actions (styles, fonts, etc.)
- Most projects done with tools (replacing, etc.)
- Most drawing actions (dragging, filling, etc.)

Suppose you have a large document with dozens of different paragraph styles. There are bold headings, indentations, several different fonts, various line- and paragraph-spacing schemes, and so on. You select all of the text and accidentally reformat it as Normal. Poof. A week's work looks like guacamole. Indentations are gone, headings look like body text—what a mess! A quick trip to the *Edit* menu would reveal the choice *Undo Formatting*, as shown in Figure 25.1

Choosing *Undo Formatting* (or pressing the ⌘-Z shortcut) would restore everything to the way it was.

But there's a *big* gotcha here. Frequently, you need to catch your mistakes *immediately* after you make them. For instance, if you type even a *single character* after accidentally reformatting your pride and joy, the *Undo* choice will change to *Undo Typing* and you will not be able to restore the formatting.

Occasionally, you will see a message like the one in Figure 25.2. Word can't always undo your mistakes.

That's why it is a good idea to save early and often. Then, when things like this happen, you can close the messed-up document either by saving it under a

Figure 25.1
The *Undo* menu choice changes based on what you've last done.

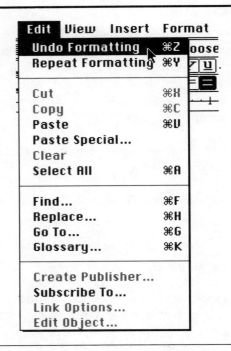

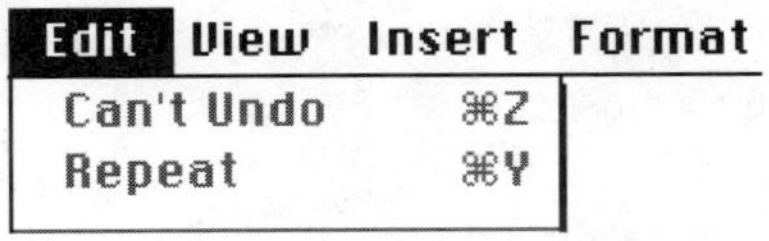

Figure 25.2
Undo is dimmed when Word can't restore your work.

different name (with *Save As...* from the *File* menu) or close the document *without saving the changes* (don't save mistakes). Next, open the earlier version that is hopefully in better shape. Sometimes you can save time by cutting and pasting between the earlier version and portions of the new (messed-up) work if you've saved it under a different file name.

The best approach is to stop and think immediately after you notice a big, potentially time-consuming mistake. Get help. Sometimes more experienced Word users or Microsoft's telephone support staff can talk you through time-saving repair techniques. Microsoft's free phone-support number is in the materials that came with your Word packaging. The less you fiddle after noticing a big mistake, the better your chances of salvation. If you are a new user, don't be embarrassed to ask for help *right when you notice your mistake!*

By the way, it is possible to undo an *Undo*. Immediately after you undo, the *Undo* command changes to *Redo*, letting you flip back and forth.

REPEAT

This feature was called *Again* in Word 4, and it had a different keyboard shortcut. *Repeat* is located on the *Edit* menu and the Word 5 shortcut is ⌘-Y. *Repeat* watches you work, and attempts to remember and recreate your actions on demand. Suppose, for instance, you move the pointer to a paragraph and apply a new style. If you have several other paragraphs scattered around your document that also need to be reformatted the same way, you can move the insertion point to each paragraph and use the *Repeat* feature. Some people find this repeating quicker than visiting the *Style:* list on the ruler. If you find yourself applying certain styles over and over, consider assigning keyboard shortcuts to the styles by using the ⌘-Option- + (plus on the keypad) trick instead of using *Repeat*.

Like *Undo*, *Repeat*'s name changes based on what you have last done, and it works with most Word actions immediately after you take them. *Repeat* works with typing and many other actions. Experiment.

THE REVERT TO STYLE COMMAND

Suppose you have an established paragraph format, and type text in that format. Then you apply character formatting to embellish the text. You underline a few words, italicize some others, and so on. Figure 25.3 shows an example of this.

But suppose you realize you've really overdone it? Word's *Revert to Style* command (found on the *Format* menu) will remove the *character formatting* (underline and italics in the example) without changing the other style elements (margins, paragraph characteristics, etc.). The keyboard shortcut is ⌘-Shift-Spacebar.

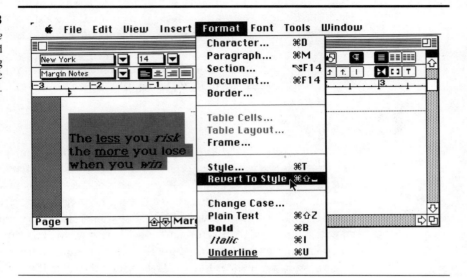

Figure 25.3
Revert to Style removes applied character formatting while retaining style characteristics.

CHAPTER 26

Finding and Replacing

FEATURING

- Ways to quickly find text and formats
- Ways to quickly change and reformat your work
- Tips and techniques for finding and replacing

Every contemporary word-processing product, including Word 5, has a way to quickly *locate* and *replace* specific *text strings* (collections of words, numbers, and other characters). Lawyers use replace features like these (sometimes called *global replace* features) to do things like finding each occurrence of *Thelma* in a contract and replacing it with *Louise*.

Some typists enter shorthand or acronyms for lengthy items when they draft. Then, while polishing the document, they replace the shorthand with the actual text. For instance, you might initially type *DRD* in the draft of a government document, then have Word find and replace each occurrence of DRD with *Department of Redundancy Department*.

With Word 5 you can search for and replace or remove *special characters* like paragraph marks, optional hyphens, or footnote-reference marks.

A form of *wild-card* searching is permitted, letting you insert question marks in search requests to work-around minor spelling variations. Asking Word to find *Sm?th,* for instance, would find both *Smith* and *Smyth.* You can search for ranges of numbers using a similar technique. Word's designers refer to this process as searching for *unspecified letters* and *unspecified digits* respectively.

Occasionally, Word's find and replace features can be used to *reformat* documents. You might, for instance, search for all occurrences of two consecutive spaces and replace them with a single space. But Word 5 can do much more than that. It will help you find all or selected paragraphs formatted with a particular *style* and apply a different style.

It is even possible to use find and replace to *remove* things. Simply tell Word to search for the item you wish to delete, and replace it with nothing. Word can search your entire document or selected portions. You specify the direction of the search (up or down).

Word provides two separate menu items called *Find...* and *Replace....* Both are located on the *Edit* menu. The *Find...* keyboard shortcut is ⌘-F and *Replace...* is ⌘-H. *Find...* is really just an evolutionary predecessor to *Replace....* In fact, if you are careful, you can use *Replace...* instead of *Find...* for everything.

THE ART OF FINDING

The *Find...* feature helps you quickly locate text, formats, special characters and *combinations* thereof. It lets you search *selected* parts of your document or the whole enchilada.

Simple find requests can locate text regardless of format, or you can ask Word to locate only very specific things, like occurrences of the word *Liberace* formatted in bold, blue, 24-point New Century Schoolbook.

You need not limit your searches to *text.* You can look for section marks, graphics, paragraph marks, and more.

When using the *Find...* command (as opposed to *Replace...*), Word *finds* what you've requested, then scrolls the found item and surrounding text into view, *but it does not modify anything.* You must click in the document window to work with the found item. You can leave the Find dialog box out on your screen as you work, flipping between it and your document window. Figure 26.1 shows the Find dialog box and its three drop-down menus.

To do a search, follow these general steps:

1. Choose *Find...* (or *Replace...*) from the *Edit* menu.
2. Specify text and special characters (if any) to find.
3. Specify formatting characteristics (if any) to find.
4. Tell Word where to search and in which direction.
5. Click Find Next to start the search.
6. When Word finds what you want, return to the document.
7. To find again, press = (the "equals" sign) on the numeric pad (if you're still in the document) or Find Next.

Like any good computer program, Word 5 takes your requests quite literally, so you will need to understand each *Find...* option fully to locate exactly what you want.

For example, if Word searches by using the criteria specified in Figure 26.1, it will find *B B King*, but not *B.B. King, BB King,* or *Burger King*.

There are ways to get Word to find each of these text strings, of course. Just realize that you may need to carefully formulate and *test* your search strategy. In some cases, you will need to perform *multiple* searches to find similar but subtly different text strings.

Realize also, that Word does not automatically search in headers, and footers, or footnotes. You must open and perform separate searches in them! For multi-section documents, you may need to open and search headers and footers in *each* section. If your search plans include things like paragraph marks or hidden text, the hidden text must be visible on the screen.

Consider proofing your document or at least running the spell-checker before important, major searches. If you spell *banana* correctly six times and incorrectly once, Word will find only six of your seven *bananas...*

Finding and Replacing

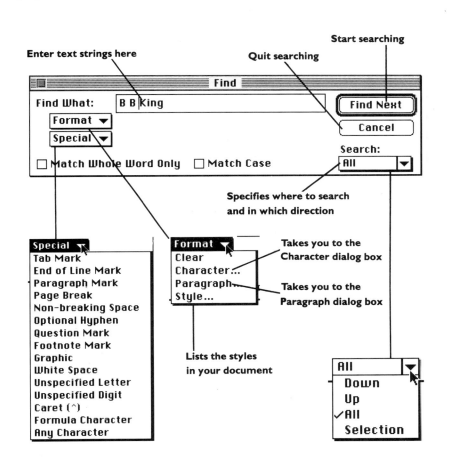

Figure 26.1
The *Find...* command is located under the *Edit* menu. It lets you specify search criteria

Finding Text

Choose *Find...* from the *Edit* menu. Move to the text area of the Find What: box and type enough text (a maximum of 255 characters) for an accurate, unambiguous search. For instance, suppose you wanted to find the word *man*. Entering *man* in Find What: would cause Word to find the words *man, Man, Mansfield, reprimand, manhole,* and *man* at the end of a sentence (followed by a period, question mark, etc.). Placing a *space* after *man* in your find request would eliminate the unwanted *Mansfield, reprimand,* and *manhole,* but would also prevent you from finding *man* at the ends of sentences because periods, question marks, and such are not spaces.

That's the reason for the *Match Whole Word Only* checkbox in the Find dialog box. If you type *man* (no space) in the Find What: area and check *Match Whole Word Only,* Word will locate only *man, Man,* and *man* at the end of sentences.

The *Match Case* checkbox instructs Word to look for *exact* capitalization matches. If you type *postscript* in the Find What: area and check *Match Case,* Word will not find *POSTSCRIPT, PostScript,* or even *Postscript* at the beginning of sentences.

Extra spaces, non-breaking spaces, and forced page breaks can also get in the way of searches. See *White Space* later in this chapter to see how to work around this.

Finding Special Characters

The *Special* drop-down list is a convenient way to enter certain special characters like tab marks, non-breaking spaces, etc. when constructing a search request. Place the insertion point where you want the special character to go and choose the desired character from the drop-down list.

Find... requests can combine regular text and special characters. For instance, you could ask Word to search for occurrences of *Bob* followed by two tab marks. Many of the special characters in the drop-down list are self-explanatory. Let's look more closely at the ones that are not. Some are extremely useful.

White Space   Here's one to keep you awake nights. Suppose that you are searching for two words together like *Microsoft Corporation.* Suppose further that sometimes you used non-breaking spaces to separate the two words. Other times you've just typed regular spaces. Occasionally, you typed *two* spaces between the words by mistake. And one time you intentionally forced a *page break* between *Microsoft* and *Corporation.* Unless you use Word's *White Space* feature, you will not find the occurrences of *Microsoft Corporation* containing non-breaking spaces or two spaces, nor will you find the one split by the page break!

So, to do it right, insert Word's White Space special character in your search string. In our example, you'd start by typing *Microsoft* in the Find What: box. Then, without touching the Spacebar, choose *White Space* from the *Special* menu. The White Space code (^w) will appear next to Microsoft. Type *Corporation*. Your finished search string would be *Microsoft^wCorporation*. That should do it.

Unspecified Letter   The *Unspecified Letter* character lets you overcome some nasty problems too. Suppose you've used accented characters sometimes but not always. *La Cañada* and *La Canada* are not the same thing to Word when it searches. A search for *La Ca^*ada* will find both. Enter the Unspecified Letter character from the *Special* drop-down menu the same way you entered the White Space character.

Unspecified Digit   This special character will sometimes help you find numbers within ranges. It might be helpful for finding specific groups of part numbers or zip codes.

For instance the search string *99^#* would find any number between 990 and 999. The specification *1^#* would find the combinations *101* and *11* in *111*. It would also find *1000*, but not *1,000*, since Word treats numbers as *text*, not numeric values, in searches like these. Commas confuse things. Ah, computers...

THE ART OF REPLACING

To replace, follow these general steps:

1. Choose *Replace...* from the *Edit* menu or press ⌘-H.
2. Create search criteria using the techniques discussed above.
3. Specify the desired replacement text, formats, etc.
4. Tell Word where to search and in which direction.
5. Click Find Next or Replace All to start the replacement.
6. Confirm the replacements.

It is a good idea to save your work before using the *Replace...* feature. If you are working on a complex, important project, you might want to use a *copy* rather than the original document.

As you can see from Figure 26.2, the Replace dialog box looks like the Find dialog box, with additional features. Word lets you confirm each replacement before it happens, or it will find and replace without your intervention.

Figure 26.2
The Replace dialog box resembles the Find box, with added features.

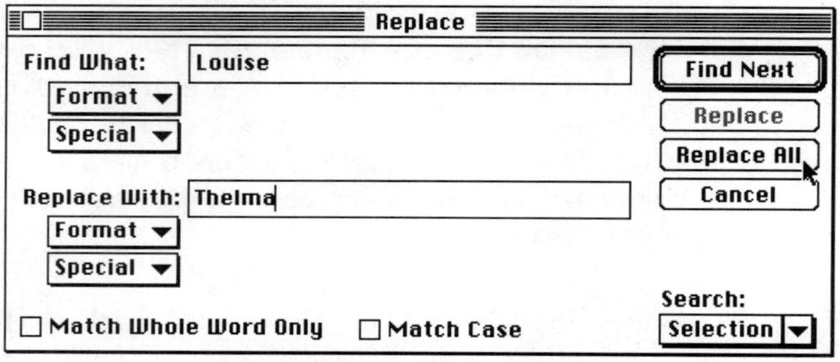

Just as you can *search* for text, formats, styles and special characters, you can *replace* them. For instance, you could replace *Thelma* with *Louise*. Or you could change each occurrence of two consecutive paragraph marks to a single end-of-line marker; or change the style of certain paragraphs from chapter-heading style to appendix style. It is even possible to replace text with graphics. Here are examples of each technique.

Replacing Text with Text

To simply replace text (like changing *Louise* to *Thelma*) without altering formats or styles, start by entering the text to find and the desired replacement text. For instance, you might enter *Louise* in the Find What: box and T*helma* in the Replace With: box.

Visit the *Search:* drop-down menu to tell Word if you want it to search the entire document, a selected portion, and so on. If you want to replace text in only a portion of the document, select the text in the document prior to beginning the replace and choose *Selection* in the *Search:* drop-down menu.

Important tip: If there are any formats or styles listed under the Find What: or Replace With: boxes, choose *Clear* from the appropriate *Format* menus. This way, Word will not alter the style or format of the document. Figure 26.2 shows what the dialog box would look like.

When the replacement instructions are complete, click Find Next. Word will search the document (or selected portion) for things matching your Find criteria and propose the next replacement. The Replace button will undim, and your document screen will scroll to reveal the first potential replacement point.

If you want Word to make the change it is proposing, click Replace. To skip the change, click Find Next. To make the change and let Word continue uninterrupted, click Replace All. Word will make the rest of the replacements nonstop, and probably too fast for you even to see them. The status area in the lower-left corner of your document window will briefly flash the number of replacements made. Check your work since *Undo* will work here.

Replacing Formatting

Suppose you have italicized words scattered throughout your text and decide to change all of them to underlined words. Start by removing any text from the Find What: and Replace With: boxes. (This is because you want Word to find *all* italicized text, not just words in the Find What: box that are italicized.)

Specify the character attributes you want Word to find (italics for example). You can do this in one of several ways.

Always start by placing the insertion point in the Find What: entry box. Then specify the Italic format either from Word's *Format* menu, or by clicking on the ribbon's Italic button. The ⌘-I shortcut works here too. (There is another other, clumsier way to specify italic: Pull down the *Word Format* menu in the Replace dialog box. From there, choose *Character,* then click in the Italic option of the Character dialog box.) As you can see, the ribbon or keyboard shortcuts are much quicker. The word *Italic* will appear beneath the Find What: box.

Next go to the Replace With: box and specify the new format—Underline in this example. Be sure there is no text in either of the text boxes. In order to prevent Word from changing the italic to *italic* underline, you must also click the ribbon's italic button until the Replace With: criteria read *Underline: Not Italic*. Figure 26.3 shows the appearance of the critical parts of the dialog box when you are ready to go. Let 'er rip! Either tell Word to Replace All or you can supervise as before.

Figure 26.3
This combination will change all italicized text to underlined text.

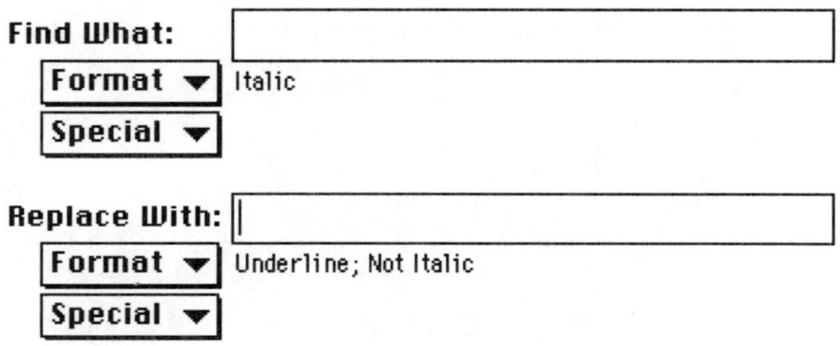

Find What:	
Format ▼	Italic
Special ▼	

Replace With:	
Format ▼	Underline; Not Italic
Special ▼	

Replacing Styles

If you want to change the style of certain paragraphs, the *Replace...* feature can help. From the Replace dialog box's *Format* menu, pick *Style...* and you will see a list of your document's styles and descriptions, as shown in Figure 26.4.

Pick styles for both the find and replace criteria, then proceed as usual. In this example paragraphs formatted with the *Appendix Heading* style will be reformatted using the *Chapter Heading* style.

Combining Replacement Tasks

Within reason, it is possible to combine search and replace instructions to restrict actions. For instance, assuming you had a document with appropriate styles, you could italicize all occurrences of *Gone With The Wind* in the *body text* of your report, while leaving the same words alone when they appear in headings, table-of-contents, and index. You would do this by typing *Gone With The Wind* in the Find What: box, and restricting the find to the *body text* style.

Finding and Replacing

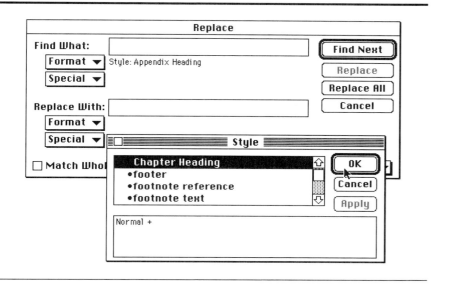

Figure 26.4
Specify styles to find and replace with the two drop-down *Format* menus.

Then you'd have to type *Gone With The Wind* again in the Replace With: box and specify Italic as the format. (If you forget to enter *Gone With The Wind* in the Replace With: box, Word will replace *Gone With The Wind* with *nothing*.... Computers are very obedient but not very clever. *Undo* may work if you spot the problem immediately. Work on *copies* of important documents.

Search:

You have several choices as to how Word will search your document for words you wish either to find or replace. These options are found under the *Search:* drop-down menu in the Find and Replace dialog boxes. *Up* searches back toward the beginning of the document, while *Down* searches toward the end. *All* searches the entire document, as you would expect. *Selection* will appear if you have any text highlighted when you give the *Find...* or *Replace...* command; this option will search only the selected text.

USING THE CLIPBOARD WITH FIND AND REPLACE

The Clipboard can be used for several interesting *Find...* and *Replace...* tasks. For instance, you can copy text from your document to the Clipboard, then paste it into the Find What: or Replace With: boxes. This is a great way to paste long passages or obscure characters like umlauted letters or math symbols. It is even possible to overcome the 255 character limitation this way.

Word also lets you replace text with graphics if you place the graphics on the Clipboard. Figure 26.5 illustrates how that is done.

Figure 26.5
It is possible to replace text with graphics on the clipboard.

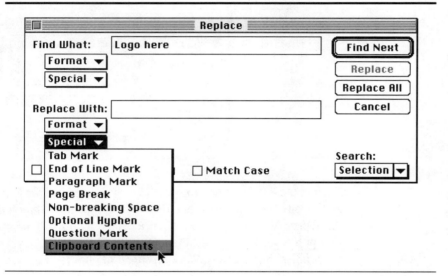

Replacing Tips

- The *Replace...* command uses considerable memory if you make a lot of changes. It is a good idea to perform a normal save after assuring that your replacements are satisfactory.

- *Undo* will undo all changes if you use Replace All, but only your last change if you have been supervising with the Find Next button...

- If you've used styles in your document, you may find it easier to make wholesale style changes by redefining or reapplying styles rather than by using Replace.

Finding and Replacing

- You can specify any Macintosh character in Find or Replace strings by typing ^*n* where *n* is the ASCII (decimal) code for the character of interest. Check your Apple manuals for ASCII code charts.

- Remember to click Clear when specifying new search criteria in the Find What: and Replace With: boxes.

CHAPTER 27

Navigating through a Document

FEATURING

- Going back and forth within a document
- Going to a specific page or section
- Moving between multiple documents
- Keyboard navigation shortcuts.

Word has a slightly overwhelming collection of tools to help you move from point A to point B in your documents. Many of these tricks automatically move the insertion point so that you are ready to type when you get to where you are going. You can use keyboard shortcuts, dialog boxes, and mouse tricks.

You've probably already read about and used many of these tools elsewhere in this and other books. If you are a newcomer, you might want to make a list of your favorite shortcuts and stick it next to your computer until you become thoroughly brainwashed.

Navigating through a Document

Navigating with Your Mouse

Word uses all of the standard Macintosh mouse-navigation tricks, and there's no need repeating them in detail here. Scroll boxes, horizontal and vertical scroll bars all work as you'd expect.

One unusual Word mouse trick worth mentioning is the technique for moving from page to page in Page Layout view.

Click on the small arrows at the bottom of the document windows. Clicking on the up arrow moves you to the previous page, clicking on the down arrow moves you to the next page in the document. See Figure 27.1.

Figure 27.1
Page Layout view has two small arrows for moving from page to page.

The Go To Feature

When editing big documents, and particularly when you have a marked-up paper copy in your hand, it is useful to be able to scoot quickly to a particular page or to a specific page within a certain section. If you know page and section numbers, Word makes this easy.

Press ⌘-G or select *GoTo...* from the *Edit* menu. You'll see a dialog box like the one in Figure 27.2.

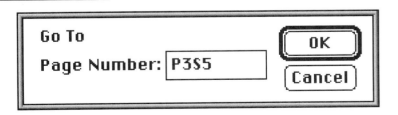

Figure 27.2
Type page and optional section numbers here, and away you'll go.

The entry area is already highlighted and waiting for you to type. In single-section documents, or documents where page numbers do not restart in each section, just type the desired page number and press Enter or Return. (Clicking OK works here too, but it will take you longer to reach the mouse than it will to hit Enter or Return.) Quicker than you can say *amen,* Word will take you to the requested page, and place the insertion point at the beginning of the first line on the page.

To specify a section number, type an *S*. For instance, typing *S4* would take you to the beginning of Section 4, (assuming you document *has* a Section 4).

To specify a particular page *and* section, type *P,* the page number, *S,* and the section number. Thus, *P3S5* would take you to the third page in the fifth section. Curiously, *S5P3* will not do the same thing. Go figure!

Go Back

Here's a handy but often confusing gizmo. When you edit, it is sometimes necessary to bounce from one part of a document to another part of the same document. Or, if you have two different documents open, you may find yourself repeatedly moving from one document to the other.

Word remembers the last three places you have done editing, plus the current insertion point. The Go Back feature lets you quickly return to those edit points. There are two keyboard shortcuts. Numeric-keypad owners will find the zero key the most convenient go-back button, assuming that you leave Num Loc off. The other keyboard shortcut is ⌘-Option-Z. The Go Back command is not on Word 5's standard menus, but you can add it from the Commands dialog box. Incidentally, simply moving the insertion point somewhere in a document does not necessarily add that point to the places in the Go Back list. Generally, you need to edit something there.

Using Find to Navigate

Here's a great way to zoom in on an area needing work. If you are looking at a printout containing a typo you want to fix, use the *Find...* command to get to the corresponding spot on your screen. Pressing ⌘-F and typing the typo, followed by Return or Enter, will quickly get you to the first occurrence of the typo.

This trick works for finding correctly typed things too. Using Find to move to a unique or uncommon word near the area of interest will place you in the right neighborhood.

MOVING BETWEEN DOCUMENT WINDOWS

You've already seen how Go Back can help you flit from one document to another. There are two other techniques worth noting—the first a Mac trick, the second a Word menu feature.

When working on multiple documents, resize and arrange the document windows so that their edges stick out like a sloppy pile of papers on a desk. Or drag a few document windows nearly off the edges of your screen. Figure 27.3 illustrates this concept.

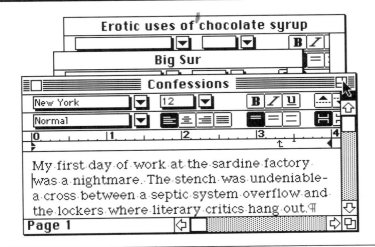

Figure 27.3
To move quickly from one document to another, stack small windows containing documents, click on the document of interest, then zoom to resize.

When you want to bring a document to the top of the pile just click on it. Hit the Zoom box in the document's upper-right corner and the project will fill your screen. Click there again to shrink it.

The Word *Window* menu offers another way to jump from document to document. As you can see in Figure 27.4, Word 5's *Window* menu lists the available documents. Pick the one you want to bring forward.

Figure 27.4
If you have several Word documents open, Word lists them in the *Window* menu. Pick the one you want.

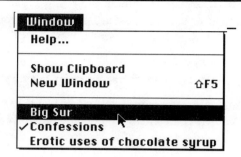

Keys for Navigation

Not only does Word have a lot of navigation shortcuts, but also, when you hold the Shift key down while using the shortcuts, they will *select* text for you. For example, ⌘-Shift-right arrow selects the next word and the space following it. There should be a keyboard shortcut that lists all of Word's keyboard-navigation shortcuts, but there isn't. (If you have *memorized* them all, it is time for you to take a very long vacation.) Table 27.1 lists most of the popular shortcuts.

TABLE 27.1
Keyboard Shortcuts: Moving, Scrolling, and Editing

Scrolling	To move to...	Press...
	Up	↑ or 8 (keypad)
	Down	↓ or 2 (keypad)
	Left	← or 4 (keypad)
	Right	→ or 6 (keypad)
	Previous Word	⌘-left arrow or ⌘-4 (keypad)
	Next Word	⌘-right arrow or ⌘-6 (keypad)
	Beginning of line	7 (keypad)
	End of line	1 (keypad)
	Previous sentence	⌘-7 (keypad)
	Next sentence	⌘-1 (keypad)

Navigating through a Document

TABLE 27.1 Keyboard Shortcuts: Moving, Scrolling, and Editing (continued)	Scrolling	To move to...	Press...
		Next page	⌘-Page Down
		Previous page	⌘-Page Up
		Beginning of current paragraph	⌘-up arrow or ⌘-8 (keypad)
		Beginning of next paragraph	⌘-down arrow or ⌘-2 (keypad)
		Top of window	Home or ⌘-5 (keypad)
		Bottom of window	End
		Start of document	⌘-Home or ⌘-9 (keypad)
		End of document	⌘-End or ⌘-3 (keypad)
		Scroll up one screen	Page Up or 9 (keypad)
		Scroll down one screen	Page Down or 3 (keypad)
		Scroll up one line	or * (asterisk on keypad)
		Scroll down one line	+ (plus sign on keypad)
	Moving in a Table or in Page Layout View	**To move to...**	**Press...**
		First table cell or page element	⌘-Option-7
		End of table or last page element	⌘-Option-1
		Next cell in table	Tab or ⌘-Option-3
		Previous cell in table	Shift-Tab or ⌘-Option-9
		Next page element	⌘-Option-3
		Previous page element	⌘-Option-9
		Cell or page element above	⌘-Option-8
		Cell or page element below	⌘-Option-2
		Cell or page element to the left	⌘-Option-4
		Cell or page element to the right	⌘-Option-6

TABLE 27.1

Keyboard Shortcuts: Moving, Scrolling, and Editing (continued)

Editing	To...	Press...
	Select the entire document	⌘-A
	Delete character before cursor or selected text	Delete (Backspace)
	Delete character after cursor or selected text	⌘-Option-F or Del
	Delete previous word	⌘-Option-Delete (Backspace)
	Delete next word	⌘-Option-G
	Insert formula character	⌘-Option-\ (backslash)
	Copy text	⌘-Option-C
	Move text	⌘-Option-X
	Insert glossary entry	⌘-Delete
	Copy formats	⌘-Option-V
	Insert special character (symbol)	⌘-Option-Q
	Copy as picture	⌘-Option-D

CHAPTER 28

Glossaries

EATURING

- Ways to save and quickly insert boilerplate
- Word's Standard glossary entries
- Special purpose glossaries
- Merging glossaries

Imagine pressing a couple keys to call up and insert entire paragraphs, complete mailing addresses, or properly formatted letter closings, including your signature. Those are just a few of the things Word's glossary feature will help you do. It can also save and recall voice annotations, graphics, memo distribution lists, tab settings, and just about any element of a Word document. Glossaries are also useful for *boilerplate* text. Boilerplates are standard clauses, paragraphs, or even entire documents that you use frequently. Creating new glossary items is quick and easy. Each saved item is called an *entry*. Collections of entries are called *glossaries* or *glossary files*. Glossary files are saved to disk. You can have different glossaries for different tasks, and switch between glossaries as necessary. It is also possible to *merge* entries from different glossary files.

Word's default glossary comes with a number of pre-defined *standard entries*. These let you quickly insert dates, times, author's names, and other useful variable information. For example, there is one standard glossary entry that will print the current date. Another automatically enters the author's name from the document's Summary Information record.

Finally, Microsoft has provided several *special-purpose glossaries* for things like page-layout projects or documents requiring complex math formulas.

DEFINING YOUR OWN GLOSSARY ENTRIES

To create glossary entries, simply select (highlight) the items in your document that you want to define as glossary entries, then call up the *Glossary dialog box*. Use either the *Glossary...* command from the *Edit* menu or the ⌘-K shortcut. Your screen will look something like Figure 28.1.

In this example, an entire letter closing has been selected. It contains several different paragraph formats, a severe left indent, and a scanned signature which has been previously pasted from the scrapbook using Word's graphics capabilities. All of these elements are one glossary entry that can be quickly recalled.

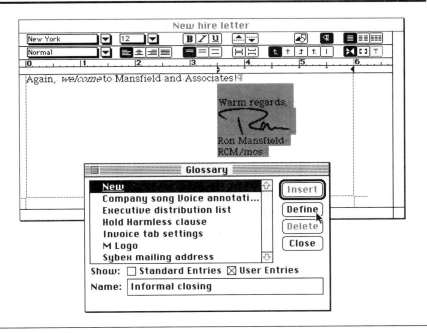

Figure 28.1

Define glossary entries by selecting items, then opening the Glossary dialog box (choose *Glossary...* from the *Edit* menu or press ⌘-K).

Type a meaningful name in the Name: box (*Informal closing* in the example), then click on the Define button to add the entry to your glossary. Then close the box.

Inserting Glossary Entries in Your Documents

Once an item is in your glossary, there are several ways to paste it into *any* document you are working on.

The obvious method is to place the insertion point where you want the glossary item to appear, then open the Glossary dialog box (*Glossary...* on the *Edit* menu). Highlight the entry of interest (scrolling first, if necessary) and click the Insert button.

The desired entry will appear at the insertion point in your document and the dialog box will vanish.

But there's a quicker way to insert entries from the Glossary dialog box. Once you have scrolled to locate the desired entry, *double-click* on the entry name, as shown in Figure 28.2. This will insert the entry and close the dialog box.

Figure 28.2
Double-click on an entry name to place it at your document's insertion point.

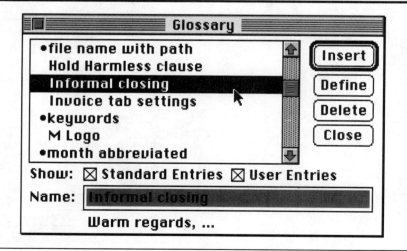

Glossaries

By the way, if you have chosen a text item, a portion of the first line text may appear at bottom of the Glossary dialog box when you select the entry. This often helps to remind you of what's contained in the entry. You can see an example of this in Figure 28.2. Graphics, sound, and other non-text entries are represented with small boxes.

Inserting Glossary Entries from the Keyboard

There are several time-saving keyboard tricks for inserting glossary entries. The first is similar to the one used to apply styles quickly. First, place the insertion point. Then press ⌘-Delete (or ⌘-Backspace). The information area at the bottom of your document window will ask for a glossary entry name. Type enough of the entry name to uniquely identify it and press Return. (In Figure 28.2 *inv* would be enough to describe *Invoice tab settings*, while *inf* would get you the informal closing. If you type an ambiguous abbreviation (*in*, for instance) Word will beep or bark or bleat at you. Try again and be more specific.

Assigning Keyboard Shortcuts to Glossary Entries

You can assign keyboard shortcuts for frequently used glossary items and insert glossary entries with a couple of keystrokes.

Open the Glossary dialog box. Hold down ⌘, Option, and the plus key on the *numeric* keypad (not on the main keyboard). The pointer will turn into a large ⌘ symbol. Click once on the name of the desired glossary entry (scroll to display it, if necessary). Word will ask you to demonstrate the shortcut-key combination. Use any previously unassigned key combination, or confirm the overwriting of an existing one. Then close the dialog box. (There's more information on assigning keystrokes in *Chapter 10*.)

Adding Glossary Entries to Work Menus

Frequently used glossary entries can be added to your *Work* menu. With the Glossary dialog box displayed, hold down ⌘, Option, and the plus on the *main* keyboard (not the numeric keypad). The pointer will turn into a large plus sign. Click on the name of the glossary entry you want added to the *Work* menu. Close the Glossary window. See *Chapter 10* for more about *Work* menus.

CHANGING AND DELETING GLOSSARY ENTRIES

To delete glossary entries, open the Glossary dialog box, highlight the undesirable entry, and click the Delete button. You will be asked to confirm.

To modify an entry, insert the item needing work into your document, make the necessary changes, and highlight it. Open the Glossary dialog box. Highlight the corresponding entry name. Click Define. Your modified entry will *replace* the old one.

WORD 5'S STANDARD GLOSSARY ENTRIES

Word comes equipped with nearly forty standard glossary entries. Word's Standard Entries all begin with a bullet (•). You cannot delete them, but you can hide them.

View standard entries by opening the Glossary dialog box and checking Show: *Standard Entries*, as illustrated in Figure 28.3. You can hide Standard Entries by unchecking the box or pressing ⌘-S, or hide your personal entries by unchecking *User Entries* or pressing ⌘-U. This makes it easier for you to find the type of entries you need. Note that ⌘-S won't save here because of its pre-assigned function.

Figure 28.3
Word's standard glossary entries all begin with bullets (•).

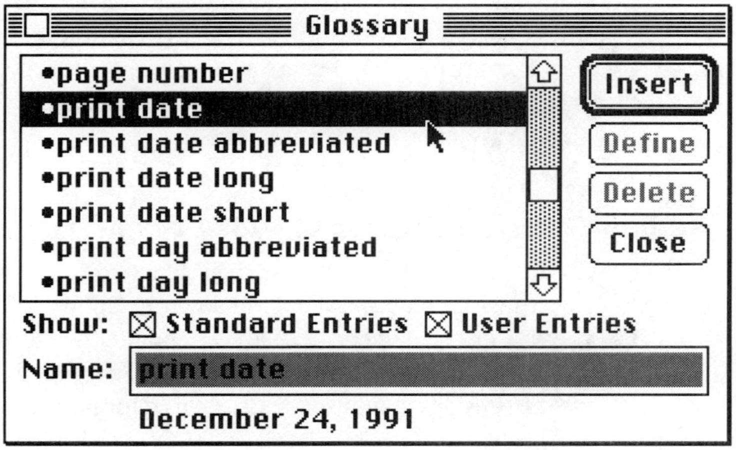

Many standard entries are self explanatory. You can often see what will be inserted by highlighting an item in the Glossary dialog box and looking at the example displayed near the bottom of the box.

Some standard entries are *date-* or *time-dependent*. For instance, in Figure 28.3 The •*print date* entry will cause the current date to print in your document, using the format shown. The date will change, depending on the date you *print* the document. In fact, all standard entries that begin with the word *print* instruct Word to check you Mac's internal clock and calendar each time a document is printed. The current date or time of printing will be inserted in your document wherever these glossary entries have been placed. Consider placing such entries in headers or footers, for instance.

Other standard entries get information from the Summary Information box you fill out when you first save a document. This is a handy way to insert things like the author's name, document-version information (draft, final, etc.), document title, and so on.

How and where glossary entries are stored

Word's default glossary is named *Standard Glossary*, and it is stored in a folder called *Glossaries*. Normally this folder is stored inside the folder containing Word 5 itself and it's a good idea to leave it there.

When you first make glossary changes, they are not immediately stored to disk. Custom entries reside in your computer's RAM only, until you save them to disk or abandon them. The changes will be available for every document you work on until you quit Word. When you quit Word, it will ask if you want to save the glossary changes, as illustrated in Figure 28.4.

Figure 28.4
When you quit Word, it will prompt you to save any changes to the glossary.

If you answer No, Word discards your changes. If you answer Yes, Word will propose saving the changes to the glossary you've been using. If you agree to save your changes there, you will be asked to confirm the replacement of old glossary information with the changes.

It is also permissible to specify a different file name and location for your new glossary. Use standard Macintosh file-saving techniques to accomplish this.

Simply closing a *document* will not start this process. You must either quit Word or ask Word to save glossary changes, which we will describe in a moment. If you have made significant changes to your glossary, you may wish to save them long before you quit Word. That way, if you experience a computer malfunction, you will not lose your glossary work.

Here's how: *First* display the Glossary dialog box. Then, visit the *File* menu on the Word menu bar (the ⌘-S shortcut will *not* work here). Choose *Save*. Instead of saving your Word document, you will be prompted to save your glossary.

You are not stuck with only one glossary; you can create additional glossaries of your own by simply saving them under different names. Open them using the techniques described next.

Special Purpose Glossaries

You or your associates can create your own special-purpose glossaries, as described above. Your copy of Word may also have been shipped with several special-purpose glossaries from Microsoft. One is used to insert desktop-publishing–page-layout entries like PostScript codes for crop marks, landscape mode, page numbers, and more. Another Microsoft glossary is useful when you create complex mathematical formulas. These special glossaries can usually be found in the Word 5 Glossaries folder. They are accompanied by Word files explaining their entries and uses.

Opening Special Purpose Glossaries

Switch to the desired glossary by choosing *Glossary...* from the *File* menu or pressing ⌘-K. This will bring up the Glossary dialog box. Next, chose *New*

(⌘-N) from the *File* menu. You will be asked if you want to remove all non-standard glossary entries. Click Yes. This removes the non-standard entries from the glossary list, but not from your standard glossary itself.

Next, locate the desired special glossary and double-click on its name or use the *File* menu's *Open* command. The selected special-purpose glossary will be added to the standard entries and will be available for your use.

You can also open a special glossary file by double-clicking on its icon. This will make it available for you to use during your Word session. If you make changes to a glossary opened this way, when you quit, Word will prompt you to save your changes. If you click Yes, a standard Save dialog box comes up, allowing you to save the glossary under its old name (thus replacing the old file) or under a new name (thus creating another special glossary). At this point, you could even save it as Standard Glossary, in which case, the file replaces your old Standard Glossary. Exercise caution if you wish to do this, though.

MERGING GLOSSARIES

This one's a piece of cake! To merge special entries with an existing glossary, simply open the existing glossary and then open the special glossary *without* removing the non-standard choice first.

If the two glossaries have entries with identical names, Word will use the entries from the second glossary you open.

GLOSSARY ENTRIES AND STYLES

Remember that *all* glossary entries are available, regardless of what document you are working on. Thus, glossary entries you've *created* in one document may use styles that do not exist in the document you are currently working on. When this happens, Word will add the necessary style to the current document's style sheet.

The usual cautions regarding different styles with the same name apply when you insert glossary entries containing style information. See *Chapter 17* for details.

Printing Glossary Entry Lists

It is possible to print glossary items by opening the Glossary dialog box and picking *Print* from the *File* menu. (⌘-P works here too). You will get a useful but not perfectly formatted collection of glossary entries. (Word prints everything using your default font).

CHAPTER 29

Stationery and Insert File...

FEATURING

- Ways to save time with reusable documents
- A new way to assemble documents from boilerplate
- Customizing Microsoft's stationery samples

Word 5 offers two simple but powerful new features that may forever change the way you work. The first gives you the ability to save Word documents as *stationery*. Think of this as a high-tech replacement for blank forms, letterhead paper, printed envelopes, and pre-printed memo stationery, among other things. Microsoft has even provided some samples to get you started.

The second feature—the *File...* command in the *Insert* menu lets you place the entire contents of documents directly into the document you are working on, without time-consuming cutting and pasting. It's the perfect way to assemble complex documents from *boilerplate* text.

WHY STATIONERY?

You've always been able to re-use word-processing documents by opening them, replacing old information with new, and then saving the work using a new file name. But as anyone who has done this will tell you, it is easy to forget to *rename* the new document before you save it. Generally this results in destroying your earlier work, since the new document overwrites the content of the old file. Not a pretty picture.

Word 5's stationery feature prevents this from happening. When you first create a letterhead, form, memo, or other file that you know you will want to use repeatedly, save it as stationery. When you open a document thus saved, you actually work on and save to a *copy* of the file, not the original file itself. Word 5's drawing tools and formatting features make it easy for you to create professional-looking letterheads, envelopes, newsletters, proposals, reports, and more. With the stationery feature, you can design these things once and re-use them without deleting old text or having to remember to change file names when you save.

Creating Stationery

You start by creating a new document including any necessary formats, styles, page-numbering choices, section decisions, graphics, and re-usable text. Before you start typing the main text, though (a letter on the new letterhead or stories in your newsletter design), save the *incomplete* work using Word's *Stationery* choice. It's found in the *Save File as Type* menu.

Figure 29.1 shows how to save files as stationery. Name the file, then before clicking *Save* or pressing Return, pick *Stationery* from the drop-down menu, available in both the *Save* and *Save As* (*Save...* and *Save As...* on the *File* menu) dialog boxes.

System 7 users will notice that stationery documents in Word act like System 7's *stationery pad items*; they even have the *Stationery pad* box checked when you do a *Get Info*.

Using Stationery

Documents saved as stationery have different icons from regular documents, making them easy to distinguish. The icons look like pads of paper with a corner turned up. In Figure 29.2 the icon on the left is stationery and the one the right is a letter created with the stationery.

Figure 29.1
Choose *Stationery* from Word's drop down *Save as File Type* menu.

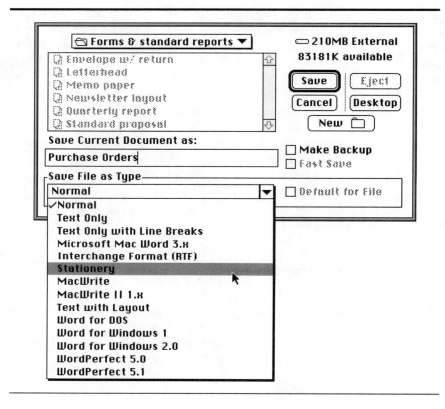

Figure 29.2
Stationery icons like the one on the left look like pads with a turned-up page.

To work with stationery, double-click on a stationery icon to open an un-named copy to work with, or use Word's Open dialog box.

To quickly spot stationery while in the Open dialog box (*Open...* from the *File* menu), pick *Stationery* from the *List Files of Type:* drop-down list, as shown in Figure 29.3. The scrollable file list will contain only stationery items and folders.

Incidentally, it is possible to put stationery documents on your *Work* menu. See *Chapter 10*. System 7 users can create *aliases* of stationery, as well.

Whichever way you open stationery, the file name for the new document will start out as *Untitled*. The first time you save a project started from stationery, Word will ask for a file name and summary information, just as if it were a new document you had created from scratch. The resulting file will be saved as a normal Word 5 file (*not* stationery), unless you instruct Word otherwise.

Modifying and Deleting Stationery

Delete stationery files as you would any other Macintosh files. They are not write-protected unless you protect them using your system features.

To *modify stationery*, open an untitled copy in the usual way. Make the desired changes and then use either the *Save...* or the *Save As...* command (both on the *File* menu). Choose *Stationery* from the drop-down *Save File as Type* menu. (This is very important.) Then, equally important, when asked for a file name enter the *exact same* file name you originally used for the stationery. You will be asked to confirm the replacement of the old stationery with the new. Click Replace to save your changes.

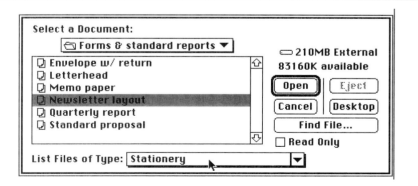

Figure 29.3
The Open dialog box can be restricted to showing only stationery.

Microsoft's Sample Stationery

Many of the sample documents provided with Word 5 were saved as stationery. Feel free to modify them for your own use and resave them as stationery. The documents can be found in the *Sample Documents* folder installed with Word 5. Look in the folder containing the Word program itself or search for *sample documents* using the *Find File...* feature, described in *Chapter 30*.

Combining Documents and Boilerplate with Insert File...

In the past, if you wanted to place the entire text of one document into another, you needed to open both documents, select all the text in one window, copy it to the Clipboard, then switch to the other window and paste it in.

Word's new *File...* feature in the *Insert* menu greatly simplifies this.

Place the insertion point where you want the contents of the file to appear. Then, pick *File...* from the *Insert* menu. You will see a standard Open dialog box. Find the file you want using the usual Macintosh folder-navigation techniques and click Open or hit Return. The entire contents of the chosen document will be inserted immediately.

Warning! The usual Word style and glossary merges occur as well. That is to say, any necessary new styles and glossary items will be added to the document receiving the insertion. This could lead to problems if there are duplicate style names.

This feature is perfect for attorneys and others needing to assemble documents from boilerplate text. Create separate files for each piece of boilerplate, then *Insert* away as needed.

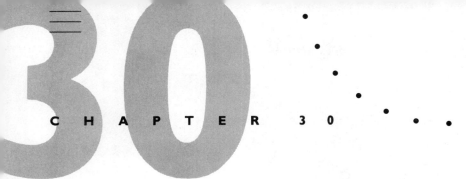

CHAPTER 30

Managing Your Files

FEATURING

- Ways to locate lost files
- Word's new Find File... command
- Managing files with Summary Info
- A review of paths

Your hard disk can contain hundreds or even thousands of files. If you work in a large, networked organization, you may have access to ten times this many documents. If you've ever misplaced a file, you know how frustrating and time-consuming trying to find it can be.

Word 5 provides two new features to help you organize and locate files. They are called *Find File...* and *Summary Info...*, both found on the *File* menu. For those of you new to the Mac, we'll start with a quick review of the concept of files and folders, and something related called a *path*.

FILES, FOLDERS, AND PATHS

Your Macintosh lets you arrange your files in a hierarchical structure. *Files* (Word documents, for instance) can be stored in *folders*. Folders can be also be stored within folders. Figure 30.1 shows an example of this.

Managing Your Files

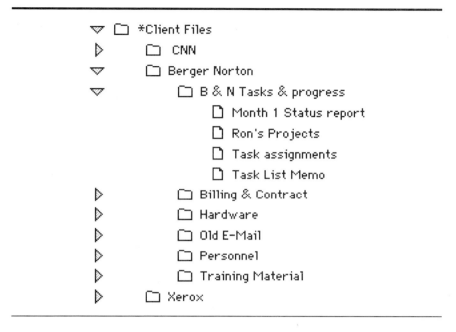

Figure 30.1
A hierarchical folder arrangement contains folders within folders.

In the example, there is a folder called *Client Files. It contains *all* of the client-related folders and files for this computer. Within the Client folder there are three client folders, one for each client (*CNN*, *Berger Norton*, and *Xerox*). Each of these client folders contains *additional* folders and files relating to the particular client. For instance, the Berger Norton folder contains the *B & N Tasks and progress* folder, in which project-related memos, lists, and reports are stored. The Berger Norton folder also contains other folders with billing and contract information, hardware information, etc. If you were to open the Xerox folder, you might find a similar arrangement of Xerox-specific files.

This hierarchy makes it easy to store and find things. It also provides good hiding places for lost files. For instance, you'd need to open three folders to find Ron's Projects file.

The steps that you take to find a file take you down a *path*. To get to Ron's Projects or the Task List Memo, for example, you would start by opening the hard disk containing the folders, then you would open the *Client Files folder. Next you would open the Berger Norton folder and *finally* the B & N Tasks &

progress folder. You can do this from the Finder by double-clicking on folders, or you can do it from within Word itself by using the *Open...* command on the *File* menu (⌘-O).

Word's Open Command

When you pick *Open...* from the *File* menu, you will be presented with a dialog box with the prompt *Select a Document*. It will look something like the one in Figure 30.2.

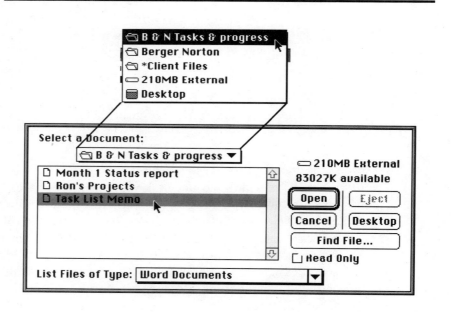

Figure 30.2
From the Open dialog box, use the drop-down menu to open the folder containing the document you need.

You "show" Word the path to your document by successively opening folders until the file that you desire is visible in the scrollable document list. To open folders, scroll through the drop-down list, picking folders to be opened. In cases where you have folders within folders, you will need to visit the drop-down list more than once.

Managing Your Files

If you open one folder too many, re-visit the list and choose the folder above the one you last opened.

When you see the file (the document) that you want to work with, double-click on the document name or just click on it and press Return. Your Macintosh manuals and Apple's disk-based tutorials contain more information on this subject and practice exercises if you need additional help. If you click *Read Only*, you will not be able to make any changes to the file; you will be asked to save any edits to a new file.

Notice that Word's Open dialog box has two devices you may not have seen in the Open dialog boxes of other Macintosh programs. The first is a drop-down menu titled *List Files of Type:*. This menu lets you restrict the *types* of files that you will see in the scrollable list. For instance, you can ask to see only stationery files, or only Word documents, or only MacWrite documents, and so on.

The second new choice in the Open dialog box is a button labeled Find File.... This takes you to a Word feature that helps find lost files and round up collections of files meeting specific criteria.

Find File...

Don't confuse Word 5's Find File... feature with the *Find File* desk accessory found on some *Apple* menus.

Word's *Find File...* (reached by choosing *Find File...* from the *File* menu) is a powerful tool that helps you locate, list, sort, examine, open, and print documents based on simple or complex search criteria. You can examine your Mac's hard disk(s) or even search a server or shared drive over a network. Both Word and non-Word files can be located by using this feature.

Suppose for instance, that you recall creating a list of projects for a client, but you don't remember where you saved the list. Find File... can help.

Start by choosing *Find File...* from the *File* menu or by clicking the Find File... button in Word's Open dialog box. You will see a Search dialog box that looks something like Figure 30.3.

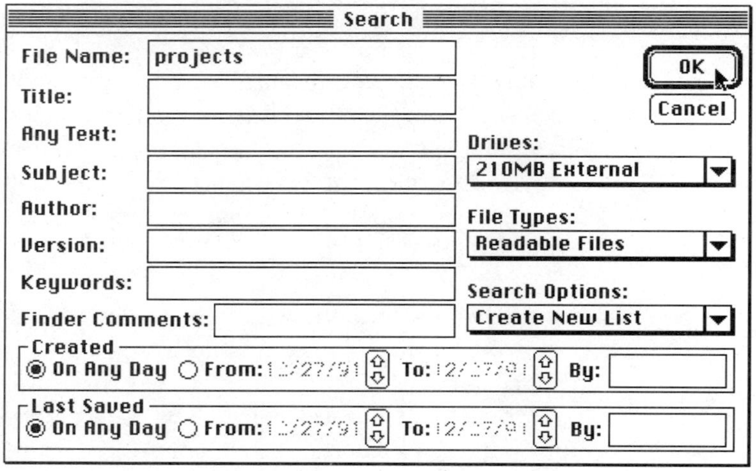

Figure 30.3
Don't confuse Word's Find File... feature with the Apple desk accessory of the same name. Word's Find File... does much more, including bringing up the Search dialog box.

This box gives you a number of places to type restrictive search criteria, an area to specify restrictive date and time ranges, plus three drop-down menus. As you may have gathered from Figure 30.3, Find File... lets you make *very* specific requests. Let's look at several examples.

Searching by File Names in Find File...

Continuing with the case of the missing project list, let's say you remember that the file name contained the word *projects*. Typing that word alone in the File Name: entry area of the Search dialog box and clicking OK or pressing Return will cause a rapid search of the disk specified in the *Drives:* drop-down menu (a drive called *210MB External* in Figure 30.3).

Soon you will see a new dialog box titled Find File, listing all of the files containing the word *projects*. As you can see from Figure 30.4, it's possible to learn a lot from this box.

In our example, three files have been found. By clicking on the name of a found file you can examine it more closely. The View drop-down menu lets you see the *contents* of the file or review its *statistics* (creator, creation date, size, etc.).

Managing Your Files

Figure 30.4
Find File creates a list of files meeting your search criteria.

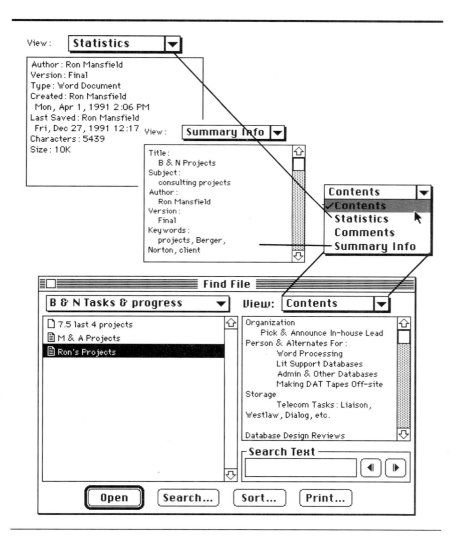

The window then displays available info. If you have entered summary information or added comments using your Mac's *Get Info* feature, you can read that information here as well.

Clicking the Open button at the bottom of the dialog box will open the document like usual. Clicking Search... will take you back to the Search dialog box

Print... opens the document and presents the Print dialog box. If you click on the folder name above the list of files, you can use the path menu to view additional files. The Sort... button is one of several devices designed to help you deal with long lists of documents meeting your criteria.

Dealing with Large Find File... Lists

Suppose we had found a *hundred* files containing the word *projects* in their names, rather than just four? You *could* click on each name in the scrollable list and manually examine the files. But there are quicker alternatives. The first is the Sort... button in the Find File dialog box. It brings up another dialog box like the one shown in Figure 30.5.

If you know the approximate time frame of a project, date sorts will help you narrow down the list to examine. If you knew this was a big document, a sort by file *size* might help, and so on. The sort feature also lets you place lists in

Figure 30.5
Find File's Sort... button lets you arrange long file lists by name, size, type, creation date, or last saved date.

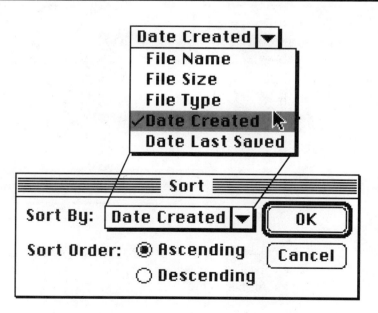

Managing Your Files

ascending or descending order. Click the appropriate radio button. When you are satisfied with your criteria, click OK or press Return.

Another alternative is to redo the search with more specific criteria. Clicking the Search... button will take you back to the Search dialog box, where you can add further restrictions by using the *File Types:* drop-down menu. For instance, you can list only files that contain specific words or phrases; or you can list just files of a specific type. If you've entered summary information, you can use it to restrict searches. Here's how.

Searching Inside Documents with Find File...

Searches on file names alone are the quickest, and are recommended as the starting point for searches of any but the smallest disk drives. But if you cannot find a file with a file-name search, or if you find too many files containing the search word, it is possible to ask Word to look *inside* each file on the disk being searched and list *only* those files containing the word or words meeting your criteria. Find File... searches entire Word documents, including headers, footers, and hidden text.

The criteria it uses is called *search text*. You enter it in the Any Text: box in the Search dialog box. When specifying search text you need to use the same care that you use with Word's *Find...* and *Replace...* commands. If you are too specific, you may miss the file you are looking for. Use too vague a search string, and you will get excessively long file lists.

Suppose, for instance you want to round up everything you've written about DAT (Digital Audio Tape). If you use *DAT* as your search text, Word will also list files containing the words *database*, *date*, and *Datsun*. This example illustrates a subtle point about search text: casing is irrelevant. Placing a space after *DAT* in the search string solves the problem.

The wildcards you read about in *Chapter 26* work here, but you will need to type them from the keyboard. For example, *Sm?th* will find both *Smith* and *Smyth*.

Once you've entered search criteria in the Any Text: section of the Search dialog box and started the search by clicking OK or pressing Return, Word will start examining the contents of your disk. This can take a while. To cancel the search use the ⌘-. (period) shortcut.

Eventually a Find File window will appear. Select the file of interest. Then, use the Search Text arrow buttons shown in Figure 30.6. Word will display and highlight each occurrence of the specified text in the view area.

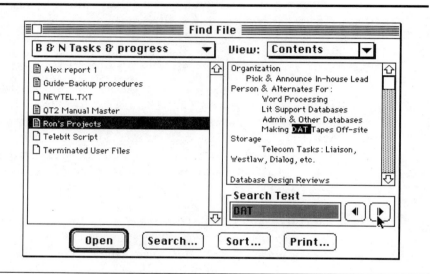

Figure 30.6
The Search Text arrow buttons let you find each occurrence of specific text within a document. This feature works regardless of how you find files.

Incidentally, the Search Text arrow buttons work regardless of how you find files. You need not first specify text in the Any Text: portion of the Search dialog box. Simply type in any text string you want to search for and press the searching arrows.

Using Find File... with Summary Info...

If you and your colleagues have been religious about entering *consistent* summary information, you can use the Find File... feature to search on those summary-info entries. That's the purpose of the Title:, Subject:, Author:, Version:, and Keywords: entries in the Search dialog box.

Just remember that if you've created documents and failed to put your name in the author box when creating summary info, or if you sometimes type your whole name and other times use your initials, you run the risk of *missing* documents when your Find File... search criteria include summary info search restrictions.

Naturally, documents created with other programs (like Word 4) that do not collect summary info will be ignored as well.

Multiple Searches

There are times when you will want to do *multiple searches*. For instance, in our earlier example, you may discover that sometimes you referred to DAT in documents by the complete name and not the acronym. You'd need to search once for *DAT* and a second time for *Digital Audio Tape* to find each relevant document. If you use multiple disk drives, you will need to perform multiple searches.

Combining Searches

The classic combined search works like this. Search for the first criterion of interest (Any Text: = *DAT* for instance). Review the list in the Find File window.

Then click Search... to return to the Search dialog box. Pull down the *Search Options:* menu near the lower-right corner of the dialog box. Choose *Add Matches to List*. Change the search criteria (to *Digital Audio Tape*, for example). Then run the new search. The resulting list will contain documents meeting either criteria.

You can combine the results of different types of searches. For example, you can search first by file name, then by author, and so on.

Searching Multiple Disks

If you have more than one disk drive on your computer, or if you want to search both your computer's disk and other drives on a network, you must do multiple searches. The results of the searches can be combined using the techniques discussed in *Combining Searches* to give you one list for all drives. Here's how that works.

Search your first drive. Re-visit the Search dialog box and pick a new drive from the *Drives:* list. Be sure to change the *Search Options:* choice to *Add Matches to List*. Run a new search on the second drive. Repeat as needed until all drives have been searched.

Using Multiple Searches to Restrict Lists

So far, you've seen multiple searches used to make lists longer. It is possible to use the *Search Only In List* on the *Search Options:* menu to make lists *shorter*.

Do your search, then click Search... to return to the Search dialog box. Pick *Search Only In List* from the *Search Options:* menu.

The next time you search, Word will only examine files listed in the previous search list. It is a way to narrow down your search without time-consuming trips through irrelevant files and folders.

DELETING FILES FROM WITHIN WORD

Here's a worthwhile addition to your Word menu. Add the Delete... command by visiting the *Commands...* command in the *Tools* menu (⌘-Shift-Option-C). (See *Chapter 10* if you've forgotten how to add menu items.)

The Delete... command lets you delete unwanted documents without returning to the Finder, as shown in Figure 30.7

Important Tip: both Yes and No eventually return you to the Delete dialog box, so be careful; this is an easy way to accidentally delete files!

Managing Your Files

Figure 30.7
Delete... is a useful file management tool. Add it to your Word *file* menu with the *Commands...* command.

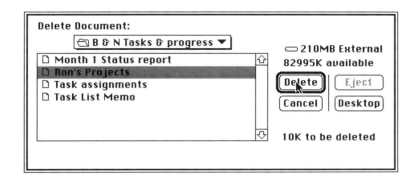

PART V

WORKING WITH GRAPHICS

Regardless of what you do these days, there's competition. We are all *so* bombarded with printed words that, like it or not, we are drawn to attractive presentations. Documents containing graphics not only get your point across more effectively, they get *read*.

Your Macintosh is well equipped to create attention-getting graphic images. If you are not an artist, you can purchase Word-compatible, low cost, disk-resident clip art from many sources.

This section will show you how Word and your Mac can put *punch* in your presentations. Even if you are not in marketing, you need to make yourself visible. Ask any successful middle manager, student, lobbyist, or minister. Here's how to go about it.

CHAPTER 31

Positioning Graphics

FEATURING

- Ways to position graphics, text, and other objects
- Word 5's replacement for the *Position* command

Word makes it easy to position graphics and text just about anywhere in your documents. A new device called a *frame* gives you impressive control over *where* objects are placed and how much white space surrounds them. Since frames can also contain text, they are ideal tools for placing text in unusual places like the margins of your documents or in the middle of other text. Users of earlier Word versions may remember the *Position* command. *Frame...* is the '90s replacement for that sometimes awkward feature.

Many items can be positioned with the techniques described here, including text, artwork, equations from the Equation Editor, tables, spreadsheets, and charts from spreadsheet packages.

It is worth noting that the command *Frame...* appears on *two* Word 5 menus, *Insert* and *Format*. The two choices do very different things, as you will soon see.

Positioning Graphics

THE EASY WAY

Whether you create a graphic with Word's *Picture...* command or paste something from your Clipboard, Word places it in a rectangular, non-printing box called a *picture frame*. Figure 31.1 shows a small picture frame containing a scanned signature.

The size of a picture frame is determined by the size of your graphic and other decisions you make. For instance, you can drag any of the small frame handles to increase the white space around the graphic.

Notice the paragraph mark at the right edge of the frame. Framed objects can often be treated like text paragraphs. For example, paragraph features like borders work with frames. You'll see an example of this in a moment.

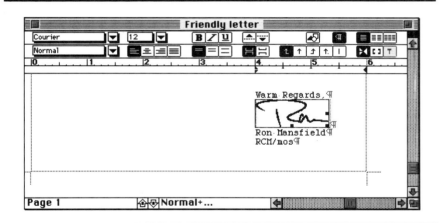

Figure 31.1
The scanned signature has been pasted into Word. It is automatically surrounded by a *picture frame*.

In Figure 31.1, the signature frame is indented just like the text above and below it. Paragraph positioning techniques (like center, align left, etc.) work just fine with framed objects. But to really take control of paragraph positioning, you'll want to use Word's *Frame...* commands on the *Insert* and *Format* menus.

Frame... on the Insert Menu

Word lets you drag frames just about anywhere in your document and, if you leave enough room, will flow text around framed objects. You *do* the actual dragging in Print Preview. But *first*, you *must* select the object you wish to move and use the *Frame...* command on the *Insert* menu. Suppose, for instance, that you wanted to drag the framed graphic in Figure 31.2.

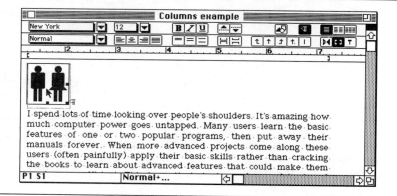

Figure 31.2
Select a framed object then choose *Frame...* from the *Insert* menu. Word will switch to Print Preview and let you drag the framed object into its new position.

Click once on the framed object to select it. You'll see the three handles used for resizing the frame. With the graphic selected, choose the *Frame...* command from the *Insert* menu. (Don't confuse this with the identically named command on the *Format* menu!) Word will place the object in a frame.

Word will automatically switch to Print Preview, where you will be able to drag your object just about anywhere, including into the margins. Point to the graphic and drag an outline of it, as shown in Figure 31.3. The top of your screen will display statistics indicating the distance from the left edge of your frame to the left edge of the page. A similar statistic is provided for the top of the frame and page.

When you release the mouse button, Word will move text as required, then recompute all of the line and page endings necessary to accommodate the new graphic position. Eventually, it will redraw the page with your graphic in place. Be patient. This is no small task.

Figure 31.3
Drag the outline to reposition your graphic.

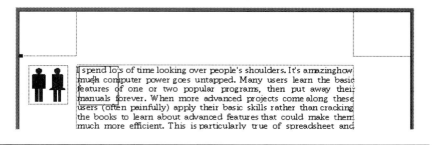

THE FRAME DIALOG BOX

While the dragging process just described is fine for most uses, it is possible to be much more precise by using the Frame dialog box, reached with the *Frame...* command on the *Format* menu (*not* the *Insert* menu). The example in Figure 31.4 was created by selecting the graphic, choosing *Frame...* from the *Insert* menu, and then using the Horizontal and Vertical positioning menus to center the graphic on the page. (It would also have been possible to type specific measurements into these boxes, instead.) Click on OK.

This dialog box also lets you specify how *wide* the frame will be and lets you force exact distances between the frame and surrounding text.

Using the Frame dialog box, you can specify positions relative to columns, pages, or margins, thanks to drop-down menus. Incidentally, the double border around the graphic in Figure 31.4 was created using Word's Paragraph Border feature. Clicking Position takes you to Print Preview. Unframe removes the frame.

FRAME POSITIONS AS STYLES

The positioning information you create when you position frames is stored with the paragraph mark following the graphic. Positioning information like this can be defined as a *style* and used over and over with different graphics!

For instance, you could select the graphic in Figure 31.4 and define a new style called *Center Frame in Page* or whatever. Then the next time you wanted to

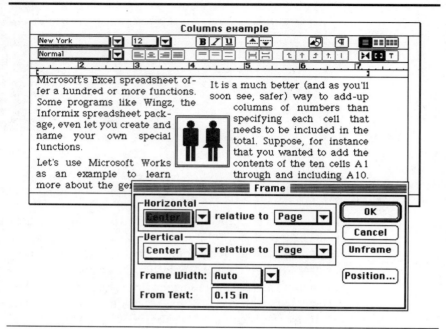

Figure 31.4
The Frame dialog box (reached by choosing *Frame*... on the *Format* menu) lets you specify precise positions, frame widths, and white space.

center a graphic in a page, you would select the graphic and apply the style. Quicker than you could say "Bill Gates has a nice house," Word would position the graphic in the center of the page.

DELETING FRAMED OBJECTS

To delete a framed object, you need to delete the object and the frame itself. Select them one at a time and press delete.

REPEATING FRAMED OBJECTS ON MULTIPLE PAGES

If you want a logo or other framed object to appear on every page of your document (or within a section), place the *frame* in a header or footer. Position the *object* wherever you want it either by dragging in Print Preview or by using the Frame dialog box, reached by choosing *Frame*... from the *Format* menu. Figure 31.5 shows an example of this.

Figure 31.5
Place the frame in a header or footer then position the object anywhere you want. It will print on all pages.

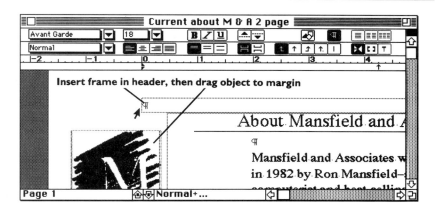

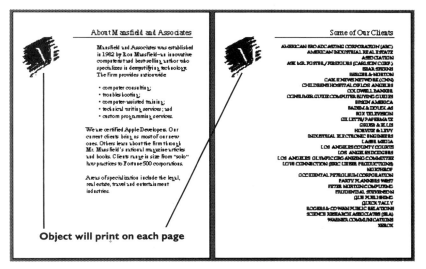

To position objects properly on mirrored pages, use the Frame dialog box to specify the object's *horizontal* position as *Outside* (or *Inside*) relative to the *Page*.

FRAMED OBJECTS IN VIEWS

Work in Normal view when you don't need to see framed objects in their correct positions. Use Page Layout view or Print Preview to see objects in position.

You can drag frames around in Print Preview and edit their contents in Page Layout view.

When you have toggled ¶ on in Normal view, a small box appears at the left of framed objects, indicating that they have formatting information that may not be apparent until you switch to Page Layout view or Print Preview.

CHAPTER 32

Importing Graphics

FEATURING

- Formats that Word 5 supports
- Ways to import clip art, scanned images, and more

Word's built-in drawing capabilities make it easy for you to draw your own illustrations, logos, and the like. But what if you want to use commercially prepared clip art, or scanned copies of your company logo, or photos from a video-capture device? Images like these are stored in files on disks. They can be moved from one program to another via your clipboard. Word 5 can accommodate images from many sources. Here are just a few of the graphic formats supported by Word 5:

- PICT and PICT2 (drawing programs)
- Bitmap files (paint programs and scanners)
- EPS (Encapsulated PostScript) files
- TIFF files

Importing Graphics

Types of Graphics

Whole books have been written about the various graphic standards now supported by computer makers. The nice thing about standards is that there are *so many of them*. With apologies to the technically inclined, here is a *brief* overview of the kinds of graphics files Word 5 can import. The general advice is to try loading any graphic file that interests you. Word will tell you if it cannot convert it. It is a good idea to *save your work* before experimenting with graphic importing, since memory problems and other gremlins can occasionally lock up your machine when unusual graphic files are encountered.

Bitmap

The original Mac standard—*bitmap* images—is found everywhere. Paint programs like MacPaint create them. Programs like SuperPaint create bitmap images in their paint layers.

Scanners create bitmap images. Shareware companies and users groups distribute disks containing all manner of bitmap graphics from pictures of farm animals to things that would make a sailor blush. Mail-order catalogs runneth over with them. Bitmap pictures are made up of tiny dots. Word supports 8-bit images and can convert others (24-bit, 32-bit, etc.) to 8-bit.

PICT

PICT and *PICT2* files are Apple-standard files created by drawing programs like MacDraw and in the draw layers of programs like SuperPaint.

TIFF

There are many variations on the *TIFF* format. Word supports many but not all of the growing number of TIFF variants. Screen-capture programs and video boards often create TIFF files. Some TIFF formats include file compression techniques that may not be compatible with Word. Word converts these to the PICT format.

PostScript (EPS)

PostScript graphic files are created by programs like Adobe Illustrator and Aldus FreeHand. Most of these images consist of two parts—the PICT file you see on-screen and the embedded PostScript file sent to your printer. Word can use both. There is even a PostScript style choice in Word, useful for inserting PostScript printing files into your Word documents. Be aware, though, that PostScript files can get pretty big.

IMPORTING WITH PICTURE...

Start by positioning the insertion point where you want to place the graphic. The *Picture...* command (located on the *Insert* menu) reveals a dialog box like the one in Figure 32.1. Use it to locate and insert graphics files.

Figure 32.1
The *Pictures...* command lets you load graphic files from disk and place them at the insertion point in your document.

Scroll if necessary to select the graphic of interest, then double-click on the file name or click once on it and then click on the Insert button. A copy of the graphic will be placed at the insertion point.

If a newly inserted graphic image seems cut off or incomplete, it's because the box in the document is smaller than the actual graphic. To see the entire graphic, select it and visit the Paragraph dialog box. Choose *Auto* from the drop-down *Line:* menu.

Importing with Your Clipboard

If you can get a graphic to your Clipboard, Word 5 can probably display and print it. This is a great way to move things if you have System 7 or MultiFinder and enough RAM to run Word and your graphics program simultaneously.

Importing PostScript Images

Many programs like Adobe Illustrator let you copy both PICT and embedded PostScript to the Clipboard simultaneously. Generally, this is done by holding down the Option key when copying. See the manuals that came with your graphics programs for details.

When you insert files like these, you get both screen and printer versions (PICT and EPS).

PART VI

POWER TOOLS

Anyone who has chopped a cord of firewood with a hand ax will tell you that a chainsaw can be a welcome, albeit noisy timesaver. You'll feel the same way about the Word 5 features described in this section.

Word's impressive spell checker will save you countless trips to that old Funk and Wagnell. The thesaurus will impress (and dazzle *and* affect *and* stir *and* persuade...) you. Word will help you grapple with your grammar and writing style. Its legendary table features are now more powerful than ever. Word can help you sort things out, organize your thoughts, check your math, create a table of contents, generate an index, and slice tomatoes. (Just kidding about the *last* one.)

Finally, this section will introduce you to the art and science of the print merge—a technique for creating personalized bulk mail and much more. Read about Word 5's power tools, warts and all, here in Part Six.

CHAPTER 33

Checking Spelling and Counting Words

FEATURING

- Word 5's much improved spell checker
- How to customize the spelling dictionary
- Word's *Word Count...* command

W ord 5 provides a powerful *spell checker* that lets you check an entire document, including headers, footers, and hidden text. You can also use the feature to check a single word. Unlike the printed dictionary on your desk, Word's checker does *not* contain definitions. It does not consider words in context. While it knows that *two*, *too*, and *to* are all proper spellings, it cannot warn you of their improper use. For instance, Word's spell checker would not object to the sentence *She went two the bank too get a to dollar bill.*

What it can do is offer suggested spellings with uncanny accuracy. Misspellings are usually replaced with just a mouse click or two. You can add and edit your own *custom dictionaries*, which might contain proper nouns, technical terms, and other specialized words or numbers. You'll learn how to use all of these features in this chapter.

We'll also explore the *Word Count...* command. It's a way for authors to quickly determine the number of characters, words, lines, and paragraphs in documents and footnotes.

CHECKING SPELLING

Start the spell checker with the ⌘-L shortcut or by picking *Spelling...* from the *Tools* menu (F15 on extended keyboards). A dialog box appears like the one in Figure 33.1.

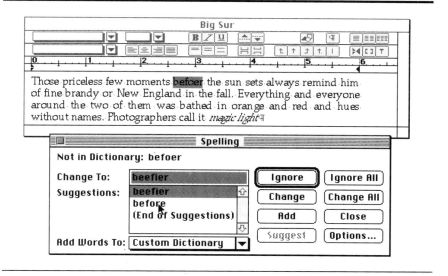

Figure 33.1
The spell checker lets you pick suggested replacement words, type your own corrections, ignore unrecognized words, or add them to custom dictionaries.

Unless you've selected only a portion of your document to check, Word scans down, beginning at the insertion point, and will ask if you want to go back to the top of the document to continue checking, if necessary.

It looks for words that it cannot find in its open dictionaries. When it spots a word in your text that it can't match, Word highlights the questionable characters, scrolls the document so that you can see the problem word in context, and offers you a number of choices.

Typing Your Own Changes

If you want to change the word only once, you can *type* a replacement in the highlighted Change To: box and press Return or click the Change button. Word will replace the problem text with the new text you have typed in the Change To: box and then continue spell checking. To change the word throughout the document that you are checking, click Change All instead of pressing Return or clicking Change. (If the new word you've typed is something you want Word to recognize in *all* of your documents, see *Custom Dictionaries* later in this chapter.)

Word's Suggested Changes

If you have suggestions enabled (check the *Always Suggest* choice in the Spelling category of the Preferences dialog box), Word will usually list one or more possible spellings, placing what it thinks is the best guess in the Change To: box. (If the default is *not* enabled, you can always ask for suggestions by clicking Suggest.) Other suggestions, if any, will be listed in the scrollable Suggestions: box. This may take a moment. You'll know Word is finished looking for alternative suggestions when you see either *(End of Suggestions)* or *(No Suggestions)* in the Suggestions: list.

If you agree with Word's best guess, simply click the Change button to change this occurrence or use the Change All button to change this and all succeeding occurrences of the word. The spell checker will replace the word and continue examining your document.

Word's best guess is usually but not always right, as you can see in Figure 33.1. If one of the alternative suggestions is correct (the word *before* in Figure 33.1), simply double-click on the desired word to replace the misspelled word, or click once on the desired word in the list to move it to the Change To: box, *then* click the Change or Change All button as necessary.

Overruling Suggestions

Sometimes Word won't make correct suggestions, or you might want to correct the problem yourself without retyping the entire word or phrase. For instance, Word may spot two run-together words like the ones shown in Figure 33.2.

Figure 33.2
Problem text can be moved to the Change To: box for editing without retyping it.

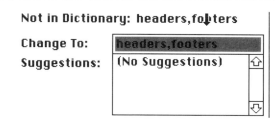

When it has no suggestions, Word moves the problem text to the Change To: box where you can edit it yourself. You can force the problem text to move down sooner by pointing at it with your mouse. The pointer will turn into the arrow you see in Figure 33.2. Click once, and the text will move down for editing.

Ignoring Words Flagged by the Checker

Sometimes Word will spot a word that is properly spelled but that isn't in its open dictionaries. Proper nouns, technical jargon, and typesetting codes are examples.

If you want Word to *ignore* the text only once, click the Ignore button. Word will leave the word or other text string as you typed it and continue spell checking. To ignore the word throughout the document you are checking, click Ignore All. (If the word is something you want to ignore in *all* of your documents, you may want to add it to a custom dictionary.)

CUSTOM (A/K/A USER) DICTIONARIES

Most of the words used by the spell checker are located in a dictionary that comes with your Word program. In the U.S., Word is shipped with a dictionary called U.S. English Dictionary. It is kept in the Commands folder. You cannot make changes to this dictionary.

It is possible, however, to maintain one or more of your own dictionaries. In Word 4 these were called *User Dictionaries*. In Word 5 they are called *Custom Dictionaries*. Word checks only open dictionaries. The more dictionaries you have open, the slower spell checking will be.

The Standard Custom Dictionary

When you install Word, the installation program places an empty Custom Dictionary in your Commands folder. The default name for the dictionary is *Custom Dictionary*. It is opened and used whenever you spell check, unless you instruct Word otherwise. This is where you will want to keep most proper nouns, trademark names, etc.

Word will place things in the Custom Dictionary whenever you click the Add button while spell checking. (The first time you add a word, you will be asked to create a custom dictionary.) You can overrule this default use of the Custom Dictionary by using the drop down Add Words To: list to specify a different dictionary.

Custom dictionaries handle capitalization as follows. If you add a word to a dictionary as all lowercase, it will be *recognized* later, regardless of whether it is typed as all lowercase, all uppercase, or with a beginning capital letter. If you enter a word with only the first letter capitalized, Word will recognize the word when it later appears in all caps or with a leading cap, but will question the word if it is all lowercase. Unusual capitalizations like *VisiCalc* will be questioned unless they are stored in the dictionary the way they should appear in the text being checked.

Creating Additional Custom Dictionaries

If you work on unusual projects that involve technical jargon, typesetting codes, etc., you might want to create one or more additional, specially named custom dictionaries, which you can turn on or off in the Spelling category of the Preferences dialog box.

To create a new custom dictionary, visit the Spelling category of the Preferences dialog box. Do this either by choosing *Preferences*... from the *Tools* menu or by clicking the Options... button in the Spelling dialog box. Figure 33.3 shows the Spelling category.

Click New... to create a new dictionary. You will be prompted for a dictionary name. In Figure 33.3 A new dictionary called *Sybex Typeset Codes* has been added.

Figure 33.3

Reach the spelling preferences category either from the *Tools* menu or by clicking the Options... button in the Spelling dialog box.

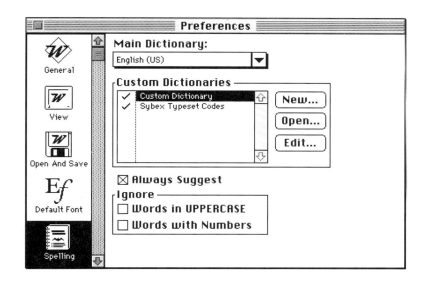

Opening and Closing Custom Dictionaries

To make a dictionary available to the spell checker, it must be open. The checkmarks next to both custom dictionaries in Figure 33.3 indicate that both are open and available for the spell checker to use. Click in the area next to the desired dictionary to open or close it. A checkmark means it's open.

To open dictionaries that are not in the folder containing the main dictionary, click the Open... button. Show Word where the desired dictionary is by using standard Macintosh folder-navigation techniques.

Editing Custom Dictionaries

To add items to a custom dictionary, click Add when the spell checker encounters a word of interest, or type a Word document containing all of the words you want to add. Spell check the document, adding each unrecognized word.

If you accidentally add a word to a custom dictionary, it is a good idea to delete it, since extra words mean more searching time during your spell checks.

Removing words from a custom dictionary is slightly more involved than adding them. Choose the dictionary you wish to edit from the Spelling category of the Preferences dialog box. Then click the Edit... button. A dialog box will appear, listing all the words in the selected dictionary, as shown in Figure 33.4. Click any words you want to delete and then click the Delete button. When you are finished, click OK.

THE WORD COUNT COMMAND

The *Word Count...* command is found in the *Tools* menu. If you have an extended keyboard, the keyboard shortcut is Option-F15. Click Count in the Word Count dialog box to start the process. Figure 33.5 shows typical results.

Figure 33.4
You remove words from a custom dictionary by clicking Edit... in the Spelling category of the Preferences dialog box and then deleting the unwanted words.

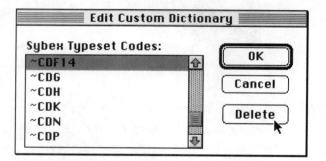

Figure 33.5
The Word Count feature also counts characters, lines, paragraphs, and words, both in the main text and in footnotes.

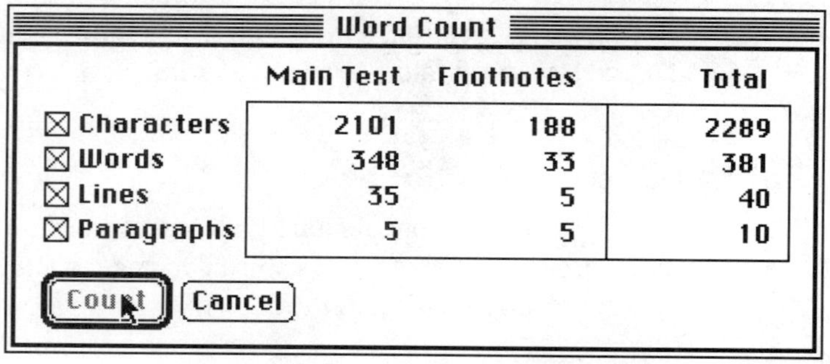

The command will scan an entire document or just text you've selected. It can count characters, lines, paragraphs, and footnote text. It does *not* count words in headers and footers. Clicking the Cancel button closes the dialog box. Click on any of the Count checkboxes to disable counting of its feature.

CHAPTER 34

The Grammar Checker

FEATURING

- Word's grammar and style checker
- How to turn off grammar and style rules

W ord's *Grammar...* command can help you spot many common writing errors. It evaluates *style* and points out many, but not all *grammatical errors*. It can often suggest changes, and even make some of them for you. Word uses two collections of *rules* when analyzing your documents. You can turn off specific rules that annoy you or cramp your style. Word will explain and demonstrate the rules for you. *Statistics* and *readability indexes* are created at the end of a grammar checking session. These help you determine if the writing style is appropriate for your audience.

Since the grammar checker needs to work with properly spelled documents, it sometimes activates Word's spell checker when it encounters unfamiliar words.

The Grammar Checker

Word's grammar checker is not a complete replacement for a human editor. For instance, it will not catch things like missing periods at the end of sentences or double spaces between words.

The fact that Word considers parts of speech when checking grammar might make you believe that it "understands" what you've written. This is not the case. For instance, the nonsense phrase *Eye sea sum tins knot write hear* passes the grammar check successfully.

None the less (oops, Word prefers *Nonetheless*), nonetheless, the checker will help you spot many common problems, and can help you polish your style.

The *Grammar...* command requires as much as 1 Mb of RAM over and above the RAM normally used by Word. You may not be able to run it on a 2 Mb Mac using System 7.

Checking Grammar and Style

You will want to *save* your document just prior to grammar checking, or run the check on a *copy* of your masterpiece. While grammar and style changes are often reversible with *Undo,* this is not *always* the case.

To check grammar and style, choose *Grammar...* from the *Tools* menu or use the ⌘-Shift-G keyboard shortcut. Unless you select a portion of your document, Word will attempt to check the whole thing.

Working from the insertion point, Word will highlight a portion of your prose (usually a sentence) and evaluate it. There may be a slight delay. If Word spots questionable spellings, you will be provided the opportunity to correct them or tell Word to ignore them, using the techniques you learned in *Chapter 33*. Once spelling issues have been dealt with, Word will use its Grammar dialog box to point out questionable style and grammar issues. The text being considered is listed in the scrolling Sentence: box. Suggestions and observations are made in the scrolling Suggestions: box. For example, in Figure 34.1 the grammar checker finds the ramblings of a few old politicians a tad wordy.

Figure 34.1
Word finds this document wordy.

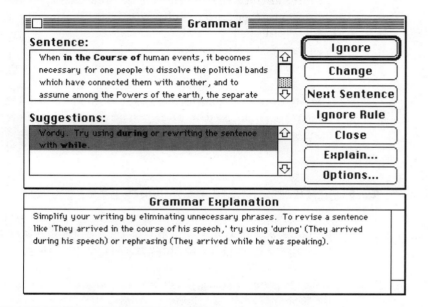

To get clarification of the rule or style suggestion Word is offering, click the Explain... button. A new window, called Grammar Explanations, will open with additional information, as shown in Figure 34.1.

Accepting Word's Automatic Grammar Suggestions

In Figure 34.1, Word is suggesting *during* as a replacement for the phrase *in the course of human events*. Here you can rewrite history with a few mouse clicks, because, when Word makes specific suggestions like this, you can double-click on its suggestion or click the Change button to apply the change. In the example in Figure 34.1, pointing to *during* and double-clicking would change the first sentence to read *When during human events....*

Before making changes like these, it is possible to try them out by just pointing to the suggestion of interest in the Suggestions: box. As you move the mouse into the Suggestions: box, the pointer turns into a hand. Use the hand to point to the suggestion you want to preview and hold down the mouse button (but don't double-click yet). The Sentence: box above will temporarily change to illustrate the effect of the suggested change. When Word is unable to make changes by itself, the Sentence: box will display the phrase *No correction available*. In either case, releasing the mouse button returns the prose in the Sentence: box to its original state, and does not modify your document.

Making Manual Changes

Many of the problems the checker spots need your intervention. To make *manual* changes, you'll need leave the grammar checker temporarily. To do this, click in your document window to activate it, then use the usual word-processing techniques to fix your work. Return to the grammar checker either by clicking on it's window or by using the menu or keyboard shortcuts. The grammar checker will pick up at the sentence nearest the insertion point.

Incidentally, leaving the Grammar dialog box and making typing changes this way *resets* the Undo feature. Suppose you've made ten or twenty changes based on Word's automatic suggestions and then left the Grammar dialog box to type a manual change in the document window. You would no longer be able to undo the changes you have made from within the Grammar dialog box, since the Undo menu would read *Undo Typing* rather than *Undo Grammar*. This dilemma often arises with the *Grammar...* command, since you frequently need to stop and restart it. That's the reason it is advisable to work on a *copy* of important documents.

Ignoring Suggestions

The Ignore button in the Grammar dialog box instructs Word to ignore the current occurrence of a problem; but will not prevent the grammar checker from pointing out similar problems in the future.

You can skip to the next sentence without making changes to the current one by clicking on the Next Sentence button.

Clicking Ignore Rule in the Grammar dialog box tells Word to stop using the current rule with the current document. For example, to stop reminders about passive voice, click the Ignore Rule button the first time Word points out a passive construction. To turn off passive-voice checking for all your projects, turn off the rule (called *Passive Verbs Usage*) in the Grammar category of the Preferences dialog box, as described next.

CHANGING PREFERENCES

You can turn rules on and off from the Preferences dialog box. Reach it via the *Preferences...* command in the *Tools* menu or simply click on the Options... button in the Grammar dialog box. Your screen will look like Figure 34.2, although your Grammar Explanations window may not be open.

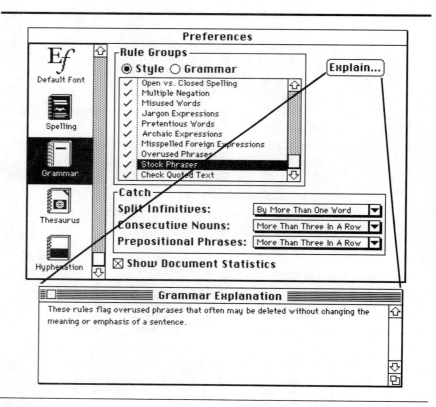

Figure 34.2
Reach the Grammar category of the Preferences dialog box from the *Tools* menu or by clicking Options... in the Grammar window.

The Grammar Checker

Here you can fine-tune Word's grammar pickiness. Rules are listed in two categories—Style and Grammar. Pick a list to scroll by clicking on the appropriate button. Checkmarks next to a rule mean the rule will be enforced. Clicking near a checkmark toggles it on and off. For more information about a rule, highlight it and click on the Explain... button.

The Catch area of the dialog box contains three drop-down menus that help you specify where Word should draw the line on things like split infinitives and consecutive nouns. An *X* in the *Show Document Statistics* box enables the document statistics feature, described next.

Document Statistics

There are liars, damned liars, and statistics. Word can provide the latter, as illustrated in Figure 34.3. Document statistics appear after the grammar checker has finished scanning your document.

The grammar feature will count words, paragraphs, and sentences, then *average* them to give you the average number of characters-per-word and similar trivia.

Several readability statistics are computed, including a count of passive sentences, two Flesch indexes, the Flesch-Kincaid index, and a Gunning Fog Index.

Use Table 34.1 to decode the Flesch findings.

TABLE 34.1	Reading Ease	Grade Level	Reading Ease
Flesch Index Levels	90–100	4	Very easy
	80–90	5	Easy
	70–80	6	Fairly easy
	60–70	7–8	Standard
	50–60	Some secondary school	Fairly difficult
	30–50	Secondary school, some higher education	Difficult
	0–30	Higher education	Totally gnarly

Figure 34.3
Word can try to quantify your writing style.

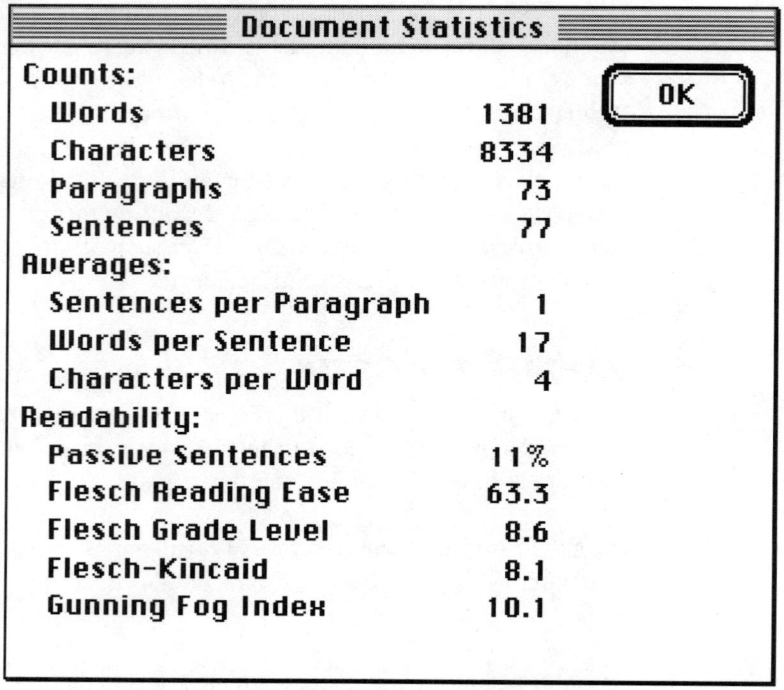

```
========== Document Statistics ==========
Counts:
    Words                           1381          [ OK ]
    Characters                      8334
    Paragraphs                        73
    Sentences                         77
Averages:
    Sentences per Paragraph            1
    Words per Sentence                17
    Characters per Word                4
Readability:
    Passive Sentences                11%
    Flesch Reading Ease             63.3
    Flesch Grade Level               8.6
    Flesch-Kincaid                   8.1
    Gunning Fog Index               10.1
```

The Flesch-Kincaid index assigns a (US public school) grade level. Gunning Fog assumes that long sentences are hard to understand, as are multisyllabic words. The higher the index, the tougher the reading.

Imagine how much better Shakespeare might have been, given tools like these...

CHAPTER 35

The Thesaurus

FEATURING

- Finding just the right word
- Locating antonyms
- Spelling help from the thesaurus

English is a rich language. There are many ways to say the same thing, yet we all tend to use a few words and phrases repeatedly. Word's *thesaurus* can help you add interest and texture to your prose. It gives you lists of *synonyms*, (similar words), then lets you quickly replace your original word with the alternative of your choice. Sometimes Word can offer *antonyms* (words with opposite meanings). Word's thesaurus also contains common phrases like *in consideration of* and *at rest*.

The *Thesaurus...* command lives on the *Tools* menu, and has no keyboard shortcut. (If you spend a lot of time writing, you might want to add a *Thesaurus...* keyboard shortcut of your own.)

LOOKING UP WORDS AND PHRASES

Highlight the word or phrase you wish to replace, or position the insertion point in a word before you choose *Thesaurus...* from the *Tools* menu. If you fail to highlight a word and the insertion point is not in a word, the thesaurus feature will pick the word *closest* to the insertion point. In any case, a dialog box will appear similar to the one shown in Figure 35.1.

The Thesaurus

Figure 35.1
Word's thesaurus suggests synonyms and antonyms for highlighted words or phrases.

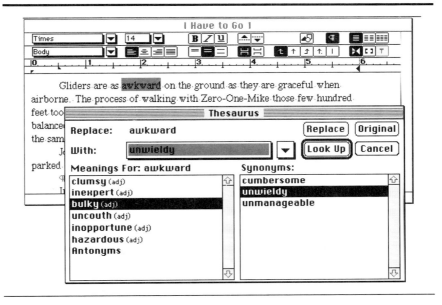

If you haven't done so already, Word will highlight the word in your document and place it in the Thesaurus dialog box next to the Replace: label. This word (or phrase) is referred to as the *original word*.

If your original word has more than one meaning, the various meanings and their parts of speech will appear in the Meanings For: scrollable list. Clicking on a meaning in the Meanings For: list displays related synonyms in the Synonyms: scrollable list. In Figure 35.1 the thesaurus offers six meanings for *awkward*. Clicking on *bulky* displays the synonyms for *bulky*.

Clicking on a particular synonym for *bulky* (*unwieldy*, for instance), places the synonym in the editable With: area of the Thesaurus dialog box. If you don't like any of the choices, clicking Cancel will close the Thesaurus window and take you back to your unchanged document.

REPLACING WORDS AND PHRASES

After exploring the various potential replacement words or phrases suggested by Word, highlight the one you like best (placing it in the With: box), then click the Replace button in the Thesaurus window. Word will replace the highlighted text in your document with the contents of the With: box; then the Thesaurus window will disappear. The *Undo Thesaurus...* command is available if you act immediately.

If you highlight a *phrase*, like *at rest*, Word may extend the highlighted area when you open the Thesaurus window. (Try it with the sentence *The ball was at rest in the driveway*.) Watch carefully when you highlight phrases and replace them using the thesaurus. You may need to make some minor repairs to your document after you close the Thesaurus window.

Related Words and Phrases

Frequently, Word's thesaurus will not contain an exact match for your original word. This can happen if you've misspelled a word. In that case, you will probably see an alphabetical list of words in place of the Meanings For: list. Pick the correct word from the list, or return to your document, correct the spelling error and then try the *Thesaurus...* command again.

You will also have trouble matching certain tenses of words. For instance, if you attempt to replace *ambled*, Word will tell you to seek related words, as shown in Figure 35.2, since the thesaurus contains the word *amble*, but not *amble*d.

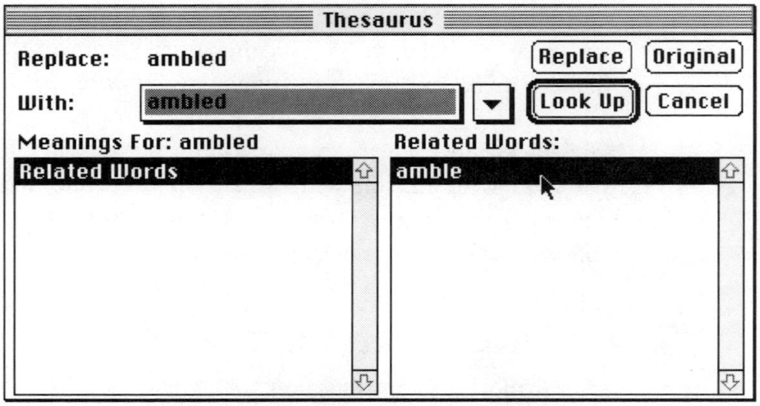

Figure 35.2
You may need to use a related word in the thesaurus and then edit it.

The Thesaurus

Clicking on a related word in the scrollable Related Word: list will place it in the With: dialog box. For instance, clicking on *amble* in the Related Words: list will replace *ambled* with *amble*, as shown in Figure 35.3. Once you have the related word in the With: box, click on the Look Up button to find synonyms and antonyms.

Figure 35.3
With the related word moved to the With: box, click Look Up and you'll be able to peruse a list of synonyms for the related word.

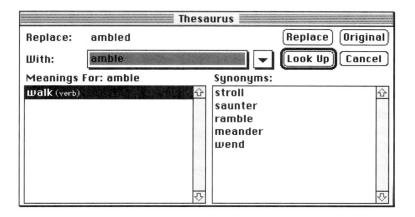

When you find a related word (*saunter*, for instance), click on it to move it to the With: box, then edit the word to suit your needs before clicking Replace. For instance, you'd probably want to add *ed* to *saunter* in our example.

Clicking on the Original button will replace the related word with your original word. Word also keeps track of any previous replacements made since you last opened the Thesaurus window, and you can frequently restore earlier "With:" words by pulling down the *With:* drop-down list. Click on the arrow to the right of the With: box to view the list if there is one.

FINDING ANTONYMS

Frequently, Word can help you find antonyms. When they are available, the word *Antonyms* appears at the bottom of the scrollable Meanings For: list. Click on *Antonyms* to display a list of them in the right-hand, scrollable-list area of the Thesaurus window. As you can see in Figure 35.4, the name of that list changes from *Synonyms:* to *Antonyms:*, and the list contains potential antonyms for the word in the With: box.

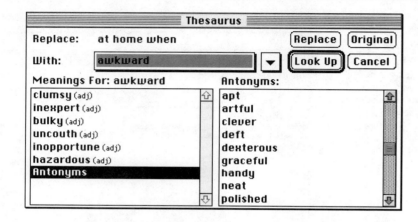

Figure 35.4
The thesaurus can suggest antonyms too.

Spelling Help from the Thesaurus

While Word's thesaurus doesn't actually contain definitions, you can sometimes use it to help pick the appropriate spelling of confusing words like *which* and *witch* or *weather* and *whether*. Look up the words in question and compare synonyms to help you pick the right spelling.

Exploring the Thesaurus

- It is possible to *really* meander around in the Thesaurus! A single click on any word (either in the Meanings For: or Synonyms: list) places it in the *With:* box. *Then* you can click on Look Up, and go from there.

- Double-clicking on a synonym places that word in both the With: and Meanings For: spaces.

- Double-clicking on a Meanings For: word places *just* that word in *With:* space.

Multiple Columns

FEATURING

- Creating snaking newspaper-style columns
- Changing column widths and spacing
- Creating banner heads on columns

ost people find short lines of text easier to read than long ones. That's one reason newspapers and book designers frequently use side-by-side *snaking columns*. Text flows from the bottom of one column to the top of the next until a page is filled, then it flows onto the next page. Word makes it easy for you to arrange your text in columns like these. The *ribbon buttons* let you choose single, double, or triple columns. (Single is the default.) Moreover, the *Columns* portion of the *Section dialog box* lets you specify up to one hundred columns. It also provides a way to adjust the amount of *white space* between columns.

In a single-section document, all of your pages must have the same number of columns. But, by breaking a document into multiple sections, you can have as many different column designs as you have sections.

Word automatically adjusts column widths to accommodate your chosen page size, orientation, and document margins. You can overrule these decisions.

Multiple Columns

It is possible to use indents within columns. You can edit columnar text just as you do any other. When you work in Page Layout view, you will see *side-by-side* columns as they will print. When working in Normal view, you will see text in the appropriate column *width*, but you will not see the columns in position next to each other.

Word's column feature requires all columns in a section to be the same width. (You can create different column widths with *tables*. See *Chapter 37* for details.)

MULTI-COLUMN DOCUMENTS FROM THE RIBBON

The easy way to create columns is to click either the double- or triple-column button on the right edge of the ribbon. As you can see in Figure 36.1, they contain pictures of the column styles they produce.

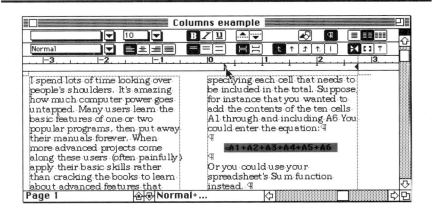

Figure 36.1
The ribbon puts two- and three-column text a click away.

Clicking the button to the left of the two column button restores the text to a single column. When you use the ribbon column buttons, Word automatically determines the appropriate width of columns and the amount of white space between columns based on the page and document settings. Changing margins, page size, orientation, indents, and related settings will cause corresponding changes in column widths and spacing.

The zero point on the ruler is always at the left edge of the column containing the insertion point. In Figure 36.1, it is at the left edge of the *right* column. Clicking in the left column would move the zero point of the ruler to the left edge of the *left* column.

Indents work as you'd expect within columns. For example, in Figure 36.1 the two-column ribbon button has been used to create two column text. Then, the highlighted text has been indented using Word's indent feature.

MULTICOLUMN DOCUMENTS FROM THE SECTION DIALOG BOX

You can "force" more than three columns and specify the desired amount of white space between by using the Columns portion of the *Section* dialog box. Reach the Section dialog box by choosing *Section...* from the *Format* menu or use the Opt-F14 shortcut if you have an extended keyboard. Figure 36.2 shows the specifications for twelve columns spaced ¼" apart. The actual column width will be determined by Word, based on the available text area.

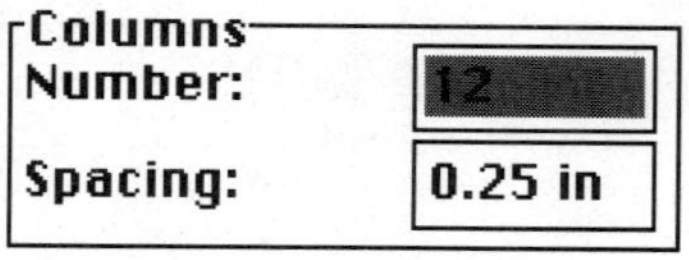

Figure 36.2
You can precisely specify the number of columns and the spacing in the Section dialog box.

```
┌Columns─────────────────
 Number:    [ 12 ]
 Spacing:   [ 0.25 in ]
```

COLUMN BREAKS AND SECTIONS

As you learned in *Chapter 23*, each section of your document can have its own column layout. Since you can break a single page into multiple sections, it is possible to have different column layouts on the same page. This is how you create *banner heads* and similar effects for newsletters and brochures.

Insert a section break (from the *Insert* menu) wherever you want to change the number or spacing of columns, as illustrated in Figure 36.3.

It is easiest to insert and delete section breaks while in Normal view, but you will want to use Page Layout view and Print Preview to fine-tune your work

Multiple Columns

Figure 36.3
Insert section breaks where you want to change column specifications. The first section here is single-column text, the second double-column text. (You see double columns side-by-side in Page Layout view.)

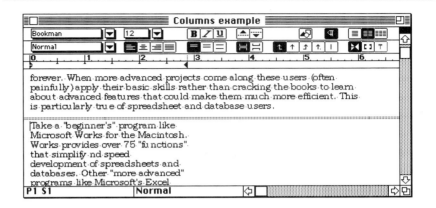

before you print! For instance in Figure 36.4 there is a problem with the spacing between the single column and two-column portions of the page. The Spacing Before paragraph feature has been used on the two-column text to place space between the single and double column text. Unfortunately, the first line of the right-hand column is not the first line of a paragraph. (It is the continuation of a paragraph.) As a result, the left column has space before it, but the right column does not. Placing space *after* the single column paragraph and no space *before* the two-column paragraphs will fix this.

Figure 36.4
Creating different column layouts using section breaks can lead to problems, as shown here. The extra space is the result of heedless use of the Paragraph Before feature.

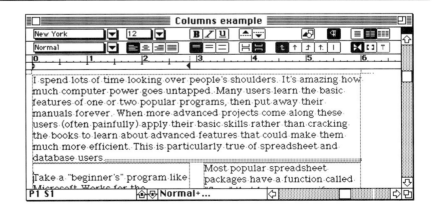

Controlling Column Width from the Ruler

As you know, Word 5's column feature requires that all side-by-side columns within a section be the same width. And, you know that Word initially sets the widths and spacing for you. It's possible, however, to drag columns to different widths using margin markers. Here's how. Follow along in Figure 36.5.

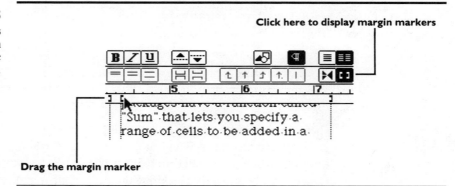

Figure 36.5
Drag margin markers to change column widths in Page Layout view.

Place the insertion point in the desired column. From Page Layout view, display the ruler if it isn't already on screen (⌘-R). Click on the Margin Marker button (the facing arrows) in the ruler to display the margin markers. Drag any marker and the all columns will adjust to the same width. If you need to have side-by-side columns of differing widths, see *Chapter 37*.

Controlling Column Breaks

Use Word's *Keep Lines Together* and *Keep with Next* paragraph features to prevent unwanted breaks. Sometimes, you will want to *force* breaks. For example, the last page of a two column document may end with uneven columns since Word will completely fill the left column before putting text in the left column.

Use Word's *Insert Page Break* command to force *column breaks*. Place the insertion point where you want the column break, then visit the *Insert* menu or use the Shift-Enter keyboard shortcut. You remove breaks by highlighting them and pressing Delete.

An alternate and perhaps more elegant way is to add another section after your last "real" text (this *last* section will be empty, of course—specs are No Break and the number of columns won't matter). Then, if you add more "real" text, your columns will automatically adjust and match up at the bottom and you *won't* have to redo your Insert Page Break, etc.

CHAPTER 37

Tables

FEATURING

- How to create and edit tables
- Borders and other table formatting enhancements
- Converting text to tables and vice versa
- Table tips and tricks

Tables help you organize complex columnar information. Use them to create such diverse documents as forms, television scripts, financial reports, parts catalogs, and resumes. You can insert tables anywhere you need them in Word documents. Word 5's table feature and the terminology used to describe it will remind you of a spreadsheet.

Word tables consist of horizontal *rows*, and vertical *columns*. You do the typing in areas called *cells*. Cells can contain *text*, *numbers*, or *graphics*. Text is edited and embellished as usual in cells. For instance, Word's ribbon and ruler are available when you're typing and editing in tables.

A number of table-specific features let you control the size, shape, and appearance of cells. Border and shading features are available. It is also easy to insert and delete rows and columns.

Tables

Tables can be created from existing text without needless retyping. Or, you can use the table feature to organize information and then convert your table to text. You can even import and export spreadsheet data.

Parts of a Table

Figure 37.1 shows a typical table. This example consists of three rows, each containing two columns, for a total of six cells.

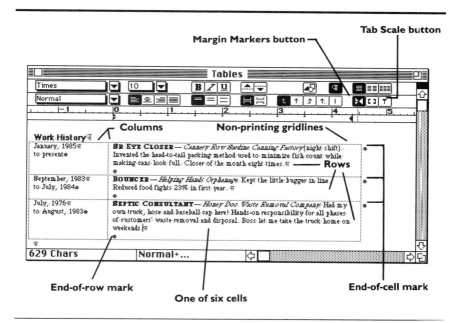

Figure 37.1
A table containing three rows, two columns, and six cells. The dotted cell gridline will not print.

The dotted lines around each cell represent non-printing table gridlines. You can add printing borders with the *Borders...* command. The larger dots are end-of-cell and end-of-row marks. Click the *Show ¶* button in the ribbon or use the ⌘-J shortcut if you can't see them on your screen.

Creating a Simple Table

Place the insertion point where you want to insert a table. Choose the *Table...* command from the *Insert* menu. (There is no standard keyboard shortcut, but you can assign one.)

The Insert Table dialog box will appear. Enter the desired number of columns and rows for your table. Don't worry if you are uncertain about the exact number of columns or rows you'll need. You can always add or delete them later. Figure 37.2 shows dialog-box entries for six four-column rows.

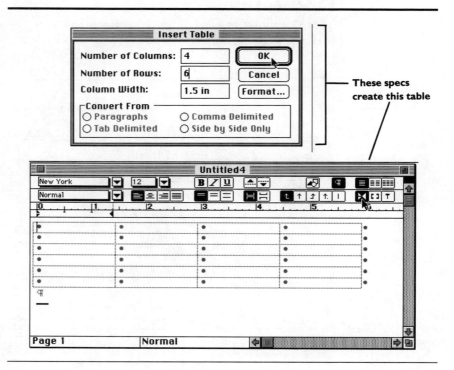

Figure 37.2
The Insert Table dialog box and the resulting four-by-six cell table it creates.

Word computes a column width automatically, taking into consideration the available text area in your document and the number of columns you've specified. Initially, all table columns are the same width, but you can change column widths using techniques described later in this chapter.

ENTERING AND EDITING TEXT IN A TABLE

With only the few exceptions noted in this chapter, you navigate, enter, and edit table text just as you do any other Word 5 text. Use your mouse or arrow keys to position the insertion point then type normally. Think of the cell borders as margins. Word will automatically wrap text within the cell as you reach the right edge. Rows will automatically grow taller as necessary to accommodate your typing.

To move from cell to cell within a table, either use your mouse or use the *Tab* key to go forward and *Shift Tab* to go backward. The insertion point will move left and down to the next row when you press Tab in the last column on the right side of a table; and it will move right and up one row when you *Shift Tab* past the the last column on the *left*. If you press Tab in the last cell of the last row, you will create a new row.

Here's an important tip: Since you use the Tab key to navigate in tables, you cannot simply press Tab to enter *tab characters* in cells. Instead, you need to hold down the Option key while pressing Tab.

You can apply the usual character formatting to all or selected characters in a table. For example, in Figure 37.1 several font sizes and bold and italic embellishments have been used in portions of some cells. The familiar ribbon, ruler, and menu features all work here.

Paragraphs in Cells

First-time table users are sometimes unaware of the important role *paragraphs* play in tables. A cell can contain more than one paragraph. Create paragraphs in the usual way. While typing in a cell, press the Return key.

You can apply all of Word's *paragraph formats* to paragraphs in cells. Since cells can contain multiple paragraphs, they can also contain multiple paragraph *formats*. Thus, within a *single* cell, you can have several different indent settings, tab settings, line-spacing specifications, styles etc.

SELECTING IN TABLES

You can select characters, words, and other items in table cells using Word's usual mouse and keyboard features. In addition, Word also provides table-specific selection tools enabling you to choose whole cells, entire rows, columns, or areas, as Figure 37.3 illustrates.

Figure 37.3
Word provides a number of table-specific selection tools.

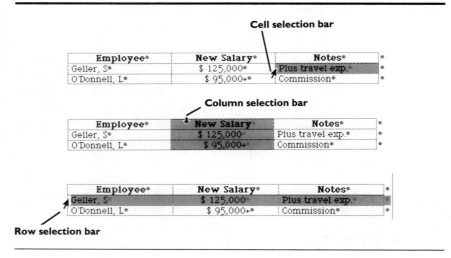

Selecting Single Cells

The area between the first character in a cell and the left edge of the cell is called the *cell selection bar*. Clicking on it selects the contents of the entire cell.

You can also select an entire cell by dragging with the mouse. Just be sure you include the end-of-cell mark in your selection.

Selecting Columns

To select a column, move the mouse pointer to the area at the top of a column called the *column selection bar*. You'll know you've arrived when the pointer changes into a large, down-pointing arrow, like the one in Figure 37.3. Click to select the entire column.

Holding down the Option key while clicking anywhere in a column will also select the entire column. Selecting the bottom or top cell in a column and dragging up or down is somewhat tedious, but will also work.

Selecting Rows

Double-clicking any cell selection bar will select the entire row. Selecting the left-most or right-most cell in a row and dragging will also work.

Selecting Adjacent Groups of Cells

To select groups of adjacent cells, either drag through the cells or click in one cell and Shift-click in the others. For instance, to select all but the employee column in Figure 37.3, you could click in the *New Salary* cell then Shift-click in the cell containing the word *Commission*. The right-most six of the table's nine cells would be selected.

Selecting the Whole Table

To properly select an entire table, hold down the Option key and double-click anywhere in the table. If your document contains *multiple* tables and they are not separated by paragraph marks, this technique will select all adjacent tables.

Do not use Word's *Select All* command to select a table, since this will also select paragraph marks and other things outside of the table.

MODIFYING TABLE DESIGNS

While Word's default table settings may be fine for simple typing tasks, you will eventually want to change column widths, overall table width, cell spacing, and so on. You'll want to insert, delete, and move rows and columns. As you can see from Figure 37.4, it is even possible to create professional-looking forms by modifying Word's standard tables.

Figure 37.4
Create professional-looking forms by adding borders and adjusting row and column sizes.

Creating complex tables like this can be a little frustrating at first. It is a good idea to *save* your work before you experiment with new table formats. Beginners should consider working on *copies* of important documents. That said, let's look at a number of ways to modify standard table designs.

Table Borders that Print

An easy way to dress up a table is to add printing borders. The form in Figure 37.4 is an example of this. Select the cell or cells you wish to surround, then choose *Borders...* from the *Format* menu. Pick the desired combination of line thicknesses and apply the borders just as you would add them to Word 5 paragraphs (see *Chapter 15*).

Adding Rows at the End of a Table

To add a row at the *end* of an existing table, place the insertion point anywhere in the *last cell* (the one in the *lower-left corner* of your table) and press the Tab key. Word will insert a new row using the styles of the cells immediately above.

Adding Rows in the Middle of a Table

To insert a single row in the middle of a table, place the insertion point in the row *below* where you want the new row. Then, use either the keyboard shortcut, ⌘-Control-V, or the Insert Row feature, found in the Table Layout dialog box shown in Figure 37.5. (You reach this dialog box by choosing *Table Layout...* from the *Format* menu.)

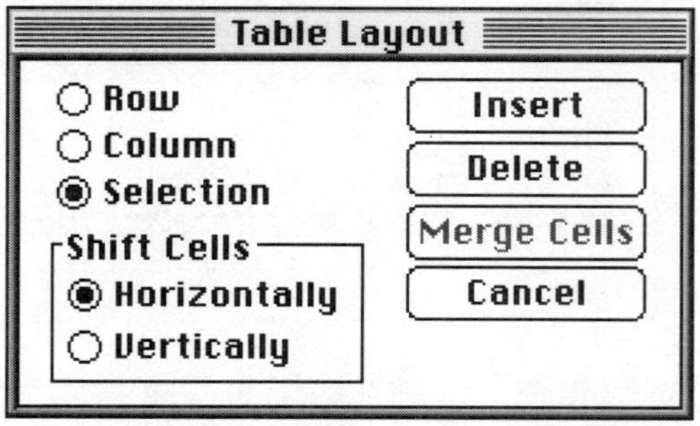

Figure 37.5
The *Table Layout...* command on the *Format* menu lets you insert, delete, and merge cells.

The *Table Layout...* command is available on the *Format* menu whenever your insertion point is in a table. To insert a row this way, activate the Row button, then click on the Insert button. You can also add the Insert Rows command to the *Format* menu.

To add multiple rows, either repeat the ⌘-Control-V shortcut as many times as you need to, or try this alternate approach.

Select as many existing rows as you want to insert new ones *before* making the insertion. In other words, if you want to add three rows, select the three existing rows beneath the desired insertion point, *then* use ⌘-Control-V or visit the Table Layout dialog box. Word will insert three rows.

Changing Row Heights

Normally, Word sets the height of each row *automatically* to accommodate the cell containing the tallest entry. For instance, if *one* cell in a row needs 2.0″ to accommodate the text or graphic it contains, *all* of the cells in that row will be 2.0″ high. All cells in a row *must* be the same height, but different rows can have different heights.

You can overrule Word's automatic row-height (and column-width) settings via the *Table Cells...* command located on the *Format* menu. This is one way to create forms with fixed-sized entry areas.

There is no standard keyboard shortcut for the *Table Cells...* command, but experienced table typists often add their own. Figure 37.6 shows the Table Cells dialog box and its menus.

Place the insertion point anywhere in the row whose height you wish to specify. If you want multiple rows to share the same height, you can select all of them.

Open the Table Cells dialog box and enter a row height and unit of measure (*1 in*, *12 pt*, etc.) in the entry box next to the *Height:* drop-down menu.

Click OK to make the change and close the dialog box to see the results of your choice without closing the dialog box. *Undo Table Cells* (⌘-Z) works here if you use it immediately.

Figure 37.6

The *Table Cells...* command on the *Format* menu brings up the Table Cells dialog box, where you can specify row heights and column widths. For a discussion of these options, see the section *The Table Cells... Command and Cell Widths*.

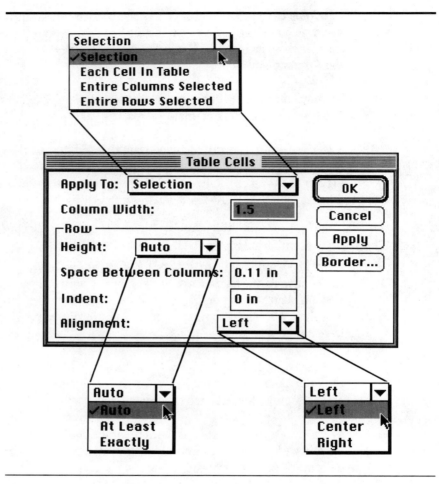

The drop down *Height:* menu lets you specify a minimum row height or an exact height. If the exact height is too small to accommodate the biggest entry in a row, the excessive text or a portion of the too-tall graphic will be cropped when printed.

Deleting Rows

Delete rows either from the Table Layout dialog box described earlier (and illustrated in Figure 37.5) or by using the ⌘-Control-X shortcut. Start by placing the insertion point in the unwanted row or by highlighting multiple doomed rows. *Undo* does work here. You can add the Delete Rows command to the *Format* menu.

Changing the Spacing between Rows

To change the amount of *white space* between rows, you must change the *before* and *after* spacing of the first or last paragraphs in the cells. (Don't confuse this with changing the *height* of rows, which is something else entirely.) Use the same techniques you use to add space between non-table paragraphs (see *Chapter 15*): Select the paragraph of interest and use the ruler's spacing buttons to add or remove space before paragraphs in cells. Or choose the *Paragraph...* command on the *Format* menu and specify before and after spacing. The keyboard shortcut for the Paragraph dialog box is ⌘-M.

Inserting Columns at the Right Edge of a Table

To insert a column at the right edge of a table, place the insertion point between the right edge of the right-most column and the end-of-row mark.

Visit the Table Layout dialog box (*Table Layout...* in the *Format* menu) and activate the column button. Click Insert. Word will add a new column but will not change the width of the earlier columns to accommodate it. In order to make the enlarged table fit on your page you will probably need to adjust margins, column widths, or page orientation. New columns retain the format of the old right-most columns, but borders will not transfer.

Inserting Columns in the Middle of a Table

To insert a single column in the middle of a table, place the insertion point in the column *to the right* of where you want the new column to appear. Then, once in the Table Layout dialog box (shown back in Figure 37.5), activate the Column button and click Insert.

To insert multiple columns, either repeat the process (perhaps using *Repeat Insert...* from the *Edit* menu—⌘-Y), or *select* as many existing columns as you want to insert new ones *to the right* of the desired location of the new columns. In other words, if you want to add three columns, select the three existing columns to the right of the desired insertion point, *then* visit the Table Layout dialog box. Word will insert three columns. You can also add the Insert Columns command to the *Format* menu. All new columns retain the format of the column to their right.

Deleting Columns

To delete columns, select the column or columns to be removed. Choose *Table Layout...* from the *Format* menu to bring up the Table Layout dialog box. (See Figure 37.5.) Activate the Column button if necessary and click Delete. Like the other commands, you can add Delete Columns to the *Format* menu.

Changing Columns Widths

You can change the widths of entire columns or selected cells within columns. Most changes can be made by dragging column markers on the table scale in the ruler. But you can make precision adjustments in the Table Cells dialog box.

Changing Column and Cell Widths with the Ruler

To change the width of an *entire column*, select all cells in the column you want to work with. This is an important step! If you fail to select the entire column, your changes will affect only one cell.

With the column selected, display the *table scale* on the ruler. To do this, click on the *Table Scale button* in the upper-right corner of the ruler. The table-column markers will display on the ruler, ready for dragging, as shown in Figure 37.7.

When you drag the markers in this way, markers to the right will also move, changing the overall size of the table. To preserve the positions of all markers, hold down the Shift key when dragging column markers.

As you can see in Figure 37.8, it is possible to change the size of just one cell by placing the insertion point in the cell then dragging its column marker. Here too, holding Shift while dragging will preserve the markers' positions.

Undo Formatting is available if you need it. Visit the *Edit* menu or use the (by now familiar?) ⌘-Z shortcut.

Tables

Figure 37.7
Drag the column markers to change column or cell widths.

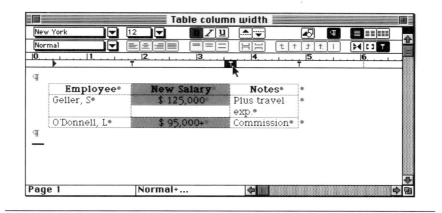

Figure 37.8
You can change individual cell widths by selecting only one cell before dragging.

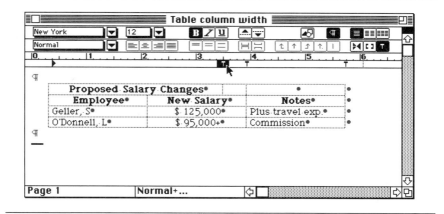

When you are just learning, it's pretty easy to mess things up while dragging cell and column borders around this way, particularly if you change cell widths when you meant to change column widths. If *Undo* can't fix the problem and you don't have a better previously saved version, perhaps the *Table Cells...* command can help.

The Table Cells... Command and Cell Widths

The *Table Cells...* command, discussed earlier, can also be used to define cell and column widths. It will either use the cell containing the insertion point as a sample, or you can type in a column-width specification. Take a look at the "before" mess in Figure 37.9. Several cell widths have been changed and nothing lines up.

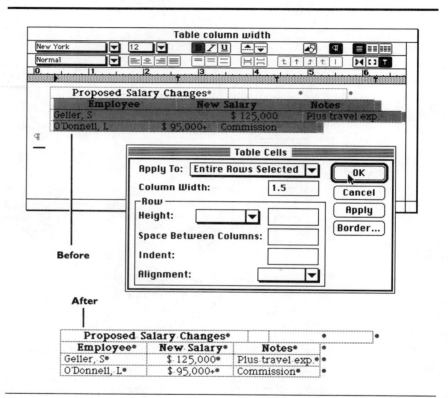

Figure 37.9
Table Cells feature can help bring order (bottom) to chaotic cell and column widths (top).

The *Table Cells...* command brings up the Table Cells dialog box shown in Figure 37.9. The drop-down *Apply To:* menu is a powerful weapon in cleaning up problems. With the rows needing identical cell widths, we've entered a column width of 1½". After clicking OK, the cells align themselves as shown in the "after" portion of the figure.

There's another trick worth noting. As shown in Figure 37.10, you can type the word *Auto* in the Column Width: box of the Table Cells dialog box. This evens out the right edge of the table.

Tables

Figure 37.10
Typing *Auto* in the Column Width: box will make unequal rows (top) the same width (bottom).

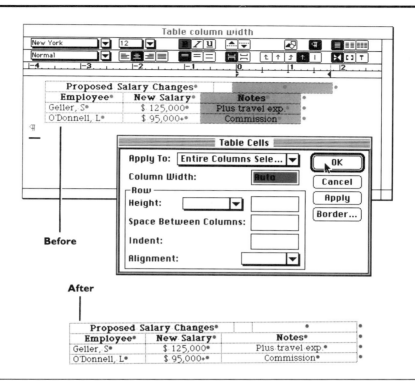

Aligning Tables

The Table Cells dialog box, shown in Figures 37.6 and 37.9, has an *Alignment:* drop-down menu that lets you specify how you want selected rows or entire tables aligned with relation to your document's left margin. The choices are *Left*, *Center*, and *Right*. Choices you make here do not affect alignment of things in table cells.

Merge Cells

Use the Merge Cells feature to combine the contents of multiple cells. This is a common way to make a heading in one cell span an entire table or selected group of columns. As shown in Figure 37.11, you select the cells to merge, then choose Selection in the Table Layout dialog box (reached from the *Format* menu). Click Merge Cells and the contents of the designated cells will merge.

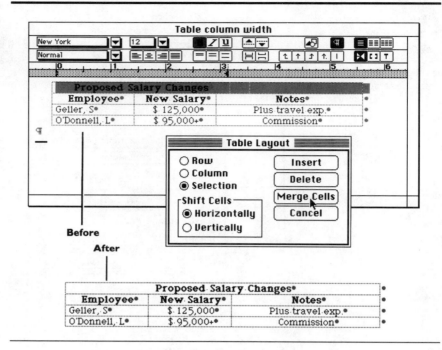

Figure 37.11
The contents of several cells (top) can be merged together (bottom) with the Table Layout dialog box.

You may need to reformat text merged this way. To split ("un-merge") cells, place the insertion point in a merged cell and re-visit the Table Layout dialog box. The Merge Cells button will be replaced with *Split Cells*. (Some formatting may be lost—cell borders for instance.) Click to restore the separate cells.

Changing the Space between Columns

Word assigns cell widths based on the available text area and the number of columns you request. In the process, it sets aside a small amount of unprintable space between (actually within) each cell. This space takes away from the usable cell space. For instance, a 1½" column with ¼" inch column spacing would have 1¼" of usable space in the middle of each cell.

To change the space between columns, select the columns of interest, then type a new specification in the Space Between Columns: box, found in the Table Cells dialog box. (Choose *Table Cells...* from the *Format* menu.) Refer back to Figure 37.6 if you've forgotten what this dialog box looks like.

Tables

CONVERTING TABLES TO TEXT AND VICE VERSA

Sometimes you'll start a project using tabs and wish you'd created a table—or a co-worker will give you some tabbed text. Other times, you will want to export things you've typed using Word 5's table feature for use with a database and other programs that expect tab- or comma-separated (*delimited*) input. Word has solutions for all these contingencies.

It's fairly easy to convert back and forth from tables to text. You may need to do some cleanup before or after conversion though. Always work on *copies* of your documents when you do this!

Converting from Text to Tables

Highlight the text in your document that you want to turn into a table. Choose *Text to Table...* from the *Insert* menu and click the appropriate Convert From button as described below.

Tab-Delimited Text

Click the Tab Delimited button in the Insert Table dialog box. Lines of text separated by paragraph marks or line breaks will become *rows* in your table. Tab-separated strings of text *within* those lines will become cell entries in the row. Word will automatically create the necessary number of columns based on the maximum number of tabs in a line.

For instance,

> **Sony Corporation [Tab] 800-222-7669 [Return] SYBEX, Inc. [Tab] 415-523-8233 [Tab] Publisher [Return]**

would create two rows with three columns, even though the last cell in the first row would be empty.

Comma-Delimited Text

Click the Comma Delimited button in the Insert Table dialog box. Lines of text separated by paragraph marks or line breaks will become *rows* in your table. Comma-separated strings of text *within* those lines will become cell entries in the row. Word will automatically create the necessary number of columns based on the maximum number of commas in a line.

For instance,

> **Sony Corporation [Comma] 800-222-7669 [Return] SYBEX, Inc. [Comma] 415-523-8233 [Comma] Publisher [Return]**

would create two rows with three columns, even though the last cell in the first row will be empty.

Warning: Beware of commas that might create unintentional cells like the one between *SYBEX* and *Inc.*

Converting from Paragraphs

Click the Paragraphs button in the Insert Table dialog box. If you ask Word to convert paragraphs to tables, it will propose a single column and create as many rows as you have paragraphs. Changing the number of columns will distribute paragraphs among the columns from left to right. In a two-column layout, the first paragraph would end up in the top-left cell of the new table, the second paragraph in the top-right cell, the third in the left cell of row two, and so on.

Converting Text Placed Side by Side

Word 3 users can convert text formatted as side-by-side text using this converter. Don't try to use it for other conversions.

Converting from Tables to Text

Select the table cells you wish to convert or use the Option-double-click trick to select the whole table.

Choose *Table to Text...* from the *Insert* menu. Word will provide a Table to Text dialog box which asks if you want the table converted to *Paragraphs*, *Tab-delimited*, or *Comma-delimited* text. Pick one. If you pick the Comma or Tab options, Word will convert each row of your table into one line (a paragraph, actually). Cells in your old tables will become tab- or comma-separated items on the lines.

Remember that in-text commas will confuse Word. It would treat *SYBEX, Inc.* as two distinct entries. If you choose tab text you will probably need to set new tabs after the conversion.

Choosing the Paragraph option will convert each old table cell into at least one paragraph. If cells contain multiple paragraphs, the paragraph marks are retained during the conversion, so some cells will create more than one new paragraph.

TABLE TIPS

Here are some tips to help make you a more productive table editor. They cover a variety of subjects.

Rearrange Rows in Outline View

With a table onscreen, switch to Outline view from the *View* menu. Move the pointer to the left edge of your table. The pointer shape will change, as shown in Figure 37.12.

Figure 37.12
Drag rows in Outline view to rearrange tables.

You can drag rows to new positions using Word's Outline features. See *Chapter 42* for more information about Outline view. You can also use Drag-and-Drop text editing to move rows up and down. This is sometimes easier to do than going to Outline view and moving rows. Unfortunately, this method will not work for moving columns.

Moving Cell Contents

To move the contents of cells, first find or create new empty destination cells in the appropriate quantity and configuration to hold the items you plan to move. For instance, if you plan to move a four row by six column collection of cells you will need the same number of available cells in the same configuration (4 × 6) to receive the moved items.

Copy or cut the items of interest by highlighting them and using *Copy* or *Cut* from the *Edit* menu or the keyboard shortcuts—⌘-C and ⌘-X.

At this point you can either *select* the same cell configuration at the destination (four rows of six columns each in our example) or you can try a shortcut. Simply place the insertion point in the upper-left destination cell. (If you use this shortcut, do *not* select the cell.) Be sure to place the insertion point before the end-of-cell mark, then paste. All of the cells will flow into their new destinations, bringing their formatting information with them.

Undo Paste (⌘-Z) works here if you spot trouble immediately. Delete unused columns using the *Table Layout...* command if necessary.

Styles and Tables

Word will use the current style (at the insertion point) when creating a new table. You can change the style of the whole table or apply different styles to different portions of the table.

Consider creating multiple *styles* if you plan to play with table formatting. For instance, you might have a style for table headings, another for standard text, another for decimal-aligned numbers, and so on. See *Chapter 17* for more detail on styles.

Apply the new style to all appropriate paragraphs in your table by selecting the paragraphs and using the ribbon's *Style:* menu. From then on, simply changing a style will change all table text formatted with the changed style.

Memory, Tables, and Speed

If Word slows to a crawl in large tables, try quitting and increasing the amount of memory allocated to Word in the Get Info box. Sometimes this helps. See your Macintosh manual for details. You might also consider turning off *Show Table Gridlines* (found in the View category of the references dialog box).

Repeating Headings on Multipage Tables

To repeat column headings on each page of a multipage table, create a separate *section* for the table. Place the table headings in the section's *header*.

Start by placing the insertion point in the first row of your table. Create a new section by inserting a Section Break (from the *Insert* menu).

Copy the heading rows from your table and paste them into the section header. Adjust paragraph before and after spacing if necessary. Page Layout view will help you see what's going on. For more on sections, refer to *Chapter 23*.

Place Table Layout Choices in Your Menu

If you create tables frequently, you can use Word's *Commands...* command to place table-related commands and choices in your menus. You can even add commands to bypass multiple choices in the table Layout dialog box. For example, an Insert Columns command is available. *Appendix B* lists all of Word 5's commands.

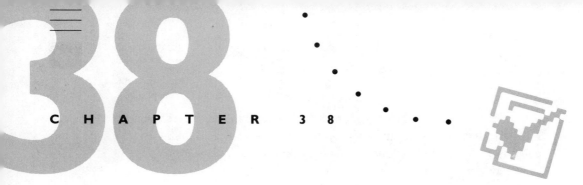

Sorting

FEATURING

- Sorting items in Word documents
- Date sorting tricks

Have you ever created something like an *alphabetical list* of employees and their phone extensions, then needed a list of phone extension assignments sorted by extension number? Most of us have many lists like these, and they always seem to be in the wrong order.

You could retype the old list or cut and paste, but Word's *Sort...* command, found under the *Tools* menu, might be a better solution.

Don't throw away your database software just yet, though. The Sort feature has limitations, many of which can be overcome with a little planning.

Word can sort lines of tabular text, items you've entered in tables, or even paragraphs in a document. The Sort command can be quite helpful when preparing data files for Word's Print Merge feature (discussed in *Chapter 40*).

As with other Word features, Sort can make substantial changes to your document (read: ruin your hard work), so it is best to save before you sort. Consider practicing on *copies* of important files.

Sorting

Simple Sorting

Word 5's Sort feature will attempt to alphabetically sort any selected text. To sort this way, first *select* all the lines you want to rearrange (and no others!). Unselected lines will not sort.

Next, pick *Sort...* from the *Tools* menu. The selected items will be rearranged in ascending order for you. *Undo Sort* is available. Take the list of employee names, phone extensions, and birthdays in Figure 38.1, for instance. Word has sorted them by first name, which might not be desirable.

Figure 38.1
Highlight the text to be sorted and choose *Sort...* from the *Tools* menu (top). Word will sort alphabetically, using the first character (bottom).

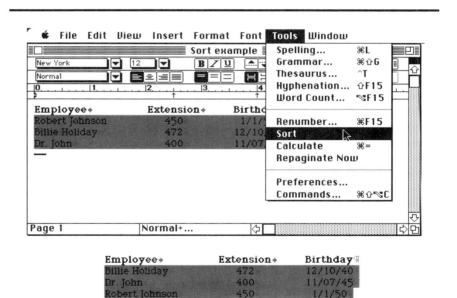

Notice that Word has rearranged the three highlighted lines alphabetically, using the *first character* in each line. If there had been two names in the example starting with *R* (*Robert* and *Robbie*, for instance), Word would have considered as many characters following as necessary to sort properly.

Sort order

Normally, Word sorts *alphanumerically* in *ascending order* based on each character's *ASCII code*. That is to say, the default sort would start with numbers 0–9, then progress from uppercase *A* to lowercase *z*.

If you hold down the Shift key when visiting the *Tools* menu, the choice will be *Sort Descending*. (You must press the Shift key *before* pointing to the *Tools* menu, and hold down the shift key at least until the menu appears.) A descending sort will progress from lowercase z to uppercase *A*, then from *9* to *0* (zero). As you will see in a moment, numbers in dates and part numbers containing letters may require special handling.

Lines beginning with special characters (*, ©, etc.) will appear at the top of ascending sorts and the bottom of descending sorts.

Accented characters are treated like their non-accented equivalents. Thus *ñ* and *n* are the same for sorting purposes.

Sorts based on portions of lines

As you can see in Figure 38.2, you need not sort on the first characters in a line. In fact, you can base sorts on nearly anything you can select. Just be sure you select *all* text you want to sort.

Figure 38.2
This sort is based on extension numbers (top). Hold the Option key while dragging to select areas like this. Even with just this "column" selected, Word sorts entire rows (bottom).

Employee	Extension	Birthday
Robert Johnson	450	1/1/50
Dr. John	400	11/07/45
Billie Holiday	472	12/10/40

Employee	Extension	Birthday
Dr. John	400	11/07/45
Robert Johnson	450	1/1/50
Billie Holiday	472	12/10/40

Sorting

You can see from the "before" and "after" portions of Figure 38.2 that Word sorted *entire rows* based on the highlighted extension numbers, not just the highlighted text. The illustration contains tab-separated text, but the technique works fine with items separated by spaces.

To select areas like the ones in Figure 38.2, hold down the Option key and drag the mouse. *Tip:* To make selecting columns easier, separate the items with a lot of white space (by using Tabs, for example).

SORTING DATES, NAMES, AND PART NUMBERS

There is no chronological sort-order option built into Word, so you will need to use some forethought when typing *dates* you plan to sort. Figure 38.3 illustrates the problem.

Figure 38.3
Word will not properly sort dates entered in most American formats.

Employee	Extension	Birthday
Billie Holiday	472	12/10/40
Dr. John	400	11/07/45
Robert Johnson	450	1/1/50

Before

Employee	Extension	Birthday
Robert Johnson	450	1/1/50
Dr. John	400	11/07/45
Billie Holiday	472	12/10/40

After

Employee		Extension	Birthday		
Robert	Johnson	450	01	01	50
Dr. John		400	11	07	45
Billie	Holiday	472	12	10	40

The solution

Since the year appears last in most American date formats, it is impossible to sort dates like the ones in Figure 38.3 without separating the month day and year into separate columns. So the solution is to turn the list into a *table* and sort by the last column.

You can have similar problems with alphanumeric part numbers. Names are a problem, too, if you've entered first names before last names or if you've included someone's title with his first name.

One solution is to break items like these into rows and insert them in a table, as shown at the bottom of Figure 38.3. Word sorts entire *rows* based on the specified sort *column*. So in the table shown at the bottom of Figure 38.3, the rows containing peoples' names are sorted by birth year.

MULTILEVEL SORTS

When you place items in a table, it is possible to have Word automatically do multilevel sorts, as shown in Figure 38.4. First, select the columns you wish to sort. Then select *Sort...* from the *Tools* menu. In this case Word has sorted by first name, then last name within first name.

Figure 38.4
Word has sorted by first name then last name *within* first name in this example.

Employee		Extension	Birthday		
Billie	Holiday	472	12	10	40
Dr. John		400	11	07	45
Robert	Johnson	450	01	01	50
Robert	Benson	425	04	15	47

Employee		Extension	Birthday		
Billie	Holiday	472	12	10	40
Dr. John		400	11	07	45
Robert	Benson	425	04	15	47
Robert	Johnson	450	01	01	50

CHAPTER 39

Math and Formula Features

FEATURING

- Basic math with the *Calculate* command
- *Calculate* command tips and traps
- Formula typesetting commands
- Introduction to the Equation Editor program

Word 5's built-in *Calculate* command will add, subtract, multiply, and divide numbers you've typed in your documents. It is perfect for creating simple financial reports or for proofreading columns of numbers. The feature has some peculiarities, however, so if you plan to use it extensively, review the examples in this chapter and create some of your own before your next rush project.

Word also provides ten formula-creation commands called *formula-typesetting commands* for displaying and printing equations containing radicals, brackets, and integrals, among other things. Some of the commands are useful even if

Math and Formula Features

you are not a scientist or a mathematician. These commands are demonstrated in this chapter.

Finally, Word 5 comes with a separate program called Equation Editor, manufactured by Design Sciences Inc. It will be of particular interest to scientists and academicians. Microsoft ships a customized version of the program designed specifically for use with Word 5. This chapter introduces you to the Equation Editor and tells you how to obtain additional information or an even more robust version of the program.

Word's Built-In Math Capability

How often have you typed an important memo and made a math or typing error in a column of numbers? Word's Calculate feature can minimize mistakes like these. In its simplest capacity, the command adds columns or rows of numbers, as shown in Figure 39.1. As you will see in a moment, it can do much more than add.

Adding with Calculate

The Calculate feature performs addition on selected columns or rows of numbers. For simple addition, highlight the numbers you wish to add, then choose

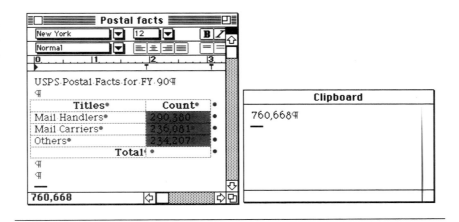

Figure 39.1
The Calculate feature gives Word 5 limited but useful math capabilities.

Calculate from the *Tools* menu or use the ⌘-= shortcut. (Press the equals sign on the main keyboard; don't use the one on the numeric keypad unless you have Num Lock engaged.)

Word will add (sum) the selected numbers and place the answer in the lower-left corner of your document window *and* on your Clipboard.

Two things should be obvious to you at this point. First, since the answer is on the Clipboard, you can paste it into your document. Second, since the answer is on your Clipboard, whatever else was previously there is *gone*. There is no *Undo* here, so if you have your life's best work residing on the Clipboard only, save it somewhere else before calculating.

Incidentally, nearly anything you do after issuing the *Calculate* command will overwrite any information in the status area at the lower-left corner of your screen. Even if the results of your calculation disappear from the status area, don't panic. Your answer will remain on the Clipboard until you copy, cut, or perform some other operation that alters the Clipboard.

You need not place plus signs between numbers you wish to add. Thus, if you were to highlight *2400 1000,* Word would place *3400* on your Clipboard.

Word ignores most but not all selected words, symbols, and punctuation as you will see in a moment. It will attempt to include commas in *answers* if commas are extant in the *original* numbers. Answers will be formatted using the maximum number of decimal places in the selected text. Thus, typing, highlighting, and calculating *2,400 + 1000.000* would result in *3,400.000,* since one of the numbers contained a comma and the other had three decimal places in the modulus.

Word treats numbers surrounded by parentheses as negative numbers, so if you highlight *2400 + (1000),* the answer will be the sum of the positive and negative numbers, *1400*.

Multiplication, Division, Percentages, and More

Word supports more complex math, within reason. If you type *2400 – 1000,* the answer will be *1400.* Placing an asterisk between two numbers—like *2 * 2*

Math and Formula Features

and highlighting both numbers will effect multiplication, giving the answer *4*. Division works as you'd expect. The string *2400/2* would yield *1200*.

There is even a percentage function of sorts. The string *80 * 10.0%* would result in *8.0*.

These features are nowhere near as robust or predictable as a full-blown spreadsheet, so you will need to keep an eye on them. For instance, you might expect that *2400 – 10%* would produce *2160* (the result of 2400 – 240). But Word doesn't work like that. Figure 39.2 shows some examples of correct and incorrect uses of the various Calculate features. The *Calculate* command was used to create all of the results that were then pasted into the right column in Figure 39.2. Creating your own examples is a good way to understand this feature's strengths and limitations. A *table* was used in Figure 39.2, but you need *not* type your examples in a table. Calculate will attempt to compute any group of numbers you highlight, whether they are in tables, tab-separated blocks, or even sentences.

Notice that in lines 1 through 6, Word provides the results you'd expect. Line 7 has a problem, apparently due to the parentheses used to surround the text. Changing the parens to brackets solves the problem, as you can see in line 8.

Figure 39.2
Use care when calculating.

	Highlight and calculate:	Result:
1	2400+1000	3400
2	2400 1000	3400
3	2400-1000	1400
4	2400 (1000)	1400
5	$2,400-$1,000	1,400
6	2,400.000-1,000.00	1,400.000
7	$2400-$1000 (this is selling price-discount)	0
8	$2400-$1000 [this is selling price-discount]	1400
9	2400/1000	2
10	2400/1000.00	2.40
11	2,400*1,000	2,400,000
12	2400*10%	240.0
13	2400-10%	2399.9
14	2400-(2400*10%)	2160.0
15	2400+100*2	5000
16	2400+(100*2)	2600
17	2400+(200)	2200

Notice the percentage computations in lines 13 and 14. In order to get the right answer you must first have Word compute 10% of 2400 and then have it subtract the answer from 2400. Parens work for this purpose. Word first does the math in parens, then works outside of them. But there's a potential gotcha as you can see in line 17. Since Word always treats single numbers in parens as negative numbers, the results on line 17 are quite different from those in line 16. Use parens with care, or better still, do the fancy work in a spreadsheet then copy and paste it into your Word document. *Chapter 44* will show you how to link Word documents and spreadsheets and how to use System 7's publish and subscribe features. These are often better ways to place complex math results in Word documents.

Formula Typesetting Commands

If you need to type complex formulas, Word now gives you the choice of using its built-in *formula typesetting commands* or the more fully featured *Equation Editor*. In this section we'll explore the ten built-in commands that let you construct complex equations. Some of these commands, like *Box* and *Fraction* may be of interest even if you don't create complex formulas.

Syntax for Formula Commands

You type formula-typesetting commands directly into your documents. They all begin with a special character created by holding down the ⌘, Option, and backslash (\) keys simultaneously. This special character tells Word that the text that follows contains special formatting instructions. For instance the command string \X(Let Me Out) tells Word to draw a box around the words *Let Me Out*. The Command .\F(1,2) tells Word you want to create the fraction ½. A *command string* consists of several parts. For instance, in the string .\F(1,2) the .\ tells Word that a formula-typesetting command follows. The letter *F* is the Word 5 command for *Fraction*, and *(1,2)* are the *arguments* used by the command. Many commands have *options*. There are rules about which arguments and options can be used together, and in what order. Sometimes there are command limitations. For instance, Word's arrays can have no more than 39 arguments. Collectively, the rules and guidelines described above are called the command *syntax*.

Math and Formula Features

To type and view a *command string*, place Word in Normal view with *Show* ¶ turned *on*. To see how the command string will *print*, choose the *Hide* ¶ command either using the ribbon, the *View* menu, or the ⌘-J shortcut. Switching to Page Layout view will also show you how command strings will print. When you get proficient with the commands you may find yourself working in Page Layout view for "instant" gratification.

Microsoft recommends that you type these commands at the beginning of new lines (paragraphs), but you may find that they'll work in the middle of lines too.

Figure 39.3 shows examples of all ten commands and the results they produce. The first column contains the command name and the basic command code. The second column shows a typical command string—examples of things you might type. Column three shows the results of the command when printed or displayed in Page Layout view or in Normal view with Show ¶ off. You may want to refer back to Figure 39.3 as you read more about each command and its options and syntax. Commands are shown in uppercase, but lowercase will work as well.

Array (.\A)

Use this command to create one- or two-dimensional arrays (usually columns of numbers). An array command can contain a maximum of 39 arguments. There are array options that let you specify the number of columns, the alignment of numbers (left, right, or center), and options for specifying vertical and horizontal spacing of the numbers.

Option	Notes
.\AL	Aligns left
.\AR	Aligns right
.\AC	Aligns center
.\CO$n$	Sets the number of columns to n
.\VS$n$	Vertical spacing between lines in n points
.\HS$n$	Horizontal spacing between column in n points

Box (.\X)

Use this command to draw a box around whatever you type in parentheses—the argument. The default command draws all four box sides. You can have word draw only specified sides (like just the top or just the left and right sides) by specifying the desired sides as options. As you can see in Figure 39.3, it is possible to embellish text in the argument. Word will accommodate for large type sizes, bold characters, etc. Here are the options for the box command.

Option	Notes
.\BO	Draws the bottom line
.\LE	Draws the left line
.\RI	Draws the right line
.\TO	Draws the top line

Bracket (.\B)

This command places brackets alongside your arguments. You can specify the character to use for bracketing (usually { }, [], or < >). If you don't specify a character, Word will use parentheses. As you can see in Figure 39.3, it's possible to specify brackets on both sides of arguments by using the .\BC option with a left bracketing character like { or [or (. If you use other characters with the .\BC option, they will repeat on both the left and right side.

Option	Notes
.\LC.\c	Puts the character c on the left of an argument
.\RC.\c	Puts the character c on the right of an argument
.\BC.\c	Puts the character c on both sides of an argument

Displace (.\D)

Use this command to move the next character horizontally relative to the preceding character. The empty parens are required, as shown in Figure 39.3.

Option	Notes
.\FO$n$	Spaces forward n points
.\BA$n$	Spaces backward n points
.\LI	Draws a line from the preceding to the next characters

Math and Formula Features

Figure 39.3
Word provides ten built-in formula commands for use in scientific and other applications.

Command	Example	Results
Array (.\A)	.\A.\CO2.\HS4(5,10,15,20,25,30)	5 10 15 20 25 30
Box (.\X)	.\x(BOX!)	BOX!
Bracket (.\B)	.\B.\RC.\}(.\A(5,10,20))	$\left. \begin{array}{c} 5 \\ 10 \\ 20 \end{array} \right\}$
	.\B.\BC.\[(.\A(5,10,20))	$\begin{bmatrix} 5 \\ 10 \\ 20 \end{bmatrix}$
	.\B\BC.|(.\A(5,10,20))	$\begin{vmatrix} 5 \\ 10 \\ 20 \end{vmatrix}$
Displace (.\D)	.\X(BOX!).\D.\FO20()Look! .\X(BOX!).\D.\FO20.\LI()Look!	BOX! Look! BOX!____Look!
Fraction (.\F)	.\F(50,100)	$\frac{50}{100}$
	.\F(Miles,Gallons)	$\frac{Miles}{Gallons}$
	X=.\F(1+.\R(-23),6)	$X = \frac{1+\sqrt{-23}}{6}$
Integral (.\I)	.\i.\su(i=0,m,i)	$\sum_{i=0}^{m} i$
List (.\L)	.\L(Curly,Larry,Mo)	Curly,Larry,Mo
Overstrike (.\O)	.\O(c,l) .\O.\AL(c,l) .\O.\AR(c,l)	¢ ₵ d
Radical (.\R)	.\R(20,50)	$\sqrt[20]{50}$
	.\R(12)	$\sqrt{12}$
Super/Subscript (.\S)	Base.\S(Super,Sub)	Base$_{Sub}^{Super}$

Fraction (.\F)

Here's an easy way to create good looking fractions. The command syntax is .\F(*numerator,denominator*). Remember to place the numerator *first* in your argument. Arguments can be numbers, text, other equations, or combinations thereof. Figure 39.3 shows some examples.

Integral (.\I)

This command creates an integral containing three arguments in the order (*lower limit*, *upper limit*, *integrand*) Integrals of simple radical equations like square roots align with the equation centered vertically. Complex equations center on the radical value.

Option	Notes
.\SU	Creates a capital sigma (Σ)
.\PR	Creates a capital pi (Π)
.\IN	Specifies in-line format with limits displayed to the right rather than above and below
.\FC.\c	Specifies a fixed-height character (*c*) as the operator
.\VC.\c	Specifies a variable-height character (*c*) as the operator— height matches the integrand's height

List (.\L)

Since Word uses commas to separate items in an argument, there needs to be a way to create commas that display and print without confusing the typesetting feature. This is it.

Overstrike (.\O)

This command draws arguments on top of each other. You can adjust the character alignment using three options.

Option	Notes
.\AL	Aligns the left edges of character areas
.\AR	Aligns the right edges of character areas
.\AC	Centers alignment

Radical (.\R)

This draws one- and two-argument radicals. Figure 39.3 has examples of each.

Super or Subscript

This command places things a specified number of points above or below the baseline. If you don't specify options, Word uses a 3-point default. You cannot use these commands in conjuction.

Option	Notes
.\UP$n$	Places arguments n points above the baseline
.\DO$n$	Places arguments n points below the baseline
.\AI$n$	Alters the space allowed above the baseline n points
.\DI$n$	Alters the space allowed below the baseline n points

Creating Complex Formulas

As you can see in the Fraction example in Figure 39.3, it is possible to combine commands and formulas to create complex notations. You may need to surround some formulas and commands with parentheses.

Formula Glossary

Microsoft may have provided a formula glossary with your copy of Word. Look for it in the Glossary folder within the Commands folder wherever you installed your Word program. If you find a formula glossary, you can use it to explore sample equations and to simplify formula creation. For more on glossaries, see *Chapter 28*.

Printing Problems

A formula must be able to fit within the specified margins, indents, or table-cell width where you ask Word to place it. Otherwise it will not display or print. If you have problems, adjust margins, indents, or cell widths as necessary, or break up the formula.

Introducing the Equation Editor

The Equation Editor is a more elegant way to create complex formulas. It helps you build formulas using *palettes* of math symbols and templates. The feature "understands" formula typesetting rules and conventions, and will do much of the formatting for you.

Starting the Equation Editor

The Equation Editor is a separate program that runs under Word 5's supervision. The program and related help file should be installed in your Commands folder. They are shown in Figure 39.4.

Figure 39.4
Equation Editor and its related help file should be installed in your Word 5 Commands folder.

Equation Editor

Equation Editor Help

Normally, Word's installation program will put them where they belong. You can double-click to launch the program under System 7 or Multifinder, but it is better to use the *Object...* command on Word 5's *Insert* menu instead. As shown in Figure 39.5, the Insert Object dialog box will present you with several choices.

Figure 39.5
Start Equation Editor from the Insert Object dialog box, reached from the *Object* command on the *Insert* menu.

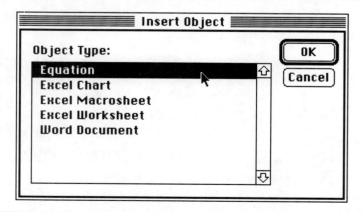

Math and Formula Features

Either double-click on Equation or highlight it and click OK. You will see an Equation Editor Window like the one in Figure 39.6.

You assemble equations by typing text and picking templates and symbols from the palettes. Equation Editor has a number of keyboard shortcuts which are detailed in the program's context-sensitive help screens.

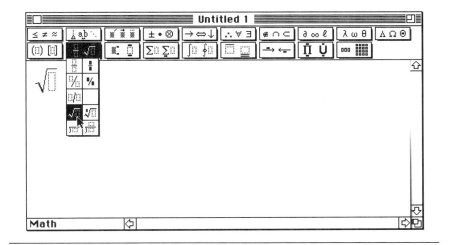

Figure 39.6
The Equation Editor window contains template and symbol palettes.

To receive online help about a particular palette or symbol, press your Mac's Help key if it has one, or choose *Help* from the *Apple* menu. You will see a window like the one in Figure 39.7

Closing the Equation Editor window pastes the equation you've created into your Word document at the insertion point. For more information about Equation Editor, refer to the separate *Equation Editor User's Guide* that came with Word 5. If you work a lot with equations, there is an even more powerful version of this program available from Design Sciences, Inc. Their address is 4028 Broadway, Long Beach, CA, 90803. Or phone (800) 827-0685.

Figure 39.7
Reach the Equation Editor's help screens from the *Apple* menu or press Help on your Mac's keyboard.

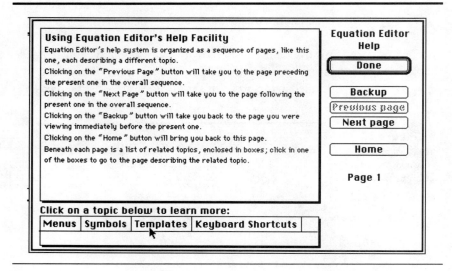

CHAPTER 40

Print Merge

FEATURING

- Ways to create personalized form letters
- Other uses for the print merge feature
- Intro to Word's envelope and label stationery

Word 5's *print merge* feature facilitates the creation of personalized correspondence and other documents. It does this by helping you combine or *merge* information from two different files. For instance, you might have a list of names and addresses in one file (called the *data document*) and use the data to address a form letter (called a *main document*) to selected people in the data file. Wherever you want data from the data document to appear in your main document you insert *data instructions*. For instance, to create personalized salutations in letters you would create a *salutation* field in your data document. In your main document you would insert the data instruction «*salutation*» after the word *Dear* and before a comma or colon. Word 5's *Print Merge Helper* has drop-down menus to guide you through this and other print-merge applications.

Once both the main and data documents are ready, the *Print Merge...* command on the *File* menu gets the ball rolling. Merged letters can be sent directly to your printer or they can be placed in *RAM*, then saved to disk for further editing and later printing.

Print Merge

Figure 40.1
A print-merge project requires a *data document* and a *main document*. It produces multiple new documents containing information from both the data document and the main document.

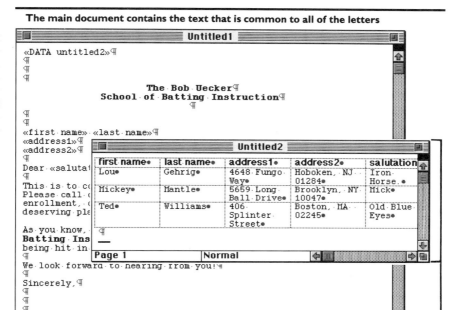

In either case, Word will automatically take care of things like word wrap and pagination for each new letter. Figure 40.1 shows an overview of the elements in a print merge project.

If you need to include personalized information not contained in the data file, Word will stop at appropriate points in the print-merge process and ask you to enter the information from the keyboard, thanks to something called the *ASK...* feature. A variation of ASK... called *SET...* makes it easy to insert common things in every copy of a particular project. Print Merge can also perform simple *math* calculations. For instance if your data document contains customers' invoice and payment amounts, each letter can contain a unique, *calculated* balance-due amount based on the data in the data document.

Print merge can make simple decisions as it encounters certain conditions. For instance, you can tell it to print a company name in the inside address of a letter *IF* the data for a customer in the data file contains one, or *ELSE* close-up what would otherwise be blank space in the letter when there is no company name. The devices that make this possible are referred to as *merge instructions*.

Before we dive into the details of *Print Merge...* and its helper, we should mention that, while most people use print merge for personalized correspondence, it can be just as easily used to create custom forms, print name tags, assemble legal documents, or crank out mailing labels. Keep this in mind as you explore the wealth of print-merge features offered by Word 5. Once you understand these powerful tools, you'll probably think of many new uses for them.

By the same token, a few people try to use Word's print merge features when they should switch to a more powerful database program like FileMaker with its robust data entry, management, and selection features. Moreover, some Word print merge features require the use of simple programming statements and techniques. While anyone can learn these things, it will take time and experimentation. Unfortunately, a book this size cannot cover all of the problems or contain recipes for every merge application you are likely to encounter. Sometimes it will be quicker to cut and paste than to set up a new merge design. Remember the old expression: *When you get a new hammer, everything looks like a nail*. If you are starting a big, data-intensive project, be sure you are using the right hammer.

About Data Documents

Data documents are organized collections of information (they're databases actually). As you will soon see, Word 5's Print Merge Helper can quickly lead you through the creation of a new data document. It automatically stores data document designs as Word *tables*.

Word can also use imported data stored in paragraphs or data from other programs like Excel or FileMaker as data documents.

Regardless of their origin, data documents contain *records* and *fields*. For instance, in an employee data document there is usually one *record* for each *employee*. Each record contains multiple *fields*, which do *not* change from record to record. There might be one field for the employee's *name*, another for her home phone number, a third for a work phone extension, etc.

Overview of a New Print Merge Project

For each new project you'll need to

- Create a new data document with Data Document Builder
- Enter information into the data document
- Type and proof the text of your main document
- Insert Data Instructions in your main document
- Check for design and data-entry errors
- Merge and print multiple documents.

You need not follow this order exactly. For instance, you can create the main document first and then create a data document, or vise versa. Since data documents are simply Word documents containing tables, you can edit information in them at any time prior to doing the actual merge. Once you feel comfortable with print-merge concepts, feel free to do things in any workable order that pleases you.

Design Data and Main Documents

You need not type your main document first, but it is often helpful to sketch one out or type a draft to get a sense of which information you will need from data documents and where to insert it. Perhaps the most important part of a new project is the thoughtful design of a useful, easy-to-maintain data document.

Plan Ahead When Designing Data Documents

If you are clever, you can use the same data document for more than one project. For instance, you might use a single, properly designed employee data document with *different* main documents to print mailing labels, phone lists, personalized memos, and name tags for the company picnic. The trick is to *think ahead* when creating new data documents.

For instance, if you plan to use an employee data document to send employees letters or memos, you might want one field for the employee's full legal name, and another for an informal salutation. That way you could address mailing envelopes to *Dr. Norman Tirebiter* and have the salutation of your letters or memos read *Dear Norm* or *Dear Doc*.

On the surface, there doesn't appear to be anything wrong with creating a single field for all the address information needed for letters and labels. Many people do this. Then they type everything—the recipient's name, company name, street address, city, state, and zip—in that single field. But you should consider breaking an addressee's data up into multiple fields. For instance, create *separate* fields for recipients' *first* and *last* names. This will come in handy if you ever plan to use Word's sort feature to produce alphabetized lists or labels sorted by last name. Putting ZIP codes in their own field will let you save money by sorting bulk mailings by ZIP code, and so on.

Space limitations preclude a thorough exploration of the science of database design—and that's what you are really doing here. If this is your first merge project, experiment with *small* data documents containing a dozen or so representative records. Try your sample data document with a number of different main documents, or have an experienced print-merge user look over you new design before spending hours entering data into your first data document.

Print Merge

CREATING A DATA DOCUMENT FIRST

For your first few projects, start with data documents. Here are the steps.

Open an empty, untitled Word document (*New* from the *File* menu or ⌘-N). Make sure the insertion point is at the *very beginning* of the empty document. You'll see why later.

Next, choose *Print Merge Helper...* from the *View* menu. You will see a modified Open dialog box something like the one at the top of Figure 40.2. It is asking if you want to locate an *existing* data document or create a new one. Click the *New* button to bring up an empty *Data Document Builder* dialog box, similar to the one shown in the bottom of Figure 40.2.

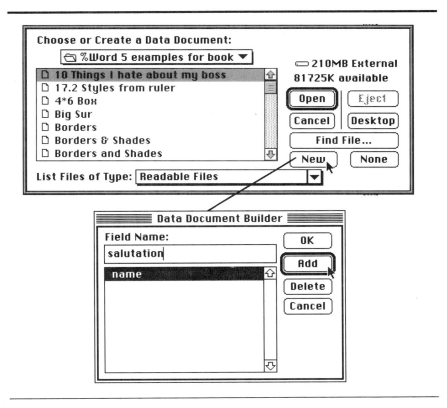

Figure 40.2
Create new data documents with Print Merge Helper. Start by telling the helper which field names you plan to use.

Type the name for your first field (the salutation in the example), then press Return or click the Add button. Type the next field name, and continue adding field names until you are finished. The order of field names is unimportant. Be sure to click add for the last field. This is easy to forget!

Field names can be up to 253 characters long, but shorter is usually better. Don't use commas in field names if you are using the U.S. version of Word. Don't use colons in non-U.S. versions. Do not use identical field names in the same data document. When using Print Merge Helper, you can define a maximum of 31 fields.

To *delete fields*, highlight the unwanted field name in the Data Document Builder's scrollable list, then click the Delete button. To *edit names*, delete the undesirable name and add the correct one.

Saving New Data Document Designs

To save your new data document design, click OK. To quit without saving the design, click Cancel. When you click OK a new untitled document will appear. This will be your new *data document*. At the same time, a standard Save dialog box will ask you for a name and storage location for the new data document. Name the document and specify a storage location if you don't like the one Word has proposed, then click Save.

Here's where things get a little confusing. In the blink of an eye, Word will open another *new* untitled document and use it to create your data document (a *table*) using the field names you've provided. Click Save. The new table will flash on your screen momentarily, then disappear. This can be rather alarming, so be prepared.

Your earlier, untitled document (soon to be your main document) will *reappear* and Word will insert the name and location of your new data document at the top of this main document.

At this point you will have at least two documents listed in your *Window* menu—the data document and this new untitled main document. If you view them together at this point, they might look something like the ones in Figure 40.3.

Word has created a table with field names at the top (called the *header record*) and one empty row, ready for you to enter the data for your first data record.

Print Merge

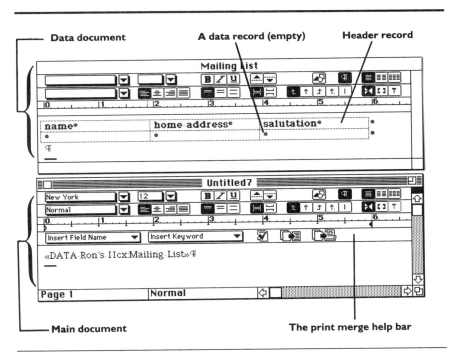

Figure 40.3
Typical data and main documents when you create a data document first. Note the data document's name and path in the main document.

In addition, it has placed the name and location of the data document (the path) in what will become your main document. Notice the new bar below the Ruler. It is called the print merge help bar. You'll use it later to create main documents.

ENTERING AND EDITING DATA IN A DATA DOCUMENT

Enter, edit, and navigate in data documents as you would in any other Word table. *Save early and often*. Place the insertion point in the first empty cell of the data document (under *name* in Figure 40.3) and type the data. Tab to the next field needing information (*home address* in our example). If you are using a single field to capture multiple lines of data (like the multiline address field in Figure 40.3) type the first line then press Return or use Shift-Return to enter a new line in the same field. (Whatever you do, be consistent.) When all of the lines have been entered in a field, tab to the next. When you reach the end of a record, tabbing again will create a new row for your next record.

CHAPTER 40

Creating a Main Document

Main documents contain the following things:

- The name and location of the associated data document
- Text and punctuation (the body of your document)
- Data instructions used by Word to merge data

Figure 40.4 shows a main document for creating a class-enrollment form letter. We'll discuss the various elements in detail.

The Data Statement—Path to Your Data Document

Each main document must begin with the (non-printing) name and location of the associated data document. This path needs to come *first* in a main document. It is called the *DATA statement*. You must place it before even your letterhead or other design elements.

As you saw earlier, Print Merge Helper can place this information at the beginning of the document for you if you properly position the insertion point in your main document before using Print Merge Helper to create a data document.

In Figure 40.4, Word will merge data from a data document called *Student Welcome Data* located in the *%Word 5 examples for book* folder on the hard disk *210MB External*.

Text in Main Documents

Use Word 5's word-processing and graphics arsenal to create text and design elements in your main documents. For example, the new student-enrollment letter shown in Figure 40.4 contains a letterhead that was created using paragraph shading, borders, white type, expanded characters and airplane symbols. The standard glossary entry •*Print Date* was also inserted.

The body of the letter was typed as usual, except that information to be supplied from the data document was left out. In its place, we inserted *data*

Print Merge

Figure 40.4
This typical main document contains a path to the data document, text, and data instructions.

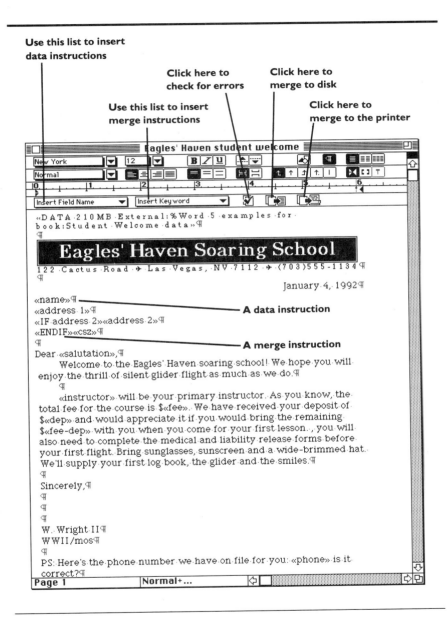

instructions containing field names and other merge devices like the *IF* instruction in the inside address and the *computation* instruction used to determine how much money students should bring with them.

Inserting Data Instructions in Main Documents

Print Merge Helper makes it easy to insert field names and other data instructions in your main documents. Place the insertion point where you want to insert a data instruction, then pull down the appropriate list from the help bar and pick the item to insert. For example, to insert the salutation field name in Figure 40.4, you would place the insertion point between the *space after* the word *Dear* and the comma. A quick trip to the *Insert Field Name menu* on the print merge help bar would insert the field name *salutation* and the required *print merge characters* (« and ») on either side of the file name.

When preparing the text of a main document, don't forget to include things like the space before a field name and any required punctuation following it.

To create the calculation required in the sample letter, it was necessary to insert a calculation command, reached from the *Calculations...* command on the *Insert Keyword* menu. Figure 40.5 shows typical *Insert Field Name* and *Insert Keyword* menus. They are both located on the print merge help bar. (See the *Merge Instructions* section later in this chapter to learn more about these advanced merge features.)

Before continuing, save your main document to disk.

Figure 40.5
Typical *Insert Field Name* and *Insert Keyword* menus, located on the print merge help bar.

TESTING AND PROOFING BEFORE PRINTING

Before cranking out a hundred or even a dozen letters, it is a good idea to *proofread* your work. Use Word's spell checker and grammar tools. Make any necessary corrections.

Then, run Print Merge Helper's *error checking program* by clicking on the checkmark icon in the print merge help bar. It will inspect your data and main documents looking for problems like missing data fields in the data document and misspelled field names in your main documents.

As a final check, you may want to merge some or all of your documents to a file and inspect them rather than printing out the whole batch. You'll learn how to do this next.

PRINTING MERGED DOCUMENTS

Records are always merged and printed in the order they occur in your data document. If necessary, sort your data document before merging. It is possible to restrict printing to only records containing certain data by using IF commands, explained later in this chapter in the section *Merge Instructions*. With your data in the desired order, start the merge process by making your main document the active document (click in it if necessary).

You can either print directly to your printer by clicking on the right icon in the print-merge help bar, or you can ask Word to create a new, untitled document containing all of your merged documents. Click the middle icon to do this. If you merge to a new untitled document, you can inspect everything on screen and print later.

All three of the print merge help buttons merge every record in your data document. Visiting the Print Merge dialog box (*Print Merge...* from the *File* menu) gives you a little more control over how many records get merged. You will see a dialog box like the one in Figure 40.6.

Here you have the same choice of testing for errors, printing to the printer, or creating a new, untitled document, but you also have some say in *how many* records are merged. Specify a range using the From and To boxes. For instance,

Figure 40.6
To merge, click on the appropriate print merge help bar icon or visit the Print Merge dialog box, shown here.

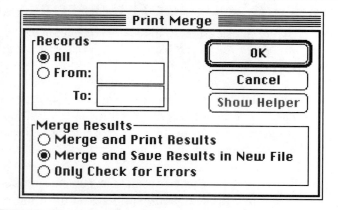

you could specify from *1* to *10* or from *25* to *50*. Each new record generates a new page.

To stop merging press ⌘-. (period) or the Escape key.

Merge Instructions

Word provides a number of ways to change its behavior based on the contents of individual records in your data document. For instance, it can insert special text if certain conditions are met or stop during each merge to let you enter unique text from the keyboard. Be prepared to spend some time experimenting and troubleshooting if you decide to use these features.

Calculations...

Calculation instructions let you insert numbers in merge documents based on the contents of records. You saw it in use in the student letter example. When creating a main document, use the Print Merge Helper to insert the Calculation instruction at the insertion point in your document. Choose *Calculations...* from the *Insert Keyword* menu. You will see a dialog box like the one in Figure 40.7.

Print Merge

Figure 40.7
Use the Insert Calculation feature to compute and insert numbers in merged documents.

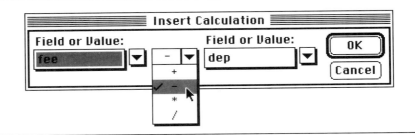

Use the drop-down menus in the Insert Calculation dialog box to specify fields or values and the type of calculation you wish to perform. In Figure 40.7 Word will subtract the deposit found in the *dep* field from the fee found in the *fee* field. You can use calculations with other instructions as you will see in a moment. For instance, it is possible to print text if the results of a calculation warrant it.

ASK...

The ASK feature will cause Word to stop during the merge process to ask you for keyboard input to be printed. It will stop each time a new *record* is merged and prompt you for a keyboard entry.

This feature is normally used to include data in *main documents* that has not been stored in the *data document*. Suppose, for example, that you were creating ten new-student welcome letters like the one in our example, and that you wanted to enter a date and time for each student's first lesson. Suppose further that your data document does not contain a field for first lesson dates and times.

Setting Up an ASK Entry

When designing your *main document*, move the insertion point to the beginning of a line near the top of your document (following the DATA statement). Then pick *ASK...* from the *Insert Keyword* menu on the print merge help bar. Word displays a dialog box like the *top* one in Figure 40.8.

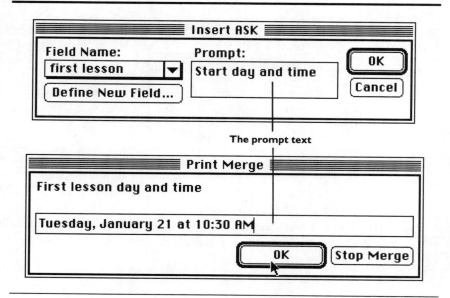

Figure 40.8
The Insert ASK feature (top) creates prompts for keyboard entries when you merge (bottom).

You would use this dialog box to create a new field unique to the *main* document (not the *data* document). Click on Define New Field, then type a new, legal merge field name (*first lesson* in our example). You can also enter a message that you want to see whenever you are expected to type from the keyboard. In Figure 40.8 the prompt would be *Start day and time*.

Next, insert the corresponding field name («*first lesson*» in our example) in your main document wherever you want the contents of the ASK entry to print. The ASK instruction goes beneath DATA near the beginning of the document, while the field names themselves are embedded.

Using ASK

When you actually merge your documents (ten letters, for instance) Word will ask you for ten lesson dates and times—one for each student's letter. You'll see a dialog box like the one at the bottom of Figure 40.8 for each student. Here, you enter the day and time then click OK or press Return.

(In a moment you will see a finished document including this feature and the results it produces. First let's look at *SET*....)

SET...

SET... works like *ASK...*, except that you are prompted *once* at the beginning of a merge print, and your keyboard entry is used for *all* documents being created. For instance, you could use it to insert *Winter* in the semester field in winter, *Summer* in summer, and so on.

Inserting a SET... Field Name

When designing your *main document*, move the insertion point to a line near the top of your document (following the DATA statement). Choose the *SET...* choice from the *Insert Keyword* menu on the print merge help bar. Word displays a dialog box like the one in Figure 40.9.

Figure 40.9
The Insert SET dialog box

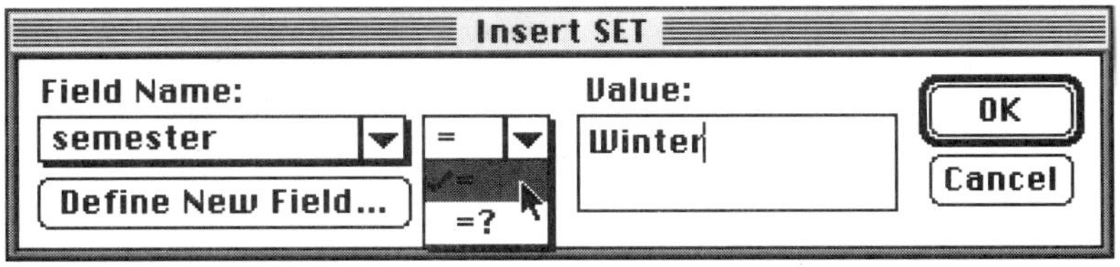

Use this dialog box to create a new field unique to the *main* document (not the *data* document). Click on Define New Field, then type a new, legal merge-field name (*semester* in our example). If you check the *equals sign* in the drop down menu, and type a value in the value box (*Winter*, for example) Word will print that value in each document until you change the Insert SET statement. If you choose the =? choice on the drop-down menu, Word will ask for a SET value each time you use the *Print Merge...* command on the *File* menu.

You can also enter a message that you want to see whenever you are expected to type from the keyboard.

Using SET...

When you actually merge your documents (ten letters, for instance), Word automatically prints the defined SET value in each student's letter at the points where you've inserted the field names.

Samples of SET and ASK at Work

Figure 40.10 shows a main document containing SET and ASK instructions near the top of the document, below the DATA line. The body of the letter contains the field names *semester* and *first lesson* where you want the SET and ASK information to print. The bottom part of Figure 40.10 shows the results.

Figure 40.10
SET and ASK place variable information in your merged documents.

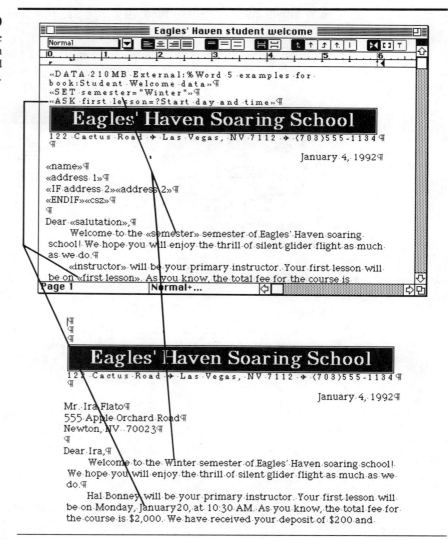

Eliminating Blank Lines Caused by DATA, ASK, and SET

Notice the three blank lines (paragraph marks) at the top of the sample merged document in Figure 40.10. They're caused by the DATA, SET, and ASK lines in the top of the main document. To prevent this, highlight all three paragraph marks in the main document and use the Character dialog box to define the marks as *hidden text*. Or use the hidden text keyboard shortcut, ⌘-Shift-X. You must also make certain that *Show Hidden Text* is not checked in the View category of the Preferences dialog box.

IF..., ENDIF..., and ELSE

You use *IF...*, its required companion *ENDIF...*, and frequently *ELSE* to cause Word to do different things, based on conditions it finds in fields in your data documents. For instance, you could have Word check the data document to see *IF* the deposit the student paid was equal to the total fee for the course. If the student had paid the total amount due you might have Word insert a sentence in her letter thanking her for the total payment; otherwise, *ELSE* would calculate the amount due and print a sentence requesting the balance.

IF statements can be used to prevent the printing of blank lines if a field is empty in a record. Figure 40.10 contains an example. In this case, Word checks to see if the «address2» field is empty.

IF statements can also compare numbers or text. IF uses the following standard comparison operators:

= (equals)

< (less than)

< = (less than or equal to)

> (greater than)

> = (greater than or equal to)

< > (not equal to a number or non-matching text)

Field Not Empty (checks for non-empty fields)

AND (a record must meet multiple conditions)

OR (a record must meet at least one condition)

NOT (the specified field must not meet the condition)

You can construct IF-ELSE statements in a number of ways. For instance, Figure 40.11 illustrates an IF-ELSE combination that does a math comparison on numbers in two fields and prints different sentences based on what it finds. Notice that the ELSE sentence contains more math.

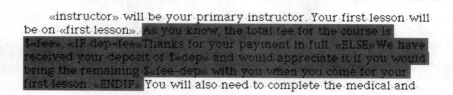

Figure 40.11
A typical IF-ELSE combination prints different sentences based on numbers found in the data document.

Place IF statements where you want them to work. Do this by moving the insertion point to the appropriate place in your main document. For instance in Figure 40.11 the insertion point was placed after the period and space following «*fee*».

Use the *Insert Keyword* drop-down menu choices to speed the construction of IF, ELSE, and ENDIF combinations. For instance, when you choose *IF... ENDIF...* or related choices you will see a dialog box like the one in Figure 40.12. It is asking for the name of a field to compare in your data record, and a value to compare.

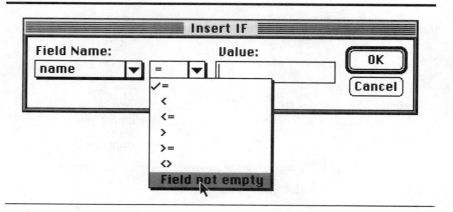

Figure 40.12
The *Insert Keyword* menu contains choices that bring up this dialog box to speed construction of IF statements.

A drop-down menu in this dialog box lists all of the available field names. When you click OK, the statement and *merge marks* will be inserted in your document. While these shortcuts can help you construct IF statements, you may *still* need to edit them from the keyboard.

INCLUDE...

Include is like an automated version of the *Insert File...* command. It will place the entire contents of a specified external file in your Word main document when you run a print merge. For instance, if you created a student phone-list document, and wanted to include that list in the body of each student letter, you could place an INCLUDE command at the appropriate spot in the main document.

When you insert the INCLUDE command using Word's Print Merge Helper, Word will present a File dialog box and ask you to locate the desired file.

Documents you include can also contain INCLUDE statements, making it possible to "nest" INCLUDEs.

NEXT

NEXT is useful when you want Word to move on to the next record in a data document without starting a new page. You might want to use this to print different labels on a page or to create a list. Place the insertion point at the location in your document where you want Word to switch to the next record and choose *NEXT* from the drop-down *Insert Keyword* menu on the print merge help bar.

ATA...

The *DATA...* choice on the *Insert Keyword* menu lets you replace the DATA statement at the top of your main document, thereby changing the data document used with the main document. You can have only one DATA statement in a main document.

This command will highlight your old DATA statement, then present a File dialog box, which you use to select the desired data document. Word will insert the replacement DATA statement, including the word DATA, the path, and the required merge marks.

IF YOU DON'T USE PRINT MERGE HELPER

It is possible to construct everything you need for a merge project without using the new Print Merge Helper. Just be sure you follow the merge rules. Data statements must be at the very top of your main document, merge marks must appear where required and so on. To manually insert merge marks « and », do not use greater than and less than characters. Use the keyboard combinations *Option-* and *Shift-Option-* to insert « and ».

RESTARTING STOPPED MERGES

If you are running a merge project and must stop before all documents have been printed due to a printer error or other problem, it is often possible to pick up where you have left off. The best way is to count the number of successful documents printed then enter the next number in the From area of the Print Merge dialog box (shown in Figure 40.6). For instance, if you tried to print ten letters and had a printer problem after the sixth letter printed, place 7 in the From box.

WORD'S PREDESIGNED LABELS AND ENVELOPES

Word is shipped with stationery for various kinds of blank labels and envelopes. Look for them in the *Mailing Labels* and *Envelopes* folders in the *Sample Documents* folder. You can use this stationery to create main documents for your mailing projects. Follow the instructions in the Readme files, also found in those folders.

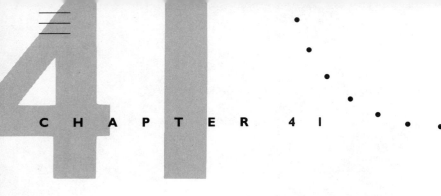

CHAPTER 41

Creating a Table of Contents and an Index

FEATURING

- Quick TOCs and Indexes
- Fancy TOCs and Indexes

Word will help you create a table of contents (TOC) for your documents. If you format your headings using Word's *standard heading styles* or *Outline* feature, the *Table of Contents...* command on the *Insert* menu will quickly *compile* (create) a simple but very usable table of contents and place it in a new section at the beginning of your document. It is also possible to *manually* select items to appear in your table of contents. You do this by identifying words and phrases in your document using *hidden text codes* called *TOC Entry* codes. You can control the appearance of the table of contents as well. Your TOC can have one or multiple levels.

Word's *Index Entry, Index...,* and hidden Index codes work together to produce equally simple or distinctive *indexes* at the end of your document.

Creating a Table of Contents and an Index

QUICK TABLE OF CONTENTS

Figure 41.1 shows a simple table of contents containing only *paragraph headings,* created using Word 5's standard *heading 1* through *heading 3* styles

Notice that Word has placed the TOC in its own new section at the beginning of the document. It has automatically inserted tabs, leading dots, and page numbers. To format and indent the new table of contents, it has used *toc styles* corresponding to the standard-heading styles. Thus, headings in the document formatted with standard *heading 3* will appear in the TOC formatted with a standard style called *toc 3*.

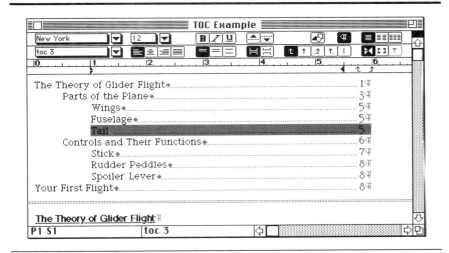

Figure 41.1
You can produce simple multilevel TOCs using Word's standard heading styles.

To create a TOC like this, begin by formatting your document's headings with Word's standard-heading styles. (These styles can be added to your ruler's drop-down style list by visiting the Style dialog box. Be sure to hold down Shift when clicking on the ruler's style menu. See *Chapter 17* for more about styles.)

When you have typed and proofed your document, and are happy with margins, headers, footers and other design elements affecting page breaks, pick *Table of Contents...* from the *Insert* menu. You will see a dialog box like the one in Figure 41.2.

Figure 41.2
The Table of Contents dialog box

Use the default choices shown in Figure 41.2 (Collect: Outline, *Show Page Numbers* and Level: All. Click Start or press Return.

Word will *compile* the new TOC. It starts by repaginating your document. Then it will create a new section at the top of your document and place the TOC in it.

You can edit the resulting TOC as you would any other text in your document. Feel free to embolden characters, change line spacing, etc. As you'd expect, changing the *style definitions* for standard styles *toc 1* through *toc 9* will change the appearance of your TOC.

If you already have a table of contents when you try to create a new one, Word will ask if you want to replace the old one or create an additional one. Sometimes it is a good idea to create an additional TOC and then delete the old one once you've determined the new one is satisfactory.

Creating Quick TOCs if You Outline

Documents created using Word's *outline* feature can quickly create simple TOCs too. *TOC levels and styles* will correspond to the *outline levels* you use, because outline levels are automatically formatted as heading styles (heading 1, heading 2, etc.). Polish the content and pagination of your document, then use the default Table-of-Contents... command settings described above. See *Chapter 42* for more about outlining.

Elegant TOCs

While the simple steps above are fine for most documents, there may times when you will want to create more complex TOCs. For instance, you might want to include items in the TOC that are not paragraph headings, or to suppress page numbers for a particular heading. You do these things by using *TOC-entry codes* instead of heading styles to define TOC entries.

Contents codes are *hidden-text markers* placed before and after the text you want to have appear in your TOC. A complete TOC entry consists of three parts: the *contents code*, the *text* of the entry itself, and the *end-of-entry code*.

Handy Tip: As you will see, for both TOCs and indexes, Word uses hidden codes to mark entries. You can save a lot of time by assigning keyboard shortcuts to the commands that enter the codes.

Suppose you need the *Theory of Glider Flight* heading to appear in the TOC without a page number and you want the next two entries to appear as they did in our first example; but you want to add another level containing entries gleaned from the text of the document.

Figure 41.3 shows a portion of a new TOC and the coded text that created it. Examine the figure, then read on to see how to easily add codes like these.

Adding Hidden TOC Codes

Start by making sure that the Show Hidden Text preference has been *enabled* using the View category of the Preferences dialog box. (See *Chapter 9* for help with preferences.)

Select (highlight) the text you want to use as a TOC entry (*The Theory of Flight*, for instance). Pick *TOC Entry* from the *Insert* menu. Word will insert a TOC code at the beginning of the entry and, if necessary, an end-of-entry code at the end of the selected text. There is no need for the end code if your selection ends with a paragraph mark.

To suppress page numbers insert a colon (:) between the last character in your text and the end-of-entry or paragraph mark. You can see an example of this in the first entry in Figure 41.3.

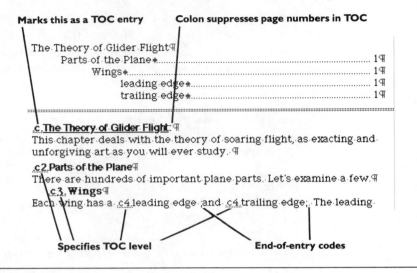

Figure 41.3
Here's a portion of a TOC shown with the text and hidden codes that created the TOC entries.

To assign *levels* to entries, insert numbers between the hidden *C* and the hidden period in TOC-entry markers, as shown in the rest of the entries in Figure 41.3. As you can see from the example, a 1 is optional.

To compile a coded TOC, use the *Table of Contents...* choice on the *Insert* menu, but click the *.C. Paragraphs* button in the Collect box. Alas, you cannot combine *Outline* and *.C.* coding to create a single TOC.

Restricting TOC Levels

If you want to supress the printing of one or more TOC *levels*, specify the From: and To: levels you wish to print in the Table of Contents dialog box (see Figure 41.2). For example, you could create a TOC showing only section and chapter headings. This is a great way to create a second "contents at a glance" TOC for big documents. You could create a second, more in-depth TOC down to the paragraph level and print them both in your document. Answer *No* to the *Replace existing table of contents?* prompt when compiling multiple TOCs like this. Word will place the most recently compiled TOC first.

Printing Colons and Semicolons in Your TOC

If you use coded TOC entries and want to print colons or semicolons in your TOC text (*Chapter 10: Annie Feels Her Oats*, for instance), surround the text with *single*, *hidden* quotes. Thus, our Chapter 10 example would read .c. *'Chapter 10: Annie Feels Her Oats',* with the single-quote marks coded as hidden.

INDEX

Automatic indexes are created using hidden codes much like the ones used to code TOC entries. There are more codes, however, since indexes can be more complex than TOCs. Word compiles indexes on demand and places them at the end of your document in new sections which it creates for this purpose.

Quick Indexes

Quick indexes might be an oxymoron. *Simple* indexes can be created by using the *Index Entry* choice on the *Insert* menu to code selected (highlighted) words and phrases you want to appear in your index. Word can then compile an unembellished index. Here's how to do that.

As with coded TOC entries, start by making sure that you are done proofing, fiddling with margins, page endings, and the like. Be certain that the Show Hidden Text preference has been *enabled* in the View category of the Preferences dialog box. (See *Chapter 9* for details help with preferences.)

Then select (highlight) a word or phrase you want to use as an index entry (*wing*, for instance). Pick *Index Entry* from the *Insert* menu. Word will insert an index code (.i.) at the beginning of the entry and, if necessary, an end-of-entry code (;) at the end of the selected text. There is no need for the end code if your selection ends with a paragraph mark.

When you have coded *all* (yes *all*) occurrences of *each* word you want to see in your index, choose *Index...* from the *Insert* menu. You'll be rewarded with as dialog box like the one in Figure 41.4.

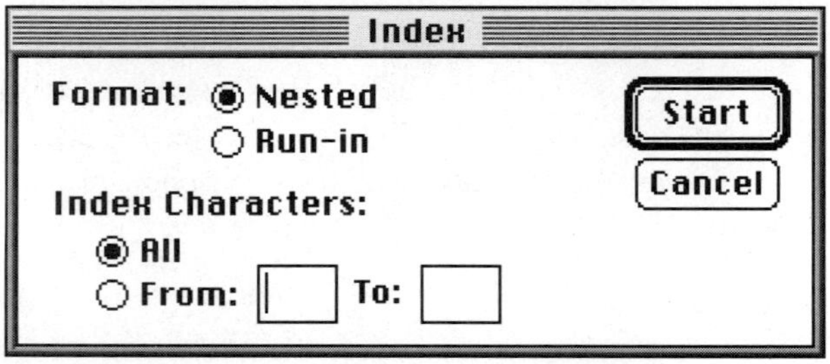

Figure 41.4
The Index dialog box starts the compilation of an index.

Index Coding Shortcuts

Place coded words and phrases in your Glossary. Insert them rather than typing and coding each time. Copy and paste works here too. In existing documents, rather than visiting *each* occurrence of *every* indexable word in your document, consider coding every first occurrence, then using Word's *Replace...* command to replace identical uncoded words and phrases with coded ones. You'll not want to use the Replace All button, however. Supervise each replacement yourself.

Fancy Indexes

Word offers quite a bit of control over the appearance of indexes. You can create multilevel indexes, italicize parts of entries, and more. Here are the tricks you need to know.

Index Subentries (Nesting)

To create sub-entries under a *common* heading, you need to retype (or copy and paste) the *common heading* at each occurrence of a word or phrase that you want to include in your index. Up to seven levels are possible. Note that levels are separated by colons. Figure 41.5 illustrates the technique for a three-level subindex. The top part of the example is the coded document text. The resulting index is shown at the bottom of the figure.

Notice that the first occurrence of *plane parts* is coded as an index entry, but the words *plane parts* are not coded as hidden text. That's because we want them to *print* at that point in the document. Subsequently, the words *plane parts* are coded as hidden text, since they are part of a nested index entry and you don't want them to print in these other places in the document.

Figure 41.5
Nesting under common terms entails repeating the common term at each occurrence of a sub-entry.

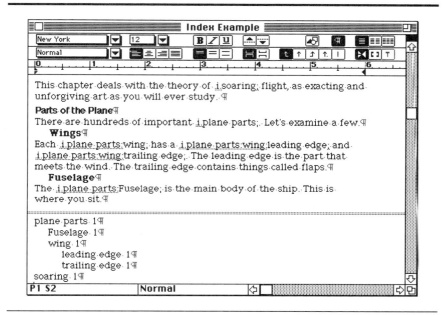

If you do a lot of this, make friends with the keyboard shortcut that toggles hidden text (⌘-Shift-X). Plan to visit the View category of the Preferences dialog box to turn hidden text on and off, since it can be pretty hard to read a document full of nested index codes like these.

Look carefully at the semicolons at the end of each coded index entry. See how they are not curly? That's how you tell that they are hidden text. If your indexed document contains unexpected semicolons or other characters, check to be sure you've defined all the codes as hidden text.

Text in Index Entries

You can type text in index entries. This has a number of benefits. Two are shown in Figure 41.6.

Earlier, we had defined the words *plane parts* in text as the common heading for *Fuselage, wing,* etc. Because we *selected* (highlighted) the lowercase words *plane parts* to define them as index entries, Word used exactly what we highlighted, lowercase and all. To place a capitalized *Plane parts* in the index, we

Figure 41.6
Typing text in index entries lets you capitalize index entries and refer readers elsewhere.

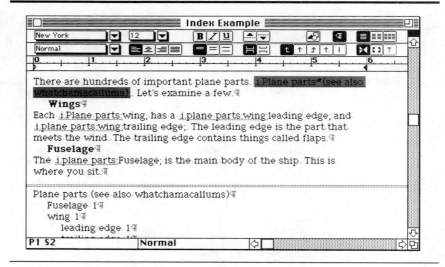

could have defined a *hidden capitalized* version of *plane parts* and defined *it* as the index instead of the actual body text. Understand here that *...hundreds of important plane parts* is not the entry now. This technique is illustrated in Figure 41.6.

Typing hidden text within an index mark is also a way to place *notes* (like *see also*) with your entries. Notice the change in the index itself resulting from the new entry technique. Notice in the figure that you must use the number symbol (#).

Cross Indexing with Text in Index Entries

You can do a form of cross referencing by typing several related hidden index words (like *.i.Plane parts;*, *.i.Parts, plane;*, and *.i.Air Frame;*) and have a separate entry appear at the appropriate place in your index. Figure 41.7 shows this at work.

Type carefully when you do this. Remember, each index item in your collection must start with *.i.* and end with a *semicolon*. Notice the use of a *comma* in the Parts, plane entry. It prints just fine here. Remember that index entries must be formatted as hidden text. Compare the resulting index in Figure 41.7 with the one in Figure 41.6. Indexing is hard work, but often worth it.

Creating a Table of Contents and an Index

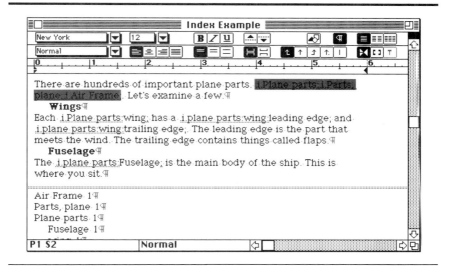

Figure 41.7
Type several index entries in the same place to create a form of cross referencing.

Formatting Index Entries

Word provides ways to italicize or make bold an index's page numbers. To make a page number bold, place the letter *b* between the *i* in the index code and the period (*.ib.Planes,* for instance). Use an *i* in place of the *b* for italics (*.ii.Planes*), or both (*.ibi.Planes*) if you want to *really* emphasize an entry.

Printing Colons and Semicolons in Index Entries

If you want to print colons or semicolons in your index text (*Glider Materials: metal, wood, fiberglass* for instance), surround the text with *single*, *hidden* quotes. Otherwise Word treats colons as indications of sub-entries. Thus, the Materials example above would read *.i. 'Glider Materials: metal, wood, fiberglass'* with the single quote marks coded as hidden.

Printing Page Ranges in Index Entries

It is possible to index selected portions of your index (A–M, for instance). Use the Index Characters: choice in the Index dialog box (revealed when you choose *Index...* from the *Insert* menu). Place the first and last letters in the From: and To: boxes respectively.

CHAPTER 42

Outlining

FEATURING

- How to organize your writing
- How Outline view speeds major renovations

Word's *Outline view,* located on the *View* menu (⌘-Option-O), is really more than a view. It's a collection of tools designed to help you plan, create, and reorganize long documents. It does this by letting you expand or decrease the amount of detail you see in on your screen. Figure 42.1 illustrates this.

The top window in Figure 42.1 shows part of a document in Normal view. The bottom window shows the same document in Outline view, with all of the body text *collapsed* (not revealed). Since only paragraph headings are visible in the bottom window, it's easy to see the overall organization (the *outline*) of the document. As you will soon find out, Outline view lets you control how much detail you see. For instance, you can view the first line of text following each heading if you wish.

Notice also that headings in Outline view are indented, giving you a better idea of the document's organization. Each new level is indented ¼" from the preceding one.

It's a snap to reorganize documents in Outline view. If you want to move all of the paragraphs having to do with *Landing gear* up, so that they appeared before *Tail*, simply drag the Landing gear heading using the Outline views special pointer. This will move all corresponding paragraphs, called *subtext*.

Outlining

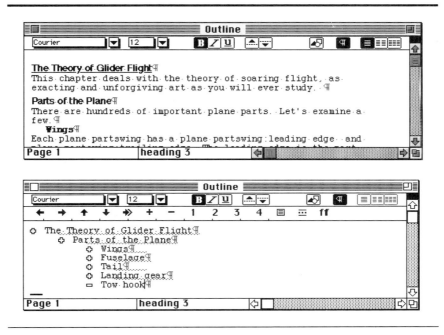

Figure 42.1
Outline view (bottom) lets you get a birds-eye view of large documents (top).

Finally, you can quickly *promote* or *demote* portions of your document using the Outline view tools, found on the *Outline bar.*

STYLES AND OUTLINES

In order to use Outline view, your headings need to be formatted using Word's standard-heading styles (•*heading 1* through •*heading 9*). If you didn't use these styles when you created a document, it is easy to reformat with them. And, as you probably know, you can change the appearance of standard headings if you don't like Word's standard styles. (See *Chapter 17* for more about styles.)

THE OUTLINE VIEW'S TOOLS

Outline view provides a number of unique tools. They are found on the Outline bar at the top of the screen. There is a new pointer shape indicating the pointer's ability to move large collections of text. It looks like a compass.

As you can see in Figure 42.1, on-screen text is often underlined with an unusual line style. This does *not* indicate text that will be underlined when printed. Rather, it indicates that there is collapsed subtext beneath it.

Plus Signs, Dashes, and Boxes

Large *plus signs, boxes,* and *dashes* appear next to many headings in Outline view. Boxes tell you that you are looking at body text; pluses indicate headings containing subtext; and minuses denote headings without subtext.

Finally, Outline view includes the *Outline bar,* with its special heading and body-text symbols.

The Outline Bar

Figure 42.2 summarizes the Outline bar's unique tools. They promote and demote heading levels, hide or reveal body text, and turn formatting on and off.

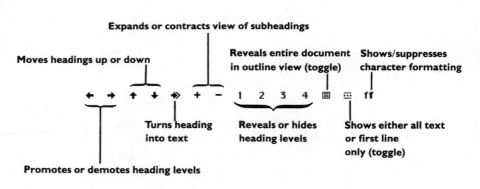

Figure 42.2
Tools on the Outline bar promote and demote headings and reveal and hide text and formatting.

The best way to understand the effect of these tools is to open a document containing standard Word headings in Outline view and experiment. If you don't have a document of your own, create one or use *Business Report* from the *Sample Documents* folder. The rest of this chapter describes the various Outline view tools, offering tips on how to use them.

CREATING NEW OUTLINES

When you start typing a new document in Outline view, Word assumes the first thing you want to type is a level 1 *heading*. Each new paragraph you type will take on the heading level of the previous paragraph.

One strategy is to type all of your top-level headings first, and then go back and insert headings in progressively lower heading levels. Another approach is to type all your document's headings in sequence, promoting and demoting as you go. It is even possible to type the entire document (all headings and text) in Outline view, without doing a traditional outline first.

The approach you choose is largely a matter of personal preference. In any scenario, you will need to know how to promote and demote headings and text.

PROMOTING AND DEMOTING

The two arrows at the left end of the Outline bar are used to promote and demote headings. Place the insertion point in the heading you wish to promote or demote. Click the right arrow to demote. Figure 42.3 shows this at work on a new outline originally typed with everything at level 1.

Here, we placed the insertion point in the *Parts of the plane* heading and clicked the right arrow once. Then we highlighted the headings *Wings* through *Tow hook* and clicked the right arrow *twice,* which demoted them two levels. The results are shown at the bottom of Figure 42.1. We have left the *Theory of Glider Flight* heading at the top level; *Parts of the Plane* is now the next level down, and *Wings* through *Tow hook* are at heading level 3. (You could confirm this by switching to Normal or Page Layout view.)

Promoting works as you'd expect. With the insertion point in a heading, click the left arrow to turn a level 3 heading into a level 2 heading, and so on.

Figure 42.3
Selecting headings and using the right arrow demotes them. The left arrow promotes.

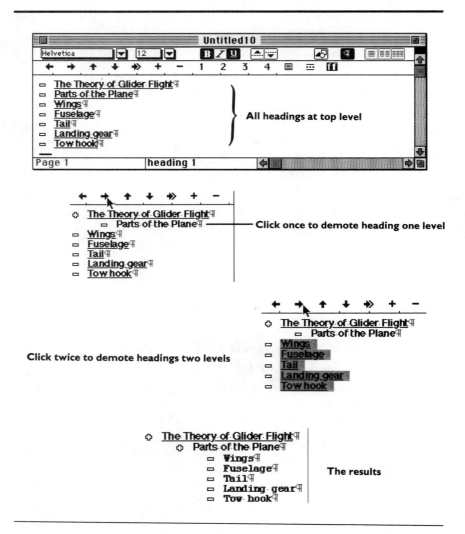

Outlining Existing Documents

Open your document in Outline view. You will see the first line of each paragraph. Place the insertion point in each heading and promote or demote them as desired. Then save your work. Use the viewing techniques described next to view and understand the organization of your document.

Expanding and Collapsing Outlines

One of the main reasons to use Outline view is to get a collapsed overview of a document's contents. Do this by expanding and collapsing views with the numbers on the Outline bars and the buttons to their right.

For instance, Figure 42.4 shows our Glider book in a bit more detail than the view in previous figures. The first line of text beneath each heading has been revealed. This was accomplished by clicking on the Show/Hide Body Text icon in the Outline bar. (Clicking the Show All icon reveals all document text.)

Figure 42.4
Click the box icon next to the 4 in the Outline bar to show the first line of text beneath each heading.

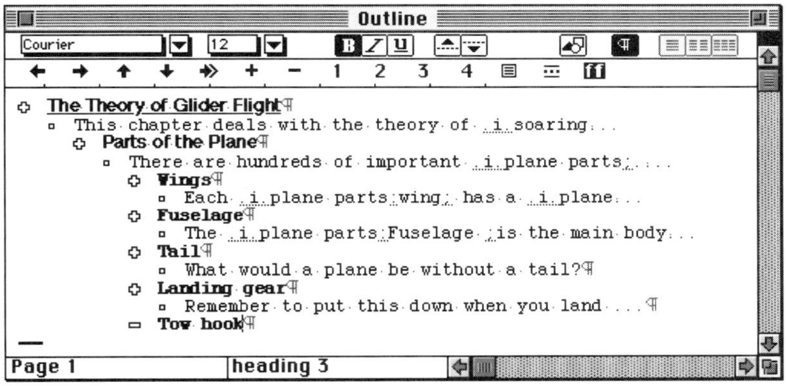

The document's true heading styles are apparent in Figure 42.4. The *ff* button at the end of the Outline bar turns character formatting on and off.

Clicking on the numbers *1* through *4* in Outline view hides or reveals the levels of your document. For instance, in our sample document, clicking on *1* will reveal only level 1 headings (the *Theory of Glider Flight*). Clicking on the *2* would reveal both level 1 and level 2 headings (*Parts of the Plane*). Clicking Show All on the outline bar, shows all text.

Split Views

Figure 42.5 illustrates a strategy for working on large documents. You can split the screen and show your document in Normal view in one half of the window and Outline view in the other.

Figure 42.5
Splitting the screen lets you work in Outline and Normal views at the same time.

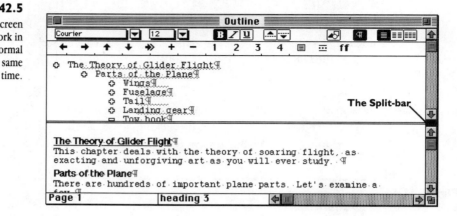

To split a window this way, double-click on the Split-bar. Then drag it up or down to change the size of the two areas. Double-clicking on the Split-bar in a split window returns you to a single window. Each part of the screen has its own scroll bars.

Moving Paragraphs

With the outline collapsed, you can move collections of paragraphs (also called subtext) by moving their associated headings. This facilitates the movement of entire chapters without needing to highlight them. Think of this feature as Drag-and-Drop on steroids. Figure 42.6 shows how it works.

Placing the pointer over the left edge of a heading changes the pointer's shape. It will look like a compass. Click and drag, and a large right arrow will appear along with a dotted line, like the ones shown in Figure 42.6. Drag the line and the pointer to where you want to move the text. Release the mouse button and the document will be reorganized.

The up and down pointing arrows on the Outline bar will also move items up and down. Highlight the headings, then click on the appropriate arrow.

Figure 42.6
Drag outline headings to move them and all their related subtext.

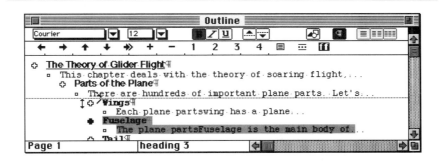

PRINTING OUTLINES

Printing in Outline view creates a document containing only the levels you see on the screen. Collapse the document to the desired level then use the *Print* command (on the *File* menu) or ⌘-P shortcut. Even if just the first line of text appears, Word will print the whole paragraph.

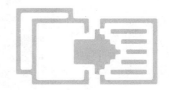

Working with Large Documents

FEATURING

- Connecting and printing a series of documents
- Page, paragraph, and footnote numbering in a series

One person's large document is another's small one. Word has the ability to create documents of virtually any length. At some point, however, you will find that Word's performance degrades as your document size increases. This is particularly true on older, slower Macs with limited RAM.

When performance (scrolling speed, spell checking, etc.) becomes disappointing, you might want to split a *single* document into *multiple* documents. Microsoft's published rule-of-thumb is to split a document every twenty pages. This seems conservative, given the speed and capacity of today's machines: Many people routinely work with documents containing hundreds of pages. So the choice is yours.

Another reason to split documents is to have different people work on different parts of the project. After everyone is done, you'll probably want to print the whole body of work as if it were one document.

After you've split a document (regardless of the reason), there are three ways to print the completed work. You can recombine all the parts and treat the resulting large document as a single entity. Or, you can keep the document broken into multiple sections and print the pieces separately. Finally, you can leave the work in pieces and have Word print them as a *series*. There are two things to watch, regardless of which approach you choose: consistency of appearance and correct numbering across document parts.

PLANNING FOR LARGE DOCUMENTS

If you know you are going to create a large document, create stationery, glossary entries, and possibly a *Work* menu first. Then use these tools to create the multiple parts.

If other people will be working on parts of the document, provide them with copies of your stationery and possibly copies of your custom glossaries, spelling dictionaries, settings files, and special fonts. You will definitely want to provide them with your various styles. The more alike your machines are, the fewer problems you will have during the crunch.

Develop a strategy. Consider making logical breaks at the beginning of chapters or sections. Publish a brief author's guide to ensure that everyone uses the same abbreviations and typing techniques.

CONNECTING MULTIPLE PARTS IN A SERIES

Word can treat pages from different files as a *continuous* series of pages for purposes of page numbering, indexing, TOC creation, and so on. To create a series, you need to show Word which documents to use and what order to use them in. The first document in a series "remembers" the name of the next in the series. Document two "remembers" the file name of document three, and so on.

You can connect a series of documents using the general technique described below. But modify the steps based on your page- and line-numbering needs. (Since page and line numbering are affected by the way you connect files, read about numbering issues before actually connecting your documents. See *Chapter 19*.)

General Steps for Creating a Series

Carpenters have a saying: "Measure twice. Cut once." In a strange way, that saying applies when creating a series. It is very important to *proofread* your work *before* connecting a series of documents. Anything that changes pagination after documents are connected can have a major ripple effect in a series. Measure twice. Cut once.

Once you have finished working on all of the separate documents (finished spell checking, paginating, footnoting, etc.), open the *first* document in your series. Use the *Document...* command in the *Format* menu to bring up the Document dialog box. Click on the *File Series...* button in the lower-right corner of the dialog box. You will be visited by the File Series dialog box, shown in Figure 43.1.

Figure 43.1
Use the File Series dialog box to connect separate documents.

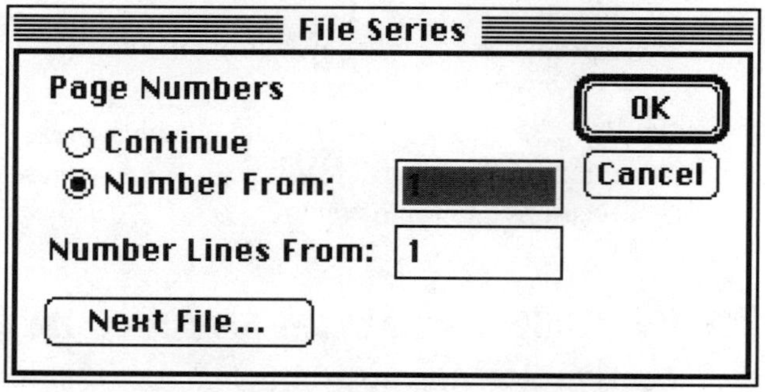

Click Next File.... You will see an Open dialog box. Locate the next document in your series and open it. The name of the file you've picked will appear near the bottom of the File Series dialog box. Click OK to close the dialog box, then click OK in the Document dialog box. Save the first document you opened. You have created a series consisting of the first and second documents.

Working with Large Documents

To add a third document to your series, open the *second* document and use the steps above to point to the third document. Save the second document, thereby instructing it to remember the name and location of the third. Continue to connect as many documents as you desire.

Numbering Issues

When you connect a series this way, Word will let you restart page numbers at the beginning of each separate document or let you create continuous numbers from beginning to end. Word can generate an index and TOC using information gleaned from all the documents in your series.

Line and paragraph numbering can be continuous or restart at the beginning of each document in the series. These techniques are described next.

Page Numbering

Assuming that you want page numbers to run continuously from the first page in the first document to the final page of the last, click *Continue* under the Page Numbers label each time you call up the File Series box.

If instead you want to define a specific starting number for the first page in each new document, specify the new starting number in the Number From: box each time you call up the File Series dialog box. See Figure 43.1. Remember to do this for *each* document.

Line Numbering

If you want line numbers to run continuously from the first page in the first document in your series to the last page of the last document in your series, you must check each document to see the last line number it contains, then type the *next* number in the Number Lines From: box in the next file's File Series box. See Figure 43.1. There is no way to effect continuous line numbering automatically.

Footnote Numbering

If you want footnote numbers to run continuously, you must check each document and note its last footnote number; then you type the *next* number in the

Footnote section's Number From: box in the *next file's* Document dialog box. See Figure 43.2. If you want more detail, see *Chapter 21*.

Figure 43.2
Open the preceding document to determine the last footnote number.

```
┌Footnotes─────────────────────────┐
│ Position: [Bottom of Page    ▼]  │
│ ○ Restart Each Page              │
│ ⦿ Number From: [12|  ]           │
└──────────────────────────────────┘
```

Paragraph Numbering

Use the same open and look technique to determine starting numbers for paragraphs. Open the next document and manually number its first paragraph. Use the *Renumber...* command on the *Tools* menu to renumber the rest of the paragraphs. Then note the last paragraph number and visit the next document in the series, if necessary.

TOC and Indexes

Once you have all of your documents connected in a series (and all index items marked in all documents), Word will create a TOC and index across all members of the series. Be sure to give the command from the first document in your series. Create them as usual (see *Chapter 41*). Be patient.

PRINTING MULTIPART DOCUMENTS

To print all the documents in a series, open the first one and print as usual. Be sure the *Print Next File* box is *X*'d in the Print dialog box (*Print...* from the *File* menu). You can print individual documents in a series separately by removing the *X* from the *Print Next File* box.

Publish and Subscribe, Link, and Embed

FEATURING

- Three ways to keep your documents current
- Publish and subscribe
- Embedded objects
- Links

System 7 users now have access to three new features: *publish and subscribe* (Apple Edition Manager); *linking* (DDE); and *embedding*. They all do similar things, but in significantly different ways. Their primary use is to keep documents up-to-date when information changes elsewhere. You can use any of them by yourself, on your own computer.

They also help you *share* information with other people. Publish and subscribe works over a network. All three can share information if you exchange diskettes containing the appropriate files.

WHICH, WHEN, AND WHY?

Publish and subscribe is the most capable of the trio. Programs capable of *publishing* (like Word 5 and Microsoft Excel) create information that you can insert in your Word 5 documents, making them the *subscribers*. Changes made in published documents will be reflected in your Word documents.

This even works over a network, making it possible for people to collaborate. If you don't have a network, publish and subscribe runs under *SneakerNet* (also called "pass the floppy").

If you are just a subscriber, your computer does *not* need to have a copy of the publisher programs in order for you to subscribe to it. For instance, you would not need Excel on your machine to receive updates of a co-worker's Excel projects.

A minimum of *three* files are created when people publish and subscribe. (You'll learn about them in a moment.) Since, in simple situations, you may only need to run Word to publish or subscribe, RAM requirements are minimal (if you consider 2 Mb minimal...). As you'll see in a moment, embedding and linking are more RAM hungry.

If you work alone, you can still use publish and subscribe by being both a publisher and subscriber.

Embedding is another way to keep your Word document current. It lets you paste *objects* into your Word documents containing not only the results of work done elsewhere, but also the file information needed to create the work. Thus, you can *double-click* on an embedded object in your Word document and Word will launch the program that created the object (Excel or the Equation Editor, for instance), and let you work in it. When you finish, and quit the program, your Word document is automatically updated.

If you save the resulting *Word document* to a diskette and give it to someone else with both Word and Excel on their machine, they can open the Word document and double-click on the embedded spreadsheet object. This will launch *their* copy of Excel and let them make changes to the *spreadsheet*. If they don't have Excel, they may even be able to use an Excel-compatible product. This is a great way to take work back and forth between home and office, since you can keep all related spreadsheets and documents together as one file. Computer dealers rejoice: when you embed, everyone involved needs enough RAM to simultaneously run both Word and the other programs that created the embedded objects if they plan to modify the objects.

Linking is a lot like embedding, but you use multiple, separate files. Typically, your Word document is the *destination* file and external information comes from *source* files. You *must* have all of the programs used to create document parts on *your* machine. Moreover, you must have enough memory to run *both* Word and the other program *simultaneously*. Linking is a good way to update part of a document when another part of that same document changes. Linking creates two files—a Word file and a file from the other program.

Publish and Subscribe

Let's start with the most powerful and confusing of the trio. To publish and subscribe you use three files:

- A subscriber document (a Word file in our example)
- A publisher document (an Excel spreadsheet for example)
- A third intermediate document (called the edition)

Suppose that someone else in your organization regularly updates rain statistics in an Excel spreadsheet. She creates and saves this spreadsheet file on her machine. In the process, she publishes a portion of that spreadsheet, creating a second file called the *edition* file.

Suppose further that *you* write a monthly memo containing some of those ever-changing statistics. You save your memo as a regular Word document that knows it is a subscriber to your friend's spreadsheet (because you tell it as much). You and your partner-in-crime are on the same network (though you need not be). Whenever you get ready to write the latest version of your monthly memo, Word will obtain your co-worker's current spreadsheet data, contained in the edition file (*and* sent over the network, in this scenario). Word automatically *inserts* the latest data at the appropriate location in your Word document. You don't even need to have a copy of Excel on your computer for this to work.

Publish and Subscribe, Link, and Embed

Incidentally, you are not limited to subscribing to Microsoft Excel spreadsheets; you can subscribe to any document created by any program that can publish (including Word 5).

Not all programs can publish yet, so check your manuals or contact software manufacturers for details regarding publish-and-subscribe–savvy software. Here are the steps for publishing and subscribing.

Publishing

To make a document a publisher, you save it normally, and (with the document on-screen) select the pertinent information and *publish* it. In the case of Word or Excel, that means a trip to the *Edit* menu for the *Create Publisher...* command. This will bring up a dialog box similar to the one in Figure 44.1.

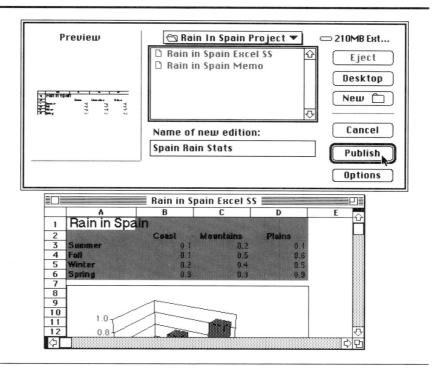

Figure 44.1
To publish, select the pertinent items, choose *Create Publisher...* to bring up this dialog box, name the *edition file*, and click the Publish button. Excel's publish feature is illustrated here. Word's is identical.

An Excel Publish dialog box is illustrated here, in keeping with our spreadsheet example. Word's Publish dialog box is reached the same way and is virtually identical to Excel's.

The publisher names the edition file (the *third* file required for publishing and subscribing). This file will contain just the selected information being published.

Use standard Mac techniques to specify a folder location for the publication, then click Publish. It's a good idea to save your original file at this point.

If people will be accessing your edition files over a network, be sure to store them in folders with appropriate access privileges. Contact your network administrator for assistance, if necessary.

Subscribing

To subscribe to an edition, open the Word document where you want to insert the published information. Place the insertion point at the desired spot. Then pick *Subscribe To...* from the *Edit* menu. You will see a dialog box like the one in Figure 44.2.

Figure 44.2
Use Word's subscribe dialog box to locate edition files and subscribe to them. Notice the unusual icon for edition files.

Using standard Mac folder-navigating techniques, locate the edition file of interest. They have unusual, fuzzy, brick-like icons, as you can see in Figure 44.2. If you are searching over a network, be sure the publisher has granted appropriate access privileges. Contact your network administrator for assistance, if necessary.

Once you've located the desired edition file, double-click on its name or highlight the name and click *Subscribe*. Soon, a copy of the published information will be placed in your Word document at the insertion point. This may take a moment if you are subscribing to a large file over a busy network. Remain calm. Figure 44.3 shows the rewards of patience and technology—copies of Excel spreadsheet cells automatically inserted into a Word 5 table. What a country!

Figure 44.3
When you subscribe, the published Excel spreadsheet cells (will appear) in your Word document.

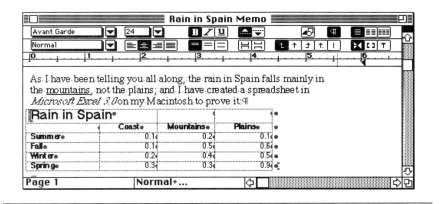

After you've first subscribed, save your Word document. Inasmuch as publish and subscribe is a new science (make that *art*), you will need to experiment with published information to see what happens regarding character embellishments, margins, styles, font incompatibilities, and the like. In our example, the font information came from Excel without difficulty. Moreover, centered spreadsheet cells became centered table cells. Experiment!

But if you make changes to the resulting Word table, you may be in for a surprise when you save, close, and reopen this Word document. For instance, if you apply table borders, adjust the table's indents and so on, these changes will all *disappear* the next time you update your subscription. Try to make the most of your style decisions on the publishing end. When necessary, create styles on the subscriber's end to speed the inevitable manual reformatting process. (Even if Word is both the publisher and subscriber, it does not send new styles with edition files unless you copy paragraph marks.)

Updating or Cancelling Your Subscription

If you are a subscriber, you *do* have control over when your document gets updated. But, unless you tell Word otherwise, it will attempt to update each time you open a subscriber document. *Undo* will not undo an automatic update.

When you open a document that subscribes, the command *Subscriber Options...* appears near the bottom of your *Edit* menu when you select a subscribed element. Choosing it brings up a dialog box like the one in Figure 44.4.

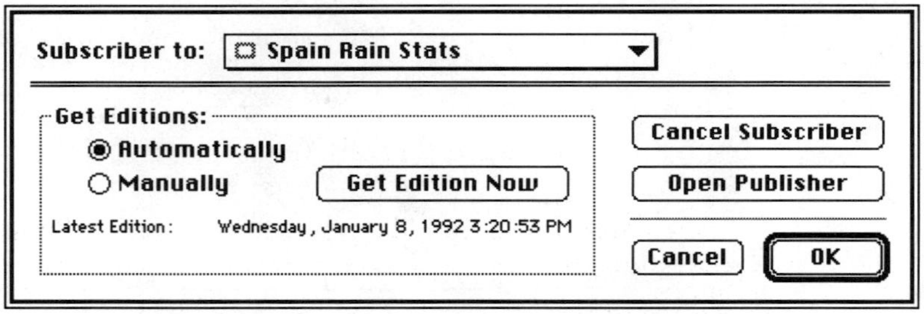

Figure 44.4
Use the *Subscriber Options...* command on the *Edit* menu to control updates and cancel subscriptions.

If you click the Manually button and save the file, automatic updates no longer occur. Thereafter, it becomes your personal responsibility to update your document. Any time you want an update, select the subscribed element and visit this dialog box and click Get Edition Now, which updates your document immediately. This dialog box also tells you when an edition was last modified—right down to the second...

Clicking *Cancel Subscriber* breaks your document's association with the publisher entirely. You are asked to confirm this. You must do this to delete information placed in your document from a publisher. Canceling a subscription does not remove the last version of the edition placed in your Word document.

Publishers have choices similar to those shown in Figure 44.4. Reach them by choosing *Publishers Options...* on the bottom of publisher's *Edit* menus.

If a subscriber can't find an edition, an abrupt dialog box announces that the edition can not be located because it is "missing". Check with the publisher to see if the document has been moved, renamed, deleted, or had its access privileges changed.

You may need to turn off automatic subscribing to edit certain kinds of objects. For example, Excel spreadsheet tables can be edited only when auto-subscribe is off.

Embedding

To *embed* existing information in a Word document (embedding a spreadsheet in Word document, for instance) you must have both applications running. Place the insertion point in the Word document that will receive the embedded information. In our example, you would then switch to the spreadsheet and select the information to embed. Copy it to your Clipboard.

Switch back to Word. Hold down the *Shift* key and choose *Paste Object* from the Word *Edit* menu. (The choice will only appear when you hold down the Shift key.) The object from your Clipboard will be pasted into your Word document. Save your Word file. Figure 44.5 shows an example. Notice that this time the spreadsheet looks like a spreadsheet rather than a table. That's because this time, it *is* a spreadsheet.

Figure 44.5
Embedding can save things like spreadsheet files in your Word documents.

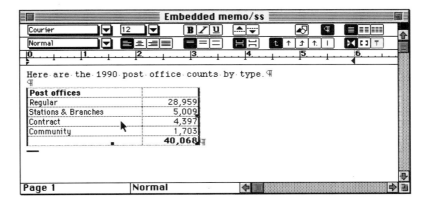

Updating Embedded Objects

Since the spreadsheet is saved as part of your Word document file, you update it by opening the Word document and double-clicking on the object. This launches the spreadsheet program (or other program that created the object). Your screen would look something like Figure 44.6.

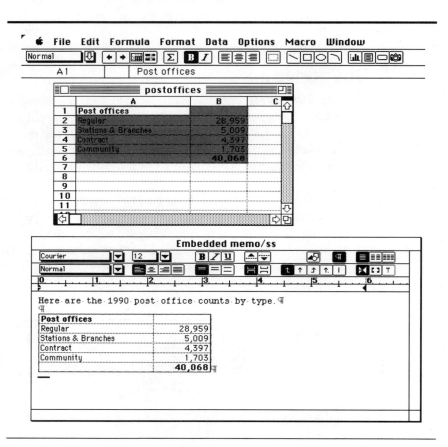

Figure 44.6
Double-clicking on an embedded object in Word launches the program that created the object.

You then edit the data in the originating program (Excel in our example) and use the *Update* command (⌘-Q) on the originating program's menu bar or paste a revised object, depending on the type of changes that you've made.

Publish and Subscribe, Link, and Embed

For example, if you simply changed the number of regular post offices in Figure 44.6, you could choose *Update* (⌘-Q) on the Excel *File* menu. Excel would move the revised spreadsheet numbers to your Word document and quit.

But suppose you made changes like those shown in Figure 44.7. Here you've added three extra lines and highlighted them.

Figure 44.7
Changes to objects sometimes require an additional trip to the *Paste Object* command (on the *Edit* menu).

	A	B	C
1	Post offices		
2	Regular	28,959	
3	Stations & Branches	5,009	
4	Contract	4,397	
5	Community	1,703	
6		40,068	
7			
8	Employees	760,000	
9	Employees per office	19	
10			
11			

Merely highlighting the additional lines and using the *Update* command in Excel will *not* add the new rows to your Word document. You must copy the new spreadsheet area to the Clipboard while in Excel, then use the Shift key in Word to reach the *Paste Object* command. A general rule-of-thumb is that if an embedded object changes in *size*, it will probably have to be re-embedded. Saving your Word document to disk saves the spreadsheet in the Word document file.

Creating New Objects

To create a new object while working in Word, pick *Object...* from Word's *Insert* menu. You will see a list of available object types, similar to the one in Figure 44.8.

Double-clicking on the desired object type (an Excel worksheet, for example) will launch the necessary program and let you create information to be pasted, using the previously described embedding procedures. Remember to save your file.

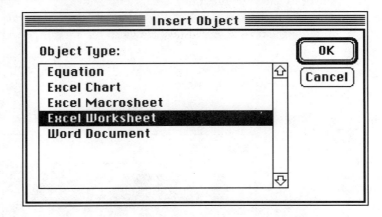

Figure 44.8
Choosing *Object...*
from the *Insert* menu
lists the available
object types.

Programs that can create objects will automatically show up in this list, but only after you have run the program at least once on your machine. For instance, if you have never run the Equation Editor program it will not show up in your list.

Cancelling Embedding

Use care when cancelling embedding. In some cases it will be irreversible. The way you cancel embedding is to convert an object to a picture with the Freeze Picture choice in the Object Options dialog box, reached with the elusive *Object Options...* command, sometimes found on Word 5's *Edit* menu. You must first select an object before visiting the *Edit* menu. Figure 44.9 is from a recent sighting.

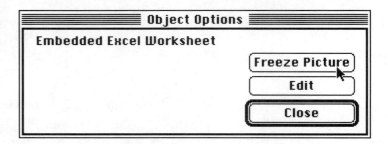

Figure 44.9
Freezing permanently
converts objects to
pictures. Use with
caution.

If you convert a spreadsheet to a picture this way, the equations will no longer be stored with your Word document file. Since your Word document is the *only* place the equations were stored, you will lose them forever unless you undo in time or have a backup of your Word document containing the equations.

When you double-click on an object after freezing it Word's draw program will open. That's because the object is now a graphic.

Link

Link works a lot like embedding. You copy things to your Clipboard, then paste them at specific spots in other documents. You can link two Word documents together or link Word documents with other programs that support this feature. When the linked information changes in the originating document, it changes in other documents that you've linked to the source. Generally, linked files are smaller.

Start by copying the text or other items of interest to your clipboard. For example, suppose you want to create a memo containing a new-hire's name and update phone lists and other documents needing the new hire's name all at once. Figure 44.10 shows an example of this.

In our example you would highlight Ferd's name in the Word memo and copy it to the Clipboard, then move to the phone list (another Word document in this example). Place the insertion point where you want to place the linked information, then hold down the Shift key and choose *Paste Link* from the *Edit* menu. Save your documents.

The information in the two documents will be linked. Fuzzy square brackets surround linked text. Then, whenever you hire a new marketing manager (or make a last-minute hiring decision change), the phone list will be updated.

Notice that the document receiving the text gets font, size, and style information from the originating document (12-point Courier, in the example). There is no easy way to force the incoming information to the receiving document's special format or style (14-point Helvetica here). You *can* paste unformatted text, in which case the receiving document will display and print incoming text in Word's default form (typically, but not necessarily, 12-Point New York).

Figure 44.10
Changing the name in the memo updates the phone list, thanks to linking. Notice what happens to character formatting.

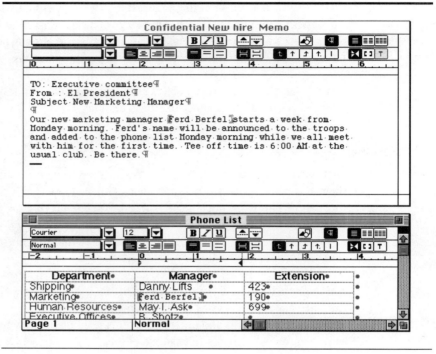

Paste Special Links

The way to paste unformatted text is to use the *Paste Special* choice on your *Edit* menu instead of the *Paste Link* command. You will see a dialog box like the one in Figure 44.11. Choosing Unformatted Text will cause the receiving document to apply the Normal style to incoming text.

Picture pastes incoming information as a picture, and picking choices like Word Document will embed objects.

Link Options

The Link Options dialog box, shown in Figure 44.12, lets you control how often links are updated and lets you cancel a link or quickly reach the original document.

Figure 44.11
Paste Special gives you a little more control over the format of incoming information.

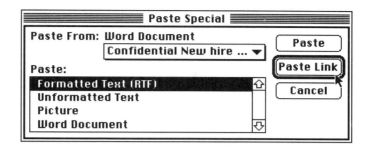

Figure 44.12
Highlight linked items and choose *Link Options...* from the *Edit* menu to get this dialog box.

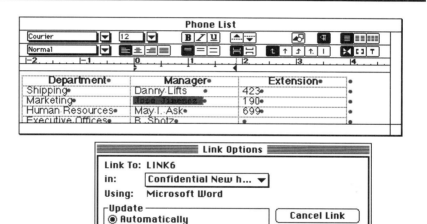

To reach this dialog box, you must open a document containing a link. Place the insertion point at the link of interest (the linked info will become highlighted, as shown in Figure 44.12). Then choose *Link Options...* from the *Edit* menu. The Update area lets you specify when links are updated. The *Format* menu provides the available format choices (typically RTF, Unformatted Text, and Picture). Open

Source takes you to the originating document. If the Source is other than Word, the button will attempt to launch the source program (Excel, for instance). You must have the source program on your machine and enough RAM to run both the Source program and Word in this case. Edit Link lets you tie the receiving link to a different source link.

E-Mail

FEATURING

- Sending e-mail (electronic mail) from within Word
- Enclosing Word documents with e-mail
- Receiving notes and enclosures from within Word

If you are on a network and your organization uses Microsoft Mail for in-house electronic communications, you can use the *Open Mail...* and *Send Mail...* commands on your *File* menu to access mail and send copies of your Word documents to others.

Word 5 is compatible with most Microsoft Mail versions, including 2.0 and 3.0. You must have Microsoft Mail installed on your Mac to use these commands. Read the *Users* booklet that came with your copy of Microsoft Mail. Contact your system administrator or mail manager for assistance.

Generally, you will want to use the Microsoft Mail command on your *Apple* menu rather than the Word mail commands for most e-mail (electronic mail) tasks. The primary advantage of using the Word 5's *Send Mail...* and *Open Mail...* commands instead of using the *Apple* menu choice is that the Word commands eliminate a couple of steps when you exchange Word documents with other Word users.

SENDING MAIL AND WORD DOCUMENTS

With your Word document saved to disk and displayed on screen, choose *Send Mail...* from the *File* menu. If your mail server is up and running, and if you are properly attached to you network, you will see a Send Document dialog box. The exact appearance of the dialog box will vary, depending upon which version of Microsoft Mail is installed on your machine. The Mail options you've chosen also affect the appearance of this screen. Figure 45.1 shows a typical but very simple mail window, running under Microsoft Mail version 2.0.

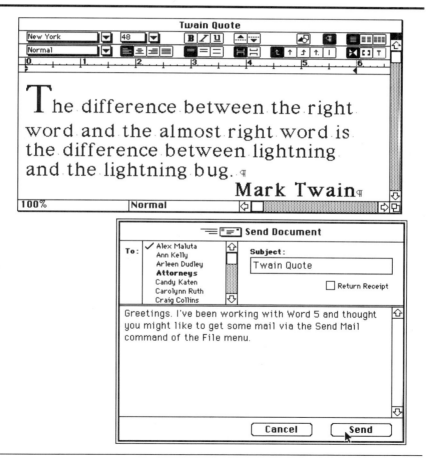

Figure 45.1
A typical Send Document window reached from Word's *Send Mail...* command. Yours may look different.

Somewhere on your screen there will be a list of potential addressees, a place for you to type the subject of your message, and a message area. There may be other checkboxes for return receipts, urgent handling, and so on.

Pick the intended recipients and type a message in the message area. Click send to transmit *both* the *message* and the *Word document* to the recipients.

Remember, if you are typing a list of ten things you hate about your boss and decide to send her an e-mail message, this is *not* the feature to use. Your note will arrive with a copy of your typing project. In this case, use the regular Microsoft Mail features on the *Apple* menu instead.

Opening Mail

Choose *Open Mail...* from the Word *File* menu. Messages with enclosures will be listed in the mailbox. Little paper-clip symbols indicate enclosures. Select the message of interest. Read the comments by clicking the Comments button. You can also open and view enclosures. When you close them, Word will prompt you to save them. Save "keepers" using the usual Word Save techniques.

APPENDIX A

INSTALLING WORD 5

WHAT YOU NEED

You can install Word on any Macintosh that has a hard drive and an 800 K or a 1.2 Mb disk drive. System 6 users will need a minimum of 1 Mb of RAM or 2 Mb if they want to run Word's grammar checker. If you have only 1 Mb of RAM, the Installer will not install the grammar feature.

System 7 users need a minimum of 2 Mb of RAM, with 4 Mb required to run Word with the grammar checker.

Your hard drive will need to have a minimum of between 5 and 7 Mb free at the time of installation, although Word will not need all of that *after* the installation. (The Installer program will inform you if you need to free up additional hard-disk space.)

Word is shipped on five 800 K diskettes:

Install
Program
Converters

APPENDIX A

Proofing Tools

Commands

The files are compressed, thus they cannot simply be dragged onto your hard disk. You need to run the Installer program, which will walk you through the simple installation steps.

Preparing Your Mac

Start by turning off any virus-protection software you are running, and disable GateKeeper if you are using it. If you have a Radius Rocket board installed, turn it off before running the Installer, as the two may not be compatible. You can turn it back on after a successful installation. If you are running System 7 or MultiFinder, quit any other programs you are running before starting the installation.

Running the Installer

Insert the *Install* disk and double-click to open it. Start by reading any ReadMe files on the disk, then return to the *Install* disk window and double-click on the *Installer* icon, shown in Figure A.1.

Figure A.1
Double-click on the Installer icon found on the *Install* disk to launch the installation program.

If this is the first time you've used the *Install* disk, you will be asked to personalize it. Enter the necessary information.

You will be reminded to send in your registration card. Acknowledge the reminder. You will be reminded about turning off virus protection and GateKeeper. If you have done that already, continue. Otherwise quit. Then rerun

Installing Word 5

Installer after turning things off. Soon you will see a dialog box like the one in Figure A.2.

The lower-left corner of the gray, dotted box shows which hard disk the Installer plans to use. If you have more than one hard disk, pick the one you want to install Word on by clicking the Switch Disk button. If you try to install on the disk used to start your Mac, Word will warn you to quit other programs before continuing. It will assist with orderly shut-downs of your various programs.

Figure A.2
Choose Easy Install for most situations.

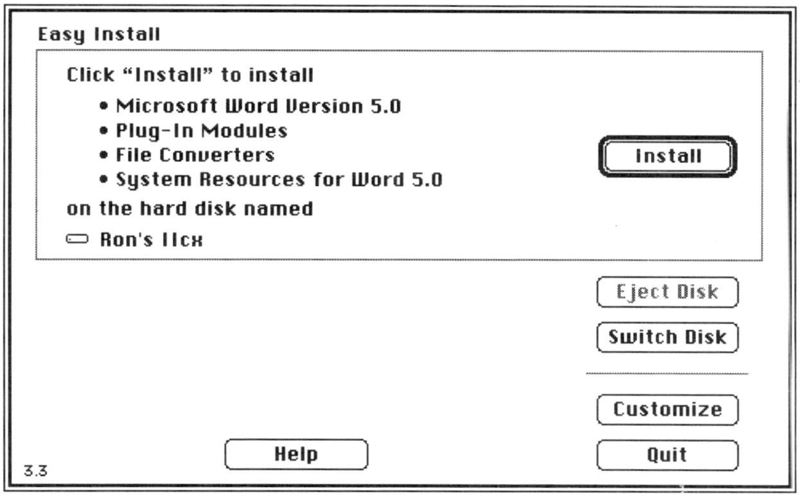

```
Easy Install

  Click "Install" to install
    • Microsoft Word Version 5.0
    • Plug-In Modules
    • File Converters                    [ Install ]
    • System Resources for Word 5.0
  on the hard disk named
  ⊂⊃ Ron's IIcx

                                         [ Eject Disk ]
                                         [ Switch Disk ]

                                         [ Customize ]
              [ Help ]                   [ Quit ]
  3.3
```

Unless you have very limited hard-disk space, it is advised that you use the Easy Install option. Clicking the Install button will determine which Microsoft installation disks are required and ask you to pick a folder to hold your new Word 5 files. Normally, you will want to create a new one. Click on the New Folder button and you will be prompted for a folder name as shown in Figure A.3.

Type a folder name and click Create. Click the Install button. If all goes well, Word will ask you for the necessary disks to complete the first part of the installation. Feed them to your Mac in the order requested.

Figure A.3
Create a new folder for Word 5 with the Installer's help.

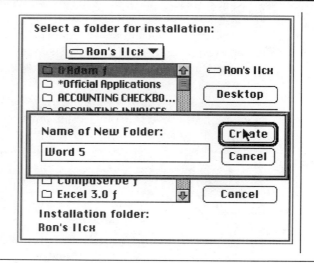

Because the files are compressed they need to be "unstuffed". The Installer does this for you, but be prepared to wait fifteen minutes or more for the process to end. You will see a series of boxes like the one in Figure A.4 as unstuffing progresses.

Near the end of the process you will get an opportunity to pick a default font. Word proposes New York. If you plan to use a laserprinter, consider choosing a laser font (such as Times or Palatino). You can change this later if you wish.

Figure A.4
The Installer will keep you posted as it unstuffs your files.

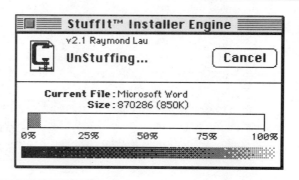

WHAT GETS INSTALLED?

Eventually you will be informed of a successful installation. The Installer will have placed the following files and folders on your disk:

Microsoft Word

Word 5.0 ReadMe

Conversion Information

Standard Glossary

Word Commands (folder)

    Word 5 Help

    Word 5 Command Help

    Find File

    Mail

    Voice Annotation

    Symbol

    Picture

    Equation Editor

    Equation Editor Help

    Grammar

    U.S. English Grammar

    Spelling

    U.S. English Dictionary

    Custom Dictionary

    Thesaurus

    U.S. English Thesaurus

    U.S. English Hyphenation

    EPS/TIFF/PICT

    MacWrite II Converter

Text with Layout
Windows Metafile Converter
Word for DOS 5.x
Word for Windows 1
Word for Windows 2
WordPerfect for DOS 5.x
MS Word Conversion Options

Glossaries (folder)
Date and Time Glossary
Formula Glossary
Formula Glossary Information
Page Layout Glossary
Page Layout Glossary Info

Settings Files (folder)
MacWrite II Settings
Short Menu Settings
Word 4.0 Settings (5)
Word for Windows (2) Settings
Word Settings (5)

Sample Documents (folder)
Brochure
Business Letter
Business Report
Employment Form
Memo
Newsletter
Resume

Installing Word 5

>   Envelopes (folder—see disk for folder contents)
>
>   Practice Documents (folder—see disk for folder contents)
>
>   Mailing Labels (folder—see disk for folder contents)

The following files are *not* installed with the Easy Install option:

>   Works for Macintosh 2.x
>
>   RFT-DCA Converter

If you need them, use the custom Installer to *add* them later.

Running Word After Installation

You will need to restart your Mac to use Word 5. The Installer will provide congratulations and a Restart button.

USTOM INSTALLATION

If you choose not to do an easy installation, you can tell the Installer which items you want to install. This is helpful if you have limited disk space or if one of your non-essential disks is damaged. For instance, you could live without the converters disk until Microsoft sends a replacement. Click on Customize when starting the installation (see Figure A.2). Optional installation items include:

>   Spell checker
>
>   Grammar checker
>
>   Thesaurus
>
>   Hyphenation
>
>   Mail
>
>   Equation Editor
>
>   Picture (the drawing feature)
>
>   Find File
>
>   Voice annotation
>
>   Insert Symbol

It's a good idea to install the sample documents and glossaries, as they contain helpful files and examples. If you choose not to install certain features (like the wonderful new spell checker), they will either not appear on your Word menus or will always be dimmed. You can always return to the Installer later and install *just* the items you left off when you last did a custom installation.

Using Old Dictionary and Glossary Files

If you have old custom dictionaries and settings files from Word 3 or 4 scattered around your hard disk, you may be able to use them with Word 5. To round them up, use Word 5's new *Find File...*, *Preferences*, and *Settings* features.

The discussion and handy tip that follow assume you know about Word 5's new Preferences dialog box, dictionary features, *Find File...*, and the Commands dialog box. (You may want to read about them *first*, then come back here.)

To find dictionaries, visit the Preferences dialog box and open the Spelling category. Click *Open...* then Find File... on the resulting Open dialog box, similar to the one shown in Figure A.5.

Figure A.5
A special Find File feature will help you locate old custom Word dictionaries and settings files for possible use with Word 5.

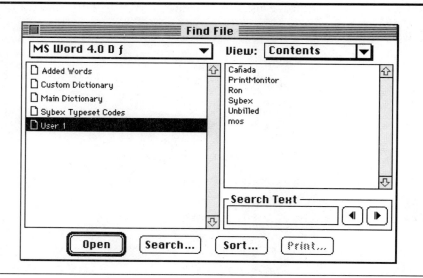

Installing Word 5

To find settings files, visit the Commands dialog box and follow the same basic steps. The Find File dialog box will list all of the dictionaries (or Settings files) it finds. Opening them from Find File... makes them available to you in Word 5.

APPENDIX B

WORD 5 COMMANDS

Word 5 has a bewildering number of commands, many of which have similar names or similar functions. To help you find commands quickly, we have listed most of the Word 5 commands in this appendix in two formats. First, you will find each command in a function-specific table (Tables B.1–B.7). Second, we have listed the commands in an alphabetized glossary. In this glossary, we have noted a keyboard shortcut if there is one; if the command appears on a menu by default, the menu is listed as well. Happy hunting!

TABLE B.1 Choosing Commands with Key Combinations

	To choose...	Press...	...Or
Menu Shortcuts	Add to menu	⌘-Option-+	
	Remove from menu	⌘-Option-–	
	Assign to key	⌘-Option-+ (keypad)	
	Unassign key	⌘-Option-– (keypad)	
File	New	⌘-N	F5
	Open...	⌘-O	F6
	Close	⌘-W	
	Save	⌘-S	F7

TABLE B.1
Choosing Commands with Key Combinations (continued)

	To choose...	Press...	...Or
	Save As...		Shift-F7
	Print Preview...	⌘-Option-I	Option-F13
	Page Setup...		Shift-F8
	Print...	⌘-P	F8
	Quit	⌘-Q	
Edit	Undo	⌘-Z	F1
	Repeat	⌘-Y	
	Cut	⌘-X	F2
	Copy	⌘-C	F3
	Paste	⌘-V	F4
	Paste Object		⌘-F4
	Paste Link		Option-F4
	Select All	⌘-A	
	Find...	⌘-F	
	Replace	⌘-H	
	Go To...	⌘-G	
	Glossary...	⌘-K	
View	Normal	⌘-Option-N	
	Outline	⌘-Option-O	Shift-F13
	Page Layout	⌘-Option-P	F13
	Ribbon	⌘-Option-R	
	Ruler	⌘-R	
	Show/Hide ¶	⌘-J	
	Footnotes	⌘-Option-Shift-S	
Insert	Page Break	Shift-Enter	
	Section Break	⌘-Enter	
	Footnote...	⌘-E	

Word 5 Commands

TABLE B.1
Choosing Commands with Key Combinations (continued)

	To choose...	Press...	...Or
Format	Character...	⌘-D	F14
	Paragraph...	⌘-M	Shift-F14
	Section...		Option-F14
	Document...		⌘-F14
	Style...	⌘-T	
	Revert To Style	⌘-Shift-Spacebar	F9
	Plain Text	⌘-Shift-Z	Shift-F9
	Bold	⌘-B or ⌘-Shift-B	F10
	Italic	⌘-I or ⌘-Shift-I	F11
	Underline	⌘-U or ⌘-Shift-U	F12
Font	Up	⌘-]	
	Down	⌘-[	
Tools	Spelling...	⌘-L	F15
	Grammar...	⌘-Shift-G	
	Hyphenation...		Shift-F15
	Word Count...		Option-F15
	Renumber...		⌘-F15
	Calculate	⌘-=	
	Commands...	⌘-Option-Shift-C	
Window	Help	⌘-/ or Help	
	New Window		Shift-F5
Other Commands	Zoom Window		⌘-Option-]
	Move To Next Window	⌘-Option-W	
	Split Window	⌘-Option-S	

APPENDIX B

TABLE B.2
Outliner Keyboard Shortcuts

To...	...Press this in Outline view
Switch to Outline view	⌘-Option-O
Switch from Outline to Normal view	⌘-Option-N
Promote heading (←)	Option-←
Demote heading (→)	Option-→
Move heading up (↑)	Option-↑
Move heading down (↓)	Option-↓
Demote to body text (→)	⌘-→
Show/Hide text below all headings	Option-Shift-→
Show/Hide text below selected heading	Option-Shift-← or – sign (numeric keypad)
Display or hide character formatting	Option-Shift-↑ or / (numeric keypad)

TABLE B.3
Choosing Options in Dialog Boxes

To do this...	Press...
Select next text or scrolling box	Tab
Select previous text box	Shift-Tab
Move right or left within a text box	→ or ←
Select next option (list, check, or button)	⌘-Tab
Select previous option (list, check, or button)	⌘-Shift-Tab
Select next item in list box	↓
Select previous item in list box	↑
Choose check box or button ∗	⌘-Spacebar or ⌘-*character*
Display list in list box	⌘-Spacebar ∗ ∗
Choose item in list box	Return or Enter
Choose the outlined button	Return or Enter
Cancel the command	Escape or ⌘-. (period)

TABLE B.3
Choosing Options in Dialog Boxes (continued)

To do this...	Press...
Open folder	⌘-↓
Close folder	⌘-↑

* Only works if the checkbox or button has a unique initial letter.
** Have to press ⌘-Tab first to choose the appropriate list.

TABLE B.4
Mouse Shortcuts

To...	Double-click on...
Open the Tabs dialog box in the Paragraph dialog box	A tab stop marker on the ruler or one of the tab buttons
Open the Paragraph dialog box	An indent marker on the ruler
Open the Go To dialog box	The page number in the status area (lower-left screen corner)
Open the Style dialog box	The style name in the status area (left of the scroll bar)
Open the Section dialog box	Any section mark
Open the footnote window at a desired foonote	An automatically numbered reference mark
Open the Document dialog box	Outside the margins in the page corners in Page Layout view
Open the Character dialog box	The ribbon between boxes or buttons
Split the current window in half, unsplit windows	The split box
Zoom into or out from a window	The window's title bar
Return to an embedded object's application	The embedded object in the Word

APPENDIX B

TABLE B.5 Character Formatting

For this format...	Press...	...Or
Bold	⌘-B* or ⌘-Shift-B*	F10*
Italic	⌘-I* or ⌘-Shift-I*	F11*
Underline	⌘-U* or ⌘-Shift-U*	F12*
Word underline	⌘-Shift-]*	⌘-F12*
Double underline	⌘-Shift-[*	Shift-F12*
Dotted underline	⌘-Shift-*	Option-F12*
Strikethrough	⌘-Shift-/*	
Outline	⌘-Shift-D*	Shift-F11*
Shadow	⌘-Shift-W*	Option-F11*
Small capitals	⌘-Shift-H*	Option-F10*
All capitals	⌘-Shift-K*	Shift-F10*
Hidden text	⌘-Shift-X (or V)*	Option-F9*
Change font	⌘-Shift-E	
Symbol font	⌘-Shift-Q	
Next larger standard font	⌘-Shift->	
Next smaller standard font	⌘-Shift-<	
Increase font 1 point size	⌘-]	
Decrease font 1 point size	⌘-[	
Subscript	⌘-Shift-– (minus sign)	
Superscript	⌘-Shift-+	
Copy formatting	⌘-Option-V	Shift-F4

* Acts as a toggle (will turn feature on or off).

TABLE B.6 Paragraph Formatting

For this format...	Press...
Normal paragraph	⌘-Shift-P
Apply new style*	⌘-Shift-S

TABLE B.6
Paragraph Formatting (continued)

For this format...	Press...
Left-aligned	⌘-Shift-L
Right-aligned	⌘-Shift-R
Centered	⌘-Shift-C
Justified	⌘-Shift-J
First-line indent	⌘-Shift-F
Nest paragraph	⌘-Shift-N
Unnest paragraph	⌘-Shift-M
Hanging indent	⌘-Shift-T
Double space	⌘-Shift-Y
Open spacing **	⌘-Shift-O
Copy formatting	⌘-Option-V or Shift-F4

* You still then need to type a style name.

** Toggles Space Before between 0 and 12 points.

TABLE B.7
Keyboard Shortcuts: Moving, Scrolling, and Editing

Scrolling	To move to...	Press...
	Up	↑ or 8 (keypad)
	Down	↓ or 2 (keypad)
	Left	← or 4 (keypad)
	Right	→ or 6 (keypad)
	Previous Word	⌘-← or ⌘-4 (keypad)
	Next Word	⌘-→ or ⌘-6 (keypad)
	Beginning of line	7 (keypad)
	End of line	1 (keypad)
	Previous sentence	⌘-7 (keypad)
	Next sentence	⌘-1 (keypad)
	Next page	⌘-Page Down

TABLE B.7
Keyboard Shortcuts: Moving, Scrolling, and Editing (continued)

Scrolling	To move to...	Press...
	Previous page	⌘-Page Up
	Beginning of current paragraph	⌘-↑ or ⌘-8 (keypad)
	Beginning of next paragraph	⌘-↓ or ⌘-2 (keypad)
	Top of window	Home or ⌘-5 (keypad)
	Bottom of window	End
	Start of document	⌘-Home or ⌘-9 (keypad)
	End of document	⌘-End or ⌘-3 (keypad)
	Scroll up one screen	Page Up or 9 (keypad)
	Scroll down one screen	Page Down or 3 (keypad)
	Scroll up one line	or * (asterisk on keypad)
	Scroll down one line	+ (plus sign on keypad)

Moving in a Table or in Page Layout View	To move to...	Press...
	First table cell or page element	⌘-Option-7
	End of table or last page element	⌘-Option-1
	Next cell in table	Tab or ⌘-Option-3
	Previous cell in table	Shift-Tab or ⌘-Option-9
	Next page element	⌘-Option-3
	Previous page element	⌘-Option-9
	Cell or page element above	⌘-Option-8
	Cell or page element below	⌘-Option-2
	Cell or page element to the left	⌘-Option-4
	Cell or page element to the right	⌘-Option-6

TABLE B.7
Keyboard Shortcuts: Moving, Scrolling, and Editing (continued)

Editing	To...	Press...
	Select the entire document	⌘-A
	Delete character before cursor or selected text	Delete (Backspace)
	Delete character after cursor or selected text	⌘-Option-F or Del
	Delete previous word	⌘-Option-Delete (Backspace)
	Delete next word	⌘-Option-G
	Insert formula character	⌘-Option-\ (backslash)
	Copy text	⌘-Option-C
	Move text	⌘-Option-X
	Insert glossary entry	⌘-Delete
	Copy formats	⌘-Option-V
	Insert special character (symbol)	⌘-Option-Q
	Copy as picture	⌘-Option-D

GLOSSARY OF WORD 5 COMMANDS

About Microsoft Word Shows Word version and serial number. Gives access to on-line help.

Activate Keyboard Menus (⌘-Tab or keypad-. (period)) Lets you use keystrokes to pull down menus and make choices. When Menu bar blackens, type first character of menu name (*F* for *File,* etc.) When menu appears, type letters or use arrow keys to highlight desired function, press Return or Enter to execute. Feature self-cancels if not used soon after activated.

Add to Menu (⌘-Option-= or ⌘-Shift-Option-=) Adds selected command to the default or "home" menu.

All Caps (⌘-Shift-K or Shift-F10) Toggles appearance of selected text to all caps or not. Underlying characters retain original capitalization.

Allow Fast Saves Lets you turn the Fast Save feature on and off from the menu bar.

Always Interpret RTF Toggles automatic conversion of Rich Text Format documents when opened by Word.

Always Make Backup Files Toggles automatic backup copy feature.

Apply Style Name: (*Work* menu) Applies indicated style to selected paragraph(s).

Assign to Key (⌘-Option-keypad + or ⌘-Shift-Option-left arrow) Used to assign a key combination to a command.

Background Repagination Toggles automatic repagination, which activates during typing pauses. Turn off if repagination causes bothersome delays or "keyboard stuttering."

Backspace (*Delete* on the *Edit* menu) The Backspace key.

Bold (⌘-B or ⌘-Shift-B or F10, on the *Format* menu) This toggle command makes text appear and print darker and thicker by applying Word's bold character format. There is also a ribbon button for this feature. Note that the key combination has changed from Word 4.

Border... (*Format* menu) Used to apply and remove selected cell and paragraph borders. Provides different dialog boxes for tables or paragraphs. Brings up Border dialog box.

Calculate (⌘-= , on the *Tools* menu) Computes numerical expression(s) in selection and places results in Clipboard. Use the *Show Clipboard* command or *Paste* to see results.

Cancel   (⌘-. or Clear) Stops current command actions like Print, Sort, etc. Can't be added to menus.

Centered   (⌘-Shift-C) Centers text or graphics between left and right indents (not margins!). There is a ruler button for this feature.

Change Case...   (*Format* menu) Changes selected text to UPPERCASE, lowercase, Title Case, Sentence case, or tOGGLE cASE.

Change Font   (⌘-Shift-E) Changes font of selected text when you type a valid font name and press Return.

Change Style   (⌘-Shift-S) Changes style of selected paragraph(s) when you type a valid style name and press Return.

Character...   (⌘-D or F14, on the *Format* menu) Brings up Character Formatting dialog box.

Clear   (*Edit* menu) Deletes selected text or graphics without moving them to the Clipboard.

Close   (⌘-W, on the *File* menu) Closes the active document window. Will ask to save new changes, if any.

Collapse Selection   In Outline view collapses selection to hide selected headings or text regardless of their level.

Collapse Subtext   In Outline view hides subordinate levels or next highest level if entire heading is selected.

Columns 1   Reverts multicolumn text to a single column. There is a ribbon button for this command.

Columns 2   Converts text to two columns. Use Page Layout view or Print Preview to see results. There is a ribbon button for this command.

Columns 3   Converts text to three columns. Use Page Layout view or Print Preview to see results. There is a ribbon button for this command.

Columns 4   Converts text to four columns. Use Page Layout view or Print Preview to see results. There is *not* a ribbon button for this command.

Command From Key Assignment   Great on-line help for learning keyboard shortcuts. You type key combinations; this feature tells you what they do.

Commands...   (⌘-Shift-Option-C, on the *Tools* menu) Displays Commands dialog box. Lets you add, delete, and move menu items. Don't remove this choice from your menu bar! If you do, use its keyboard shortcut to bring up the Commands dialog box, then reinstate the *Commands* menu choice.

Condensed 1.5 pt   Reduces intercharacter spacing by an amount you specify when adding this item to the menu. Must be between 0.5 and 1.75 points and will be rounded to the nearest .25 points. Default is 1.5 pt.

Copy   (⌘-C or F3, on the *Edit* menu) Copies selected text graphics or sounds to Clipboard, replacing previous Clipboard contents. Undo will revert if done immediately.

Copy as Picture   (⌘-Option-D) Places selection in the Clipboard in MacDraw-compatible format.

Copy Formats   (⌘-Option-V or Shift-F4) Copies character formatting or entire paragraph formatting if paragraph is selected. Applies formatting to subsequently selected text.

Copy Text   (⌘-Option-C or Shift-F3) Either copies selected text to a new location or copies text you select after choosing this command to the current insertion point location. Watch status area at lower-left of screen. Cancel with ⌘-. (period) or *Clear.*

Create Publisher... (*Edit* menu) System 7 feature lets you share a document or portion thereof with others on your network.

Cut (⌘-X or F2, on the *Edit* menu) Removes selected text graphics or sounds and places on Clipboard, replacing previous Clipboard contents. Undo will revert if done immediately.

Default Font... Lets you quickly set default font.

Delete Cells, Shift Left In tables, deletes selected cell(s), then moves remaining cells to the left. Deletions do *not* go to Clipboard.

Delete Cells, Shift Up In tables, deletes selected cell(s), then moves remaining cells up. Deletions do *not* go to Clipboard.

Delete Columns In tables: deletes column containing insertion point or selected column(s). Deletions do *not* go to Clipboard.

Delete Forward (⌘-Option-F or Del) Removes one character to the right of the insertion point. Some keyboards have both a Delete and Del key. This is the Del key. Deletions do *not* go to Clipboard.

Delete Next Word (⌘-Option-G) Removes word or partial word to right of insertion point. Deletions do *not* go to Clipboard.

Delete Previous Word (⌘-Option-Delete) Removes word or partial word to left of insertion point. Deletions do *not* go to Clipboard.

Delete Rows (⌘-Control-X) In tables: deletes row containing insertion point or selected row(s). Deletions do *not* go to Clipboard.

Delete... Deletes unopened documents from disk.

Demote Heading In Outline view lowers selected paragraph(s) to next outline level.

Different First Page   Lets you turn off page number of first page of section and create special first page headers and footers.

Document...   (⌘-F14, on the *Format* menu) Displays Document formatting dialog box.

Dotted Underline   (⌘-Shift-\ or Option-F12) Applies/removes the dotted underline character format to selected text.

Double Underline   (⌘-Shift-[or Shift-F12) Applies/removes the double-underline character format to selected text.

Down   (⌘-[or ⌘-Shift-<, on the *Font* menu) Decreases font size by one point. Works with selected text or text typed at insertion point after you issue the command.

Drag-and-Drop Text Editing   (*Tools* menu) New Word 5 feature lets you select items, then drag them to desired location and insert by releasing mouse button at desired insertion point. Will *not* work between Word windows, between split window segments, or between different programs.

Edit Link (QuickSwitch)   (⌘-, (comma) or Option-F2) Automatically switches you to another (the source) application.

Edit Object...   (*Edit* menu) Runs application that created the selected object.

Even Footer   Opens footer for even-numbered pages in the current section. Lets you view and edit.

Even Header   Opens header for even-numbered pages in the current section. Lets you view and edit.

Expand Subtext   In Outline view shows either all lower levels or next lower level if entire heading is not selected.

Expanded 3 pt   Expands intercharacter spacing by an amount you specify when adding this item to the menu. Must be between 0.5 and 14 points and will be rounded to the nearest 0.25 points. Default is 3 pt.

Extend to Character   (⌘-Option-H or keypad –) This selection shortcut will extend an existing selection area up to and including the first occurrence of the next letter that you type. Watch lower-left of screen for prompts. Cancel with ⌘-. (period).

File...   (*Insert* menu) Brings up the Word File dialog box and inserts the *entire* selected file at the insertion point.

Find...   (⌘-F, on the *Edit* menu) Brings up Find dialog box. Lets you search for text, special characters, formats, and styles.

Find Again   (⌘-Option-A or keypad =) Repeats searches for text or formats performed with Find or Replace commands.

Find File...   (*File* menu) Helps locate lost files by searching on summary info, filename dates, and text content.

Find Formats   Searches for matching character or paragraph formats, based on selection.

First Footer   Opens footer for first page in current section. Lets you view and edit.

First Header   Opens header for first page in current section. Lets you view and edit.

First Line Indent   (⌘-Shift-F) Sets indent of selected paragraph(s) to first tab stop.

Footer   (*View* menu) Opens a standard footer window in the current section. If you are in Page Layout view, footers are shown with regular text; in Normal view, they're displayed in a separate window.

Footnote... (⌘-E, on the *Insert* menu) Inserts a footnote reference marker at the insertion point and opens a footnote window. Moves insertion point to footnote text area when in Page Layout view.

Footnote Cont. Notice... Lets you type a footnote continuation notice.

Footnote Cont.: Notice Default (⌘-H, on the *Edit* menu) Returns footnote continuation notice to Word 5's default (no continuation notice).

Footnote Cont. Separator... Lets you change characters used to separate footnotes continued from preceding page and body text.

Footnote Cont. Sep.: Default Returns footnote continuation separator to Word 5's default (6", 1 pt. line).

Footnote Separator... Lets you change characters used to separate footnotes from body text.

Footnote Separator: Default Returns footnote separator to Word 5's default (2", 1 pt. line).

Footnotes (⌘-Shift-Option-S, on the *View* menu) Displays all footnotes related to any "visible" footnote reference markers.

Fractional Widths Toggles LaserWriter fractional-width feature document-wide.

Frame... (Format) (*Format* menu) New Word 5 feature. Opens dialog box used to position selected paragraphs on current page. Do not confuse this with its cousin, who lives on the *Insert* menu.

Frame... (Insert) (*Insert* menu) New Word 5 feature. Inserts a positioned paragraph, called a frame, at the current selection or insertion point. Opens Print Preview to let you drag the frame into position. Don't confuse this with its cousin, who lives on the *Format* menu.

Full Repaginate Now   Forces a repagination even if there were no edits since last pagination.

Glossary...   (⌘-K, on the *Edit* menu) Improved Word 5 feature. Opens Glossary dialog box. Lets you insert existing Glossary entries, create new entries, or switch Glossary files.

Go Back   (⌘-Option-Z or keypad 0) Powerful navigation aid. Quickly moves you to previous selection or to the insertion point (last three editing places in the document).

Go To...   (⌘-G, on the *Edit* menu) A dialog box that lets you specify a page and/or section number, then takes you there quickly.

Grammar...   (⌘-Shift-G, on the *Tools* menu) New Word 5 feature. Checks grammar and document readability, offers suggestions, aids editing. File called "Grammar" must be installed in the Word Commands folder.

Hanging Indent   (⌘-Shift-T) Indents lines after first line in paragraph(s) to first tab stop.

Header   (*View* menu) Opens a standard header window in the current section. If you are in Page Layout view, the insertion point will move to the header window as well.

Help...   (*Window* menu) A scrollable list of on-line help topics and related help info.

Help (Context Sensitive)   (⌘-/) Displays help information for open dialog boxes and commands. This command cannot be added to the menu bar.

Hidden Text   (⌘-Shift-V or ⌘-Shift-X or Option-F9) This toggle formats text as hidden or not hidden.

Hyphenation...   (Shift-F15, on the *Tools* menu) Presents hyphenation dialog box and offers suggestions for soft hyphen placement.

Include Endnotes in Section   Forces footnotes to end of section when enabled.

Include Formatted Text in Clipboard   Toggles Rich Text Format (RTF) for Clipboard contents. Determines if style (bold, italic, etc.) will be retained by Clipboard.

Index . . .   (*Insert* menu) Causes Word to generate an index of your document.

Index Entry   (*Insert* menu) Inserts index entry code either at insertion point or before and after selected text.

Insert Cells Down   In a table, inserts equal number of empty cells above selected cells. Selected cells are pushed down.

Insert Cells Right   In a table, inserts equal number of empty cells to the left of selected cells. Selected cells are pushed right.

Insert Columns   In a table, inserts empty column(s) to the left of the column containing the insertion point or to the left of selected columns.

Insert Formula   (⌘-Option-\) Inserts the special formula character required when using math formula codes.

Insert Glossary Entry   (⌘-Delete) Asks you for name of an existing Glossary entry, then inserts the contents of that Glossary item at the insertion point.

Insert Non-breaking Hyphen   (⌘-`) Creates a required hyphen that will prevent line breaks at the hyphen. (Keeps items on same line.)

Insert Non-breaking Space   (Option-Spacebar or ⌘-Spacebar) Creates a required space that will prevent line breaks at the space. (Keeps items on same line.)

Insert Optional Hyphen (⌘- –) Creates a hyphen that is printed only if a word is broken at the hyphen.

Insert Rows (⌘-Control-V) In a table, inserts empty row(s) above the row containing the insertion point or above selected row(s).

Insert Tab (Tab or Option-Tab) Inserts a tab character.

Insert ¶ Above Row (⌘-Option-Spacebar) In a table, inserts a paragraph marker (Normal style) above the row containing the insertion point or above selected row(s).

Italic (⌘-I or ⌘-Shift-I or F11, on the *Format* menu) Makes text appear italicized by applying Word's italic character format. There is also a ribbon button for this feature. Note that the key combination has changed from Word 4.

Italic Cursor Toggles slanted insertion point in italic text, which some find hard to use.

Justified (⌘-Shift-J) Justifies text on both right and left edges between indents by adjusting spaces.

Keep Lines Together Prevents page breaks within the selected paragraph and its successor.

Keep with Next ¶ Prevents page breaks between the selected paragraph and its successor.

L Thick Paragraph Border (⌘-Option-2) Applies heavy left border to selected paragraphs.

Larger Font Size (⌘-Shift-> or ⌘-Shift-. (period)) Increases selected character(s) to next larger point size.

Line Break   (Shift-Return) Inserts a nonprinting line-ending marker and moves insertion point to beginning of next line. Often better than pressing Return to separate paragraphs. Used in conjunction with paragraph spacing features.

Line Numbers By Page   (*Format* menu) Turns on line numbering for current section and restarts line numbers at 1 on each new *page*.

Line Numbers By Section   Turns on line numbering for current section and restarts line numbers at 1.

Line Numbers Continuous   Turns on line numbering for current section and continues line numbers from preceding section.

Line Numbers Off   Turns off line numbering for selected text.

Line Spacing: 1 and ½   Creates 1½ line spacing (18 pts. between lines) for selected paragraphs. May not work with type sizes greater than 24 pts. In this case use character spacing instead.

Line Spacing: Double   (⌘-Shift-Y) Double-spaces selected lines (24-point line spacing). There is also a ruler button for this feature.

Line Spacing: Single   Applies single-line (12 pt.) spacing to selected text.

Link Options...   (*Edit* menu) Opens a dialog box with linking choices under System 7 or MultiFinder.

List All Fonts   Displays all fonts on Word *Font* menu.

List Recently Opened Documents   New Word 5 feature. Appends names of last four Word documents you've used to bottom of *File* menu for easy relaunching.

Lowercase   Changes current selection to all lowercase.

Make Backup Files Toggles automatic backup of saved documents. When on, backup is made when document is saved. Limit the length of file names when using this feature.

Make Body Text In Outline view converts selected text to body text.

Margin Page Numbers Toggles auto page numbering for current section.

Measurement Unit: Cm Changes default unit of measurement to centimeters.

Measurement Unit: Inches Changes default unit of measurement to inches.

Measurement Unit: Picas Changes default unit of measurement to picas.

Measurement Unit: Points Changes default unit of measurement to points.

Merge Cells In tables, combines selected cells in a row into a single cell.

More Keyboard Prefix (⌘-Option-') Used with original (small) keyboards. Amplifies extent of subsequent key action.

Move Down One Text Area (⌘-Option-keypad 2) In text, moves insertion point down to next text line. In tables, moves insertion point down 1 cell. (Page Layout view.)

Move Heading Down In Outline view, moves selected heading or text below next paragraph in the outline.

Move Heading Up In Outline view, moves selected heading or text above preceding paragraph in the outline.

Move Left One Text Area   (⌘-Option-keypad 4) Moves insertion point to the text area to the left or to next cell to left in tables. (Page Layout view.)

Move Right One Text Area   (⌘-Option-keypad 6) Moves insertion point to the text area to the right or to next cell to right in tables visible in the window. (Page Layout view).

Move Text   (⌘-Option-X or Shift-F2) Moves text, graphics, or sound without disturbing Clipboard contents.

Move to Bottom of Window   (End) Places insertion point after last character visible in window.

Move to End of Document   (⌘-keypad 3 or ⌘-End) Places insertion point after last character visible in document.

Move to End of Line   (keypad 1) Places insertion point at end of current line.

Move to First Text Area   (⌘-Option-keypad 7) Moves insertion point to first text area or to first cell in tables.

Move to Last Text Area   (⌘-Option-keypad 1) Moves insertion point to last text area in Page Layout view or to last cell in tables visible in the window.

Move to Next Cell   In tables, moves insertion point to next cell to right. Wraps left and down at end of row.

Move to Next Character   (right arrow or ⌘-Option-L or keypad 6) Moves insertion point right one character.

Move to Next Line   (down arrow or ⌘-Option-, or keypad 2) Moves insertion point down one line.

Move to Next Page   Moves insertion point to beginning of next page.

Move to Next Paragraph   (⌘-down arrow or ⌘-Option-B or ⌘-keypad 2) Moves insertion point to beginning of next paragraph.

Move to Next Sentence   (⌘-keypad 1) Moves insertion point to beginning of next sentence.

Move to Next Text Area   (⌘-Option-keypad 3) Moves insertion point to beginning of next text area in Page Layout view or next cell in table.

Move to Next Window   (⌘-Option-W) Moves insertion point to the next document window.

Move to Next Word   (⌘-right arrow or ⌘-Option-; or ⌘-keypad 6) Moves insertion point after current or next word.

Move to Previous Cell   (Shift-Tab) In tables moves insertion point to preceding cell.

Move to Previous Character   (left arrow or ⌘-Option-K or keypad 4) Moves insertion point back one character.

Move to Previous Line   (up arrow or keypad 8) Moves insertion point up one line.

Move to Previous Page   (⌘-Page Up) Moves insertion point to beginning of previous page.

Move to Previous Paragraph   (⌘-up arrow or ⌘-Option-Y or ⌘-keypad 8) Moves insertion point to beginning of current or previous paragraph.

Move to Previous Sentence   (⌘-keypad 7) Moves insertion point to beginning of current or previous sentence.

Move to Previous Text Area   (⌘-Option-keypad 9) Moves insertion point to beginning of previous text area in Page Layout view or a cell in a table.

Move to Previous Word   (⌘-left arrow or ⌘-Option-J or ⌘-keypad 4) Moves insertion point to beginning of current or previous word.

Move to Start of Document   (⌘-keypad 9 or ⌘-Home) Places insertion point before first character in document.

Move to Start of Line   (keypad 7) Moves insertion point to beginning of current line.

Move to Top of Window   (⌘-keypad 5 or Home) Places insertion point before first character in active window.

Move Up One Text Area   (⌘-Option-keypad 8) Moves insertion point to beginning of previous text area in Page Layout view or up one cell in tables.

Nest Paragraph   (⌘-Shift-N) Shifts indent of selected paragraph(s) right one tab stop.

New   (⌘-N or F5, on the *File* menu) Opens a new untitled document.

New Paragraph   (Return or Enter) Inserts a nonprinting paragraph marker and moves insertion point to beginning of next line.

New Picture   Inserts an empty graphics frame and opens the Picture window.

New Window   (Shift-F5, on the *Window* menu) Opens an additional window for the active document.

New ¶ After Ins. Point   (⌘-Option-Return) Inserts a new paragraph marker (after the insertion point) without moving the insertion point.

New ¶ with Same Style   (⌘-Return) Overrides "Next Style" feature and opens a new paragraph with the same style as the current one.

No Paragraph Border (⌘-Option-1) Turns off paragraph border for selected paragraph(s).

Normal (⌘-Option-N, on the *View* menu) Switches to Normal view, which is quick, but does not easily show headers, footers, or footnotes.

Normal Character Position Applies normal text baseline position to selected text or text typed at insertion point.

Normal Character Spacing Applies normal character spacing to selected text or text typed at insertion point.

Normal Paragraph (⌘-Shift-P) Applies Normal style to selected paragraphs or paragraph containing insertion point.

Numeric Lock (keypad Clear) Toggles Num Lock to permit dual use as number entry or navigation tool.

Object... (*Insert* menu) New Word 5 feature. Brings up dialog box listing objects that Word can embed (Excel spreadsheets, etc.). Lets you insert these objects in Word documents.

Odd Footer Opens footer for odd-numbered pages in current section. Lets you view and edit.

Odd Header Opens header for odd-numbered pages in current section. Lets you view and edit.

Open... (⌘-O or F6, on the *File* menu) Presents the Open dialog box containing a list of files from which you choose. Also lets you change folders or launch Find File to locate lost documents. You can use this command in conjunction with the Glossary or Style dialog boxes.

Open Any File... (Shift-F6) Lists all available files even if they are not Word-compatible. Lets you attempt to open them.

Open Documents in Page View   Lets you control whether Word opens all documents in Page Layout view or Normal view.

Open Documents With Ribbon   Lets you control whether Word opens all documents with or without a ribbon.

Open Documents With Ruler   Lets you control whether Word opens all documents with or without a ruler.

Open Mail...   (*File* menu) Opens messages in your Microsoft Mailbox if they contain Word-readable enclosures.

Other...   (*Font* menu) Takes you directly to the Character dialog box from the *Font* menu. Lets you specify color, character spacing, etc.

Outline (Format)   (⌘-Shift-D or Shift-F11, on the *Format* menu) This toggle shows the letters of text as thin outlines, like stencils.

Outline (View)   (⌘-Option-O or Shift-F13, on the *View* menu) Changes display to Outline view. Helps organize and rearrange complex documents.

Outline Command Prefix   (⌘-Option-T) Lets you use the keyboard to create actions in outlines (such as demoting headings).

Outline View On/Off   Toggles Outline view on and off.

Page # Alphabetic Lowercase   Formats page numbers a–z, aa–zz, etc.

Page # Alphabetic Uppercase   Numbers pages A–Z, AA–ZZ, and so on. All caps.

Page # Arabic   Numbers pages 1, 2, 3, and so on.

Page # Roman Lowercase   Formats page numbers as lowercase Roman numerals (i, ii, etc.).

Page # Roman Uppercase   Selects uppercase Roman numerals for current section.

Page Break   (Shift-Enter, on the *Insert* menu) Inserts a hard (manual) page break.

Page Break Before   Inserts a hard page break just before selected paragraph.

Page Layout   (⌘-Option-P or F13, on the *View* menu) Changes to Page Layout view, which shows how the page will look when it is printed.

Page Layout View On/Off   Toggles Page Layout view.

Page Number   Inserts automatic page numbers based on Glossary.

Page Setup...   (Shift-F8, on the *File* menu) Brings up Page Setup dialog box where you enter paper size, orientation, and printer effects based on chosen printer.

Paragraph...   (⌘-M or Shift-F14, on the *Format* menu) Brings up standard Paragraph dialog box, where you define Spacing before and after paragraphs, line numbers, and more.

Paragraph Aligned Left   (⌘-Shift-L) Aligns selected text with left indent. There is also a ruler button for this feature.

Paragraph Aligned Right   (⌘-Shift-R) Aligns selected text with right indent. There is also a ruler button for this feature.

Paragraph Border...   Brings up Paragraph Border dialog box, used to place borders around paragraphs. Choose standard borders or design your own.

Paste   (⌘-V or F4, on the *Edit* menu) Inserts Clipboard contents at insertion point or replaces selected items with Clipboard contents.

Paste Cells   Only available when table cells are on the Clipboard. Pastes cells.

Paste Link   (Option-F4) Lets you paste items from other documents (Excel spreadsheets, for example) into Word documents and have the Word document updated when the external items change.

Paste Object   (⌘-F4) Pastes items (usually from spreadsheets, drawing programs, etc.). Pasted objects cannot be modified by Word.

Paste Special...   (*Edit* menu) Brings up a dialog box that lets you specify whether Clipboard contents should be pasted in Rich Text Format (RTF), as unformatted text, or as a picture.

Paste Special Character   (⌘-Option-Q) You type the decimal value of a character and Word pastes the corresponding character in the current font.

Picture...   (*Insert* menu) Brings up a dialog box that lets you use Word's Picture window to either draw your own graphics or import them from other sources. Closing the Picture window pastes the graphic into your document.

Plain Text   (⌘-Shift-Z or Shift-F9, on the *Format* menu) Removes optional character formatting, including bold, underscore, italic, and so on, from selected text.

Preferences...   (*Tools* menu) Brings up a dialog box that lets you change your name and initials for the Summary Info fields; define custom paper sizes; change units of measure; toggle smart quotes, background pagination, Clipboard features, the Drag-and-Drop feature, etc.; specify default views, Open... and Save options, default fonts, spelling, grammar, thesaurus, and hyphenation settings; and more!

Print . . . (⌘-P or F8, on the *File* menu) Brings up the Print dialog box to let you print entire documents, selected portions of documents, outlines, open glossaries, and style sheets.

Print Date   Inserts current date using Glossary format *Month date, year.*

Print Merge Helper . . .   (*View* menu) Toggles print merge help bar. Helper also assists in the creation and editing of data for print merge projects (name and address lists, etc.).

Print Merge . . .   (*File* menu) Combines documents and data to create personalized form letters and such.

Print Preview . . .   (⌘-Option-I or Option-F13, on the *File* menu) Powerful tool that shows one or two pages as an on-screen representation of how your document will print. Shows margins, line numbers, etc. Lets you change margins, manage page numbers, and so on.

Promote Heading   In Outline view, this command moves selected paragraphs up one outline level.

Prompt for Summary Info   Toggles the Summary Info dialog box. When enabled, you will see a new Summary dialog box whenever you create a new document.

Quick Record Voice Annotation   (Control-⌘-R) Shortcut for recording voice annotations (dialog box must be showing). Press ⌘-. (period) to stop recording.

Quit   (⌘-Q, on the *File* menu) Ends your Word session and removes Word from RAM. Prompts you to save unsaved changes to documents, glossaries, and dictionaries.

Redefine Style From Selection   Use to change a style. Based on the style of a selected paragraph.

Remove From Menu (⌘-Option- –) Removes a selected command from the menu.

Renumber... (⌘-F15, on the *Tools* menu) Brings up a dialog box that lets you specify renumbering options, then renumbers automatically.

Repaginate Now (*Tools* menu) In Normal view, repaginates your entire document. In Page Layout view, repaginates from beginning of document to current page.

Repeat Repeats your last command or text you've typed since the command was executed.

Replace... (⌘-Y, on the *Edit* menu) Brings up a "search and replace" dialog box that lets you find and replace text, formats, and styles. Much improved over Word 4 version!

Restart Page Numbering at 1 Toggles feature that restarts page numbering at 1 for current section only.

Revert To Style (⌘-Shift-Spacebar or F9, on the *Format* menu) Returns selected text to the style for the paragraph (removes manual changes to font, styles, indents, etc.)

Ribbon (⌘-Option-R, on the *View* menu) Toggles display of ribbon in document, header, and footer windows.

Ruler (⌘-R, on the *View* menu) Toggles display of ruler in document, header, and footer windows.

Same As Previous Copies contents of previous section's header or footer into current header and footer windows.

Save (⌘-S or F7, on the *File* menu) Saves the active document using the most recent Save As dialog-box settings (quick save, file locations, etc.).

Save As... (Shift-F7, on the *File* menu) Brings up a dialog box that lets you specify a new document name, format for saving the document, new location, etc.

Save Copy As... Saves a copy of the active document under a new name, then lets you continue to work on the original document, not the copy.

Screen Test A built-in "screensaver" that displays changing geometric shapes to prevent screen burn-in while you are not typing. Has user-definable patterns and colors. Starts as soon as you choose the *Screen Test* menu item. Click the mouse button to change the settings or cancel.

Scroll Line Down (⌘-Option-/ or keypad +) Scrolls up one line. If out of view, it brings next line into view at bottom of screen.

Scroll Line Up (⌘-Option-[or keypad *) Scrolls down one line. If out of view, it brings next line into view at top of screen.

Scroll Screen Down (⌘-Option-. (period) or keypad 3 or Page Down) Scrolls down one full window. If out of view, it brings next window into view.

Scroll Screen Up (keypad 9 or Page Up) Scrolls up one full window. If out of view, it brings next window into view.

Section... (Option-F14, on the *Format* menu) Brings up the Section dialog box, where you can specify breaks, column numbers, header/footer positions, page numbering, and more.

Section Break (⌘-Enter, on the *Insert* menu) Inserts section break at insertion point.

Section Starts on Even Page Forces sections to start on even-numbered pages.

Section Starts on New Column   Forces sections to start in next column on same page, unless current and preceding sections have a different number of columns, in which case text starts on next page.

Section Starts on New Page   Forces current section to start on new page.

Section Starts on Odd Page   Forces sections to start on odd-numbered pages.

Section Starts with No Break   Does not force a new page for current (new) section.

Select All   (⌘-A or ⌘-Option-M, on the *Edit* menu) Selects contents of entire document.

Send Mail...   (*File* menu) Lets you send the current Word document via Microsoft Mail if your computer is so equipped. Brings up the MS-Mail Send window.

Sentence Case   Capitalizes the first word in the selected text using periods as its guide. Does not change existing capital letters.

Separator   Inserts dashed line at bottom of selected menu. Used to group related menu choices.

Set Indent Ruler Scale   Switches ruler tools to those used to manipulate paragraphs. There is also a ruler button for this menu choice.

Set Margin Ruler Scale   Switches ruler tools to those used to manipulate the entire document. There is also a ruler button for this menu choice.

Set Table Ruler Scale   Switches ruler tools to those used to manipulate tables. There is also a ruler button for this menu choice.

Shadow   (⌘-Shift-W or Option-F11) Character format changes letters to white with black, shadowed outline.

Show All Headings　In Outline view, this displays all levels of headings and text (the entire document).

Show Body Text　In Outline view, this displays body text (the entire document).

Show Clipboard　(*Window* menu) Displays the contents of the Clipboard in a movable, sizable window.

Show Formatting　In Outline view, toggles bold, type sizes, etc. When off, all headings and body text appear plain and the same size.

Show Function Keys on Menus　Toggles listing of extended-keyboard function keys (F1, F2, and so on) in menus.

Show Heading 1–9　In Outline view, lets you decide which levels of outline to display. Show Heading 1 shows only level 1. Show Heading 3 shows levels 1, 2, and 3.

Show Hidden Text　Toggles display of hidden text on screen. This command does not affect the printing of hidden text.

Show Picture Placeholders　Displays rectangles in place of graphics to speed scrolling.

Show Styles on Ruler　Drops down a style list, but only if the ruler is displayed. An alternative to clicking on the style list triangle.

Show Table Gridlines　In tables, toggles display of nonprinting gridlines. Does not affect display of printing cell borders.

Show Text Boundaries　In Page Layout view, toggles display of nonprinting rectangles that outline text, footers, frames, etc.

Show/Hide ¶　(⌘-J, on the *View* menu) Toggles display of nonprinting characters (paragraph marks, tab marks, etc.).

Side by Side   One of several ways to specify position-related paragraphs. Largely obsolete with tables and paragraph-positioning features.

Small Caps   (⌘-Shift-H or Option-F10) Toggles small caps for selected text when the current font supports this feature.

Smaller Font Size   (⌘-Shift-< or ⌘-Shift-,) Decreases font size to next smaller standard size.

Smart Quotes   Toggles use of standard quote marks (" ") with typesetting curly quotes (" ") while typing. Does not replace previously typed quotes.

Sort   (*Tools* menu) Sorts selected text in ascending (ASCII) order, based on left-most selected character. Sorts A–Z, 0–9.

Sort Descending   Sorts selected text in descending (ASCII) order, based on left-most selected character. Sorts Z–A, 9–0.

Space Before ¶: 12 points   (⌘-Shift-O) This toggle adds 12 points of vertical white space before each selected paragraph.

Space Before ¶: None   Narrows vertical interparagraph spacing in selected paragraph(s).

Spelling . . .   (⌘-L or F15, on the *Tools* menu) Spell-checks your document if the spell checker has been installed in the Word 5 commands folder.

Split Cell   In a table, returns a merged cell to two single cells.

Split Window   (⌘-Option-S) This toggle lets you have two views of the same document. Good for flipping between distant sections of a large document.

Strikethru   (⌘-Shift-/) Toggles strikethru text formatting in the selected text.

Style...   (⌘-T, on the *Format* menu) Brings up the Style dialog box, where you define and modify paragraph styles.

Subscribe To...   (*Edit* menu) System 7 feature that lets you link your Word document with "editions" (from Excel spreadsheets, for instance). Contents of edition appear at the Word document's insertion point.

Subscript 2 pt   (⌘-Shift- –) Applies the subscript style to selected text using a point measurement you specify when installing the command.

Summary Info...   (*File* menu) Brings up a Summary Information dialog box, where you enter document-identification information (title, author, subject, etc.) Facilitates future searches for lost documents for documents meeting specific criteria.

Superscript 3 pt   (⌘-Shift- =) New Word 5 feature. Applies the superscript style to selected text, using a point measurement you specify when installing the command.

Suppress Line # in Paragraph   Turns off line numbers for selected text. (Only available if numbering option is on for section.)

Symbol...   (*Insert* menu) Displays a palette of font-specific symbol characters. Click on the desired character to place it at the insertion point.

Symbol Font   (⌘-Shift-Q) Applies the Apple LaserWriter symbol font to selected text.

Table...   (*Insert* menu) Brings up a dialog box that lets you define and insert a new table.

Table Cells...   (*Format* menu) In tables, brings up a dialog box that lets you define cell sizes, alignment, spacing, borders, etc.

Table Cells Borders...   Brings up Borders dialog box.

Table Layout... (*Format* menu) In tables, brings up a dialog box that lets you add and delete rows, merge split cells, and more.

Table of Contents... (*Insert* menu) Generates a TOC and places it at the beginning of the active document. You can use either a document's outline or TOC entries (hidden-text codes) to create the TOC.

Table to Text... In a table, converts the table to text, separated either by paragraph marks, tabs, or commas.

Tabs... Brings up a dialog box that lets you define and position tabs for the selected paragraphs.

Text to Table... Converts the selected text into a table using tabs and paragraph markers as indicators of columns and rows.

Thesaurus... (*Tools* menu) Brings up a thesaurus offering alternative words for the selected word. Only works if the thesaurus has been installed in the Word 5 commands folder and the selected word is properly spelled.

Time Inserts the current time using the Glossary's time format. (Updates the time when you print.)

Title Case Capitalizes *every* selected word.

TLBR Single Paragraph Border (*Format* menu) Used with tables to modify border of specified cell(s).

TLBR Single Shadow Paragraph Border (*Format* menu) Shades selected cells in tables.

TOC Entry (*Insert* menu) Inserts a TOC (hidden-text) code before and after the selected text.

Toggle Case Reverses the case of each highlighted letter. Caps become lowercase, and vice versa.

Word 5 Commands

Unassign Keystroke (⌘-Option-keypad –) Asks you to type a key combination (⌘-P for instance). Removes that key combination from its related command (*Print...* in our example) so the combination can be used elsewhere.

Underline (⌘-U or ⌘-Shift-U or F12, on the *Format* menu) Applies or removes the continuous underline format from selected text. There is also a ribbon button for this feature.

Undo (⌘-Z or F1, on the *Edit* menu) Watches you work and attempts to undo your most recent action (typing, formatting, deleting, etc.). Works best if used immediately after action needing reversal.

Unnest Paragraph (⌘-Shift-M) Shifts selected paragraphs left one indent.

Up (⌘-] or ⌘-Shift-<, on the *Font* menu) Increases font size by 1 point. Works for selected text or text typed after the command is issued.

Update Link (Option-F3) MultiFinder feature that updates selected linked information to match source. Source application (Excel, for instance) must be available and have enough RAM to run.

Uppercase Changes all selected text to uppercase.

Use Short Menu Names Shortens length of Word menu names to permit use of additions (clocks, etc.) on smaller Mac screens. For instance, *Format* becomes *Fmt*.

Voice Annotation (⌘-Shift-A, on the *Insert* menu) Brings up the Voice Record dialog box.

Voice Annotations (⌘-Shift-Option-R, on the *View* menu) Brings up the Voice Annotations dialog box, where you can play back voice annotations.

Word Count... (Option-F15, on the *Tools* menu) Counts and displays word, character, paragraph, and line counts for selected section or entire document. Does not count text in headers or footers.

Word Underline (⌘-Shift-] or ⌘-F12) Applies and removes single-word underline (does not underline spaces).

Zoom to Fill Screen Resizes active window to fill entire screen.

INDEX

; (end-of-entry code), 413
(¶) paragraph mark, vs. section breaks, 236
= ? choice, for SET statement, 401
~ (tilde key), 226
« and » (merge marks), manually inserting, 406
⌘ key, 17, 241
  to drag copy, 33, 51
• (bullet), for standard glossary entries, 278
¶ (paragraph mark), 160, 162. *See also* paragraph mark (¶)

About Microsoft Word, 469
Activate Keyboard Menus, 469
active window, 28
Add Space ruler button, 166
Add to Menu, 469
addition, with Calculate command, 373–374
Adobe Illustrator, 314
Again (Word 4). *See* Repeat (Edit menu)
Aldus FreeHand, 314
Alias (System 7), 48
  for stationery, 287
alignment of tables, with margins, 359
alignment of text
  in Picture window, 41
  with ruler, 165
All Caps, 470
All Styles button (Style dialog box), 186
Allow Fast Saves option, 79, 470
Always Interpret RTF option, 77, 470
Always Make a Backup option, 78, 470
Always Suggest option (Spelling), 80, 82
annotations, 59, 210–215
  hidden text for, 210–211
antonyms, 334, 337–338
Any Text (Search dialog box), 297
Apple Edition Manager, publish and subscribe, 432
"Apple" key, 241
Apple LaserWriter Effects, 122–123
Apple LaserWriter Options, 124–126
Apple portable computers, keyboard on, 240
Apply Style Name: (Work menu), 470
arc tool (Picture window), 41
Array (.\A) formula-typesetting command, 377, 379
arrowheads, in picture window, 41

ascending character, 146
ascending sort order, 368
ASCII decimal codes, 52, 155
ASK feature (Print Merge), 388, 399–400, 402
  eliminating blank lines from, 403
Assign to Key command, 470
author, of document, 55
author glossary item, 73
automatic optional hyphenation, 226–230
  preparing for, 227
  undoing, 230
automatic page breaks, on Normal view, 104
automatic word wrap, 5. *See also* word wrap

Background Repagination, 74, 107, 207, 470
Backspace key, 6, 241, 470
backup copies, Word 5 creation of, 78
banner heads, 342
bar tab stops, 172
baseline, 154
bitmap characters, 123, 156
  smoothing, 124
bitmap graphics, 313
  printed appearance of, 126
black & white, reversing, 125
blank lines, eliminating in merge, 403
blocks of text, 39
boilerplate text, 274, 288
Bold (Format menu), 470
bold fonts, 11, 157–158
borders
  for paragraphs, 168
  for tables, 347, 352
Borders (Format menu), 168, 352, 470
bound documents, white space for, 132
Box (.\X) formula-typesetting command, 378, 379
boxes, in Outline view, 420
Bracket (.\B) formula-typesetting command, 378, 379
bullet (•), for standard glossary entries, 278
bulleted lists, hanging indents for, 164

Calculate command (Tools menu), 372, 373–376, 470

calculations, in Print Merge, 388, 396, 398–399
Calculations (Insert Keyword menu), 398
Cancel command, 471
capitalization
  in custom dictionary, 322
  in style names, 181
cascading objects in picture window, 38
Catch option (Grammar category), 82
cell selection bar, 350
cells in tables, 346
  merging, 359–360
  moving contents of, 363–364
  paragraphs in, 349
  selecting, 350
  shading, 58
center tab stops, 171
Centered command, 471
centered paragraphs, 161
centering text, 5
  with ruler, 12, 165
centimeters (cm), for spacing settings, 167
Change Case (Format menu), 150, 471
Change Font command, 471
Change Style command, 471
chapters, sections as, 233–234
Character (Format menu), 149–150, 211, 471
Character dialog box, 149, 150–154
  custom point size from, 151
  gray boxes in, 152
  Hidden, 211
character formatting, 143, 187. *See also* styles
  applying and removing, 146–155
  copying and repeating, 154–155
  from Format menu, 149–150
  keyboard shortcuts for, 466
  in Outline view, 423
  removing, 154
  from ribbon, 146–147
characters, 143
  color choices for, 152–154
  count of, 325
  spacing between, 154
  special, 155
  superscript or subscript, 154
Chooser (Apple menu), 20, 118
  for printer customization, 74
  removing icons from, 118
Clear (Edit menu), 471

Clear All button, for tab stops, 176
Clear key, 242
clearing tab stops, 176
clip art, 312
Clipboard, 30-31
  Calculate and, 374
  cutting or copying to, 26
  with Find and Replace, 263-264
  importing graphics with, 312, 315
  include formatted text in, 74
  link with, 443
  pasting from, 439
Close (File menu), 471
closing custom dictionaries, 323
cm (centimeters), for spacing settings, 167
Collapse Section command, 471
Collapse Subtext command, 471
collapsed body text, 418
colon (:)
  printing in index entries, 417
  printing in table of contents, 413
color printers, 153
colors
  choices for characters, 152-154
  in picture window, 41
Column Width box (Table Cells dialog box), Auto in, 358
columns, 5, 340-345
  mixing formats for, 234
  new sections as, 235
  on Normal view, 104-105
columns in tables, 346
  adding, 355-356
  deleting, 356
  dotted lines between, 75
  selecting, 350
  space between, 360
  width of, 356-358
Columns n command, 471-472
combining documents, 288
comma-delimited text, converting to tables, 361-362
Command From Key Assignment, 472
Command Reference, 97
command sets, multiple, 99-100
command string, for formulas, 376
commands, 461-498. See also keyboard shortcuts
  description of, 88
Commands (Tools menu), 70, 241, 244, 472
Commands dialog box, 87-92, 241, 459
  Do It button, 91
  List, 244
  removing, 91-92

removing shortcuts in, 245
  Reset function, 97
Commands folder, Custom Dictionary in, 322
Commands list, in Commands dialog box, 88-89
comparison operators, for IF merge statement, 403-404
compressed files, 454
condensed character spacing, 154
Condensed 1.5 pt command, 472
condensed fonts, 157-158
connected documents, printing set of, 131
consecutive nouns, Grammar check of, 82
Context Sensitive Help, 477
continuation notices, for footnotes, 216
continuation separators, for footnotes, 222
Continue (File Series box, Page Numbers label), 429
Control key, 241
conversion
  of files from other word processors, 60
  of tables to text, 362-363
  of text to tables, 361-362
Copies (Print dialog box), 128
Copy (Edit menu), 472
Copy as Picture command, 472
Copy Formats command, 472
copy operation
  for character formatting, 154-155
  to Clipboard, 26
  for footnotes, 218-219
  from one document to another, 28
  paragraph mark (¶), 163
  for section breaks, 236
  from spreadsheet, 31
Copy Text command, 472
Courier font, 144-145
Cover Pages (Print dialog box), 129
Create Publisher (Edit menu), 435-436, 473
cursor. See insertion point; navigation
curve tool (Picture window), 41
custom dictionaries, 318, 321-324, setting preference for, 80
custom paper size, 73-74
custom point size, from Character dialog box, 151
Cut command (Edit menu), 27, 473
cutting to Clipboard, 26

dashes
  em, 226
  as leading characters, 175

in Outline view, 420
DATA, eliminating blank lines from, 403
Data Document Builder dialog box, 391
data documents, 386, 389
  changing, 403-406
  connecting to main document, 394
  creating, 391-393
  designing, 390
  entering and editing data in, 393
  saving designs for, 392-393
  sorting, 397
data exchange, tabs and, 177
data instructions, 386, 394, 396
DATA statement, 394
  replacing, 403-406
database, vs. Print Merge, 388
dates
  in headers or footers, 107
  of printing, 279
  sorting, 369-370
DDE linking, 432
decimal tab stops, 172
Default Font (Font menu), 149, 473
Default Font Category (Preferences), 80
default settings, 1, 4, 61, 66-70
  for font, setting during install, 454
  for footnotes, 217-218
  for glossary, 274-275
  for margins, 133
  storage location for, 69
  for tab stops, 176
  for views, 113
Delay Until Repeat setting, 244
Delete Cells, Shift Left command, 473
Delete Cells, Shift Up command, 473
Delete Columns command, 473
Delete Forward command, 473
Delete key, 6, 241
Delete Next Word command, 473
Delete Previous Word command, 473
Delete Rows command, 473
deletion
  of fields in data document, 392
  of files, 300
  of footnotes, 218-219
  of framed objects, 308
  of glossary entries, 278
  of hyphens, 230
  of items from menus, 87
  of page breaks, 208
  of page numbering, 206
  of paragraph mark (¶), 162
  of section breaks, 236
  of stationery, 287

Index

of styles, 189
of table columns, 356
of table rows, 354–355
of text, 6–7
Demote Heading command, 473
descending character, 146
descending sort order, 368
description of commands, 88
Design Sciences Inc., 373, 383
destination file, for linking, 434
dialog boxes, 62
  keyboard shortcuts for options in, 464–465
  keyboard tricks in, 247
dictionaries
  custom, 321–324
  setting preference for, 80
  using old with Word 5, 458–459
Different First Page (Section dialog box), 199, 474
digits, unspecified, search for, 255, 259
disabled users, 241
disks
  saving work to, 14
  searching multiple for files, 299–300
  space for sound files, 212
Displace (.\D) formula-typesetting command, 378, 379
division, with Calculate command, 374–375
Do It button (Commands dialog box), 91
Document (Format menu), 134, 176, 428, 474
Document dialog box, 128
  File Series button, 428
  margin settings in, 134, 135
  Mirror Even/Odd feature, 137
document windows, 3
  moving between, 269
documentation, of command changes, 96
documents. *See also* files; large documents; stationery
  benefits of splitting, 426–427
  combining with Insert File, 288
  double-clicking to launch Word, 47–49
  last saved listed on File menu, 48–49, 76
  list of open, 29
  margins for, and centered text, 165
  for merging. *See* data documents; main documents
  navigating through, 266–272
  opening in Page Layout view, 76

outlines for existing, 422
printing connected, 131
sending in E-mail, 449
setup for, 4
statistics on, 331–332
style sheet for, 179
subscriber or publisher, 434
summary info on, 16–17, 54–55, 73, 495
white space for binding, 132
on Work menu, 93–94
dots as leading characters, 175
Dotted Underline command, 474
double-clicking, 2
  documents to launch Word, 47–49
  to select word, 6
double-line spacing, 166
Double Underline command, 474
Down (Font menu), 474
downloadable fonts, and print area size, 126
Drag-and-Drop, 33, 51–52
  for footnotes, 218
  for text editing, 74, 474
drawing, 34–44, 57
  text in, 38–41
  text style and size in, 40
duplicate tool (Picture window), 38
duplicating objects, in picture window, 37–38

E-mail, 448–450
Easy Access, 241
Edit Link (Link Options dialog box), 446, 474
Edit menu, 8
  keyboard shortcuts for, 462
Edit Object (Edit menu), 474
editing
  keyboard shortcuts for, 469
  in Normal view, 104–105
  in Page Layout view, 105, 107
edition file, 434, 436
electronic mail (E-mail), 448–450
ellipse tool (Picture window), 41
ELSE statement (Print Merge), 388, 403–404
em dashes, 226
embedded objects, updating, 440–441
embedded PostScript (EPS) images, 127
embedding, 432, 433–434, 439–443
  cancelling, 442–443
end-of-entry code (;), 411, 413

ENDIF statement (Print Merge), 403–404
envelopes, stationery for, 406
Envelopes folder, 406
EPS (PostScript) files, 314
  importing, 315
  printing, 130
Equation Editor, 60, 373, 381–384
  starting, 382
error checking, by Print Merge Helper, 397
error correction. *See* Undo . . .
Escape key, 241
Even Footer command, 474
Even Header command, 474
even pages, new sections on, 235
Expand Subtext command, 474
expanded character spacing, 154
extended keyboard, 240
  and Word, 242–243

factory settings. *See* Microsoft Standard Settings
fast saves, 79
Faster Bitmap Printing option, 124
ff button (Outline bar), 423
field names
  in data document, 392
  inserting in main document, 396
fields, 389
File (Insert menu), 57, 284, 288, 475
file management, 290–301
File menu
  keyboard shortcuts for, 461–462
  listing recently opened documents or, 48–49, 56, 67, 76
file names, searching with Find File, 294–296
File Series dialog box, 428
  Page Numbers label, 429
files, 290–292. *See also* documents
  converting from other word processors, 60
  deleting, 300
  edition, 434
  quick access to last-used, 48–49, 56–57, 67, 76
  renaming, and Work menu, 94
  sending printing to, 130
  setting preferences for reading and writing, 77–80
  viewing contents of during search, 294
  from Word install, 455–457
fill patterns, in picture window, 41

Find (Edit menu), 55, 255-259, 475
    Clipboard with, 263-264
    navigating with, 268-269
    white space in, 258-259
Find Again command, 475
Find dialog box, Search, 263
Find File (Apple menu), 2, 55
Find File (File menu), 55-56, 475
Find File button (Open dialog box), 293-300
Find Formats command, 475
finding styles, 189-190
First Footer command, 475
First Header command, 475
First Line Indent command, 475
fixed-pitch fonts, 144
Flesch Index, 331
Flesch-Kincaid index, 332
flipping objects, in picture window, 44
Flips (Page Setup dialog box, Options), 125
Fog index (Gunning), 332
folders, 15, 290-292
    Glossary, 279
    location for edition file, 436
    Settings Files, 100
    from Word install, 455-457
Font menu, 147-149
fonts, 142-158
    bitmapped, 123, 156
    choosing with Character dialog box, 151
    default settings for, 67, 80
    in Normal view, 103
    size of, 10, 60, 117
    substitution of, 123
Footer command (View menu), 475
footers. *See also* headers and footers
    entering in Normal view, 195-196
Footnote command (Insert menu), 216, 476
footnote continuation notices, 216, 476
Footnote dialog box, 219
footnote-reference markers, 216, 217, 222
footnote reference style, 220
footnote separators, 216, 221-222
footnotes, 216-222
    continuation separators for, 222
    copying, deleting and moving, 218-219
    count of text in, 325
    default settings for, 217-218
    editing text in, 219
    numbering, 220, 429-430

positions for, 221
text style for, 220
viewing, 218
Footnotes (View menu), 218, 476
forcing page breaks, 207
Format menu, keyboard shortcuts for, 463
    Paragraph, 166, 487
formatting
    changing with Find and Replace, 255
    clearing from Replace dialog box, 261
    and Clipboard text, 74
    effect of page setup options on, 119-128
    manual, and styles, 186-188
    for page numbering, 204
    replacing, 261-262
    and sections, 234, 236
formula-typesetting commands, 372, 376-381
formulas, printing, 381
Fraction (.\F) formula-typesetting command, 379, 379
Fractional Widths (Page Setup dialog box), 126, 476
frame, 34, 304
    for graphics, 61
    paragraph mark and, 305
    positions as styles, 307-308
Frame (Format menu), 304, 307, 476
Frame (Insert menu), 304, 306, 476
Frame command, 139
Frame dialog box, 307
framed objects
    deleting, 308
    on mirrored pages, 309
    repeating on multiple pages, 308-309
Freeze Picture (Object Options dialog box), 442
front/back tool (Picture window), 43
Full Repaginate Now command, 477
function keys, 240, 242-243
    displaying on menus, 76

Galley view. *See* Normal view
GateKeeper, 452
General Preferences category, 73-74
Get Info feature, 295
global replace, 254
Glossaries folder, 279
glossary, 60, 94, 274-282
    footnote entries in, 222

for formulas, 381
section breaks as, 236
using old with Word 5, 458-459
Glossary (Edit menu), 73, 275, 280, 477
    and styles, 191
glossary entries
    assigning keyboard shortcuts to, 277
    changing and deleting, 278
    defining, 275-276
    inserting in documents, 276-277
    for large documents, 427
    printing list of, 282
    standard, 278-279
    storage of, 279
    and styles, 281
    on Work menu, 93-96
Go Back command, 477
Go To feature, 267-268, 477
grade level of writing, 332
Grammar (Tools menu), 58, 326-332, 477
    accepting suggestions from, 328-329
    Ignore button, 329-330
    manual changes in, 329
Grammar category (Preferences dialog box), 82, 330
Grammar Explanations window, 328
grammar rules, resetting to standard, 98
graphics
    formats for Word 5, 312
    frames for, 61
    importing, 312-315
    Move Text command for, 32
    positioning, 304-310
    replacing text with, 264
    speed of displaying, 75-76
    types of, 313-314
Graphics Smoothing (Page Setup dialog box), 124
gray-capable printers, 153
gray shading
    for characters, 153
    for cells, 58
    for paragraphs, 58, 168
    printing, 130
gridlines in tables, 75, 347
groups of table cells, selecting, 351
Gunning Fog index, 332
gutters, 132, 138-139

handles, 25
    to resize rectangles, 37

Index

hanging indents, 161, 477
  with ruler, 164–165
hard drive
  installing Word on, 453
  space requirements for, 451
hardware requirements, for Word, 451
Header (View menu), 477
Header/Footer method
  and page number deletion, 206
  for page numbers, 202
header record, 392
headers
  PostScript code in, 199
  placing table headings in section, 364
headers and footers, 194–199
  in margins, 139
  in Page Layout view, 76, 105, 107, 196
  in Print Preview, 23, 196–198
  search in, 256
  setting first page different, 199
headings
  in outlines, levels for, 421
  spacing for, 168
Help (Context Sensitive), 477
Help (Window menu), 477
hidden text, 477
  for annotations, 210–211
  displaying, 75
  in Page Layout view, 107
  in Print Merge, 403
  printing, 107, 130
  and searches, 256
hidden-text markers, for table of contents, 411
horizontal flipping, 125
horizontal positioning of frame, 307
Hyphenation (Tools menu), 227, 477
hyphenation, automatic optional, 226–230
Hyphenation category, 83–84
hyphens, 224
  deleting, 230
  long, 226
  typing, 225–226

.i. (index code), 413
I-beam (mouse pointer), 4, 8
icons
  in Print Preview, 23
  for stationery, 285, 286
  Word 5, 2, 3
IF statement (Print Merge), 388, 397, 403–404

Ignore button (Grammar dialog box), 329
Ignore option (Spelling), 82
Ignore Rule button (Grammar dialog box), 330
ImageWriters, 73
imported data, for Print merge, 389
importing graphics, 312–315
inches (in), for spacing settings, 167
Include Endnotes in Section command, 478
Include Formatted Text in Clipboard, 478
INCLUDE statement (Print Merge), 405
indent markers, and centered text, 165
indentation
  within columns, 342
  hanging, 161, 164–165
  vs. margins, 134
  on Normal view, 103
  in Outline view, 418
  of paragraphs, 5, 164
Index (Insert menu), 413
index code (.i.), 413
Index Entry (Insert menu), 413, 478
indexes, 413–417
  and footnotes, 222
  for series, 430
  subentries in, 414–415
  text in entries for, 415–416
Initials (General Preferences), 73
Insert Cells Down command, 478
Insert Cells Right command, 478
Insert Columns command, 478
Insert Field Name menu (Print Merge help bar), 396
Insert Formula command, 478
Insert Glossary Entry command, 478
Insert Keyword menu
  Calculations, 396, 398
  IF, ELSE, and ENDIF, 404
Insert menu, keyboard shortcuts for, 462
Insert Non-breaking Hyphen command, 478
Insert Non-breaking Space command, 478
Insert Optional Hyphen command, 479
Insert Page Break, 5
  and column breaks, 344
Insert ¶ Above Row command, 479
Insert Rows command, 479
Insert Tab command, 479
insertion
  of glossary entries in documents, 276–277
  of symbols, 52
  of text, 7–8
insertion point, 4. *See also* navigation

vs. I-beam, 8
  moving in table, 349
  and moving to new page, 107
inside margins, white space in, 138
Installer, 451–459, and custom dictionary, 322
Integral (.\I) formula-typesetting command, 379, 380
inter-character spacing, 126, 154
  and fonts, 158
inter-line spacing, and fonts, 158
international keyboard, 240
Invert Image feature (Page Setup dialog box), 125
Italic (Font menu), 479
Italic Cursor command, 479
italics type, 11, 157–158, 261
  keyboard shortcut for, 62

Justified command, 479
justified text
  optional hyphens and, 224
  ruler for, 12, 165–166

Keep Lines Together paragraph features, 344, 479
Keep With Next paragraph feature, 344, 479
kerning, 11, 154
Key Repeat Rate, 244
key words, for document, 55
keyboard(s), 240–247
  applying styles from, 181
  inserting glossary entries with, 277
  stopping merge for input from, 399
  typing symbols from, 155
Keyboard control panel (Apple menu), 243
Keyboard menus, 241
  activating, 246–247
keyboard shortcuts, 17–18, 62–63, 241, 461–469
  adding and changing, 98–99
  assigning, 88
  assigning to glossary entries, 277
  for character formatting, 149–150
  exploring and modifying, 244–246
  for hidden-text markers, 411
  for navigation, 270–272
  storage of, 245
  for voice feature, 214–215
Keys list, 98

L Thick Paragraph Border command, 479
labels, stationery for, 406
ladder, 225
landscape printing, 120–121
language, default for thesaurus, 83
large documents, 426–430
   connecting multiple parts of, 427–430
   planning for, 427
   printing in series, 430
Larger Font Size command, 479
Larger Print Area (Page Setup dialog box), 126
laserprinters, 20, 73
   minimum margins on, 126
LaserWriters, 153
launching Word 5, 2
   by double-clicking document, 47–49
leading, 11, 146
leading characters, for tab stops, 175
left aligning text, with ruler, 165
left tab stops, 171
letters, unspecified, search for, 255, 259
Level meter, for voice annotations, 213
li (lines), for spacing settings, 167
Line Break command, 480
line endings, Fractional Width and, 126
line numbers, 107
   commands for, 480
   in Print Preview, 23, 104, 110
   in series, 429
line spacing
   commands for, 480
   on Normal view, 103
   with ruler, 12, 166
line tool (Picture window), 38, 41
lines
   count of, 325
   eliminating blank in merge, 403
   sorting based on portion of, 368–369
   thickness of, in picture window, 41
lines (li), for spacing settings, 167
Link, and styles, 191
Link Options (Edit menu), 445, 480
Link Options dialog box, 444–446
linking (DDE), 432, 434, 443–446
List (.\L) formula-typesetting command, 379, 380
List All Fonts command, 480
List button (Commands dialog box), 96
List Files of Type menu, 293
List Recently Opened Documents command, 480
lists, of open documents, 29
LocalTalk connections, 119

locations, of saved files, 15
lowercase characters, changing to, 150, 480

MAC, preparing for Word installation, 452
Mac control panel, Monitor, and gray shading, 153
MacPaint, 313
MacRecorder, 212
macro programs, 87
MacroMaker, 87
magnification, in Print Preview, 23
Mailing Labels folder, 406
main dictionary, setting preference for, 80
main documents, 386, 392
   creating, 394–396
   data instructions in, 396
   designing, 390
   input from keyboard during merge, 399–400
   stationery for, 406
Make Alias (File menu), 48
Make Backup Files command, 481
Make Body Text command, 481
manual formatting, and styles, 186–188
manual page breaks, 207
   on Normal view, 104
margin brackets, on ruler, 135, 136
margin handles, dragging, 135
Margin Page Numbers command, 481
margins, 132–138
   aligning tables with, 359
   default settings for, 67
   dragging indent marker beyond, 164
   measurement unit for, 74
   in Print Preview, 23, 24–25, 110
   printer restrictions on, 126, 139
   resetting to standard, 98
   ruler for, 12
mass mailings, 59
Match Case checkbox (Find dialog box), 258
Match Whole Word Only box (Find dialog box), 258
math. *See* Calculate command (Tools menu)
Meanings For: scrollable list, 335
measurement unit, setting preference for, 74, 481
memory
   for Grammar checker, 327
   for replace command, 264
   for tables, 364
menu bar, 9
menus, 61, 86–100
   adding table layout choices to, 364

default settings for, 67
displaying function keys on, 76
revisions in, 62
short names for, 77
merge, for glossaries, 281
Merge Cells command, 481, 359–360
merge marks (« and »), manually inserting, 406
merging. *See* Print Merge
microphones, 211
Microsoft, telephone support, 251
Microsoft Mail, 448
Microsoft Standard Settings, 67–68
   reverting to, 69–70
mirror margins, 137–138
Mirror Even/Odd feature, 133–134, 137–138
mirrored pages, positioning objects on, 309
monospaced fonts, 144–145
More Keyboard Prefix command, 481
Most Recently Used List (MRU List), 48–49, 56, 67, 76
mouse
   avoiding use of, 246
   navigating with, 267
   selecting text with, 6
   shortcuts for, 465
mouse pointer, 4
   and text insertion, 8
Move Down One Text Area command, 481
Move Heading Down command, 481
Move Heading Up command, 481
Move Left One Text Area command, 482
move operation
   for cell contents, 363–364
   for files, and Work menus, 94
   for footnotes, 218–219
   for menu items, 92
   for page breaks, 208
   for tab stops on ruler, 173
   for windows, 28
Move Right One Text Area command, 482
Move Text command, 32, 482
Move to . . . commands, 482–483
moving objects
   drag-and-drop for, 33
   in picture window, 38
MRU List (Most Recently Used List), 48–49, 56, 67, 76
MS Word 5 folder, 15
MultiFinder
   display for, 3
   and importing clipboard graphic, 315
   multiple programs on, 30–31

Index

multilevel sorts, 370
multiple copies, printing, 128
multiple documents, using same styles in, 190-191
multiple pages, repeating framed objects on, 308-309
multiple searches, for files, 299-300
multiple windows, 28
multiplication, with Calculate command, 374-375

names
  sorting, 369-370
  of styles, changing, 189
  in Summary Information dialog box, 73
navigation, 266-272, through tables, 349
negative numbers, parentheses for, 374
Nest Paragraph command, 484
nesting INCLUDEs, 405
nesting indexes, 414-415
network
  choosing printers on, 118
  edition file on, 436
New (File menu), 391, 484
New ¶ After Ins. Point command, 484
New ¶ with Same Style command, 484
new page, preventing in print merge, 405
New Paragraph command, 484
New Picture command, 484
New Window command, 484
Next Sentence button (Grammar dialog box), 329
NEXT statement (Print Merge), 405
Next Style: (Style dialog box), 185
No Break, for printing sections, 235
No Paragraph Border command, 485
nonbreaking hyphens, 224, 226
nonbreaking spaces, 226
Normal Character Position command, 485
Normal Character Spacing command, 485
Normal Paragraph command, 485
Normal view, 102, 103-105, 485
  columns in, 341
  as default setting, 113
  footer entry in, 195-196
  footnotes on, 218
  formula-typesetting commands in, 377
  framed objects on, 309-310
  header entry in, 195
  section breaks in, 342
nouns, consecutive, Grammar check of, 82
Num Loc feature, 242, 485

numbered paragraphs, hanging indents for, 164
numbering in series, 429-430
numbers
  for footnotes, 217, 220
  speller checking of, 82
numeric keypad, 240
  and keyboard shortcuts, 241, 246
  and Word, 242

Object (Insert menu), 382, 441-442, 485
Object Options dialog box, Freeze Picture, 442
objects
  creating, 441-442
  groups of, in picture window, 41
Odd Footer command, 485
Odd Header command, 485
odd pages, new sections on, 235
online help, for Equation Editor, 383
Open (File menu), 95, 292-293, 485
Open and Save category, 77-80
Open Any File command, 485
Open dialog box, Find File button, 293-300
open dictionaries, 321
open documents, list of, 29
Open Documents in Page View command, 486
Open Documents with Ribbon command, 486
Open Documents with Ruler command, 486
Open Mail (File menu), 448, 450, 486
Open Source (Link Options dialog box), 446
opening custom dictionaries, 323
opening documents, in Page Layout view, 76
opening picture windows, 35
opening special purpose glossaries, 280
optional hyphens, 224, 226
  entering, 227-229
Options button (Page Setup dialog box), 125
orientation of page, for printing, 120-121
original word, for Thesaurus, 335
Other (Font menu), 149, 486
Outline (Format), 486
Outline Bar, 420-421
Outline Command Prefix, 486
outline fonts, 156-157
Outline view, 102, 110-113, 486
  character formatting in, 423
  footnotes on, 218
  keyboard shortcut for, 62

  indentations on, 418
  for rearranging table rows, 363
  tools in, 419-421
outlines, 418-425
  keyboard shortcuts for, 464
  and table of contents, 408, 410
Overstrike (.\O) formula-typesetting command, 379, 380

Page # Alphabetic Lowercase command, 486
Page # Alphabetic Uppercase command, 486
Page # Arabic command, 486
Page # Roman Lowercase command, 486
Page # Roman Uppercase command, 487
Page Backward arrow, 105, 107
Page Break (Insert menu), 207
page breaks, 207-208, 487
  forcing, 207
  moving and deleting, 208
  on Normal view, 104
  paragraph spacing and, 168
page-ending markers, reduce/enlarge box and, 121
Page Forward arrow, 105, 107
Page Layout view, 102, 105-108, 487
  columns in, 341
  footnotes on, 218
  formula-typesetting commands in, 377
  framed objects on, 309-310
  headers and footers in, 107, 195, 196
  keyboard shortcut for, 62
  mouse to move through, 267
  opening documents in, 76
  shortcuts for moving in, 468
  showing text boundaries in, 75
page numbering, 23, 487
  formats and styles for, 204
  Header/Footer method for, 202
  in headers or footers, 107, 196
  methods for, 201-204
  in Page Layout view, 76
  pagination and, 207
  with Print Preview, 110, 201
  removing, 206
  restarting with 1, 205
  with Section dialog box, 202-203
  sections and, 234
  in series, 429
  starting, 204-206
  style for, 201

suppressing first, 205
suppressing in table of contents, 411
page orientation, for printing, 120–121
Page Setup dialog box, 117, 119–128, 487
  Options button, 125
Page view. *See* Page Layout view
pages
  as multiple sections, 234
  new sections on, 235
  preventing new in Print Merge, 405
  setup for, 4
Pages: All or a Range (Print dialog box), 128–129
pagination, 200–208
  background changes in, 74
  Fractional Width and, 126
  margins and, 133
  in print merge project, 388
  printer characteristics affecting, 117–118
palettes of math symbols, 381
paper size, 4, 122
  custom, 73–74
Paper Source (Print dialog box), 129–130
Paragraph (Format menu), 166, 487
Paragraph Aligned Left command, 487
Paragraph Aligned Right command, 487
Paragraph Border command, 487
Paragraph dialog box, 161, 166–168
paragraph mark (¶), 160, 162
  deleting, 162
  displaying, 162
  for frames, 305
paragraph styles, on Work menu, 95
paragraphs, 160–163
  borders and shading for, 168
  in cells, 349
  converting to tables, 362
  count of, 325
  formatting with ruler, 163–166
  indentation of, 5, 164
  keyboard shortcuts for formatting, 466–467
  moving in outlines, 424
  numbering in series, 430
  positioning for framed objects, 305
  shading, 58
  spacing, 5
  spacing before and after, 167–168
  spacing with ruler, 166
  triple-clicking to select, 52
parentheses, for negative numbers in Calculate, 374

part numbers, sorting, 369–370
Paste Cells command, 488
Paste command (Edit menu), 27, 488
Paste Link (Edit menu), 443, 488
Paste Object (Edit menu), 439, 488
Paste Special (Edit menu), 444, 488
  and styles, 191
Paste Special Character command, 488
pasting to Scrapbook, 30
path, 16, 290, 291
percentages, with Calculate command, 374–375
performance, document size and, 426
phototypesetting machines, creating disk file for, 130
phrase, in Thesaurus, 336
picas (pi), for spacing settings, 167
PICT graphic files, 313
PICT2 graphic files, 313
Picture (Insert menu), 35, 314, 488
picture frame, 305. *See also* frame
picture placeholders, 75–76
picture windows, 34
  alignment of text in, 41
  duplicating objects in, 37–38
  items stacked in, 42–43
  object groups in, 41
  opening, 35
  rotating and flipping objects in, 44
  Tool Palette for, 36
pictures, drag-and-drop to move or copy, 51–52
Plain Text (Format menu), 154, 488
playing voice annotations, 213–214
plus sign, in Outline view, 420
point sizes, 145–146
  changing from Font menu, 147
  custom, from Character dialog box, 151
pointing to windows, 30
points (pt), for spacing settings, 167
polygon tool (Picture window), 41
port for printer, selecting, 119
portrait printing, 120–121
Position feature, 61. *See also* Frame
position of characters, 154
PostScript code, in headers, 199
PostScript (EPS) graphic files, 314
  importing, 315
  printing, 130
PostScript Type 1 outline font format, 157
power failure, 14
PowerBook notebook computers, keyboard on, 240

Precision Bitmap Alignment (Page Setup dialog box), 126
preferences, 72–84
  resetting to standard, 98
Preferences (Tools menu), 72, 330–331, 488
Preferences dialog box, 67, 72
  Grammar category, 330
  Show Hidden Text, 411, 413
  Spelling category, 458
  Spelling, Always Suggestion option, 320
  View Category, 57
  View category, Show Hidden Text box, 211
prepositional phrases, Grammar check of, 82
Print (File menu), 128, 489
Print Date command, 489
Print dialog box, 25, 117, 128–131
  Print Hidden Text, 107, 211
  Print Next File box, 430
Print Merge, 386–406, 489
Print Merge Helper (View menu), 59, 386, 391, 489
  error checking by, 397
  merge project without using, 406
Print Merge instructions, 388, 398–405
  ASK, 388, 399–400, 402
  IF, ENDIF, and ELSE, 403–404
  INCLUDE, 405
  SET, 401–402
Print Next File (Print dialog box), 131
Print PostScript Over Text (Page Setup dialog box), 127
Print Preview, 21–24, 61, 102, 110, 489
  to drag framed object, 306
  dragging margins in, 135
  footnotes in, 218
  framed objects on, 309–310
  headers and footers in, 196–198
  keyboard shortcut for, 62
  margin changes in, 134
  for page numbering, 201
  removing page numbers on, 206
Print Selection Only (Print dialog box), 130
printer driver icons, 118
Printer Effects, 122
printer port, selecting, 119
printers, 4, 117
  choosing, 117, 118–119
  selecting, 20
printing, 20–25, 117
  black & white vs. color/grayscale, 130
  documents in series, 430

Index

glossary entries list, 282
hidden text, 107, 130
inserting date or time of, 279
in margins, 139
merged documents, 397-398
outlines, 425
page orientation for, 120-121
PostScript files, 130
problems with formulas in, 381
style sheet, 183
Promote Heading command, 489
Prompt for Summary Information option, 79, 489
prompts, for keyboard input to merge, 400
proper nouns, hyphens and, 225
proportionally spaced fonts, 144-145
pt (points), for spacing settings, 167
publish and subscribe (Apple Edition Manager), 432, 433, 434-439
publisher document, 434
publishers, choices for, 438
Publishers Options (Edit menu), 438-439
publishing, 435-436

Quick Record Voice Annotation command, 489
QuicKeys, 87
Quit (File menu), 47, 489
quitting Word, 46
and saving glossary changes, 279-280
and saving menu changes, 97
quotation marks, using typesetter's, 74

Radical (.\R) formula-typesetting command, 379, 380
Radius Rocket board, 452
RAM (random-access memory), 14
for Grammar Checker, 58
for publish and subscribe, 433
readability indexes, 326
reading disk files, 77-80
ReadMe files, 452
recording
sounds to disk, 211
voice annotations, 212-213
records, 389
tabs to separate, 177
rectangle tool (Picture window), 36-37
rounded, 41
Redefine Style from Selection command, 489

Redo (Edit menu), 251
Redo Typing command (Edit menu), 7
Reduce or Enlarge % (Page Setup dialog box), 121
removing menu items, 90-91, 490
renaming files, and Work menu, 94
Renumber command (Tools menu), 430, 490
Repaginate Now (Tools menu), 108, 206, 490
repagination, 103. *See also* pagination
background, 74, 107, 207, 470
in Page Layout view, 107-108
before printing page range, 129
Repeat (Edit menu), 251, 490
Repeat keyboard shortcut, 181
repeating keys, 243-244
Replace (Edit menu), 255, 259-263, 490
Clipboard with, 263-264
for styles, 189-190, 262
tips for using, 264-265
Replace dialog box, 260
Search, 263
replacement
of special characters, 52
of styles, 53, 189-190
of text, 9
Reset function (Commands dialog box), 97
resizing document windows, 269
Restart Page Numbering at 1 command, 490
Return key, 5, 160
Revert to Style command (Format menu), 251-252, 490
ribbon, 4, 9-12, 40, 52, 76
appearance of, 75
button for hiding text, 107
character formatting from, 146-147
columns from, 340, 341-342
default settings for, 66
in headers and footers, 196
Ribbon (View menu), 490
Rich Text Format (RTF), 77
right aligning text, with ruler, 165
right tab stops, 172
rivers of white space, 166, 225
Roman numerals, for page numbers, 204
rotating objects, in picture window, 44
rotating text, 39
rounded rectangle tool (Picture window), 41
rows in tables, 346
adding, 352-353
changing height of, 353-354

changing spacing between, 355
deleting, 354-355
dotted lines between, 75
selecting, 350
RTF (Rich Text Format), 77
Rule Groups: Grammar option, 82
Rule Groups: Style option, 82
ruler, 4, 12, 40, 76
for aligning and justifying text, 165-166
appearance of, 75
applying styles from, 180
and column width, 344, 356
default settings for, 66
defining styles from, 180
hanging indents with, 164-165
in headers and footers, 196
improvements in, 60
to indent paragraphs, 164
line spacing with, 166
margin brackets on, 135, 136
measurement unit for, 74
moving tab stops on, 173
paragraph formatting with, 161, 163-166
paragraph spacing with, 166
for setting tab stops, 173
zero point on, 342
ruler margin markers, reduce/enlarge box and, 121

Same As Previous command, 490
sans serif fonts, 146
Save (File menu), 14, 490
Save As (File menu), 491
Save Copy As command, 491
Save Current Document as: box, 16
Save File as Type menu, Stationery, 285, 287
save process, 14-16, 249-250
for glossary changes, 279-280
keyboard shortcut for, 17-18
for menu changes, 97
speeding up, 79
for style sheets, 183
Save Reminder Every *n* Minutes, 79-80
scanned images, 312, 313
Scrapbook, pasting to, 30
screen, splitting, 108
screen-capture software, 313
screen display, menus on, 61
screen editing keys, 240

screen redrawing, 103
Screen Test menu choice, 90, 491
Scroll... commands, 491
scrolling
  keyboard shortcuts for, 270-271, 467-468
  pages in Page Layout view, 105
Search dialog box, 293-294
Search: menu (Find and Replace dialog boxes), 263
search text, 297
searches, multiple, for files, 299-300
Section (Format menu), 199, 234, 491
Section Break (Insert menu), 233, 491
section breaks
  copying, 236
  deleting, 236
  vs. paragraph marks (¶), 236
Section dialog box (Format menu), 234-236
  Columns, 340, 342
  Different First Page, 199
  for page numbering, 202-203
Section Starts on... commands, 491-492
sections, 232-237
  creating breaks for, 233-236
  printing page ranges from, 129
  setting strategy for printing, 235
  for table of contents, 409
Select All (Edit menu), 9-10, 492
selected text, 5-6
  searches of, 263
  for style changes, 9-10
selecting paragraphs, triple-clicking for, 52
selection tool (Picture window), 37
semicolons
  printing in index entries, 417
  printing in table of contents, 413
Send Document dialog box, 449-450
Send Mail (File menu), 448, 449, 492
Sentence Case command, 492
Separator command, 492
separator lines, on menus, 92
separators for footnotes, 216, 221-222
serial connections, 119
series
  connecting multiple parts in, 427-430
  creating, 428
  numbering in, 429-430
  printing, 430
serif fonts, 146
Set button (Tab dialog box), 175
SET feature (Print Merge), 388, 401-402
  eliminating blank lines from, 403

Set Indent Ruler Scale command, 492
Set Margin Ruler Scale command, 492
Set Table Ruler Scale command, 492
Settings files, 86
  in Commands dialog box, 88
  folder for, 100
  keyboard shortcuts in, 245
shading. See gray shading
Shadow command, 492
shape drawing, in picture window, 41-44
shared printers, cover pages for, 129
sharing information, 432
Show ¶ feature, 107
  and framed objects, 310
  and tables, 347
  and tabs, 172
Show All Headings command, 493
Show Body Text command, 493
Show Clipboard (Window menu), 30, 493
Show Formatting, 493
Show Function Keys on Menus, 493
Show Heading 1-9 command, 493
Show Hidden Text (Preferences dialog box), 75, 211, 411, 413, 493
Show/Hide ¶ choice (View menu), 107, 162, 493
Show/Hide Body Text icon (Outline Bar), 423
Show Paragraph feature, and optional hyphens, 226
Show Picture Placeholders (View category), 75-76, 493
Show Styles on Rule command, 493
Show Table Gridlines (View category), 75, 493
Show Text Boundaries in Page Layout View (View category), 75
Side by Side command, 494
single-line spacing, 166
size of text, in drawings, 40
Small Caps command, 494
Smaller Font Size command, 494
"Smart" quotes, setting preference for, 74, 494
smoothing bitmapped fonts, 124
snaking columns, 340. See also columns
solid lines as leading characters, 175
Sort (Tools menu), 366, 367, 494
Sort Descending command, 494
sorting, 366-370, in Find File feature, 296-297
sound, 211-215
  in Clipboard, 30

Move Text command for, 32
Sound quality, 213
source file, for linking, 434
Space Before ¶: 12 points command, 494
Space Before ¶: None command, 494
spacebar, 5, 170
spaces, nonbreaking, 226
spacing, 11
  for headings, 168
  inter-character, 126, 154
  of lines, with ruler, 166
  for paragraphs with ruler, 166
Spacing Before paragraph feature, 343
special characters, 155
  finding, 258
  replacement of, 52
  search and replace for, 254
  and sort order, 368
speed
  and displaying graphics, 75-76
  table size and, 364
  views and, 103
Spell checker, 60, 318-325
  and footnotes, 222
  Grammar checking and, 327
  before searches, 256
spelling, Thesaurus and, 338
Spelling category (Tools menu, Preferences), 80-82, 319, 322, 494
Split-bar pointer, 108
Split Cells feature, 360, 494
split infinitives, 82
Split Screen view, 108
  and different views, 108
split views, Outline view as one, 423-424
Split Window command, 494
splitting documents, benefits of, 426-427
spoken notes, 59
spreadsheet, copying from, 31
standard custom dictionary, 322
standard glossary entries, 278-279
standard heading styles, 408
  and outlines, 419
standard keyboard, 240
standard styles, with Word, 186
Start: menu (Section dialog box), 235-236
stationery, 284-288
  for large documents, 427
  for main documents, 406
statistics
  on documents, 331-332
  for file, 294
  from grammar checking, 326

Index

straight lines, in picture window, 38
Strikethru command, 494
Style (Format menu), 181, 495
Style button, 82
Style dialog box, 181-183
   All Styles button, 186
   defining styles in, 182
   Next Style:, 185
style sheets
   printing, 183
   saving, 183
styles, 52, 143, 178-192
   changing, 9-12
   changing, vs. replacing, 264
   clearing from Replace dialog box, 261
   copying paragraph mark (¶) and, 163
   finding and replacing, 53,
      189-190, 262
   for footnotes, 220
   frame positions as, 307-308
   glossary entries and, 281
   and outlines, 419
   for page numbering, 201, 204
   standard heading, 408
   and tables, 364
   on Work menu, 93-94, 96
Styles (Character dialog box), 152
styles of text, in drawings, 40
subject, of document, 55
Subscribe to (Edit menu), 436, 495
subscriber document, 433, 434
Subscriber Options (Edit menu), 438
subscribers, 433
subscribing, 436-437
   and styles, 191
   updating or cancelling, 438-439
subscript characters, 11, 154
Subscript 2 pt command, 495
subtext, in Outline view, 418
Summary Info (File menu), 17, 54-55, 495
   prompting for, 79
   using Find File with, 298-299
Summary Info dialog box, 16-17, 73
   and standard glossary entries, 279
Super or Subscript formula-typesetting
   command, 379, 381
SuperPaint, 313
superscript characters, 11, 154
Superscript 3 pt command, 495
Suppress Line # in Paragraph
   command, 495
switching views, 105
Symbol (Insert menu), 52, 155, 495

Symbol Font, 495
symbols, inserting, 52
synonyms, 334
syntax, for formula-typesetting
   commands, 376
System 6
   display for, 3
   and hardware requirements for
      Word, 451
System 7, 63
   Alias, 48
   display for, 3
   and hardware requirements for
      Word, 451
   and importing clipboard graphic, 315
   multiple programs on, 30-31
System Folder, Word Settings (5) file, 69

tab characters, in table cells, 349
tab-delimited text, converting to tables, 361
Tab key, 5
   for navigating tables, 349
tab markers, 172
tab stops, 170-177
   and indents, 164
   measurement unit for, 74
   moving on ruler, 173
   ruler for, 12
   setting, 172-175
   setting with ruler, 173
   vs. tables, 172
   types of, 171-172
Table Cells Borders command, 495
Table Cells command (Format menu),
   353, 495
   and cell width, 357-358
Table Cells dialog box, Alignment
   menu, 359
Table Layout (Format menu), 352-353, 496
table of contents
   creating, 409-410
   and footnotes, 222
   from Outline feature, 410
   restricting levels for, 412
   for series, 430
   suppressing page numbers in, 411
Table of Contents (Insert menu), 408,
   409-410, 412, 496
Table Scale button, 356
Table to Text (Insert menu), 362, 496
tables, 61, 346-365
   as data document design, 389, 392

   gridlines in, 75, 347
   parts of, 347
   rearranging rows in Outline view, 363
   shortcuts for moving in, 468
   vs. tabs, 172
Tables (Insert menu), 347, 495
Tabs dialog box, setting tab stops with
   173-175, 496
tabular data, entering and editing, 176-177
text. *See also* selected text
   converting tables to, 362-363
   converting to tables, 361-362
   deleting, 6-7
   drag-and-drop to move or copy, 51-52
   in drawings, 38-41
   finding, 257-258
   inserting, 7-8
   replacing, 9
   replacing text with, 260-261
   replacing with graphics, 264
text attributes, storing in Clipboard, 74
text boxes, measurement unit for, 74
Text Smoothing (Page Setup dialog
   box), 124
text strings, 254
Text to Table command, 496
text tool (Picture window), 39
Thesaurus, 334-338
   exploring, 338
   looking up words in, 334-335
   related words and phrases in, 336
   replacing words and phrases with,
      335-336
   spelling help from, 338
Thesaurus (Tools menu), 58, 334, 496
Thesaurus Category, 83
TIFF format graphics, 313
tilde key (˜), 226
time
   in headers or footers, 107
   of printing, 279
Time command, 496
Title Case, 150, 496
TLBR Single Paragraph Border (Format
   menu), 496
TLBR Single Shadow Paragraph Border
   (Format menu), 496
TOC Entry (Insert menu), 411, 496
TOC Entry codes, 408, 411
Toggle Case command, 496
Tool Palette, for picture window, 36
Tools menu, keyboard shortcuts for, 463
triple-clicking, to select paragraphs, 52

TrueType outline font format, 157
two-sided documents, margins for, 133, 137
type. *See* fonts
typesetter's quotes, 74
typesetting commands, for formulas, 372, 376–381
typestyles, resetting to standard, 98
typing habits to change, 4–5

Unassign Keystroke command, 242, 497
Underline command (Format menu), 497
Underline options, in Character dialog box, 152
underlined text
 keyboard shortcut for, 62
 in Outline view, 420
underscore button, 11
Undo (Edit menu), 249–251, 497
 and deleted styles, 189
 and Drag-and-Drop, 51
 and Grammar checker, 327, 329
 and Replace, 264
 to restore Clipboard contents, 30
Undo Formatting, for column widths, 356
Undo Hyphenation (Edit menu), 230
Undo Paste, 364
Undo Table Cells, 353
Undo Thesaurus command, 336
Undo Typing (Edit menu), 7
Unformatted text, pasting, 444
U.S. English dictionary, 321
Unlimited Downloadable Fonts (Page Setup dialog box), 126
Unnest Paragraph command, 497
unspecified letters and digits, search for, 255, 259
Up (Font menu), 497
Update Link command, 497
uppercase characters, changing to, 150, 497
uppercase words, speller checking of, 82
Use As Default check box (Page Setup dialog box), 120

Use Short Menu Names command, 497
user dictionaries. *See* custom dictionaries

variable-pitch fonts, 144
vertical flipping, 125
vertical positioning of frame, 307
View category (Preferences dialog box), 57, 74–77
View menu, 105, 294
 Footer, 475
 Footnotes, 218, 476
 Header and Footer windows, 104, 194, 477
 keyboard shortcuts for, 462
 Print Merge Helper, 59, 386, 391, 489
 Show/Hide ¶ choice, 107, 162, 493
viewing Clipboard, 30
views, 102–113, framed objects on, 309–310
virus-protection software, 452
voice annotations, 497
 playing, 213–214
 recording, 73, 212–213
Voice Impact, 212
Voice Impact Pro, 212
Voice Record dialog box, 213

weight of characters, 146
white space, 4, 132
 changing between table rows, 355
 between columns, 340
 on inside margins, 138
 rivers of, 166, 225
 in searches, 258–259
width of columns, 341
 ruler and, 344
wild cards in searches, 255, 297
Window menu, 29, 269, keyboard shortcuts for, 463
windows
 moving, 28
 multiple, 28

pointing to, 30
Word 5
 Document Button (Page Setup dialog box), 128
 enhanced features of, 60–62
 extended keyboard and, 242–243
 icon for, 2, 3
 installing, 451–459
 launching by double-clicking on document, 47–49
 new features of, 50–60
 numeric keypads and, 242
 quitting, 46
 standard styles with, 186
 window for, 4
Word Commands folder
 custom dictionaries in, 80
 Hyphenation files in, 84
 Thesaurus files in, 83
Word Count (Tools menu), 324–325, 497
word processors, converting files from other, 60
Word Settings (5) file, 72, 99, 100
 in System Folder, 69
Word Underline command, 498
word wrap, 5
 hyphens and, 224
 in print merge project, 388
 in table cells, 349
 in text blocks, 39
words
 changing during spell check, 320
 looking up in Thesaurus, 334–335
Work menu, 86, 92–96
 adding glossary entries to, 277
 for large documents, 427
 stationery on, 287
writing disk files, 77–80
writing style, 82
 evaluating, 326

Zoom box, 269
Zoom to Fill Screen command, 498

FREE BROCHURE!

Complete this form today, and we'll send you a full-color brochure of Sybex bestsellers.

Please supply the name of the Sybex book purchased.

_____

How would you rate it?

____ Excellent   ____ Very Good   ____ Average   ____ Poor

Why did you select this particular book?

____ Recommended to me by a friend
____ Recommended to me by store personnel
____ Saw an advertisement in _____
____ Author's reputation
____ Saw in Sybex catalog
____ Required textbook
____ Sybex reputation
____ Read book review in _____
____ In-store display
____ Other _____

Where did you buy it?

____ Bookstore
____ Computer Store or Software Store
____ Catalog (name: _____)
____ Direct from Sybex
____ Other: _____

Did you buy this book with your personal funds?

____ Yes   ____ No

About how many computer books do you buy each year?

____ 1-3   ____ 3-5   ____ 5-7   ____ 7-9   ____ 10+

About how many Sybex books do you own?

____ 1-3   ____ 3-5   ____ 5-7   ____ 7-9   ____ 10+

Please indicate your level of experience with the software covered in this book:

____ Beginner   ____ Intermediate   ____ Advanced

Which types of software packages do you use regularly?

____ Accounting	____ Databases	____ Networks
____ Amiga	____ Desktop Publishing	____ Operating Systems
____ Apple/Mac	____ File Utilities	____ Spreadsheets
____ CAD	____ Money Management	____ Word Processing
____ Communications	____ Languages	____ Other _____ (please specify)

Which of the following best describes your job title?

_____ Administrative/Secretarial   _____ President/CEO

_____ Director   _____ Manager/Supervisor

_____ Engineer/Technician   _____ Other _____
                                              (please specify)

Comments on the weaknesses/strengths of this book: _____

_____

_____

_____

_____

Name _____
Street _____
City/State/Zip _____
Phone _____

PLEASE FOLD, SEAL, AND MAIL TO SYBEX

SYBEX, INC.
Department M
2021 CHALLENGER DR.
ALAMEDA, CALIFORNIA USA
94501

SEAL

HIGHLIGHTS OF WORD 5 FEATURES

Fabulous is only *one* way to describe Word 5's built-in *thesaurus*.

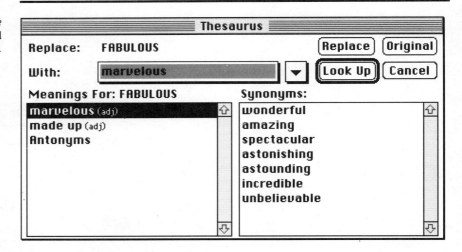

Word 5's new *spell checker* is bright, quick, and a great guesser.

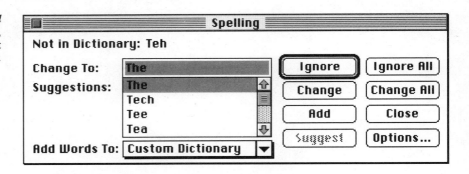

Word 5's built-in *grammar checker* looks after the details and helps you polish your prose.